AF540670

CONSUMERISM AND LEGAL PROTECTION OF CONSUMERS

With a Critical and Explanatory Commentary and Latest Case Law

CONSUMERISM AND LEGAL PROTECTION OF CONSUMERS

With a Critical and Explanatory Commentary and Latest Case Law

DR. RIFAT JAN

DEEP & DEEP PUBLICATIONS PVT. LTD.
F-159, Rajouri Garden, New Delhi-110027

CONSUMERISM AND LEGAL PROTECTION OF CONSUMERS

ISBN 81-7629-962-6

Typeset by ASHISH TECHNOGRAPHICS,
3190, Mohindra Park, Shakur Basti, Delhi-110034.

Printed in India at NEW ELEGANT PRINTERS,
A-49/1, Maya Puri, Phase-I, New Delhi-110064.

Published by DEEP & DEEP PUBLICATIONS PVT. LTD.
F-159, Rajouri Garden, New Delhi-110027.
Phones: 25435369, 25440916
E-mail: ddpbooks@yahoo.co.in • deep98@del3.vsnl.net.in
Showroom:
2/13, Ansari Road, Daryaganj, New Delhi-110002 • Telefax: 23245122

"Dedicated to my mother who inspired me in making my dream project a reality"

CONTENTS

ACKNOWLEDGEMENTS

I have no words to express my gratitude to the Almighty Allah for giving me strength and patience to complete this book.

I would be failing in my duty if I do not express my gratitude to all those who have been source of encouragement and help for me.

First of all I would like to express the gratitude of my Id. Supervisor Prof. Dr. Mohd. Ishaque Qureshi Sahib, Dean Chairman of Faculty of Law, A.M.U. who taught me the lesson of patience and positiveness in the research and inspite of being busy kept himself always available to me.

Similarly, it gives me immense pleasure to show my gratitude to the Prof. Dr. Saleem Akhter Sahib for his Alligarian nature and courtesy.

I must acknowledge my indebtedness to Dr. Faizan Mustafa Sahib (Reader) whose purely peaceful teachings shattered my idleness.

For me it is indeed a great honour to express my affectionate tribute to Late Mr. Shaheed-ud-din Sahib, Mr. Shareef-ud-din Sahib and Mr. Musharraf Alam Sahib. It is their love and affection which laid my roots successfully in the A.M.U. and I came out from home sickness.

I respectfully offer my profound thanks to the respected Retd. Prof. Mr. Zakaria Sahib, Prof. Qaiser Hayat Sahib and S.S.H. Azmi for their invaluable love and affection.

I also offer my thanks to the respected Dr. Shakeel Samnani Sahib, Dr. Javid Talib Sahib, Dr. Zubair Sahib, Dr. Zahir Sahib, Dr. Bader Alam Sahib and Dr. Mehfooz Nomani Sahib for their timely good cooperation and constant support.

I am thankful to my Brother-in-law Mr. Shahzad Shah

M. Amin Sahib who kept research a motive before me and my Brother Mr. Miya Jan Sahib whose financial assistance successfully made my research possible.

I am also indebted to my loving Sister-in-law Zamrad (Honey Jan) who accompanied me while approaching various Courts.

My special thanks and good wishes are due to Dear Mr. Irshad Ahmed Sahib, Mr. Ramesh Ji and Mr. Sheikh Tariq Sahib who had collected valuable material from various sources.

I owe a great debt to many who assisted me in brining out this work—prominent among them are Mr. Mushtaq Ahmad, Head Clerk State Commission and Bashir Ahmad for their help and good cooperation.

I cannot remain without expressing my profound gratitude to Staff members of Bar and University Libraries of Aligarh, Jammu and Kashmir and Delhi. Retd. Mr. Wajid Hussain Sahib, Mr. Roshan Sahib, Mr. Rafiq Sahib deserves my special thanks and good wishes for their nice help and cooperation.

I am immensely indebted to all the well-known scholars and writers whose work I have consulted and tested while working on my book.

I am also thankful to all those esteemed consumers, traders and other good citizens whose valuable suggestions and wise opinions are responsible for increased value of this book.

Similarly I am thankful to the Diamond Computers, Islamabad Kmr. Prop. Mr. Mushtaq Ahmad Khan Sahib who sent me a competent person Khursheed Ahmad Kathroo Sahib who computerized this book.

Last but not the least my thanks are to Deep & Deep Publications Pvt. Ltd., New Delhi, who desired and designed this work in the real sense. My good wishes are with this Corp.

I once again whole heartedly thank to the Almighty Allah who bestowed me nice things of patience, courage and a wish to live a simple, selfless and truthful life.

DR. RIFAT JAN

LIST OF ABBREVIATIONS

AIIMS	All India Institute of Medical Sciences
AIR	All India Reporter
All	Allahabad
Co.	Company
Corpn.	Corporation
CDRA	Consumer Disputes Redressal Agency
CPA/Act	Consumer Protection Act
C.P.C.	Civil Procedure Code
CPJ	Consumer Protection Journal
Cr.P.C.	Criminal Procedure Code
D.D.A.	Delhi Development Authority
D.D.	Date of Decision
Deptt.	Department
D/I	Date of Institution
Dist. Forum	District Forum
D/F	Divisional Forum
Dr.	Doctor
E.C.A.	Essential Commodities Act
Edu.	Education
eg.	For example
etc.	Etcetera
HUDA	Hyderabad Urban Development Authority
IDRA	Industries Development and Regulation Act
Imp.	Important

IPC	Indian Penal Code
J&K	Jammu and Kashmir
Jmu.	Jammu
Ld.	Learned
LDA	Lucknow Development Authority
Ltd.	Limited
M.C.A.	Municipal Corporation of Delhi
MRP	Maximum Retail Price
MRTP Act	Monopolistic and Restrictive Trade Practices Act
NC	National Commission
O/F	Original/Office File
O/P	Opposite Party
p.a	Per annum
Prof.	Professor
Pvt.	Private
Rs.	Rupees
Regd.	Registered
Retd.	Retired
RPC	Ranbir Penal Code
SC	State Commission
S.G.A.	Sale of Goods Act
Sgr.	Srinagar
Sec.	Section
SLJ	Srinagar Law Journal
U.K.	United Kingdom
U.S.A.	United States of America
U/S	Under Section
w.e.f.	With Effect From

CHAPTER

1

INTRODUCTION

Consumer is the sovereign is the slogan of our welfare State. The moment we accept it a welfare state it is appropriate to refer John Roskin's ideal—

"The last man should be our first concern."

After industrial revolution people migrated from rural to urban areas and their dependence on the traders became manifest. Unlike the earlier age when a personal relationship between a seller and buyer preceded an economic relationship, the new creed was marked by sophistication of business techniques and impersonal relations between the two. By taking advantage of the helplessness of the consumer—means foul and fair were devised by the manufacturers, distributors and the retailers to have a firm control on the market place. About the marketing it is rightly observed by the A.S.C. Ehrenberg in his book titled "consumer" that it is much more difficult, complex and variable than natural science. The study of Physics and Chemistry easily yields the absolute and invariant laws of science with which we are all so familiar. In contrast, marketing is thought to be far more complex to study. There are more factors at work. It involves intangibles, human beings and so on. Nothing is constant. Everything varies. There may never be any stable scientific laws in marketing. The marketing of goods and services is conducted through the trained business minded men in varying ways that often it becomes difficult to the consumer to judge their quality, purity and durability, etc. and this way consumers are easily cheated by well trained experts that is manufacturers and other concerned dealers. Consumer choice is just a fiction. Despite legislative and administrative measures consumer protection is a distant dream.

In this context U.N. General Assembly set forth objectives/guidelines urging all nation states—

(i) to assist member-countries in achieving or mentioning adequate protection for their population as consumers;

(ii) to facilitate production and distribution systems which meet the needs and desires of consumers;

(iii) to inculcate and promote high levels of conduct and responsibility amongst the producers and distributors of goods and providers of services to the consumers;

(iv) to help and assist countries in checking consumer exploitive trade practices at national and international levels which adversely affect the consumer interest;

(v) to assist and create congenial environment for the growth of independent and effective consumer bodies;

(vi) to help, assist and encourage such an open and competitive market regime which may offer affordable and cheaper goods; and finally

(vii) to evolve international cooperation consumer protection.

In pursuance of the guidelines issued by the United Nations General Assembly in the year 1985 our country passed Consumer Protection Act in the year 1986 and on the same and similar lines the State of Jammu and Kashmir (for constitutional reasons) passed its own Act on consumer protection. Though it is a fact that the State of Jammu and Kashmir enjoys special status Under Article 370 of the constitution but it is also true that this State is industrially poor and sick. Maximum quantity of essential commodities imported from outside are passing directly into the hands of consumers. There is no governmental or semi-governmental department or agency to check the purity and safety of goods before they can be taken and/or purchased by the consumers for their use. In the April 19, year 2000 eighty-one percent of drugs were reported to have been imported in the State of Jammu and Kashmir which were later on declared sub-standard by the Comptroller and Auditor General (CAG) of India. However, it is strange to believe that this huge quantity of drugs were already consumed by the consumers when information about their impurity reached the State. It is learnt that in the last decade of turmoil in the valley profiteering, black-marketing and hoarding, etc. have crossed almost all limits. These and many other crimes against consumers are also called socio-economic crimes, as, in socio-economic crimes in the same way money is the motive behind consumer crimes also. It is noteworthy to mention here that government has taken ample measures both legislative and administrative to curb the menace by empowering both officials/agencies and consumers to file complaints in such cases of consumer exploitation. However, only educated persons are taking benefit of beneficial enactments by filing complaints against unscrupulous manufacturers, producers, traders and service providers. Rest majority of the consumer community is illiterate and backward and lack of awareness have deprived them to know how, where and against whom action is to be initiated. In these circumstances many moot questions like what is the present position of consumer awareness in the state? Is the present existing law adequate to cope with the situation? If not, what sort of protection do consumers really need are striking my mind. All these questions together with some other issues will be considered minutely in the study to have a better view of the subject matter titled—Consumerism and Legal Protection of Consumers. Though there is wide range of statutes covering consumer disputes and huge case law is available under these enactments but in this work only those cases which are decided and diposed of under the Consumer Protection Act will be dealt. Since the Jammu and Kashmir Consumer Protection Act has large similarities with the Central Act on consumer protection and maximum number of cases delivered by the National Commission and Supreme Court have desired impact on all Consumer Disputes Redresssal Agencies of the Country including the State of Jammu and Kashmir. It is the uniform impact of these landmark judgments which will be scrutinized in this work. Further relevant case law has been surveyed and scrutinized from various sources while commenting on various provisions of the Act. In this background below mentioned objectives are conceived.

OBJECTIVES OF STUDY

- To identify the problems which are responsible for consumer exploitation.
- To have a systematic study of consumer legislation in the state of Jammu and Kashmir.
- To examine the impact of some landmark judgments on Consumer Fora in the State.
- To critically analyse the provisions of Consumer Protection Act, 1987.
- To assess and evaluate quasi-judicial attitude towards the consumer in the State.

RESEARCH METHODOLOGY

In order to achieve the above avowed objectives doctrinal method has been employed. Apart from resorting to relevant statutory material for making thoughtful study—reports, articles and commentaries of various authors on consumer protection and statutory material of some western countries has been examined carefully. Further, I have obtained material of decided cases directly from the concerned consumer forums of the state and for making future improvements in the policy and law on consumer protection I have conducted face to face interviews of some eminent jurists, experts and consumers, and others in various fields of consumer affairs.

DESIGN OF STUDY

Now before turning directly to the study work it is appropriate to comment briefly on chapters in which I have divided the study work.

The main object of the study is introduced and addressed in Chapter 1 followed by a smallest Chapter 2 which contains broad concepts of expressions—consumer, consumerism, etc. In the later part of this chapter some factors primarily responsible for consumer exploitation has been briefly pointed out and in order to curb their menace some suggestions got pointed out.

Chapter 3 deals with the evolution and development of consumer law which is in a scattered form. Chapter also carries brief account of some time-honoured doctrines and detailed account of United Nations General Assembly guidelines.

Chapter 4 deals with commentary on The Jammu and Kashmir Consumer Protection Act, 1982 and wherever possible suitable case law has been referred at the appropriate places and in the light of Consumer Protection Act, 1986 critical observations have been also made wherever possible and necessary.

Chapter 5 is comparatively big chapter consisting a variety of judgments decided by a National Commission and Supreme Court from time to time. The reason for incorporating this chapter in the study work is mainly that these judgments have simplified and widened the scope of various provisions of this Act to a large extent. Further among other things there is a overwhelming impact of these judgments on almost all Consumer Disputes Redressal Agencies of the country including the State of Jammu and Kashmir.

Study in Chapter 6 is wholly concerned to assess the quasi-judicious attitude towards the consumer in the State of Jammu and Kashmir.

Next chapter titled as "Conclusion and Suggestions" concludes on the whole study work and some suggestions have been made for the promotion and protection of legal protection to consumers.

CHAPTER

2

CONSUMERISM: PROBLEMS AND PERSPECTIVES

INTRODUCTION

Prior to Industrial Revolution the needs of human beings were very few and these were met through exchange of goods. There existed a barter system that is exchange of possession of goods of one kind with the other catering to their mutual requirements. There was no competition as the concept of market was not in vague at all. The wants of people were not many. However, the Industrial Revolution has caused radical changes in the lives of human beings as regards the goods and articles consumed by them in the day-to-day life. The consumer goods flooded the market and the traders started adopting various devices to sell the goods manufactured by them. The concept of market was also brought into existence. As more and more inventions—more and more goods and articles were manufactured and the human being started relying upon them more often. The untrained consumer is very often cheated in the quality, quantity and price of goods or services. About the marketing as already mentioned in Chapter 1 it is rightly commented that it is more complex to study and there may never be any stable scientific laws in this field. The developed countries like United States of America and United Kingdom were first to realize the need to protect the interest of consumer who became a powerful and intelligent class in the society. As in other countries of the world in our country also the concept of consumer came into existence and consumer protection became one of the primary duties of State. Inspite of various efforts both legislative and administrative to prevent the Commission and repetition of consumer crimes, these crimes which have eroded almost all vitals of society are growing at a fast rate. While this in mind, this short chapter is intended to concentrate on concepts of Consumer, Consumerism and point out the problems which are also known by the other name that is socio-economic crimes. These problems, and/or crimes are responsible for hindering the promotion and protection of consumer rights. Lastly, the chapter presents an analysis of the interaction between researcher and the actual consumers.

(A) THE CONSUMER—A CONCEPT

The word 'consumer' though looks simple to understand its meaning but for more convenience it will be understood under the following sub-headings.

(I) Ordinary Meaning

A pertinent question that first of all arises in the present context is who is a consumer? In the answer it may be pointed out that in simple words, every human being who consumes anything for survival is a consumer. For example, one who eats food, buys commodities either from a cooperative store or approved ration shop, stands in queue to buy kerosene, smokes, bidi or cigarette, travels on horse, bullock-cart, camel-cart, bus, motor-car, train or plane, hires taxi or auto-rickshaw, takes flat or house on rent, buys house, gets teeth filled or extracted, gets cloths stitched, gets cloths cleaned, buys auto-mobile or any other mode of transport, pays electricity and water charges, buys shoes or gets repaired and drinks alcohol. One is also a consumer who gets building work done, goes to doctor, lawyers or any professional, operates bank account and safe deposit value, hires architect and surveyors, goes to cinema and theatre and involves in any kind of transaction.[1]

(2) Dictionary Meaning

This word has always been defined in a specific sense, for instance, the Longman Dictionary of English Language[2] defines consumer as "one who purchases goods or services."

The Oxford Advanced Learners Dictionary[3] also defines consumer as "a person who buys goods or uses services." According to the Collins English Dictionary[4] a consumer is a "person who purchases goods and services for his own personal needs. "Whereas the Random House Dictionary[5] defines the consumer as "a person or an organization that uses a commodity or service." Similarly, according to the Oxford English Dictionary[6] a consumer is "one who purchases goods or pays for services."

(3) Statutory Meaning[7]

First of all we will begin with the Section 4 of the Consumer Protection Act, 1978 of Finland which defines consumer as a person who acquires consumer goods or service primarily for his personal use or for use in his private household.

Almost identical language has been used by Section 1 of the Draft Consumer Protection for Slovenia which defines consumer as "a person who acquire goods and service in the first place in the personal use or use in his/her household.

1. Rajendra Kumar Nayak, Consumer Protection Law in India (An Eco-Legal Treatise on Consumer Justice), 1991, Ed. 1, Bombay, N.M. Tripathi Pvt. Ltd.
2. Gurjeet Singh, The Law of Consumer Protection in India, 1996, Deep & Deep Publications, New Delhi; Seen also the Laxman Dictionary of English Language (1991), New Ed., Essex, Longman Group U.K. Ltd., p. 343.
3. *Ibid.*; Seen also The Oxford Advanced Learners Dictionary of Current English (1989), Fifth Ed., Oxford University Press, p. 252.
4. *Id.*; Seen also the Collins English Dictionary (1991) 3rd Ed.
5. *Id.*; Seen also the Random House Dictionary of the English Language (1987) 2nd Ed. New York.
6. *Id.*; Seen also Oxford Dictionary, 1989, p. 802.
7. *Ibid.*

Section 20(6) of the Consumer Protection Act, 1987 of the United Kingdom defines the term 'consumer' as under:

"Consumer"—

(i) in relation to any goods means any person who might wish to be supplied with the goods for his own private use or consumption;

(ii) in relation to any services or facilities means any person who might wish to be provided with any services or facilities otherwise than for the purposes of any of his business; and

(iii) in relation to any accommodation means any person who might wish to occupy the accommodation otherwise than for the purposes of any business.

The Molony Committee on Consumer Protection in Britain regarded a consumer as one "who purchases or hire purchases goods for private use or consumption."

Thus, in the context of the British Consumer Protection Law, the traditional view of a consumer or at least that given by the thrust of the modern consumer protection legislations is of an individual dealing with a commercial enterprise. However, according to David Oughton, it is also the case that the term 'consumer' encompasses a person who makes use of the services provided by public sector or private monopolies subject to public control.[8]

In the United States, Ralph Nader also known as the father of modern consumerism has taken the view that the term 'consumer' should be equated with the word 'citizen' . . .

Coming to the Indian Law of protection, the definition of the term 'consumer' given in the Consumer Protection Act, in its Section 2(1)(d) is fairly wide. It not only includes within its ambit any person who buys any goods or hires or avails

8. On this basis he argues, Consumer Protection Law would also cover complaints by individuals about the services provided by British Gas, British Rail, Electricity and Water Companies.

of any services for consideration it also includes any user of such goods or beneficiary of such services.[9]

(4) A Comparative View

Now if we analyze all the five definitions mentioned above, we will find some differences among them. For instance the first definition is a very simple and straight forward one. Under this definition any body who purchases goods or services is a consumer. The second and the third definitions are almost the same except that instead of the words 'purchases goods and services' the words 'pays for services' and 'uses services' have been respectively used. The fourth definition is more clear than the earlier three definitions as it specifically defines the consumer as a person who 'purchases goods and services for personal needs'. The fifth definition, however appears to be broader than all of them as it includes even an organization in the ambit of the term consumer. Thus, the judicious admixture of all these definitions would consider a consumer as a person or an organization that purchases goods or services for their personal needs. This is rather broad definition. The same is true under the statutory definitions which to some extent are similar to each other but the definition as given under Indian law is more wide and comprehensive.

(B) CONSUMER PROTECTION

It will be more suitable and convenient to know the meaning and aspects, etc. of the consumer protection under some sub-headings.

(1) Meaning

The phrase 'consumer protection' in the larger context would refer to some kind of safeguard for the members of the society from all sorts of malpractices and exploitative deeds of market operators, the incidence of which in the final analysis affect adversely the individual in the society—the consumer. Under the social conditions in which the average

9. For definition of consumer note *infra* Chapter IV.

citizen survives, he needs and required to be protected from the activities that are social evils like corruption, under payment and exploitation, ill-treatment, and exploitation, unhealthy and unhygienic working conditions, adulteration, spurious and injurious manufactures, black marketing and price hike, over charging, misguidance by false advertisements, misuse of trademarks and patents, non-labeling and mislabeling, duplications and similar other deceitful market practices. More pointedly referring to protection against duping of the consumer by the selling and distributing agencies in the market, consumer protection in its narrow import signifies remedy for and protection of the one who pays the price[10]—

(i) to ensure that the consumer gets what he has paid for in quality and in right measure; and
(ii) to enforce his rights, if the consumer does not get the right thing in right measure, for which he has paid the money value.

Thus in the narrow import, it is protection against the sale and supply of bad, sub-standard and duplicate consumer products in the market; non-supply and short supply of consumer goods; unwarranted and excessive pricing and the false and misleading advertisement camouflaging the truth. In the ordinary social terminology these activities of the market agencies are referred to by the twin term adulteration and black-marketing.[11]

It is undeniable that the onus of protecting the individual and society in general is on the government of the day. Modern governments charged with the duties of a welfare state have no escape from pursuing policies both administrative and legislative for the common good and protecting the consumers from the undesirable activities of the Shylocks in trade and commerce. Thus as the consumer protection movement gained momentum

10. P.G. Krishnan, Article, 'Consumer Protection and the Law', Consumer Protection and Legal Control (Essays and Papers, UGC National Seminar at University of Cochin), Ed. P. Leela Krishnan, Eastern Book Company, p. 123.
11. *Id.* at p. 124.

every enlightened government rose to the occasion and legislated on the matter.[12]

(2) Aspects of Consumer Protection

When we talk of consumer protection, we should bear in mind three important things, these are firstly, the physical protection of the consumer; secondly, protection of the economic interest of the consumer; and thirdly, protection of public interest. The first aspect would include measures to protect consumer against products that are unsafe or injurious to health and hygiene.

The second aspect would cover measures to protect the consumer against deceptive and other unfair trading practices and to provide him adequate means to get his grievances redressed. The third aspect would cover measures to prevent abuse of monopoly position or restrictive practices.[13]

(3) Devices of Consumer Protection[14]

There are three alternative devices of providing consumer protection in the market—

(a) Consumer Association

Consumer Unions envisage providing protection to consumer interests and rights. Consumers evolve to ensure distributive justice to consumers when the business enterprise fails to recognize its social responsibilities.

(b) Business Self-regulation

Under this system a business enterprise on its own maintains certain ethical standards towards consumer and evolves consumer-oriented marketing plans and programmes. Business by self-regulation gives a fair deal not only to a consumer but also to a retailer.

---

12. *Ibid.*
13. *Id.* at p. 25.
14. Dr. Keshav Sharma, Article, 'Consumer Movement in India', The Daily News Paper *Kashmir Times*, 15, 2001, p. 5.

(c) Consumer Legislation[15]

Consumer legislations provide statutory protection to consumers against unfair trade practices. Consumer legislation is the crudest form as well as the last resort to secure a disciplined business conduct. The government by implementing special consumer legislation ensures, competition, provision of information to consumers and fairplay through regulation of unfair trade practices. Moreover, legislation also ensures the consumer's right to represent their interest in all government regulating agencies.

(C) CONSUMERISM

After knowing consumer and consumer protection[16] the next question arises what is consumerism? Let us know about consumerism below in brief words.

(I) Meaning

Consumerism is an organized movement of citizens and government to strengthen the rights and power of buyers in relation to sellers. It is an ideology and a concept which has came to stay in business literature. The consumer is exposed to many hazardous—physical, environmental and exploitation due to unfair trade practices. He needs protection, for instance, against products which are unsafe for consumption such as drugs and adulterated food products and products which may cause badly injury such as defective electrical appliances. He needs protection against mal-practices and deceit by sellers. He should have adequate rights and the right of recourse to redressal measures against defaulting businessman. He should be protected against environmental pollution of air, water and noise and effective measures should be devised to keep the surroundings neat and clean.

---

15. For important legislation in the State note *infra,* pp. 10-93.
16. During the early years of the last century, legal protection for the consumer was the aim, but later emphasis began to be placed on the information and education. Now, the term 'Consumerism' rather than consumer protection describes the wide-ranging efforts to Aid the individual, consumer A.Q. Ahanger—Article, 'Protecting Consumer', The Daily News Paper *Greater Kashmir,* 20th July, 1999.

The consumer also needs protection against misleading or untrue information through advertisements. Consumerists have advocated and in many cases won such proposals on the right to know the true interest cost of a loan, the true cost per standard unit of competing brands (unit pricing) the basic ingredients in a product (ingredient labeling), the nutritional quality of food (nutritional labeling), the freshness of product (open dating) and the true benefits of a product (truth in advertising). They want the government to check on the safety of products that are potentially hazardous and penalize companies that are careless. Some consumerists want companies to elect consumer representatives to their boards to introduce consumer consideration into business decision makings.[17]

Unlike the U.S.A. where 100% of the consumer products and 90% of the consumer services (the only exception being the postal service) are produced, manned and maintained by the private sector, in India about seventy-five percent of consumer products and nearly hundred percent of the consumer services are produced, manned and maintained by the government sector. The government therefore, becomes the main source of all consumer problems.[18] The onus of promoting consumerism as a movement in a country like India therefore rests to a very large extent on the government and the story is no different from the countries which are like of ours and our State of Jammu and Kashmir is no exception to this.

(2) Need and Reasons[19]

The need of strong consumerism for/in our country (India) is on account of the following reasons:

(i) In a vast country like India, it is very difficult to organize the consumers. The people besides being the backward have linguistic, cultural and religious differences which make the problems quite intricate.

17. *Supra* Note 14.
18. *Ibid.*
19. *Ibid.*

(ii) Majority of our population is illiterate, uneducated, ignorant and ill-informed.

(iii) Poverty, lack of social awareness, accepting life as it is and passive outlook are some of the factors which make consumer movement difficult to thrive.

(iv) There may not be a positive common objective for the consumers except their desire for safe quality products, for reasonable price and a feeling of strong negative reactions against the products. In the wake of large scale production and the variety and choice conferred on the consumers, a consumer needs guidance which can only be appropriately provided by a consumer organization.

(v) Multiple overlapping roles of individual members with diverse interests and attitudes are often contradicting and conflicting with each other. Individual consumers are more interested in themselves for short and immediate benefits ignoring the long range common interest. This conflicting role without positive long range objectives and ready to sacrifice common interest for self-interests gives death blow to consumerism. Hence the need of the hour is that consumers should themselves rise to the occasion to check the wrong against public interest.

(vi) The advertisements bombarded on the consumers make them quite confused and hence again a need for consumer guidance.

(vii) The deceitful sellers do not give a consumer his money's worth. The goods which are sub-standard defective, inferior in performance and with high price are passed out to him. The unfair trade practices like hoarding and black-marketing on the part of the sellers is a common site in our business scenario. This is a case of clear consumer exploitation.

(viii) The various governments have themselves all been exploiters. It has always been the endeavour of each successive government at the centre or at the State to befool a voter. All issues centre around a man. The energies of any government are mainly channelized around how to retain a power? Any kind of shame on majority of our politicians is rare. They make matters vexed, earn money, indulge into the worst form of nepotism, corruption and favouritism. Their conduct is deplorable beyond description. They came again on time to masses and ask for votes, and worst is the innocent voters still vote for them and ensure election victories for these proven criminals who occupy a central stage in the political set-up. They eat almost every thing themselves by not allowing the progress to reach a commoner. The consumerists need to pass on this very important message of not letting themselves fall prey to these unscrupulous politicians.

(D) PROBLEMS AND PERSPECTIVES: A BRIEF ACCOUNT

With the rise in prices and standard of living, consumers have became cost conscious. Taking advantage of the helplessness of consumers, unscrupulous traders play with the life and happiness of consumers and millions of innocent people buy, sell adulterated articles of food, drink and drug at a cheaper rate and make huge profits. They resort to various undesirable methods of adulteration starting from the stage of manufacture to that of sale of the articles even at the risk of the consumer's, health, happiness and life. It is shocking to know that poisonous constituents are often added to articles of food and drinks and spurious drugs are sold resulting in number of deaths and causing innumerable diseases. Fake and misleading advertisements are made and published in newspapers, magazines, radio and television, etc. about the quality and effect of drugs and medicines. False assurances are given regarding the treatment of chronic diseases, etc. causing incalculable harm and irreparable damage to the health and wealth of the people. In this context let us identify the following notable consumer crimes so called socio-economic crimes which round the cloak have multiplied consumer miseries and sorrows.

(1) Adulteration

Adulteration in ordinary sense means an act of making an inferior article for a superior one in order to gain illegitimate profit. The health of its citizens ought to be the primary concern of any state. In order to secure better health to its citizens it falls upon the State to ensure that there is no adulteration in foodstuffs, drugs or cosmetics. However, food and drug adulteration is going so unchecked that a stage has reached where every doctor is having a good busy day. All violations of prescribed standards of purity and quality and orders regarding limitation of coloring or preservations are adulteration. Adulteration of food and drugs is often described as subtle murders predicted on the community. It mostly starts with the manufacturers and travels to the wholesalers and retailers.

(2) Corruption

There is a nexus between corruption and the social problems. Every social problem is in itself a state of corruption. Corruption is the cause, the problems its consequences.[20] Whether it is adulteration, hoarding, black-marketing, corruption, etc. are all remote controlled. "Jawahar Lal Nehru has on record said that the black-marketer should be hanged at the nearest pole." But alas, it remained a good quotable quote. In sheer desperation, "Mrs. Indira Gandhi under played the damage done to Indian polity by the ever increasing influence of corrupt politician and bureaucrats."[21] In recent times a number of influential people, mostly in position of power, have been let off in corruption cases because of laxity in the law or some procedural constraint.[22] Today, the institutionalized abuse of public resources for

20. *Supra* Note 16, B.N. Saqib Khan, Article, 'The Causes of Corruption', 9th of October, 2000.
21. *Supra* Note 14, N.C Joshi, 24th of January, 2000.
22. *Ibid.*

private ends, by public servants, is an all-pervasive disease sweeping all classes and sections of society. Corruption has eroded efficiency, worsened governance and induced rent-seeking in place of productive activity.[23] The horror or dropsy outburst in 1998 is still fresh in people's memory. In Delhi alone the death toll was sixty-seven due to consumption of adulterated Mustard Oil. Gujarat appears to be a major player in the field of adulteration. Being aware of the menace State government decided to come down heavily on the powerful and wealthy adulterators but there was lack of support from centre. In a case detention orders of culprits were revoked by the Centre government even before they could be arrested. So to say comprehensive and enough punishments will not suffice unless government itself will protect and promote consumer interests and collective effort on the part of consumers is needed to curb the corruption.[24]

(3) Deceptive Advertising

Another areas of consumer anxiety have been consumer credit and deceptive advertising. The word 'advertising' is derived from the French word 'adverter' which means to give notice and ordinarily in business set-up it means to give information about a new product its quality, durability, etc. but more often reverse is the case. Advertising gives fictitious information instead of meaningful information which has the evil effects on consumers and the society. In the past, there was little redress against exorbitant interest rates, fraud and deception. In advertising field, consumer can become a prey to beguiling modern techniques which today dominate electronic media, particularly. Advertising has and does enable the consumer to make some sort of choice between retailing outlets and brands by the information it provides but it has also created artificial desires and disguise superficial wants as real needs. There has been little legal control by government over the claims and methods of advertising.

23. *Ibid.*
24. *Ibid.*, M.M. Khajooria, Article, 'Food Adulteration—A Crime that Kills Silently', 15th of March, 2001.

(4) Misbranding Articles

Misbranding means to brand falsely or in a misleading way. It is an imitation of any product or substance which resembles in a manner likely to deceive another article of food under the name of which it is sold and is not plainly labeled so as to indicate its true character. Sometimes it is falsely stated to be the product of any place or country or it is sold by a name which belongs to another article of food. If it is so coloured, flavoured or coated, powdered or polished the fact that the article is damaged is concealed or if the article is made to appear of better or of greater value than it really is. Under this heading a person misrepresents his goods as the goods of another person and sometimes uses such mark, sign, symbol, device or means, etc. which can mislead a customer to purchase it. Ranbir Penal Code has also defined and prescribed punishment for using a false property mark and for possession of any instrument for counterfeiting a property mark.[25]

(5) Monopolistic Trade Practices

The right to carry on trade or business is a traditional right. It became a guaranteed right for the first time in the 13th century when it was mentioned in the Magna Carta of 1215. The right has been cherished and valued much because it helps to keep the channels of distribution open for the benefit of the consumer. Therefore, grant of monopoly by the State to or assumption of monopoly by any individual or corporation to trade in any item or items has been viewed with great alarm because it not only interferes with the right of others to carry on trade in those items but also puts a clog on the channels of distribution. Restrictive Trade Practice is concerned only with primary effect on competition but Monopolistic Trade Practice is concerned not only with primary or immediate effect on competition but also with secondary or final effect that is the effect on prices, quality of goods or technical development or capital investment. There

25. Sections 481-489 RPC; Seen also Food Adulteration Act; Drugs and Cosmetics Act which gives a comprehensive definition of the word 'Misbranded'.

is a bit of overlapping between the inherent nature of Monopolistic Trade Practice and its impact on public interest.[26]

(6) Restrictive Trade Practices

'Restrictive Trade Practice'[27] means a trade practice which has or may have the effect of preventing, distorting or restricting competition in any manner and in particular which tends to obstruct the flow of capital or resources into the stream of production or which tends to bring about manipulation of prices or conditions of delivery or to effect the flow of supplies in the market relating to goods or services in such manner as to impose on the consumers unjustified costs or restrictions. The effect of trade practice may be actual or reasonably predictable on a balance of probabilities. If the practice is in operation for some time, its probable effects may be gauged from its actual effects in the past. If the practice is merely introduced or is about to be introduced judicial prediction will be called for. In every case effect should be on competition in the relevant trade. It can be at the producers level or at the intermediate level or at the retailer's level or at the consumer's level. However, it is not every restraint of competition and not every restraint of trade that works an injury. Only unreasonable restraint of trade that has such an effect is deemed to be unlawful.

(7) Spurious Goods

Goods are sub-standard when they are not of the standard as prescribed by the law. The goods available in the market specially drugs and cosmetics are reported to be sub-standard. Even drugs of some reputed companies have been found sub-standard. Now nobody gets amazed to know about the death caused by spurious drugs. Even a natural death is now believed to be caused by a spurious drug. Many

26. MRTP Act, 1969.
27. Section 2(1)(nn) of Consumer Protection Act, 1987 which requires a consumer to buy, hire or avail of any goods or as the case may be services on a condition precedent for buying, hiring or availing of other goods or services.

cosmetics claiming to whiten the dark skins is nothing but a sales gimmick for all those gullible young and old who are spending hundreds of rupees on these products. In the long run they prove more harmful than beneficial. Similarly, sub-standard transformers and pressure cookers resulting in no power and death or physical injury are all forms and sizes of sub-standardization of goods.

(8) Unfair Trade Practices

Ordinarily an 'unfair trade practice'[28] means a trade practice which is detrimental to the interests of the consumer whether the interests are economic or in respect of health, safety or other matters which can be regarded as unfair to the consumer. Unfair trade practice in view of Section 36-A (1) Part B of the MRTP (Amendment) Act, 1984 means a trade practice which for the purpose of promoting the sale, use or supply of any goods or for the provision of any service adopts any unfair method or unfair or deceptive including practice of making any statement orally or in writing or by visible representation that the goods are of a particular standard, quality, quantity, grade composition, style or model but which are not. Similarly, if a person gives warranty or guarantee about the quality, durability which is not based on an adequate or proper test or makes a false or misleading representation, etc. are categorized as unfair trade practice.

(9) Violation of Standards of Weights and Measures[29]

A standard means a basis of measurement of quantity or quality of any thing. In order to maintain reliability in trade and commerce measuring units are prescribed and most of these measuring units have earned international recognition. These measuring units are essential not only for maintaining reliability in foreign trade but also for the protection of the consumer. Various Standard gauges, weights and measures on quantity and quality are prescribed but

28. *Id.* Clause (r) of Section 2(1).
29. Seen Violation of Weights and Measures Act.

quite often these standards are violated and faulty gauges, weights and measures are used in violation of weights and measures are no less harmful than adulteration in food, drugs and cosmetics. The two are co-related yet distinctive therefore, they have been treated under different heads.

(E) EVIL EFFECTS OF THE ABOVE CRIMES—CONSEQUENCES

In the State of the Jammu and Kashmir no serious study or survey has been conducted on the subject-matter so far. Since the State is industrially poor and sick, most of consumer goods are imported from rest of the country including the adulterated ones. It is learnt apart from hoarding and profiteering food and drug adulteration is rampant in the State of Jammu and Kashmir. Food is the first requirement of life. Food habits vary from society to society but all societies require purity of the preferred food as *sine qua non*. Mal-nutrition is the result as much of impurity of food and energy and cases of serious malnutrition do not respond to treatment. In a consumer society, the prevalence of the practice of selling adulterated food can and does rise to higher infirmity and mortality rates. Who is responsible and how to control this sorry state of affairs let us seek public opinion.

(I) Interaction with Learned Personalities—Some Views

- The Holy Quran gives a clear cut picture on the point of discussion that he who cheats or exploits others he will be sent to the Jehannum where punishment of fire is for him. So producers, traders and retailers, etc. should refrain themselves from cheating and unfairly treating or exploiting others.
  —*Mir Waiz Qazi Amanullah Sahib*

- They have unanimously expressed their concern over the States failure of not introducing consumer forums in their areas. They said there is high level of adulteration in essential eatables and goods.

The process of sending complaints to competent consumer forums through Deputy Commissioners of their respective areas is overburden on them which has discouraged consumers to redress their grievances by way of simple and speedy remedy.

—Javaid Ahmad Khawja, D.S.P., Abdul Razaq Master and others, Poonch & Rajouri.

- Consumers must make their associations in every part of the State both in urban and rural areas. Consumers in a representative character must launch a struggle for improving the lot of the consumers. Further Consumer Forums in this State need to be given due support, financially, administratively and consumer education must reach to every corner of the State.

  —Ad. Roopak Ratta, Jammu and Kashmir High Court, Jammu.

- I appeal to all those scholars, students and those who are in touch with consumer affairs in the State to organize debates and seminars especially in rural and far-flung areas so that the ill-informed and illiterate people will become aware of their rights and killing nature and effects of consumer and other socio-economic crimes, etc.

  —Deputy Registrar Co-operatives, Mr. Sonaullah Adil.

- The great Philosopher Rousseau has rightly said, "Man is born free but everywhere he in chains." By recalling the great Philosopher here I want to convey that we are all consumers in one or the other form dependent on each other. We are having wide and ample statutes and administrative rules covering fraudulent sale supply, distribution and storage, etc. of goods but unless and until we all consumers in one form or the other become conscious of our duties towards each other and the country at large we will not prosper in any way whether it is consumer movement and/or the matter of nation-building.

  —Poet & Critic Mr. Arjan Dev Majboor, Udhampur.

- We are having bundle of laws to protect the consumer but the problem is of their lukewarm enforcement. The State Consumer Protection Act has many defects which are to be removed by Amendment by incorporating many provisions of Central Act. So the immediate need is for establishment of consumer forums at district and tehsil level.

  —Announcer, Radio Kashmir, Mr. Majid Jahangir

- Police and checking squad must properly made inspections and those found guilty or indulged in unfair trade practices be punished heavily and rigorously so that they will become examples for those like-minded persons. It will not only deter the culprits from committing and repeating crimes but will go a long way in making all traders and shopkeepers conscious of their duties and afraid of police raids and they will check their goods, etc. themselves regularly.

  —Trader Mr. Mohd. Yaqoob, Sabzi Mandi, Anantnag.

- We are not exploiting our customers. People especially ladies must be enough wise to decide while purchasing household or other goods or essential commodities. We are giving them a variety of items they demand and it is their sweet choice which makes them to purchase and we are selling accordingly in due regard to their needs and requirements.

  —Shopkeepers Mr. Youser Bhat & Mr. Arif Shawl, Chanpora, Srinagar.

- Our food supply is highly adulterated with a large percentage of pesticides. Pesticides might have the effect of preventing crops and fruits from the pests and birds but they have dangerous effects on health of the consumers. So steps should be taken by the government itself to control and prohibit sale and supply of pesticides which carries a serious threat to life and safety of the people.

  —Agriculture Assistant Mr. Sheikh Mohd. Iqbal, Anantnag.

- This Kendra plans and produces programmes/ segments on consumer awareness regularly. We are telecasting various programmes on Agriculture —'Buterath', womens programme Urdu/Kashmiri, current affairs programme 'Amne Samne' and live weekly programme 'Hello DD' with phone informant. Besides, this Kendra disseminates information on consumer awareness through spots, quickies, short films, documentaries and special voice over captions from time to time.

—Coordinator for Director, Door Darshan Kendra, Srinagar.

- In our State of Jammu and Kashmir consumer exploitation has crossed all limits. It is desirable that the government should fix prices of essential prices so that the consumer would not be cheated by the hands of unscrupulous traders. Net retail price should be printed on packaged commodities and goods instead of local taxes extra.

—Z.A. Qurreshi, Jammu and Kashmir High Court, Srinagar.

- On consumer protection there is a separate Act titled 'Consumer Protection Act' which should be implemented at the grass-root level. If we want consumer welfare and better quality of life for our consumers in the state we all including the government and manufacturers, sellers and consumers must made efforts to act together for the betterment and safety of the people to ensure comfortable standards of life for all.

—Producer Mr. G.A. Rather, Doordarshan, Srinagar.

- The ways as the things are developing on the economic front one can say that our 'consumer' has became a king. He has wide variety of similar goods to choose from at competitive prices which he was denied earlier. We are having ample law, rules and regulations but the problem is their lukewarm enforcement. Consumers are not aware of their rights, government and Media must pay attention towards consumer problems only then the consumer will be real king otherwise it will amount negligence on their part also.

—*Writer Mr. Talha Jhangir, Radio Kashmir, Srinagar.*

- In our state people are not aware of their rights and law and order is collapsed. In these circumstances exposure to consumer awareness be given first priority.

—*Sobia, Hina, Orooj-ul-Islam & Iqra Jan Melanson School, Srinager.*

- We are without proper drinking water and have no irrigation facility. No government has shown mercy to us. It was during the rule of Badshah Sahib when we were provided with tubewell facility.

—*Residents of Villages Kulangam, Watpora, Hatmullah, Mughalpora, Udipora, Rajwar & Nagri, Distric Kupwara.*

- While expressing the fear and insecurity as the cholera has recently killed seven persons including two children in the surrounding villages by taking impure water, villagers shouted slogans against the government which as they said has failed to provide them water in pure and hygienic conditions. However, it is admitted that the concerned minister of their area has given them assurance that he will take the matter up to the higher authority as soon as possible.

—*Residents of Villages Yaripora, Sonigam, Tarigam, Tehsil Kulgam, District Anantnag.*

- Yes, I am habitually taking liquor and that day also I had taken a little quantity of it. When my health conditions deteriorated I was admitted to hospital. I am an illiterate man and knows nothing about the quality and contents of liquor except that I am purchasing it only when it costs me at low price rate.

—*Abdul Rashid, Taxi Driver, Camedy Adda, Anantnag.*

- We are waiting here as we want to go Jammu from this place. Though distance from Jammu to Srinager and *vice versa* is the same but these Sumo drivers without any reason and rhyme are demanding sometimes Rs. 1.50 and sometimes Rs. 300 per head on one side. We are the employees working in Secretariat but have no time to lodge complaints. You are requested to bring the matter before the concerned authority. We expect you to make the concerned authority aware and to fix fare for this route so that passengers will not be exploited in future.

  —Syed Abdul Rashid Chhanapora, Ratanlal Sharma, Goggi Bagh, Srinager.

- As a consumer I will like to say that I am taking beer as medicine but I know often this variety imported in the valley is not of the set prescribed standards. It is difficult for the people to say anything about its purity but government officials are required to check these items before it reaches in the market.

  Yes, as a good citizen I should also play my role in raising cry against any unfortunate thing which I may observe say for example adulteration or impurity in such commodities which will badly affect the health and wealth of poor consumers but you know we are living in such society where as compared to western society users of beer, liquor or any other commodity of this nature (excluding tobacco users to some extent) are not accepted by the society. In such circumstances to communicate the government officials in case any wrong thing will be personally detected in such goods is one thing but to educate consumers as to what to use, how to use and to what extent they will use. I have my personal hesitation because it will carry social stigma to me.

  —A Doctor who requested for not disclosing his identity.

- Power curtailment at the odd hours has badly

affected our studies. We are busy in the preparations for coming examinations. There is constant hike in tariff but non-supply of electricity is still our fate.

—Students of Burn Hall School, Kothi Bagh College, Srinager.

- Our area remained neglected during last 56 years and it is the time that government should take measures to make out district operational through special development schemes. The entire population of the district should be provided relief and rehabilitation packages in view of the fact that district remained worst hit by terrorism for last 14 years. While commenting on their own rights as consumers participants stressed the need that the Consumer Protection Act, 1987 be made operational at district level if we really want a powerful consumer moment.

  —Residents of Kishtwar through Noor Hasan, Haider Khan, Latif Shah, Md. Ramzan Raina and others.

- I will like to draw the attention of authorities towards unfair practices still being adopted by the business community specially the jewelers and dry cleaners of the Jammu region.

  —Fayaz Ahmad Sofi, Nazeer Ahmad, Muhstaq Ahmad, Khatika Talab, Jammu.

- Consumer awakening programmes be conducted to expose age old exploitation of consumers by the business community.

  —Mr. Tej Krishan, near Gandhi Road, Jammu.

- We have recently purchased cell phones and here maximum number of students are carrying cell phones with themselves. Please make aware the authority that there is no need for the internet or E-mail on these phones. What we really want is more hours to talk at a cheaper rate.

  —Students in the way of tour to Pahalgam.

- There is a wave of violence in our state and we all are insecure in one way or the other. In these circumstances how can we launch consumer movement which comes next to life.
  —Some Hawkers & Fishermen, Dal Lake, Nehru Park, Srinager.

- Everything comes at a price. But it is unfortunate that even after more than 50 years of independence consumer is not receiving the value of his price. It is duty of the government to march forward for achieving consumer protection.
  Tara Singh and Deedar Singh, Bohri Kadel, Srinager.

- We all are crying for consumer protection. Nothing is going to be achieved unless and until something substantial is to be done both by the government by empowering agencies to improve their lot and also by consumers to help themselves.
  —Mrs. Gulshan Nazeer, Lecturer & Gulam Nabi Engineer, HMT, Srinager.

It is important to mention here that while interacting with consumers in various public gatherings, parks and villages just to have spot assessment of the problems confronted by the consumers, their passive attitude and way of taking life as it is due to present turmoil in the valley itself gives signs of their grievances which one way or the other way are found to be related with the violation of human rights, unemployment and poverty. However, for the sake of relevance only those esteemed consumers who have answered the questions not only beyond the expectations but they discuss various aspects of consumer problems (as above mentioned) became part of the present project study. In these circumstances efforts and exhaustive tour is made of various far flung and remote areas just to know about consumer awareness in the state of Jammu and Kashmir. For perusal result of a brief organized programme will be presented here.

FIG. I

Sample Drawn from the Srinagar and Jammu Cities

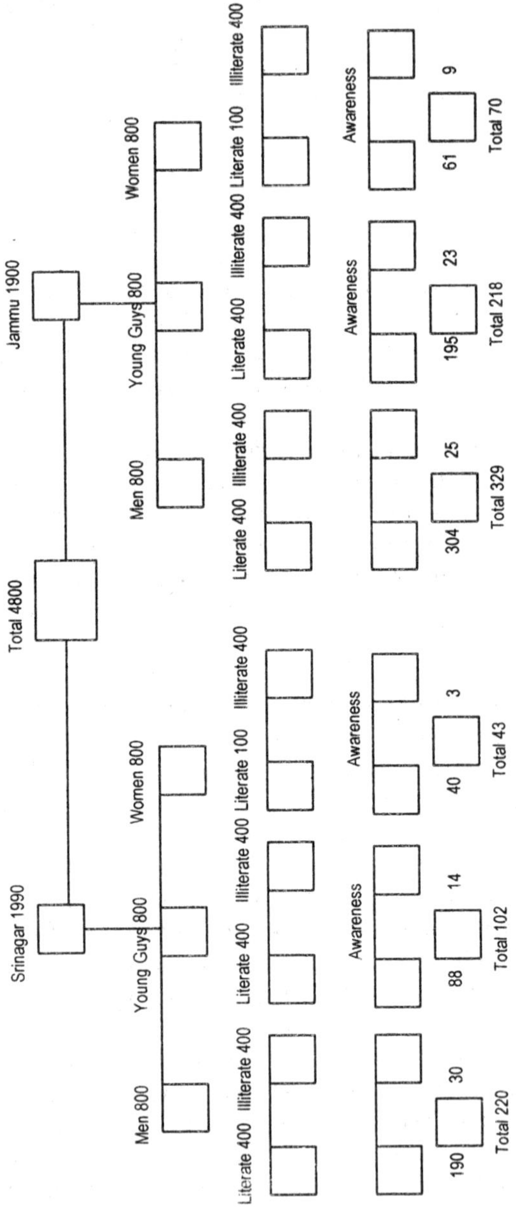

Srinagar 1990
Total 4800
Jammu 1900

Men 800
Young Guys 800
Women 800
Men 800
Young Guys 800
Women 800

Literate 400 Illiterate 400
Literate 400 Illiterate 400
Literate 100 Illiterate 400
Literate 400 Illiterate 400
Literate 400 Illiterate 400
Literate 100 Illiterate 400

Awareness
Awareness
Awareness
Awareness

190 30
Total 220
88 14
Total 102
40 3
Total 43
304 25
Total 329
195 23
Total 218
61 9
Total 70

FIG. 2

Sample drawn from Ligitants of 10 Districts during Lok Adalats conducted at Different Times in Different Court Cmplexes in the State of Jammu & Kashmir

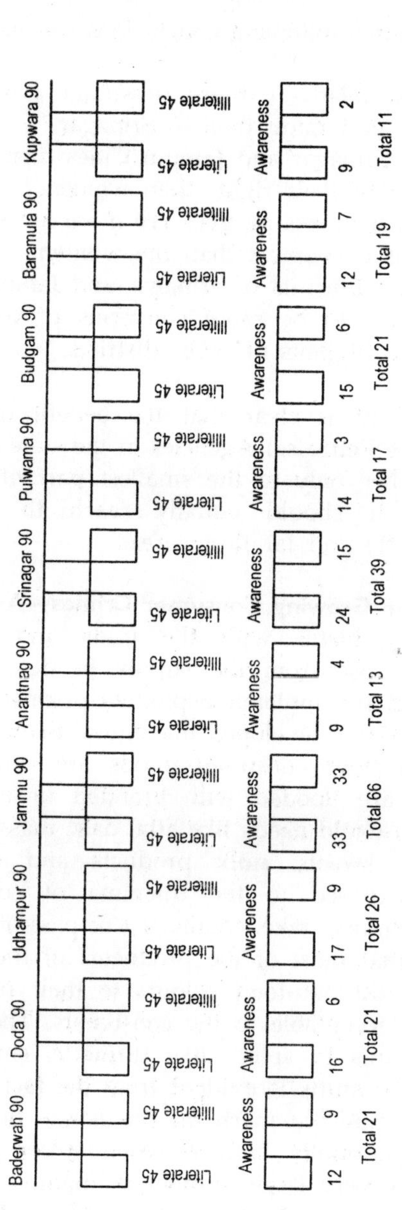

Baderwah 90 — Literate 45, Illiterate 45 — Awareness 12, 9 — Total 21
Doda 90 — Literate 45, Illiterate 45 — Awareness 16, 6 — Total 21
Udhampur 90 — Literate 45, Illiterate 45 — Awareness 17, 9 — Total 26
Jammu 90 — Literate 45, Illiterate 45 — Awareness 33, 33 — Total 66
Anantnag 90 — Literate 45, Illiterate 45 — Awareness 9, 4 — Total 13
Srinagar 90 — Literate 45, Illiterate 45 — Awareness 24, 15 — Total 39
Pulwama 90 — Literate 45, Illiterate 45 — Awareness 14, 3 — Total 17
Budgam 90 — Literate 45, Illiterate 45 — Awareness 15, 6 — Total 21
Baramula 90 — Literate 45, Illiterate 45 — Awareness 12, 7 — Total 19
Kupwara 90 — Literate 45, Illiterate 45 — Awareness 9, 2 — Total 11

From the figures following conclusions can be drawn—

- There is relatively more consumer awareness in the city of Jammu than in Srinagar.
- In both Srinagar and Jammu Cities men are more in know of their rights than women.
- Next to men, young gyes are more aware of their rights as consumers than the women.
- Similarly, litigants of Srinagar and Jammu district are found to be more conscious of their rights than the litigants of other districts.

To conclude, it is clear that the benefit of two-tier Consumer Disputes Redressal Agencies in the state of Jammu and Kashmir reaches only to the smallest part of the state though basically it should equally reach to the poor consumers of remote and far flung areas.

(2) Concern over Growing Consumer Crimes—A Comment

Consumer problems with the trade and consumer sector commonly arise from the supply of defective, sub-standard, fake and manipulated exploitive pricing. Since the State is not industrially developed maximum quantity of food commodities and other consumer goods are coming from outside. Markets are flooded with branded or un-branded items of daily household needs like atta, dals, massala, edible oils, soft drinks, sweets, milk products and what not. Consumers are exposed to the dilemma of confounding choice from the genuine, fake, counterfeit or pass-off goods. It is a known fact that most of the producers of the packages spices and dyes add non-food colours to their products to make these more acceptable to the consumers. The presence of colour adulterants in spices like turmeric, chilli-powder and other such like stuffs is evident from the fact that these colours leave an indelible mark on the hands of the users which does not normally happen when spices ground at home are used. A very large number of manufacturers and traders producing and trading in spices and condiments are reported to be indulging in adulterating their produce. Similarly, the use of organo-phosphates to curb the menace of fungal, bacterial and parasitic injections in vegetables, fruits and even in cereal crops could be a cause for the consumers to contract a variety of diseases as the traces of such fungicides, insecticides, etc. do appear in the produce.[30]

There are reports that the liquid milk imported into the valley to meet the growing demand for the commodity is not wholesome. Only educated and alert consumers are taking actions against these unscrupulous producers and traders. In this context in order to promote consumerism following suggestions are noteworthy—

(a) Self Help

Consumers have to remember that we have to pay a price for quality goods by being alert. Consumers should refuse to accept anything sub-standard. The safest way is to buy items manufactured by well-known companies. There at least one can complain and get the item replaced or money back. However, under all circumstances consumer should remember to take the cash memo and the warranty. One should see that the warranty is signed and stamped by the dealer with date. Greater consumer awareness and assertiveness in buying goods is the only way to help, improve the quality of services and goods. The onus rests squarely on the female consumers because they are the major purchasers for the families. One is witness to educated women and girls just ordering items without checking the dates of manufacture, expiry and the contents, etc. There are a number of so-called departments, stores and other elite shops which sell foreign goods like juices, chocolates, candies and other food items. Several of them are date expired but most of our customers have a craze for every thing foreign so they must be selling without a thought to food poisoning. Even hair dye have a limited life, they became ineffective if they are over the expire date. While making purchases it is good to remember that consumer grievances concerning the purchased item stands good only if he has the cash memo. So make sure consumer always get the shop receipt from the

30. *Supra* Note 20, Article, 'Playing with the Public Health', 14th of April, 2001.

seller.[31]

(b) Consumer Organisation

The consumers must unite and form an association. Unity is Strength. The consumers can bargain with the traders or suppliers when they negotiate as organized group. When consumers are educated and are well-informed, the prices fall and they can get goods of standard quality and weight. Consumers as an organization can fix up the price in consultation with experts. They can appoint experts to check up the purity of the goods and prevent adulteration of food. It can advise the consumers on the use of certain goods, food, drugs and its effects, etc. It can advise to the consumers as to the method of detecting adulteration, etc. Not only this consumer organizations or groups can educate the consumers which will make them powerful and conscious of their rights so as to prevent them from social and economic exploitation by the producers and traders.[32] Though in all developed countries and in the rest of our country also there is mushrooming of consumer organization but in the State of Jammu and Kashmir situation is totally reverse. It is learnt that a voluntary organization was set-up in the name of 'Kashmir Consumer Council' in Kashmir specifically for rural areas but it could not function smoothly due to lack of funds. So there is a need to have increased number of consumer associations here in the State also so that consumer interests will be protected at the grass-root level. If each one wants his own way then encroachments cannot be removed. Consumers should learn to live according to certain laws and principles for the common good. The consumer activist groups have a very important role to act as watch-dog and guide for the consumers.

---

31. *Supra* Note 24, Usha Kumari Jamwal, Article, 'United Efforts for Consumer Rights', 23rd of June 2000.
32. *Supra* Note 10, S.S. Alur, Article, 'Myth of Consumer Protection', p. 182.

(c) The Media

Mass communication is important and must effectively be directed towards the masses. In rural and far flung areas where people are mostly illiterate, if a message is to be effectively communicated to them it is essential that the spoken word media and the indigenous communication channel like songs, drama and other traditional cultural programmes are made use of. Through this media one can communicate his ideas to the masses, beyond imagination. It can generate fire and contrarily can calm the wildest boil also. It is quite evident that how important it is for the welfare of the society. It has the capability to highlight different practical aspects of the society. It can expose the secrets and vigil the society. It can influence the masses regarding what we do? What shall be its consequences and what we should do, etc.[33]

The Newspapers and other periodicals form a stronger media for the protection and ventilation of consumers' interest. So these agencies should take up the task of enlightening and educating the consumers. They should set aside a page or a column once in a week to air the grievances of the consumers or for educating them. This should not be difficult for the press. In the State of Jammu and Kashmir among various newspapers especially the daily newspapers 'Kashmir Times' and 'Greater Kashmir' are publishing consumer articles.

(d) Law and the Courts

In the next chapter we are going to deal with a galaxy of statutory Acts and provisions. These statutes are enacted in the public interest. However, people all over the State are not aware of these statutes and remedies available thereunder are dilatory, time consuming and expensive. Now we have Consumer Protection Act, 1987 which provide a simple, speedy and inexpensive remedy. However, government under the Act has not given District Courts in the rest of the country. Only two Divisional Forums and one State

33. *Supra* Note 31, 23rd of January, 2000.

Commission is functioning for the whole State. In order to avoid the disparity the Act needs to be amended. The Act bestows limited powers on the forums to provide relief to a consumer by removing defects in goods or services, replacement with news goods, refund the price to a consumer or the charges paid by him and award payment of compensation to the consumer for any loss or injury suffered due to negligence of the manufacturer, supplier or dealer. The law does not empower the consumer courts to give collective or policy relief. The Courts should impose a bar on the manufacture of defective goods say for example T.V. sets, cars or any other product about which there are number of complaints.[34]

(e) The Government

The role of the government in providing consumer protection is very vital. While granting licenses under the Industries (Development and Regulation Act) the government can play down the norms for maintaining standard, quality and price. Under this Act the Central Government has power for controlling supply, distribution price, etc. of any article or class of articles. While doing so the government should keep consumer benefit and interest uppermost in it's mind. It should set-up special agencies to check the enforcement of the conditions. Further, it should itself take up the task of supplying other goods. At present it is supplying though not adequately some of the consumable articles. It tries to set-up good standards, the other traders may emulate and in the process the consumer may get a good deal.

OBSERVATION

From the above discussion it is clear that there is a weak relation between the buyer and seller and their socio-economic status. The real irony of the situation is that the considerable price rise in essential commodities gives rise to blackmarketing, hoarding and adulteration which causes severe hardships to the consumers. Although hard decissions

34. *Supra* Note 14 or 17, 17th of March, 2001.

on the economic front are inevitable in view of the increasing burden of subsidy on petroleum products, the Government must keep in mind the interest of the poor consumers who belong to the weaker section of the state population. They are unable to bear even a marginal price rise in essential commodities like food grains (which is the staple diet of all Kashmiris) sugar, cooking gas, kerosene oil, passenger fare. Any increase in the price of cooking gas and kerosene may be okay with the middle and upper middle classes but for the poor consumers it increases the burden to an intolerable level. The next that needs to be emphasised is that accountability at all levels in both public and private sector is to be ensured. Further the philosophy of the new strategies should be to place peoples health in peoples hands with a pledge to ensure that the entire health service system has to be geared to respond the people by responding to their needs. But without active interest of consumers to fight for their rights and active participation of consumer associations, government, law and courts to respond consumer needs consumerism will remain a distant dream. So it is the time we all should understand social responsibility if we really want welfare of everyone. Whether in business, service or profession we all have to eat, drink, live and use the same items in the society. What is good for others is good for us and *vice-versa*. We sink and swim together. Social evils affect all of us not just individual or two. These are crimes against the society which should be punished heavily if we really want to give the consumer a fair deal.

CHAPTER

3

CONSUMER LAW: A COMPREHENSIVE VIEW

INTRODUCTION

> "A customer is the most important visitor in our premises. He is not dependent on us. We are dependent on him. He is not an interruption in our work. He is the purpose of it. He is not an outsider on our business. He is a part of it. We are not doing him a favour by serving him. He is doing us a favour by giving us an opportunity to do so."
>
> —*Mahatma Gandhi*

> "Consumer is the sole end and purpose of all production; and the interest of the producer ought to be attended to only so far as it may be necessary for promoting that of the consumer."
>
> —*Adam Smith*

Since the early writings of well known personalities, namely, John Kenneth, Gilbraith, Vance Packard, Rachal Carson, John Kennedy and Ralph Nadar consumer protection has become a serious concern all over the word. Various consumer organizations have come into existence and various enactments for protection of consumers have been passed. The General Assembly of the United Nations passed guidelines for consumer protection on April, 1985 though origin can be traced to the late 1970's urging Nation States to encourage International cooperation in this field of Consumer Protection. This chapter is an outcome of an attempt to bring together various enactments which cover diverse subjects and provide consumer protection in one or the other form. However, brief account of some time-honoured doctrines of past and consumer law of other countries from whose experience we have been benefited in framing our own consumer law and policy will be dealt in the first part of this chapter.

(A) THE LAW OF TORTS

When a person transfers goods to another person under a contract, his liability arises not only under the Law of Contract but also under the Law of Torts. If defective, unfit or dangerous goods are supplied, liability to compensate for the harm done would arise on the principle of *Donough* v. *Stevenson.*[1] Before this decision there were no proper regulation from government side to prosecute the manufacturers in relation to food products. The English Courts felt a great necessity to impose the privity requirement in *Winterbottom* v. *Wright*[2] as it was observed that the Courts would be faced with "an infinity of actions." In this case the privity requirement was extended to the negligence action of an injured driver against the supplier of a defective mail coach. This holding left the driver remediless owing to the governmental immunity of the employing post master who had contracted for the coach's. Winterbottom was generally followed in America throughout the last Century. The real departure from the application of the doctrine of privity came in 1916 with the landmark case of *Macpherson* v.

1. (1932) A.C. 562; R.K. Bangia, Law of Torts, Allahabad Law Agency, Allahabad, p. 14.
2. 152 E.R. 402 (1842); quoted H.N. Gire, Consumers, Crimes and the Law, 1987, Ashish Publishing House, New Delhi, p. 13.

Buick Motor Company[3] where it was held that an action in negligence could be maintained against a remote manufacturer of an automobile with a defectively manufactured wheel that broke, causing injury to the plaintiff. The Court found that the category of inherently dangerous products is not limited to poisons, explosives and things. . . . Which in their normal operation are implements of destruction rather if the nature of the thing is such that it is reasonably certain to place life and limb in peril when negligently made, it is then a thing of danger. Winterbottom was essentially overruled when the Court further stated:

"If to the element of danger there is added knowledge that the thing will be used by persons other than the purchaser and used without new tests, then irrespective of any contract the manufacturer of this thing of danger is under a duty to make it carefully."[4]

After half a century after this case, erosion in many jurisdiction of the privity requirement took place. This erosion was not only in negligent acts but also for breaches of warranty. Here emphasis was upon the growth of large scale manufacturers and their direct appeals to consumers through extensive advertising.[5]

In *Escola* v. *Coca Cola Bottling Company of Frexsno*[6] Justice Traynor stated that public policy demands that responsibility be fixed wherever it will most effectively reduce the hazardous to life and health inherent in defective products that reach the market. It is evident that the manufacturer can anticipate some hazardous and guard against the recurrence of others, as the public cannot.

In 1936 the law in relation to the liability of the manufacturer and vendor for the protection of consumer interest was widely discussed by Lord Wright in *Grant* v. *Australian Knitting Mills.*[7] In this important case Grant had

3. *Id.* 111 N.E. 1050 (N.Y. 1916).
4. *Ibid.*
5. *Ibid.*
6. *Id.* (Cal. 1994) 436 2nd, p. 150.
7. *Id.*, p. 15 (1936) A.C. 85.

purchased from a retailer a suit of Woolen Wear. He suffered from dermatitis which was found to have been caused by certain chemicals not properly washed out of the clothes while manufacturing. Both the retailer and manufacturer were held liable in damages for contract and tort respectively. Lord Wright held that the former liable in contract because the retailer owes a contractual obligation amounting to a condition or warranty in certain cases under the Sales of Goods Act. The liability of latter in tort was based on the principle laid down in *Donough* v. *Stevenson*.[8] In this case A went to a Restaurant with a woman friend and bought one bottle of ginger-beer manufactured by the defendants. The woman consumed part of the contents but when the remainder was poured in the glass she observed the decomposed body of a snail in it. The ginger-beer bottle being opaque and scaled, the presence of snail could not have been observed earlier. The woman brought an action against the manufacturer for negligence and alleged that by taking a part of the contaminated drink, she had contacted serious illness. The House of Lords held that the manufacturer owed her a duty to take care that the bottle did not contain noxious matter, injurious to health. Referring to the liability of the manufacturer of food articles Lord Macmillan observed:

"I have no hesitation in affirming that a person who for gain engages in the business of manufacturing articles of food and drink intended for consumption by makers of the public in the form in which he issues them is under a duty to take care in the manufacturing of these articles. That duty, in my opinion, he owes to those whom he intends to consume his products. He manufactures his commodities for human consumption; he intends and contemplates that they shall be consumed. By reason of that very fact he places himself in a relationship with all the potential consumers of his commodities, and that relationship which he assumes and desires for his own ends imposes upon him a duty to take care to avoid injuring them. He owes them a duty not to convert by his own carelessness an article which is dangerous to life and health. It is sometimes said that liability can arise

8. *Supra* Note 1.

only where a reasonable man would have foreseen and could have avoided the consequences of his act or omission. In this present case, the respondent, when he manufactured his ginger-beer, had directly in contemplation that it would be consumed by members of the public. Can it be said that he could not be expected as a reasonable man to foresee that if he conducted his process of manufacture carelessly he might injured those whom he expected and designed to consume his ginger-beer? The possibility of injury so arising seems to me in no sense so remote as to excuse him foreseeing it."[9]

Thus in this case it was concluded that the manufacturer was under a legal duty to the ultimate purchaser to consume to take responsible care that the article is free from defect likely to cause injury to his health. This of course holds true only if the purchaser or consumer cannot discover the defect by inspection, the beer was in a sealed bottle; the bottle was of dark opaque glass which under circumstances made it impossible for the consumer to discover the defect (dead snail in the beer) by inspection.[10] The rule in this case was formulated for the protection of the consumer. Liability in tort may arise because of fraud practized or due to negligence. The remedy for breach of contract is available only to the parties to the contract (and to third parties in few cases). This remedy can be contracted out by the parties. The remedy under the law of torts is available to immediate as well as ultimate transferees. This duty is imposed by law generally and is available to all those who are affected. The liability of the manufacturer is further extended to other categories of persons who create a source of danger as in Donough's case. The Rule includes people who repair, erect, assemble or supply articles of any sort or even leave such articles in place where they are likely to be a source of danger.[11]

---

9. *Id.*, p. 15.
10. *Supra* Note 8, pp. 15-16.
11. S.S. Alur, Article, 'Myth of Consumer Protection', Consumer Protection and Legal Control (Essays in papers UGC National Seminar at University of Cochin, Ed. by P. Leela Krishnan, Eastern Book Company, Lucknow.

The rule in *Donough* v. *Stevenson* was formulated for the protection of consumers.[12]

The tort of deceit enables a consumer to recover damages for the fraud practized on him by the other. The defendant makes a false or reckless statement with a view to deceive the plaintiff so as to cause him some loss— pecuniary or otherwise. So to a consumer who suffers by any such means the Law of Torts permits relief in the form of damages.[13]

In India there is freedom of trade and freedom of association (subject to fulfilment of certain conditions and by following the prescribed procedure). This right coupled with the right to combination is misused so as to cause loss to the consumer. There can be combination of traders and by combining into a group may dictate terms to the retailers and consumers. If this combination amounts to the tort of conspiracy, then the consumer has a remedy. It will be actionable only if the persons have combined with a view to cause damage followed by a consequential loss. Exclusive dealership agreements, restrictive trade practices, price maintenance agreements are instances of such agreements. Some of these practices are treated as valid by Section 38 of the MRTP Act, 1996 in the public interest. Others are actionable wrongs. The monopoly position occupied by the traders or businessman is often abused and exploited to their advantages, the victim is the poor remediless consumer.[14]

In the present age of advertisement, every manufacturer, supplier, trader, distributor and even retailers firmly believe that there is no business like show business. Therefore, each advertises in respect of his wares. They spend a lot on advertisements. In the absence of proper and adequate knowledge, the consumer falls a 'prey' to these gimmicks of the trader. The Law of Torts tolerates this 'advertisement gimmick' under the name of 'puffing of goods'. The line between 'puffing' and 'deception' is very thin only in the latter case, the consumer can succeed.[15]

---

12. *Ibid.*
13. *Ibid.*
14. *Id.*, p. 175.
15. *Ibid.*

(B) MEDIEVAL DOCTRINES

After having a brief concept of law of torts let us have a brief account about some medieval doctrines.

(I) Doctrine of *Mens rea*

The general rule of English Law is that no crime can be committed unless there is *mens rea*. This principle is also one of the main characteristics of our legal system that the individual's liability to punishment for crimes depends among other things, on certain mental conditions.[16] Consumer offences fall under the general category of public welfare offences. One of the most important problems in this area is whether the element of *mens rea* should be excluded from such offences contrary to the traditional common principles that *mens rea* is essentially for holding a person criminally responsible. The problem has for many years confronted legislators, lawyers and courts as is there any special reason for the exclusion of *mens rea* from offences created for the protection of consumer interests?[17]

To comment, in most of the offences the accused do an act, in the sense of executing some bodily movement, or omit to do an act. But to commit some offences it is sufficient to show that the accused was in some "state of being", for example was in possession of something or was in some specified place. In a number of offences it must be shown not only that the accused did an act, or omitted to do an act, but also that certain consequences resulted from that act or omission. These two categories of offences are important for the discussion because offence against consumers often belong to these categories. Where certain consequences form part of the *actus reus*, the accused must have foreseen those consequences as are likely to result from his conduct. Where some "state of being" for example being in a certain place or

16. S.N. Misra, Indian Penal Code, 5th Ed., Sanagam Law Agency, Allahabad, p. 11.
17. *Supra* Note 11, G. Sadasivan Nair, Article, '*Mens rea* in Consumer Offences', p. 290.

being in charge of or in possession of something forms part of the *actus reus* of an offence, it must be proved that the accused was voluntarily in that state and either that he must have known that he was in that state, or that he was indifferent as to whether he was in that or not.[18]

To overcome the deficiencies of the traditional doctrine of *mens rea,* the legislature, and to some extent, the courts have created crimes which exclude *mens rea*. These offences are called Strict or Absolute liability offences. Many of these strict liability offences arise under regulatory legislation, controlling such matters as the sale of food and drink, the use of false weights and measures, and the use of misleading or false trade descriptions, control of hoarding and black-marketing, etc. which may widely be classified as consumer offences. The justification for the creation of offences of strict liability is that the requirement that prosecution must prove *mens rea* makes it impossible to enforce many enactments in very many cases.[19]

However, it is to be submitted that the adoption of 'Strict Liability' rule has not succeeded in containing serious consumer offences like adulteration of food. It may be argued that the failure is because of the lapses in implementing the law and what is required is a revamping of the machinery to see that it is more rigorously implemented with the help of the strict rule. But the truth is that lack of a valid discrimination between the wicked and the not so wicked together with the ultra-modeled executive discretion, judicial helplessness and societal sympathy has made it an abusive peace of legislation. No doubt, in some consumer offences strict liability may be the rule, but it is necessary to take away the element of *mens rea* in all its forms from every consumer offence? The answer is no. What is needed is a change from the 'strict liability rule' to the 'negligence rule'. The chance of proving innocence, in the sense of either lack of *mens rea* or having taken all necessary precautions to avoid the mischief, should be given to the accused. Such position is

18. *Id.,* 291-92.
19. *Ibid.*

taken by the legislature under Consumer Protection Act, 1987.[20]

(2) Privity of Contract

The doctrine of 'privity of contract' means that only those persons who are parties to the contract can enforce the same. A stranger to the contract cannot sue.[21] This rule has been primarily designed to meet the requirement of commercial transactions. Under this rule in order to recover damages arising out of the faulty products one must be a buyer. This requirement covers a very limited class of persons who can claim relief as consumers. No member of the family of the buyer or his guest, sustaining injury or damage there from can claim relief. The Law Commission of India, which submitted its eighth report in 1958, while suggesting Amendment in the Sale of Goods Act, failed even to touch the problem of radical reform needed in this field of law. In England, the Molony Committee was constituted to study the problems of consumer transactions and protection and to suggest reform but the said committee confined its definition of 'consumer' to that of buyer only.[22]

There is also the problem of apportioning the loss arising due to faulty products. Under the Sale of Goods Act and Contract Act it is the seller who has to bear the loss for injury or damage arising even due to faulty manufacturing of goods. Here also the rule of Privity of Contract intervenes. Though ultimately in the line of chain of action, the manufacturer may be liable but this method works hard on the seller and is not in the public interest.

Though there is a radical departure from this rule under Consumer Protection Act (under which the consumer does not mean only such person who pay consideration for

---

20. *Id.*, 304.
21. R.K Bangia, Principles of Mercantile Law, 1995, 3rd Ed., Allahabad Law Agency, Allahabad, p. 52.
22. S.S.H. Azmi, A Comparative Study of Law Relating to Consumer Protection under India, British and American System, (1970) 1 S.C.J. (5-18); Seen also Sale of Goods and Consumer Protection in India 1992 Ed. 1, Deep and Deep Publications, Delhi, p. 67.

purchasing the goods or availing the services for private use or consumption but it includes all those persons who use these goods or avail the services with the permission of such persons) but the decision given by the Apex Court in *Indian Oil Corporation* v. *Consumer Protection Council, Kerala*[23] appears to have given undue rise to this rule within the ambit of the Act. In this case 'A', Dr. Kamlasanand, the Secretary of a registered society known as Consumer Protection Society, Kerala took an L.P.G. gas connection through Karthika Gas Agency an authorized distributor of the appellant. 'A' paid the amount towards the charges of obtaining LPG connection and other accessories. Due to irregularities committed by the Gas Agency, its distribution work was suspended for some time by the appellant. On revival of gas agency, a new connection was given to 'A' by it and consequently 'A' requested the appellant (the principal of gas agency) to regularize its gas connection. On refusal by the appellant to regularize the connection, the complainant filed a suit before the Consumer Disputes Redressal Forum on behalf of 'A' all Consumer Disputes Redressal Agencies directed the appellant to regularize the gas connection. On appeal the Supreme Court held that in the absence of privity of contract between the appellant and the complainant there is no deficiency of service.[24]

It is to be submitted that the application of the privity rule by the Supreme Court in this case has resulted in miscarriage of justice as it is against the letter and spirit of the Consumer Protection Act. The Consumer Protection Act has excluded this rule partially in consumer sales, so far as the commercial sales are concerned the rule applies vehemently. So it is hoped that the above decision of the Supreme Court would be disregarded by this court and Consumer Disputes Redressal Agencies in future in order to implement this consumer protection legislation in a peaceful way for the better interest of the consumer.[25]

23. *Id.*, pp. 1-6.
24. *Ibid.*
25. *Id.*, S.C.J.P. 14.

(3) Caveat Emptor

In a civilized society, each citizen has an legitimate expectation that his co-citizen will behave justly and fairly towards him, if not, he expects a suitable remedy for the unjust and unfair dealings towards him which caused, either material loss or mental stress and pain to him. For the social existence, an individual has to cater into commercial dealings either to get essential goods for his own existence or to do commercial service for the existence of others. This inter-dependant relationship in commercial dealings is described as 'seller' and 'buyer'.[26]

Traditionally a seller was kept in a high pedestal with the aid of doctrine of *Caveat Emptor*—'let the buyer be aware' which is an old medieval concept. It assumed that the consumer was responsible for protecting himself and would do so by applying his intelligence and experience in negotiating the terms of any purchase. In ancient time when the consensual nature of the contract reigned supreme, courts were in favour of enforcing the 'intention of the parties', as evident from the 'terms of the contract'. Implied terms by way of conditions and warranties were not given much importance and if interpreted very strictly but mostly not in favour of the buyer.[27] An old case,[28] is typical to illustrate this. In 1603, a gold smith sold a precious stone to Lopus for dollar 100. He told Lopus that it was a bezoar-stone while it was only a fake. The claim for damages failed. The attitude of a court is clear from the following observations:

> " . . . everyone in selling his wares will affirm that his wares are good, or the horse which he sells is sound; yet if he does not warrant them to be so, it is no cause of action . . ."

This principle may have been appropriate for transaction conducted in village markets. In early times, the

---

26. C. Manickam and K.K. Mythli, 'Unfair Trade Practices and Consumer Protection—New Trends and Issues', S.C.J., October 1996, Vol. 3, Part (2).
27. *Ibid.*
28. Chander Lal *v.* Lopus, 79 ER 3.

consumer may have to able to protect himself since the products were less sophisticated and could be inspected before purchase. It was for the buyer to make himself acquainted with the quality and defects of the goods which he intended to purchase. Lord O. Hagan said in *Ward* v. *Hobbs*[29] that although the vender is bound to employ no artifice or disguise for the purpose of concealing defects in the article sold as that may amount to a positive fraud on his part; yet under the general doctrine of *Caveat Emptor,* he is not generally bound to disclose every defect of which he may be cognizant although his silence may operate to virtually to cheat the buyer.

This rule was defended for the reason that it tended to diminish litigation.

Baron Parke said in *Barr* v. *Gibbson*[30] that in a bargain and sale of an existing chattel, the law does not, in absence of fraud, imply any warranty of the good quality or condition of the chattel so sold. Fitz Gibbon L.J said:[31]

> "*Caveat Emptor* does not mean in Latin law that the buyer must 'take chance', it means that he must 'take care'. It applies to the purchase of specific things for example a horse or a picture, upon which the buyer can and usually does, exercise his own judgment; it applies also whenever the buyer voluntarily chooses what he buys; it applies also where by usage or otherwise it is a term of the contract, express or implied, that the buyer shall not rely on the skill of judgment of the seller but it has no application to any case in which the seller has undertaken, and the buyer has left it to the seller, to supply goods to be used for a purpose known to both parties at the time of sale."

But now the conditions have changed. Many modern goods are technological mysteries. The consumer knows little or nothing about these highly sophisticated goods. In real life,

---

29. *Supra* Note, 25; (1878) 4 A.G. 13 at 26.
30. *Id.* (1838) 3M and W 390, p. 399.
31. *Id.*, Wallis *v.* Russel, (1902) 2 I.R. 585, p. 615 C.A.

products are complex and of great variety and consumers and retailers have imperfect knowledge.[32] The products are marked in a number of ways that it is often very difficult to the consumers to judge their quality adequately. The advertisements regarding the taste, flavour, style, quality standard of the commodities and services of their products by the manufacturers and dealers always allure the consumers to purchase and use when consumers have cause to complain about the product or service they are left to purchase the other better one. The consumer does not get remedy to his previous grievances. Consumers of course,. are typically in a weak bargaining position because of the disparity in knowledge and resources between the parties which narrows the consumers access to a remedy.[33]

But it does not meant that there is no remedy to eliminate or mitigate the grievances of the consumers. In a modern welfare state, the state is not only an administrator but has also assumed the positions of a Protector, Provider, Entrepreneur, Economic Controller and Arbitrator. Quite consistent with this development and to suit the change from the *laissez-faire* policy to one of more interventions by the state on the affairs of the citizens, the state and laws have been helping the consumers against 'defective goods' and 'defects on proper using of goods.' Starting with the outmoded and one sided caveat emptor rule and enforcing only the express terms, the law and law courts slowly evolved a process of providing protections to the ordinary purchaser of goods. This was achieved by a long and continuous process.[34]

(a) New Development

The changes brought out in English common law by statutory modifications and liberal judicial interpretations in the past one century gives us a model worthy of emulation.

---

32. Dr. V.K. Agarwal, Consumer Protection, 2nd Ed., B.L.H. Publishers and Distributors Pvt. Ltd, Delhi, p. 3.
33. Ross, Cranston, Consumers and the Law (1978), p. 3; *Supra* Note 2, p. 2.
34. *Supra* Note 17.

Exemption clauses introduced into the Sale of Goods Act of 1893 and successive exposition by the highest judicial authorities have resulted in very important legislative reforms in the seventies of this century. A new Sale of Goods Act was passed in 1979 incorporating the changes effected earlier particularly by the Supply of Goods (Implied Terms) Act of 1973. In short, the most important change was to protect the consumer from defective and unmerchantable goods thus compelling the seller to sell only goods which are of merchantable quality and reasonably fit for the purpose for which they are brought.[35]

Though no concerted effort was made in India in the field of quality control and consumer protection, there are a number of statutes in India[36] which indirectly provide for them. Here the development can be read under the following headings—

(i) Conditions and Warranties

The implied conditions and warranties provided for in the Sale of Goods Act[37] play an important role in quality control and consumer protection. In effect the distinction between a condition and a warranty is only to show the difference between terms which are of a fundamental nature and terms of less significance. Whether a stipulation in a contract of sale is a warranty depends on the construction of the contract. A stipulation may be a condition though called a warranty in the contract. However, in some circumstances though the contract might use the term condition, if the breach is not resulting in anything fundamental the remedy given may be only that for breach of warranty. The term conditions and warranties were used in a confused manner till codification of law and now when they are all well defined there is no question of their being used so by the parties to the contract writes Prof. S.S. Hazmi in his book titled 'Sale of Goods and Consumer Protection in India'.

35. *Ibid.*
36. See for example: The Sale of Goods Act, Sections 11-17 which deal with conditions and warranties.
37. Section 16 of Sale of Goods Act, 1930, Corresponding Provision in the English Act is 14.

However, under the present system of law, if a stipulation amounts to condition the plaintiff is entitled to repudiate such contract even if he does not sustain any damages. But if it amounts to warranty, then its breach will entitle him to claim damages, even though such damages are no consolation for the plaintiff. Repudiation of contract and rejection of the goods may be only appropriate remedy which is not available to the buyer under the present rule.

(ii) Merchantable Quality[38]

The word 'merchantable' can only mean commercially saleable. Reproducing the definition set out in the Supply of Goods (Implied Terms) Act of 1973, the new Sale of Goods Act (English Act) of 1979 has introduced the definition of 'merchantable quality'. Accordingly, Sub-section (6) of Section 14 runs as follows:

> Goods of any kind are of merchantable quality within the meaning of sub-section (2) above if they are as fit for the purpose or purposes for which goods of that kind are commonly bought as it is reasonable to expect having regard to any description applied to them, the price (if relevant) and all the other relevant circumstances.

By the definition of merchantable quality quoted above, the existing law is continued but the conditions will not apply regarding defects specifically drawn to the buyer's attention before the contract is made. The result is that the seller can no longer get rid of all responsibility for the quality of the goods. But the seller will be responsible only for such degree of quality as can reasonably be expected in the light of what he has said about the goods, together with other relevant circumstances. The price will be relevant if it is clearly different from the usual price for similar goods. A very important change effected in the English law is that in order to have the implied condition of 'merchantable quality',

38. *Id.*, Section 16(2), English Corresponding Section 14.

it is no longer required that the seller must be one who deals in goods of that description. Section 14(2) now reads:

> Where the seller sells goods in the course of a business, there is an implied condition that the goods supplied under the contract are of merchantable quality, . . .

Though the requirements merchantable and reasonable fitness overlap but they are still quite separate and distinct. When a new car or a washing machine is purchased what is expected is not only that the object of purchase should work properly, that is to be reasonably fit for the purpose but also that it would be in the normal form and appearance. The second one comes under merchantability.

The meaning of the term was subject to comprehensive review in the case of *Summer Permain and Company* v. *Webb and Company*. The Court of Appeal came to the conclusion that it simply meant that the goods comply with the description. Outer appearance is not sufficient to make the goods merchantable, if they suffer from some latent defect, not apparent on ordinary examination.

Thus, quality includes the state or condition of the goods. Merchantability extends to the labels or packages in which the goods are contained. The other requirement is that the goods must be fit for the ordinary purposes for which such goods are used. This requirement is broad-based and it means that where goods are used for many purposes, it should be fit for although ordinary purposes and not any one of them.

(iii) Fitness for Purpose[39]

'Reasonable Fitness' means fitness for general purposes as well as for specific purposes. A particular purpose is in fact a purpose which is expressly or impliedly communicated to the seller and for which the goods are bought. It is not necessarily distinct from a general purpose for example general purpose of purchasing the food for eating may also be specific purpose. Where the articles sold are described in

39. *Id.*, Section 6(1), English Corresponding Section 14(3).

such a manner as to show an intention on the part of the buyer to use them in a specific manner, then that description of the goods is a specific purpose. Where the goods are used for multipurpose then one indicated by the buyer is the particular purpose. Where the buyer omits to indicate any specific purpose, he will have no remedy, if the goods are unfit for the purpose intended by him. A purpose may be put in a wide or narrow term and it may still be a particular purpose.[40]

(b) Present Position

Thus starting with the age old rule of *'Caveat Emptor'* we have seen that the law and judges were in favour of the seller. This rule was a dominant future of the law relating to sale of goods in the nineteenth century in England. Since our Sale of Goods Act is largely based upon the provisions of English Sale of Goods Act we have also adopted this rule. But with the development of new commercial practices, new methods of trade transactions, varieties of hire purchase systems and consumer credits, self-reliance shops with sophisticated articles including those with scientific intricacies and so on, the buyer was found to be in a difficult situation. The law came to his rescue. A number of implied conditions and warranties came to be imposed as above mentioned inspite of the exemption clauses agreed to.[41] This has created a consciousness in the society which paved way for the acceptance of the theory of *'Caveat Vendetar'*—let the seller beware in the larger interest of the society.

(C) CONSUMER LAW—A CONTEMPORARY VIEW

In this part besides knowing United Nations Guidelines for Consumer Protection we will know consumer law of some Western Countries also.

40. *Supra* Note 25, p. 184.
41. *Supra* Note 10, p. 158.

(I) United Nations Guidelines for Consumer Protection[42]

The General Assembly adopted guidelines for consumer protection by consensus on 9 April, 1985. The guidelines provide a framework for governments, particularly those of developing countries, to use in elaborating aid strengthening consumer protection policies and legislations. They are also intended to encourage international co-operation in this field.

The origin of the guidelines can be traced to the late 1970s, when the Economic and Social Council recognized that consumer protection had an important bearing on economic and social development. In 1977, the Council asked the Secretary-General to prepare a survey of national institutions and legislations in the area of consumer protection. In 1979, the Council requested a comprehensive report containing proposals for measures or consumer protection for consideration by governments. In 1981, the Council, aware of the need for an International policy framework within which further efforts for consumer protection could be pursued, requested the Secretary-General to continue consultations with the aim of developing a set of general guidelines for consumer protection, taking particularly into account the needs of the developing countries.

Accordingly, the Secretary-General carried out consultations with governments and international organizations and submitted draft guidelines for consumer protection to the Economic and Social Council in 1983. During the next two years there were extensive discussions and negotiations among governments on the scope and content of the guidelines, culminating in their adoption in 1985.

(a) Objectives

(I) Taking into account the interests and needs of consumers in all countries, particularly those in developing countries, recognizing that consumers often face imbalances in economic terms, educational levels, and bargaining power, and bearing in mind that consumer should have the right of

42. *Supra* Note 32, p. 622.

access to non-hazardous products, as well as the importance of promoting just, equitable and sustainable economic and social development, these guidelines for consumer protection have the following objectives:

(i) To assist countries in achieving or maintaining adequate protection for their population as consumers;
(ii) To facilitate production and distribution pattern responsive to the needs and desires of consumers;
(iii) To encourage high levels of ethical conduct for those engaged in the production and distribution of goods and services to consumers;
(iv) To assist countries in curbing abusive business practices by all enterprises at the national and international levels which adversely affect consumers;
(v) To facilitate the development of independent consumer groups;
(vi) To further international co-operation in the field of consumer protection; and
(vii) To encourage the development of market conditions which provide consumers with greater choice at lower prices.

(b) General Principles

(II) Government should develop, strengthen or maintain a strong consumer protection policy, taking into account the guidelines set out below. In so doing, each government must set its own priorities for the protection of consumers in accordance with the economic and social circumstances of the country, and the needs of its population, and bearing in mind the costs and benefits of proposed measures.

(III) The legitimate needs which the guidelines are intended to meet are the following:

(i) The protection of consumers from hazards to their health and safety;
(ii) The promotion and protection of the economic interests of consumers;

(iii) Access of consumers to adequate information to enable them to make informed choice according to individual wishes and needs;

(iv) Consumer education;

(v) Availability of effective consumer redress; and

(vi) Freedom to form consumer and other relevant groups or organizations and the opportunity of such organizations to present their views in decision-making process.

(IV) Governments should provide or maintain adequate infrastructure to develop, implement and monitor consumer protection policies. Special care should be taken to ensure that measures for consumer protection are implemented for the benefit of all sectors of the population.

(V) All enterprises should obey the relevant laws and regulations of the countries in which they do business. They should also conform to the appropriate provisions of international standards for consumer protection to which the competent authorities of the country in question have agreed.

(VI) The potential positive role of universities and public and private enterprises in research should be considered when developing consumer protection policies.

(c) Guidelines

(VII) The following guidelines should apply both to home-produced goods and services and to imports.

(VIII) In applying any procedures of regulations for consumer protection, due regard should be given to ensuring that they do not become barriers to international trade and that they are consistent with international trade obligations.

(IX) Governments should adopt or encourage the adoption of appropriate measures, including legal system, safety regulations, national or international standards, voluntary standards and the maintenance of safety records to ensure that products are safe for either intended or normally foreseeable use.

(X) Appropriate policies should ensure that goods produced by manufacturers are safe for either intended or normally foreseeable use. Those responsible for bringing goods to the market, in particular suppliers, exporters, importers, retailers and the like (hereinafter referred to as 'distributors'), should ensure that while in their care these goods are not rendered unsafe through improper handling or storage and that while in their care they do not become hazardous through improper handling or storage. Consumers should be instructed in the proper use of goods and should be informed of the risks involved in intended or normally foreseeable use. Vital safety information should be conveyed to consumer by internationally understandable symbols wherever possible.

(XI) Appropriate policies should ensure that if manufacturers or distributors become aware of unforeseen hazards after products are placed on the market, they should notify the relevant authorities and, as appropriate, the public without delay, governments should also consider ways of ensuring that consumers are properly informed .of such hazards.

(XII) Governments should, where appropriate, adopt policies under which if a product is found to be seriously defective and/or to constitute a substantial and severe hazards even when properly used, manufactures and/or distributors should recall it and replace or modify it or substitute another product for it; if it is not possible to do this within a reasonable period of time, the consumer should be adequately compensated.

(XIII) Government policies should seek to enable consumers to obtain optimum benefit from their economic resources. They should also seek to achieve the goals of satisfactory production and performance standards, adequate distribution methods, fair business practices, informative marketing and effective protection against practices which could adversely affect the economic interests of consumers and the exercise of choice in the marketplace.

(XIV) Governments should intensify their efforts to prevent practices which are damaging to the economic interests of consumers through ensuring that manufacturers, distributors and others involved in the provision of goods and services adhere to established laws and mandatory standards. Consumer organizations should be encouraged to monitor adverse practices, such as the adulteration of foods, false or misleading claims in marketing and service frauds.

(XV) Governments should develop, strengthen or maintain, as the case may be, measures relating to the control of restrictive and other abusive business practices which may be harmful to consumers, including means for the enforcement of such measures. In this connection, governments should be guided by their commitment to set of agreed Equitable Principles and Rules for the Control of Restrictive Business Practices adopted by the General Assembly in resolution 35/63 of 5 December 1980.

(XVI) Governments should adopt or maintain policies that make clear the responsibility of the producer to ensure that goods meet reasonable demands of durability, utility and reliability, and are suited to the purpose for which they are intended, and that the seller should see that these requirements are met. Similar policies should apply to the provision of services.

(XVII) Governments should encourage fair and effective competition in order to provide consumers with the greatest range of choice among products and services at the lowest cost.

(XVIII) Governments should, where appropriate, to see it that manufacturers and/or retailers ensure adequate availability of reliable after-sales and spare parts.

(XIX) Consumers should be protected from such contractual abuses as one sided standards contracts, exclusion of essential rights in contracts, and unconscionable conditions of credit by sellers.

(XX) Promotional marketing and sales practices should be guided by the principle of fair treatment of consumers and should meet legal requirements. This requires the provision of information necessary to enable consumers to take informed and independent decisions, as well as measures to ensure that the information provided is accurate.

(XXI) Governments should encourage all concerned to participate in the free flow of accurate information on all aspects of consumer products.

(XXII) Governments should, within their own national context, encourage the formulation and implementation by business, in co-operation with consumer organizations, of codes of marketing and other business practices to ensure adequate consumer protection. Voluntary agreements may also be established jointly by business, consumer organizations and other interested parties. These codes should receive adequate publicity.

(XXIII) Governments should regularly review legislation pertaining to weights and measures and assess the adequacy of the machinery for its enforcement.

(XXIV) Governments should, as appropriate, formulate or promote the elaboration and implementation of standards, voluntary and other at the national and international levels for the safety and quality of goods and services and give them appropriate publicity. National standards and regulations for product safety and quality should be reviewed from time to time in order to ensure that they conform where possible to generally accepted international standards.

(XXV) Where a standard lower than the generally accepted international standard is being applied because of local economic conditions, every effort should be made to raise that standard as soon as possible.

(XXVI) Governments should encourage and ensure the availability of facilities to test and certify the safety, safety quality and performance of essential consumer goods and services.

(XXVII) Governments should, where appropriate, consider:

(i) Adopting or maintaining policies to ensure the efficient distribution of goods and services to consumers: where appropriate, specific policies should be considered to ensure the distribution of essential goods and services where this distribution is endangered, as could be the case particularly in rural areas. Such polices should include assistance for the creation of adequate storage and retail facilities in rural centers, incentives for consumer self-help and better control of the conditions under which essential goods and services are provided in rural areas.

(ii) Encouraging the establishing of consumer co-operatives and related trading activities, as well as information about them, especially in rural areas.

(XXVIII) Governments should establish or maintain legal and/or administrative measures to enable consumers or, as appropriate, relevant organizations to obtain redress through formal or informal procedures that are expeditious, fair, inexpensive and accessible. Such procedures should take particular account of the needs of low income consumers.

(XXIX) Governments should encourage all enterprises to resolve consumer disputes in a fair, expeditious and informal manner, and to establish voluntary mechanisms, including advisory services and informal complaints procedures, which can provide assistance to consumers.

(XXX) Information on available redress and other dispute-resolving procedures should be made available to consumers.

(XXXI) Governments should develop or encourage the development of general consumer education and information programmes, bearing in mind the cultural traditions of the people concerned. The aim of such programmes should be to enable people to act as discriminating consumers, capable of making an informed choice of goods and services and conscious of their rights and responsibilities. In developing such programmes, special attention should be given to the needs of disadvantaged consumers, in both rural and urban areas, including low income consumers and those with low or non-existent literacy levels.

(XXXII) Consumer education should, where appropriate, become an integral part of the basic curriculum of the educational system, preferably as a component of existing subjects.

(XXXIII) Consumer education and information programmes should cover such important aspects of consumer protection as the following:

(i) health, nutrition, prevention of food-borne disease and food adulteration;
(ii) product hazards;

(iii) product labeling;
(iv) relevant legislation, how to obtain redress, and agencies and organization for consumer protection;
(v) information on weights and measures, prices, quality, credit conditions and availability of basic necessities, and
(vi) As appropriate, pollution and environment.

(XXXIV) Governments should encourage consumer organizations and other interested groups, including the media, to undertake education and information programmes, particularly for the benefit of low-income consumer groups in rural and urban areas.

(XXXV) Business should, where appropriate, undertake or participate in factual and relevant consumer education and information programmes.

(XXXVI) Bearing in mind the need to reach rural consumers and illiterate consumers, governments should, as appropriate, develop or encourage the development of consumer information programmes in the mass media.

(XXXVII) Governments should organize or encourage training programmes for educators, mass media professionals and consumer advisers, to enable them to participate in carrying out consumer information and education programmes.

(XXXVIII) In advancing consumer interests, particularly in developing countries, governments should, where appropriate, give priority to areas of essential concern for the health of the consumer, such as food, water and pharmaceuticals. Policies should be adopted or maintained for product quality control, adequate and secure distribution facilities, standardized international labeling and information, as well as education and research programmes in these areas. Government guidelines in regard to specific areas should be developed in the context of the provisions of this document.

(XXXIX) *Food*. When formulating national policies and plans with regard to food, governments should take into account the need of all consumers for food security and should support and, as far as possible, adopt standards from the Food and Agriculture Organization of the United Nations and the World Heal Codex Alimentarius and to maintain, develop or improve food safety measures, including, *inter alia*, safety criteria, food standards and dietary requirements and effective monitoring, inspection and evaluation mechanisms.

(XL) *Water*. Governments should, within the goals and targets set for the International Drinking Water Supply and Sanitation Decade formulate, maintain or strengthen national policies to improve the supply, distribution and quality of water for drinking. Due regard should be paid to the choice of appropriate levels of service, quality and technology, the need for education programmes and the importance of community participation.

(XLI) *Pharmaceuticals*. Governments should develop or maintain adequate standards, provisions and appropriate regulatory systems for ensuring the quality and appropriate use of pharmaceuticals through integrated national drug policies which could address, *inter alia*, procurement, distribution, production, licensing arrangements, registration systems and availability of reliable information on pharmaceuticals. In so doing, governments should take special account of the work and recommendations of the World Health Organization on Pharmaceuticals. For relevant products the use of that organization's Certification Scheme on the Quality of Pharmaceutical Products Moving in International Commerce and other international information systems on pharmaceuticals should be encouraged. Measures should also be taken, as appropriate, to promote the use of international non-proprietary names (INNs) for drugs, drawing on the work done by the World Health Organization.

(XLII) In addition to the priority areas indicated above, governments should adopt appropriate measures in other areas, such as pesticides and chemicals in regard, where relevant, to their use, production and storage, taking into account such relevant health and environmental information as governments may require producers to provide and include in the labeling of products.

(d) International Co-operation

(XLIII) Governments should, especially in a regional or

sub-regional context:

(i) develop, review, maintain or strengthen, as appropriate, mechanisms for the exchange of information on national policies and measures in the field of consumer protection;

(ii) co-operate or encourage co-operation in the implementation of consumer protection policies to achieve greater results within existing resources. Examples of such co-operation could be collaboration in the setting up or joint use of testing facilities, common testing procedures, exchange of consumer information and education programmes, joint training programmes and joint elaboration or regulations; and

(iii) co-operate to improve the conditions under which essential goods are offered to consumers, giving due regard to both prices and quality. Such cooperation could include joint procurement of essential goods, exchange of information on different procurement possibilities and agreements on regional product specifications.

(XLIV) Governments should develop or strengthen information links regarding products which have been banned, withdrawn or severally restricted in order to enable other importing countries to protect themselves adequately against the harmful effects of such products.

(XLV) Governments should work to ensure that the quality of products and information relating to such products, vary not from country to country in a way that would have detrimental effects on consumers.

(XLVI) Governments should work to ensure that policies and measures for consumer protection are implemented with due regard to their not becoming barriers to international trade, and that they are consistent with international trade obligations.

Now let us proceed to know the consumer law of some Western countries. We have borrowed much from these countries while framing our constitution and other laws. In the same way we owe much to our Western countries regarding framing and developing concept of Consumer Protection. In this perspective it is appropriate to briefly know origin of Consumer Law in these countries.

(2) United States

The United States, as long as 1890, enacted the first anti-trust legislation, namely, The Sherman Anti-Trust Act.[43] It contains the embodiment of the law upon the subject of unlawful restraint of trade and monopolies. Section 1 of the Sherman Anti-Trust Act, 1890 states—

> "Every contract, combination in the form of trust or otherwise, or conspiracy in restraint of trade or commerce among the several states or with foreign nations, is hereby declared to be illegal."

Section 2 of the concerned Act declares—

> "Every person who shall monopolize or attempt to monopolize any part of trade or commerce among the several states or with foreign nations shall be deemed guilty of misdemeanor."

The Act provides both for civil remedies and for criminal penalties of up to one year imprisonment or fine of up to $ 5000 or both. In 1955 the Act was Amended to increase the fine to a maximum $ 50,000. But this Act could not respond to the widespread pressures for increased protection of consumers. To meet this end major legislations, The Federal Trade Commission Act, The Clayton Act were passed in 1940. The Federal Trade Commission Act is the oldest and the most prominent statute for the protection of consumers. The Act authorized the Federal Trade Commission to correct unfair methods of competition. In its

43. *Id.*, pp. 5-6, the Legal System of the United States is based on common Law of England. In the initial stages of development American Courts applied the rules of English Law as contained in the Judgments of English Courts.

implementation, the commission moved to protect consumers as an objective in and of itself, rather than as an incident that would further competition. In 1938, the Act was amended by Wheeler—Lea Act extending the scope of the Act to cover 'unfair or deceptive acts or practices' as well as 'unfair methods of competition'. Thus, the Amendment provided three separate bases for the Federal Trade Commission's jurisdiction—unfairness or deception or unfair competitive methods, 1975, The Magnusn—Mass Warranty—Federal Trade Commission Improvement Act further strengthened the commission's rule making and other authority over 'unfair and deceptive acts and practices'. The commission is organized into two principal operating Bureau, the Bureau of consumer protection and Bureau of competition. The Bureau of Consumer Protection has principal responsibility of monitoring advertising, labeling and deceptive practices.[44]

The Clayton Act, including later amendments contains four substantive provisions. It prohibits under certain conditions—price discrimination, exclusive dealing contracts and tying arrangements, mergers and interlocking corporate directorships. Exclusive dealing contracts, tying arrangements and mergers are forbidden where their effect may be substantially to lesson competition or where they tend to create a monopoly. The Robinson-Patman Act was adopted in 1936 in direct response to the growth of a few nation-wide chain-store corporation in 1920's and 1930's. Its purpose is to strengthen the provisions of Clayton Act regarding firstly, price discrimination, secondly, to prevent sellers and brokers from yielding to the economic pressures of a large buying organization by granting unfair preferences in connection with the sale of goods, thirdly, to prohibit all devices by which large buyers gain discriminately preferences over smaller ones by virtue of their greater purchasing power, fourthly, to protect small businesses, which are unable to buy in quantity against competing operation of large inter-state concern and fifthly, to insure that purchaser from a single supplier are not injured by the suppliers discriminatory practices.[45]

44. *Id.*, pp. 6-8.
45. American Jurisprudence, Vol. 54, 2nd Ed.

In addition to aforesaid legislations there are number of other legislations on consumer protection which cover, Consumer Credit Protection Act which requires certain disclosures in consumer credit sales and loans, The Consumer Leasing Act which deals with consumer leases, The Fair Credit Billing Act, which contains provision relating to credit billing practices, The Fair Packaging & Labeling Act, The Poison Prevention Packaging Act and The Consumer Patient Radiation Health and Safety Act provide protection to the consumers in several ways. Further, the Uniform Commercial Code attempts to protect purchaser of goods through a requirement of 'good faith' and a prohibition of 'unreasonable' practice. The provision of the Code have widely incorporated in subsequent uniform or Model Consumer Protection Statute for example Uniform Consumer Credit Code, Uniform Consumer Sales Practice Act, Uniform Residential Landlord & Tenant Act, Uniform Land Transaction Act, Uniform Simplification of Land Transfers Act, Uniform Condominium Act, Model Real Estate Timeshare Act, Uniform Planned Community Act, Model Real Estate Cooperative Act, Uniform Common Interest and Ownership Act.[46]

(3) United Kingdom[47]

In the United Kingdom, there are number of legislations to protect the interest of consumers. The most significant of them are the Fair Trading Act, 1973, The Competition Act, 1980 and the Consumer Protection Act, 1987. The Fair Trading Act, 1973 seeks to protect the consumers from consumer trade practices and unfair practices. The main object of the Act was to encourage competition which is fair as between one business and another, and fair towards the consumer by ensuring the trading standards are improved wherever possible and that unfair trading practices are stopped or changed, whether they be abuses of a monopoly position or practices which are, for

46. *Supra* Note 44, p. 6.
47. *Ibid.*

example, oppressive of or inequitable to consumers. Part III of the Act provides for a separate procedure for dealing with unfair practices. An unfair practices involves for a separate procedure for dealing with unfair practices. An unfair practice involves a cause of conduct which is detrimental to the interests of consumers, whether interest in respect of health, safety or other matters. The area to which Part III of the Act can apply is extremely wide. There are no specific exclusions, so that all the professions and all businesses including nationalized industries and public undertakings are within its ambit. The Competition Act, 1980 has been enacted to make provisions for the control of anti-competitive practices in supply and acquisition of goods and the supply and securing of services, to provide for the investigation of prices and charges by the Director General of Fair Trading and to make some amendments with respect to the Fair Trading Act, 1973 and The Restrictive Trade Practices Act, 1976.

The Consumer Protection Act, 1987 is a wide ranging piece of legislation, creating both civil and criminal liability. The philosophy of the Act is that the best form of Consumer Protection is to promote competition. Supplying unsafe goods or misleading consumer about the price is an unfair competition. Fair competition will not be achieved if consumers are given false or misleading information on which to base the decisions that they make in the market place. Thus, if competition is to work effectively in practice, then consumers must have sufficient information for them to make effective choices. The Act deals with three main objects—

(a) Product Liability

Part I of the Act provides a system of strict liability imposed upon a producer in respect of any damage caused by defective products. However, the complainant must still prove a casual relationship between the damage and the defect. However, Section 4(1) of the Act enables the producer to avoid liability if he can prove any one of six defenses laid down under the Act.

(b) Unsafe Goods

Part II of the Act introduces a general duty on all suppliers of consumer goods to ensure that the goods they supply are safe. A person who offers, or agrees to supply or supplies any consumer goods which fail to comply with the general safety requirement, shall be guilty of an offence under the Act.

(c) Misleading Price Indications

Part III makes it a general offence to give misleading price indications to consumers in respect of any goods, services, accommodation or facilities.

(4) Australia

In Australia, the first anti-trust legislation was adopted in 1906, The Australian Industries Preservation Act, 1906. The Act was influenced by and was substantially similar to the Sherman Act, 1890 of the United States. Although the Act was amended in 1911, to overcome some difficulties but changes in attitudes brought by two world wars and a world depression led to its being ignored for many years. It was hardly the success of the 1906-Act that promoted the 1965 legislation, namely, The Trade Practices, 1956 of the United Kingdom. Finally, the Trade Practices Act, 1974 was passed which replaced the 1965-Act. There were some minor amendments to the Act before 1977, but the first major amendments were effected in 1977. Further significant amendments have since been made in 1978 and 1980. The Act is concerned with restrictive trade practices and consumer protection. Part V deals with consumer protection and is aimed at eliminating unfair competition in trade and commerce as well as strengthening the positions of consumers. It prohibits false or misleading representation or advertisement; offering of gifts, prizes or other free items with the intention of not providing them, bait advertising. Further, a corporation is prohibited to supply goods which do not comply with the prescribed consumer products safety standard.[48]

48. *Id.*, p. 8.

Now before scrutinizing the consumer early legislation with State of Jammu and Kashmir, it would not be out of place to ascertain the law available in India.

(5) India[49]

In India following the constitutional mandate a number of legislations—Drugs (Control) Act, 1950; Drugs and Magic Remedies (Objectionable Advertisements) Act, 1954; Prevention of Food Adulteration Act, 1954; Essential Commodities Act, 1955; Prevention of Black-marketing and Maintenance of Supplies of Essential Commodities Act, 1980; Essential Service Maintenance Act, 1968; Trade and Merchandise Marks Act, 1986; Standards of Weights and Measures Act, 1976; Bureau of Indian Standards Act, 1986; The Monopolies and Restrictive Trade Practices Act, 1969 have been enacted. Some pre-independent legislations are—Indian Contract Act, 1872; Sale of Goods Act, 1930; Agricultural Produce (Grading and Marking) Act, 1937; Drugs and Cosmetics Act, 1940.

After passing of the MRTP Act which was amended in the year 1984 to incorporate new provisions—the ultimate consumers could not be protected from defective goods or deficient services, over-charging of prices and unscrupulous exploitation. For these and many other reasons the Parliament passed potentially a very important legislation—The Consumer Protection Act, 1986 to provide better protection to the interests of the consumers. The Act provides a three-tier quasi-judicial machinery at the National, State and District level for redressing consumer grievances. The Act has been amended on various times and these amendments have made positive improvements.

(D) CONSUMER LAW IN THE STATE OF JAMMU AND KASHMIR[50]

In this part of the chapter Consumer Law which is in scattered form will be assembled and discussed here briefly.

49. *Id.*, pp. 9-11.

50. Some Central Acts having their implications on the State of Jammu and Kashmir have been also discussed.

(I) The Ranbir Penal Code

This Code is the first and foremost of laws which made certain provisions to protect the interest of a consumer. The consumer under this Code gets remedy not by way of compensation but by punishing the wrongdoer. In this connection the noteworthy provisions of this Code which provide indirect and remote satisfaction to the consumer law be quoted here.

Firstly, Section 264-267 deal with offences relating to weights and measures. Under these Sections any person who makes fraudulent use of false instruments for weighing, fraudulent use of false weight and measures and any one who is in possession of false weights or measures and is involved in making or selling false weight or measures respectively shall be punished with imprisonment or fine or with both depending upon the gravity of offence.[51]

Secondly, Sections 269-271 deals with offences—like spreading of infection and thereby affecting the public health. Further, Sections 272-276 of the same chapter deal with different types of adulteration of food, drink and drugs and provide for their punishments. Also Sections 277 and 278 of the said chapter provide punishment for corrupting and fouling water of public spring or reservoir so as to render it less fit for the human consumption.[52]

Thirdly, Sections 415 and 425 deals with cheating and wrongful loss or damage to the public or to any person and provide punishment in the former case of imprisonment of either description for a term which may extend to one year, or with fine, or with both and in the latter case with imprisonment of either description for a term which may extend to three months, or with fine or with both.[53]

Fourthly, Sections 481 and 482 prescribed penalty for using a false trademark or property mark. A person is liable under the Code to punishment for falsely marking goods,

---

51. Of Chapter XIII of RPC dealing with offences relating to Weights and Measures.
52. *Id.*, Chapter XIV under title (Of Offences Affecting the Public Health, Safety, Convenience, Decency and Morals).
53. *Id.*, Chapter XVII relating to offences against property.

packages or other receptacles of food and using false property mark so as to make a customer believe that such an article is genuine.[54]

(2) The Contract Act[55]

This Act of 1977 also provides and protects consumer interests. Since this Act is similar in substance with the Indian Contract Act and Sir Fedrick Pollock said about this Act in the following words[56]:

> "The Law of Contract may be described as an endeavour of the state, a more or less imperfect one by the nature of case, to establish a positive sanction for the expectation of good faith which has grown up in the mutual dealings of man of average right mindedness. Accordingly the most popular description of a contract that can be given is also the most exact one, namely that it is a promise or set of promises which the law will enforce. The specific mark of contract is the creation of a right, not to a thing, but to another man's conduct in the future. He who has given the promise is bound to him who accepts it, not merely because he had or expressed a certain intention, but because he has so expressed himself as to entitle the other party to rely on his acting in a certain way."

In the light of the above observation and after a thorough reading of the Contract Act Section 17 seems to be noteworthy so far as the consumer interest is concerned. If a person feels aggrieved by any mode of sale say for example advertising, labeling or packaging or any other type of fraud he may invoke under the said Section of the Contract Act.[57]

---

54. *Id.*, Chapter XVIII of RPC.
55. Passed in the year 1977.
56. Pollock on contracts (1) (1889).
57. Fraud means and includes—
    (i) the suggestion as to a fact of that which is not true by one who does not believe it to be true;
    (ii) the active concealment of a fact by the one having knowledge or belief of the fact;

(3) The Sale of Goods Act[58]

This Act like the above mentioned Act provides for and applies to consumer disputes. Generally this Act does not apply to contracts for services independently but to sale of goods and other similar transactions. Since the seller sells goods in the course of a business and the buyer expressly or by implication makes known any particular purpose for which the goods are being bought, there is an implied condition that the goods supplied under the contract are reasonably fit for that purpose. This Act in open words under different Sections lays down a number of duties which a seller owes to the buyer. Some of these duties are[59]—

(i) duty to pass a good title;
(ii) duty to deliver goods specified under the contract;
(iii) duty to deliver goods of right quality, fitness and safety; and
(iv) duty to deliver goods at a reasonable time and price.

One thing pertinent to say here is that this Act is equally applicable to the sale of drugs like any other type of goods. Thus by providing the rights and liabilities of seller and buyer this Act safeguards the rights of the consumer. The implied warranties and conditions provided in this Act play an important role in quality control and consumer protection. But this protection given through implied terms in a contract is taken away if the goods are purchased under a trade or patent name or purchased after examining the goods.

(4) The Dangerous Drugs Act[60]

This Act is an important central legislation which

(iii) a promise made without any intention of performing it; and
(iv) any such act or omission as the law specially declares to be fraudulent.

58. Samvat, 1996.
59. *Id.*, Section 16.
60. Passed in the year 1930. Though State of J&K has no separate Act but the instant Act is applicable to the State as to the other states by implication.

empowers the Central Government to control certain operations relating to dangerous drugs. India participated in the Second International Opium Conference at Geneva wherein a convention relating to dangerous drugs was adopted in 1925. The contracting parties to the said convention resolved to take appropriated measures to suppress contraband traffic in and abuse of dangerous drugs, especially those derived from opium, Indian hemp and cola leaf. In order to honour their commitments, the Government of India placed the Dangerous Drugs Act on the statute book in 1930, with a view to control certain operations in dangerous drugs and to centralize and vest the same in the Central Government. The Act also aimed at increasing penalties for certain offences relating to dangerous drugs and to render uniform all penalties relating to certain operations concerning such drugs. Section 4 of the Act prohibits cultivation of any coca plant or gathering of any portion of a coca plant, manufacturing or possessing prepared opium and import and export, transit or sale of prepared opium. The Act has since been amended from time to time by the various Acts.

(5) The Drugs and Cosmetics Act[61]

This Act is mainly concerned with standards and quality of drugs manufactured in this country and controls the manufacture sale and distribution of drugs. The term 'drug' as used in the Drugs and Cosmetic Act did not include medicines and substances exclusively used or prepared for use in accordance with the Ayurvedic or Unani system of medicine. It includes all other medicines for internal or external use of human beings or animals and also substances intended to be used for or the diagnoses, treatment mitigation or prevention of diseases in human beings or animals. It also includes all substances other than food intended to affect the structure of the human body or any functions thereof, or intended to be used for the destruction of vermin or insects

61. This Act is in addition to and not in derogation of the Dangerous Drugs Act and any other law for the time being in force.

which cause disease in human beings or animals as may be specified by the central government. So the expression 'drug' includes medicine for external or internal use and the expression 'substance' includes a liquid.[62]

Thus, by widening definition of the term 'drug' this Act provides check on contaminated drugs manufactured or packed under in sanitary conditions the Supreme Court in *Swantraj* v. *State of Maharashtra*[63] observed that the Drugs and Cosmetics Act is a life saving statute. Prior to the Amending Act, 1962 there was no legislation for regulating the manufacture of Cosmetics and therefore, for doing away with the evil involved a remedy was thought for by amending the principal Act namely, The Drugs Act, 1940. For the purposes of regulating the manufacture of cosmetics, the legislature choosed to define the said term 'cosmetic' including in its import any article which is intended to be applied to the human body or any part thereof even for the purposes of beautifying and promoting attractiveness or altering the appearance of the body. Further Amending Act of 1982 introduced more stringent penalties which could be imposed on anti-social elements indulging in the manufacture and sale of such drugs.

(6) Pharmacy Act[64]

This Act is enacted to make better provision for the regulation of the profession and practice of pharmacy. The object of this Act is that only those persons who have attained a minimum standard of profession education should be permitted to practice the profession of pharmacy. It is accordingly proposed to establish Central Council of pharmacy, which will prescribe the minimum standards of education and approved courses of study and examination for

62. Law of Drugs, Medicines and Cosmetics, Revised by Ad. B.R. Beotra 1977 2nd Ed. Law Book company Allahabad, p. 11.
63. A.I.R. 1974 S.C., p. 517.
64. In State of J&K Pharmacy Act, 2011 (1955 A.D) stands designed; quoted all Samuals—Article 'Errors by the Pharmacist—legal liability, medicine, science and the law', (The Official General of the British Academy of Forensic Sciences) October 1996, Vol. 36, No. 4, p. 320.

pharmacists, and provincial pharmacy councils, which will be responsible to the maintenance of provincial registers of qualified pharmacists. The pharmacist is an ethical skilled professional person undertaking heavy responsibilities. By and large the profession gives an excellent service to the public and indeed is gradually extending and enhancing the scope of the service, taking over heavier responsibilities in conjunction with the medical professions for the health and well-being of the public.

However, an error from time to time occurs. We are all fallible, also subjects to human error. But an error by a pharmacist can have potentially very serious consequences and thus the greatest possible care must be taken to ensure that the drug given to the consumer is the correct one. As the European Directive says, there must be a high degree of consumer protection and in case contrary is proved he would be punished in terms of the Sale of Goods legislation that is unsatisfactory goods.

(7) The Drugs (Control) Act[65]

Another Act called The Drugs (Control) Act, was passed which provides for the control of the sale, supply and distribution of drugs. The object of this Act is to ensure that certain essential importing drugs and medicines are to be sold at reasonable prices. This Act enables the Chief Commissioner—

> firstly, to fix the maximum price to be charged; and
> secondly, to fix the maximum quantity that may be sold to any person in a single transaction.

However, this maximum may be different in different localities and for different classes of dealers or producers. In case any producer or dealer contravenes any of the provisions of this Act or fails to comply with any direction made under authority conferred by this Act shall be punished with imprisonment for a term which may extend to three years or with fine or with both.

---

65. *Supra* Note 60; A.I.R. Manual (16) 47-51 4th Ed. (1979).

(8) The Constitution[66]

Thought the word 'consumer' is not to be found in the constitution, the consumer breaths and peeps out through many of the blood vessels of the constitution. The constitution is a social document. It is not made only to provide a machinery of government to maintain law and order and to defend the country and here obviously to defend the State under State constitution. The founding father's of the constitution has a glorious vision of the establishment of a new society with high ideals for granting the multi-dimensional welfare of all the people.[67] with a view to identify some of the provisions in the fundamental law of the State that is in the constitution that are related directly or indirectly with the philosophy and mechanism for the protection of the interests, health and happiness of the consumer the following appears to be noteworthy—

(a) Preamble[68]

The constitution is made by the people for the people and it is of the people. This is declared specifically in the preamble of the constitution. It is a socialist constitution in which the instruments of production and the natural wealth of the State shall be either owned or controlled by the State as a trustee of society for the benefit of the people. One of the goals of the constitution epitomized in the preamble is doing justice to all the people. Justice in its simple, direct, widely and historically accepted meaning both conceptually and practically connotes the giving to every person what is due to him.

Economic justice means securing full reward materially, what is due to a person based on his work or constitution by performing a socially useful function or otherwise one is entitled for morally, socially and legally. Consumer justice implies securing to the consumer commodities or services equivalent to the payment made by him without legally or

---

66. Of Jammu and Kashmir, 1957.
67. *Supra* Note 34, P. Koteswar Rao's Article, p. 82.
68. *Supra* Note 66.

commercially prescribed or impliedly agreed or understood quantity and standard.[69]

(b) Equality[70]

Constitution guarantees equality before law to all the persons within the territory. Therefore, producers, sellers and consumers are equal before law either for receiving reward or punishment. Further constitution under this provision guarantees equal protection of laws to all the persons. This is a positive policy of the State imposing a duty on the state to positively, deliberately and actively involve and also effectively participate in the task of protecting all the persons irrespective of other considerations of status and power of money against harmful actions and omissions of others. Hence, state is enjoined constitutionally to give protection to the consumers. Constitutional consumer protection implies for preventing malpractices in trade, commerce and business, defrauding and exploiting the consumer of his due by adulteration, sub-standardization, under weighing, etc. The consumer has to be protected against creation of artificial scarcities by hoarding and manipulation of stock exchanges and black market. A number of laws like Prevention of Food Adulteration Act, Weights and Measures Act, Essential Commodities Act have been passed translating the fundamental rights into legislation.

(c) Personal Liberty[71]

This Fundamental Right as guaranteed by the constitution is relating to life and personal liberty. The word 'life' should not be construed here in a narrow sense to mean freedom from bodily restraint or confinement to prison only but something more than the mere animal existence. It includes all that is implied in this term. The right to health and medical care is a fundamental right. Health cannot be separated from (life) because life in the human body is

69. *Supra* Note 67.
70. Chapter IV, Fundamental Rights as Guaranteed under the Constitution of India, Article 14.
71. *Id.*, Article 21.

supported not only by the existence but also by the proper functioning of all the constituents of the human organism. The basic principal of public health is that every member of the community is entitled to protection in regard to his health just as in regard to his liberty.

(d) Social Order Based on Justice

Section 13 (Article 38 under the Indian Constitution) of the constitution provides that the state shall strive to promote the welfare of the people by securing and protecting as effectively as it may, a social order in which justice social, economic and political shall inform all the institutions of national life.

This Directive only reaffirms what has already been said in the Preamble according to which the function of the republic is to secure to all its citizens social, economic and political justice. Justice is to be imparted in all relations whether it is between individual and state, employer-employees, master-servant or seller and buyer.

(i) Duty to Raise Standard of Living and Improvement of Health

Section 15 of the State (Article 47 under the Indian constitution) imposes duty upon the State to raise the level of nutrition and the standard of living of its people and the improvement of public health and shall endeavor to bring about prohibition of the consumption except for medicinal purposes of intoxicating drinks and of drugs which are injurious to health.

(ii) Duty to Secure a Welfare State

Section 14 [Clause (b) and (c) of Article 39 of Indian Constitution] of the Jammu and Kashmir Constitution provides that the State is duty bound to direct its policy towards securing the distribution of the ownership and control of the material resources of the community in such a way as 'to subserve the common good' and the operation of the economic system which does not result in the concentration of wealth and means of production to common detriment. It may also be noted that though this section guarantees to all citizens the right to practice any profession or to carry on any occupation trade or business but restrictions under Article 19(6) imposes reasonable restrictions on this right. Further, the state is empowered to impose restrictions on monopoly to create a market in favour of the State excluding the private individuals in the interest of the consumer.

Thus, the identification, enumeration, amplification and elucidation of the relevant provisions of the constitution demonstrates the availability of abundant legislative and administrative power in the constitution and the possibility for progressive interpretation by the judiciary in protecting the basic, essential, legitimate interests of the consumer.

(9) The Industries (Development and Regulation) Act

The Industries Development and Regulation Act, 1951 (hereinafter referred to as IDRA) is another example on the part of the Union Government to make some attempts in implementing the objectives of consumerism. The IDRA provides a legal framework within which policies and procedures are to be worked out for the utilization of the limited resources of the country and foreign exchange available, for maximum industrialization. This Act with its registration[72] and licensing provisions[73] and provisions empowering the Central Government to make investigations,[74] to give direction,[75] to assume management and control of business[76] and to control the distribution, supply and prices of their products,[77] serves consumer interest to a great extent. Under Section 18-G, this Act empowers Central Government to regulate by licenses and permits distribution, transport, disposal, acquisition possession, use or consumption of any article or class of articles. Further under the said Section of the Act, the Central Government is empowered to regulate or prohibit any class of commercial or financial transaction of

72. IDRA. Section 10.
73. *Id.*, Section 11.
74. *Id.*, Section 15.
75. *Id.*, Section 22.
76. *Id.*, Section 18-A.
77. *Id.*, Section 18-G.

article which is considered to be detrimental to public interest. Control is exercised over substantial expansion of Industry[78] and in producing a new article. The function of development councils constituted U/S 16 of the IDRA include recommending production targets and promoting standardization of products.

(10) The Indian Standards Institution (Certification Marks) Act

From the point of view of administrative protection the Indian Standards Institution has been rendering remarkable service ever since its establishment. It provides the standardization and marking of goods which is a pre-requisite establishment of a healthy trade and to compare favourably with the established makes of foreign products. From objects and reasons of the Act it appears that the ISI is performing the following functions[79]—

(i) to prepare and promote the general adoption of standards on national and international bases;
(ii) to promote standardization, quality, control and simplification in industry;
(iii) to provide for registration of standardization marks applicable to products, commodities, etc.; and
(iv) to provide or arrange facilities for the examination and testing of commodities, etc.

The Act has been amended from time to time to make more effective provisions in order to achieve its objectives. The ISI prescribes specification for most of the commodities and manufactured articles which figured in India's export trade with foreign countries and also in the home markets.

The wide publicity given by ISI[80] has attracted attention of the enlightened purchasers, especially or organized

78. *Id.*, Section 11-A.
79. Seen statements, objects and reasons of the Act 13, A.I.R Manual 667, 4th Ed., 1979.
80. ISI has formulated a number of standards for food stuffs, drugs, cosmetics, utensils, textiles, electric appliances, paints, carpets, furniture, detergents, soaps, etc.

agencies such as the railways, the municipal corporations, the director general of supplies and disposals and defense establishments, manufacturers and industrial undertakings. The ISI has also a system of issuing product certification marks to producers who are properly equipped to undertake specified testing operations for regulating the quality of their products. The institute exercises overall supervision over the working of the scheme and it is authorized to suspend or cancel any Licence in the event of its misuse. There are other agencies too for such product certification such as the well known Agmark, established in 1937 for grading and marketing of agriculture products by the directorate of Marketing and Inspection of the Ministry of Food and Agriculture.[81]

(11) The Drugs and Magic Remedies (Objectionable Advertisements) Act[82]

This Act seeks to control the advertisements of drugs for certain purposes of remedies alleged to possess magic qualities. The statements of objects and reasons of the Act spells out its purpose which is as follows:

> "In recent years there has been a great increase in the number of objectionable advertisements published in newspapers or magazines or otherwise relating to alleged cures for venereal diseases, sexual statements and alleged cures for diseases and conditions peculiar to women. These advertisements tend to cause the ignorant and the unwary to resort to self-medication with harmful drugs and appliances or to resort to quacks who indulge in such advertisements for treatments which cause great harm."

Keeping the above purpose of the Act in view it becomes clear that this Act prohibits advertisement of only

81. *Supra* Note 67, M.V. Pylee, Article, 'Consumer Protection in a Developing Society', pp. 22-23.
82. This Section of the said Act deals with prohibition of advertisement of certain drugs for treatment of certain diseases and disorders.

certain drugs for treatment of certain diseases and disorders and puts ban on misleading advertisement relating to drugs, magic remedies for treatment and regulation of certain advertisements of Indian imports and exports. The Act prohibits only those advertisements and advertisements of only those drugs whose magically curative properties were intended to influence the organic function of the human body.

In considering the question as to whether the accused is guilty under Section 3[82] and Section 7[83] or not, if his case can fall under the provisions of Section 14, then Section 3 cannot be invoked against him. Thus, the object of the Act is to avoid self-medication by people or their being misled by various advertisements. The necessary condition, therefore, is that the advertisement must induce others into using the drugs advertised. In *Dr. Yashpal Sahi* v. *Delhi Administration*,[84] it was held that in order a person is to be penalized it is not necessary to show that the contravention brought home to him is in the nature of a habitual contravention. A single contravention proved against to a person would make him guilty under Section 7.

(12) The Prevention of Food Adulteration Act[85]

This Act is for prevention of food adulteration hazardous to human life and health. The statement of objects and reasons of the Act provides—

> "Adulteration of food stuffs is so rampant and the evil has become so widespread and persistent that nothing shall of a somewhat drastic remedy provided for in the bill can hope to change the situation. Only a concerted and determined onslaught on this most anti-social behaviour can hope to bring relief to the nation. All remedies intended to be effective must be simple."

83. The instant section of the same Act provides penalty for contravention of any of the provisions of the Act.
84. Saving clause for example, this Act will not apply to any advertisement relating to a drug printed or published by the government.
85. Of 1954, in 1970 it was made applicable to the State of J&K.

The Act in order to curb the increasing tendencies of adulteration and to make the machinery provided under it more effective was amended in various times. The Act has laid emphasis on the supply of articles of food and drink which are fit for human consumption by prohibiting the manufacture for sale or store, to sell or distribute any adulterated food, misbranded food which is prohibited for sale by health authorities to prevent the spread of diseases etc.[86] Section 2(a) of the Act elaborates in detail cases when an article of food shall be deemed to be adulterated. Section 5 of the Act prohibits import of any misbranded food either by himself or through others and Section 16 of the said Act treats misbranded article of food with adulterated article of food in respect of penalties.

In brief all the measures provided in the original Act and subsequent amendments are designed for the prevention of adulteration in food to ensure safety and health to the consuming public at large. Deterrent punishment to the extent of life imprisonment have been provided for habitual food adulterators, if the product when consumed by any person is likely to cause death or grievous hurt. A provision for summary trial for food adulteration has also been made. The offence under the Act can be tried only by metropolitan magistrates or judicial magistrates first class and serious offences have been made cognizable and non-bailable. Criminal liability has also been fixed on the officers of the company responsible for offences committed under the Act.

(13) Essential Commodities Act[87]

The most significant of laws that enables the government to deal effectively with trading activities that are adverse to the consumers is the Essential Commodities Act (hereinafter called E.C. Act). The very object of the E.C. Act as well as its predecessor enactment the Essential Supplies

---

86. In Municipal Corporation of Delhi *v.* Shiv Shanker [(1971)1 SCC 442]. The Supreme Court observed that purpose of the Act was held to eliminate the danger to human life and health from the sale of unwholesome articles of foods.

87. It is the Act of 1955, for details *Supra* Note 81.

(Temporary Powers) Act called E.S. Act are to check the inflationary trends in prices and to ensure equitable distribution of consumer commodities. For that purpose wide powers were conferred on the government by the Act. The E.C. Act and E.S. Act initially dealt with two classes of essential commodities[88]—

(i) basic non-perishable commodities like coal, textiles, iron and steel, etc., and
(ii) daily consumption perishable commodities like food stuffs, cattle feed, etc.

The primary concern of the government in issuing the control orders had been to see that the concerned commodities is in regular supply and available for consumer in right measure and at fair price. The E.C. Act vested wide powers in the Central Government to meet the objectives of the Act, and to issue control orders for the same. The powers exercisable by the Central Government, State Government or officers (to whom the centre and state can delegate powers) to ensure that the dealers display price lists and stock position extends even to introduce a ban in trade and commerce or prohibit the circulation of any particular article or commodity which in the opinion of the concerned authority is not in the interest of public consumption. The authority of the government to act on behalf of the consumer was reinforced by the Defence of India Act, 1971 and the rules made thereunder. Exercising the powers vested on the government consumable commodities of several kinds were brought under control one by one through the control orders to ensure both quality and quantity of supply.[89]

The powers conferred on the government under Section 3 of E.C. Act is of a general and particular nature and at the same time both pragmatic and purposive which any government would undoubtedly need if it were to safeguard its domestic market and economic order. The power is meant to enable the government to see the equitable distribution

88. *Id.*, pp. 129-30.
89. *Ibid.*

and the availability of commodities in the market at fair price to the consumers. In its particular nature, the government is to regulate by licenses and permits the production, manufacture, storage, transport, distribution, disposal, acquisition, use and consumption of essential commodities to control the price level, to require persons holding stocks to sell them to the central or state government to regulate or prohibit commercial and financial transaction relating to food stuffs to ensure maintenance of supply, to bring under cultivation arable and waste lands, to collect information and statistics to require person engaged in trade and commerce of essential commodities to submit their books, accounts and records for inspection. Besides, the government has the incidental and supplementary power to enter and search premises, vehicles, vessels and aircraft and seize them. It empowers the government to confiscate food grains, edible oil, seeds and oils and other consumer goods pursuant to any control order, subject only to the supervisory and bailing powers of the district collector. The orders issued by the government under Section 3 of the Act will have effect notwithstanding inconsistency with the other laws in force. Only orders contrary to the provisions of the Act itself is rendered invalid.[90]

The judicial affirmation supporting government authority in this respect is uniform whether in India or America. In 1968 in the Permian Basin Area Rate Cases, the Supreme Court had held that government is entitled to make pragmatic adjustments which may be called for by particular circumstances and the price control orders can be called unconstitutional only if it is patently arbitrary, discriminatory or demonstrably irrelevant to the policy which the legislature has adopted. So also in *Narendra Kumar* v. *Union of India* the Indian Supreme Court has held that the power of regulation and prohibition U/S 3 of the E.C. Act does not violate the fundamental rights guaranteed under the Indian Constitution.[91]

However, despite the vast powers enabling the

90. *Ibid.*
91. *Ibid.*

government to regulate, control, supply and distribute goods of normal consumption,[92] it is seen that the provisions are rendered ineffective for the lack of enforceability and the penal provisions are found meaningless. Therefore, it is felt that unless by concerted action an awareness is created on the consumers and resistance is built up, market force would continue to regulate the supply system and the consumer will have to surrender himself to be exploited by the sharks in high seas of the market economy.[93]

(14) The Medical Council Act

The main purpose of this Act is to establish a uniform essential standard of higher qualification in medicine. This is the principal Act governing the medical profession. Medical Council may direct the removal or for a specified period from the register the name of any registered practitioner who has been convicted of any such offence as implies in the opinion of the medical council a defect of character or who after an inquiry at which opportunity has been given to such registered practitioners be heard in person or has been held by medical council to have been guilty of infamous conduct in any professional respect. However, under this Act it is not open for a sufferer or consumer to make complaint before the council himself.[94]

(15) The Trade and Merchandise Marks Act

This Act[95] had been enacted with a view to protect trade interests to prevent the deception of the consumers by the misuse or abuse of the trademark. The statement of objects and reasons provides:[96]

---

92. Even though the provisions of E.C.A. have armed the government with substantial power to ensure regular supply and fair distribution at reasonable prices of a variety of consumable articles.
93. *Id.*, p. 132.
94. N.J. Modi, The Medical Council of India, 1956, Medical Jurisprudence and Toxicology, 13th Ed., Bombay, Tripathi, 1988, p. 426.
95. This Act has consolidated The Trade Marks Act, 1940 and Indian Merchandize Marks Act, 1889 and provided law relating to registration and better protection of trademarks in the country.
96. Statement of Objects and Reasons of the Act, 1948; A.I.R 33 Manual 599 (4th Ed., 1979).

> "The criminal laws relating to trademarks and trade descriptions which are contained in Chapter XVIII of the Indian Penal Code and the Indian Merchandise Marks Act, 1889 respectively, were enacted at a time when commercial advertising in this country had not been much developed. With the increase both in appeal and power of modern advertisements, afresh approach to matters relating to false trademarks and false trade description has become necessary."

The Act provides for the legislation, better protection of trademarks and for the prevention of the use of fraudulent marks on merchandise. A good trademark is the best salesman and advertiser of goods. To the purchaser a genuine trademark gives assurance of the mark and quality of the article he is buying. This Act provides enhanced punishment for offences relating to trade and merchandise marks particularly drugs and foods on grounds of public interest and public health. The Act provides for registered and un-registered trade marks, proposed use of trade mark by the company to be formed and removal from register and imposition of limitations on ground of non-use. It also provides for alteration and rectification of trade marks and correction of the registration and certification of trade marks. So the protection of the trade marks is essential not only for the honest trader, but also for the benefit of the purchasing public.

(16) The Specific Relief Act[97]

This Act has been enacted to define and amend the law relating to certain kinds of specific relief's obtainable in Civil Courts. From the consumer's point of view the Act deals with the rights and liabilities of parties of a contract specifically among others with the right to claim compensation for the breach of contract[98] and power of the Court to award compensation in certain cases.[99]

---

97. Act of 1977 (Act No. XXXVII).
98. *Id.*, 21.
99. *Id.*, Section 22.

(17) Monopolies and Restrictive Trade Practices Act

The Passing of the MRTP Act[100] (hereinafter called MRTP Act) can be said really to be the beginning towards the consumer movement. This Act came into force on June, 1970. The regulation and control of monopoly in trade and business is an effort done by governments every where to ensure distributive justice. MRTP in several ways tries to checkmate the manipulative capacity of the monopoly trades, and thus protect the consumer in an indirect way from an adverse market. The enforcement of the Act is sought to be done by the Central Government and the Monopolies and Restrictive Trade Practices Commission, an institution created under the Act. The Act, for the control of the big industrial houses, envisages that their expansion schemes, establishment of new undertakings, mergers, amalgamations and takeovers were to be processed by the government and application for that purpose should be made to the government If the government so desires, it will refer to the commission any enquiry that has to be made before taking a decision on the application of these houses.

As far as the control of restrictive trade practices are concerned, the commission is left autonomous and independent of the government. The commission is required to act either on a reference by the government or complaint from either parties or Registrar of restrictive trade agreements or on its own motion. The decisions of both the government as well as the commission on any matter is appealable to the Supreme Court. 'Restrictive Trade Practices' and arrangements which would every where prevent, distort or restrict competition in any manner especially those which tend to restrict the flow of capital or resources into the stream of production. It can also be arrangement which bring about manipulation of prices which affect flow of supply in the market of goods and services which tend to impose on the consumers unjustified costs and restrictions. Section 33 of the MRTP Act gives illustrative agreement of the kind that would be restrictive trade practices. In the TELCO case, The

100. Passed in the year 1996 and commission established under this Act has been established at centre.

Supreme Court opened that every agreement that falls within the specified types of Section 33, would not be restrictive trade practice, but only those that have the characteristic of being anti-competition and harmful for 'public good'. Within the compass of the definition of the terms 'undertaking', 'dominant undertaking', 'inter-connected understanding' and 'service', a good variety of establishment and activities are concerned, the controlling power of the government on production, distribution and supply of manufactured goods and services can be effective to a very great extent.

The MRTP commission is empowered to inquire into any restrictive trade practices on receiving a complaint from any trade or consumer's association having a membership of not less than 25 persons or more consumers. In any monopolistic trade practice the commission can make an enquiry upon a reference by the Central Government or on its own knowledge or information. The commission for the purposes of inquiry is vested with the powers of a Civil Court, and has to be deemed a Civil Court. It has the power to decide applications referred to it for further inquiry by the Central Government The commission also possess the power to register the trade agreements submitted to it for further inquiry by the Central Government The commission also possess the power to register the trade agreements submitted to it under the Act and the commission can cause the Director of MRTP to make an investigation before issuing process to parties in particular cases. Thus the entire working pattern of the MRTP commission and the Central Government as designed by the Act necessarily envisages the protection of the consumer from the evil designs of the monopoly traders and their trading practices.

However, there is a serious complaint about Sections 21 and 22 of the MRTP Act. While the large companies find the said Sections of the Act led to considerable delay in the implementation of the project, the small companies allege that the loopholes in the Section have provided the big houses the chance to expand without the commissions approval of the schemes. The Sachar Committee on MRTP Act finds that the adverse criticism of the functioning of the commission are unwarranted and unfounded and are not tenable on the face of facts.

Further it is noteworthy to mention here that MRTP did not contain the provisions directly aimed at protecting the consumer but it was intended to regulate competition in the hope that it would generate fair conduct, the effect of which would percolate to the ultimate consumer.

(18) The Hire Purchase Act[101]

It is a very important consumer legislation and a convenient and a useful legal device for acquiring goods on long terms. Section 6 of this Act provides that every hire-purchase agreement does contain certain conditions—

(i) That the hirer shall have an enjoy quite possession of the goods; and
(ii) That the goods shall be free from any charge or encumbrance in favour of any third party at the time when the property is to pass.

Sections 9, 10 and 11 of this Act entitle the hirer to purchase property at any time with rebate, to terminate agreement at any time and to appropriate payments in respect of two or more agreements respectively. Furthermore, Section 17 ensures the rights of hirer in case of seizure of goods by owner and Section 20 deals with the restriction on owner's right to recover possession of goods otherwise than by proceeding through Court of Law after a specified proportion of hire purchase price has been paid or tendered.

(19) The Code of Criminal Procedure[102]

This Code like the Ranbir/Indian Panel Code also protects the consumer interest to some extent. Sections 149-153 lays down the provisions relating to preventive action of the police.[92] Under the said provisions of the Code an officer incharge of a police station may, without a warrant enter any place within the limits of such station for the purpose of

101. Passed in the year 1972; A.I.R. 20 Manual 851 (4th Ed., 1979).

102. Such action of the police officers falls into three categories: (i) Prevention of Cognizable Offences, (ii) Prevention of injury to public property, and (iii) Inspection of Weights and Measures.

inspecting or searching false weights or measures or instruments for weighing. If he finds in such place any false weights, measures or instruments for weighing, he may seize the same and report the seizure to a Magistrate having jurisdiction.

(20) The Cigarettes (Regulation of Production, Supply and Distribution) Act

Though this Act[103] regulates supply and distribution of cigarettes but it simultaneously and sufficiently warns about the hazardous of smoking. The statement of objects and reasons read as under—

> "Research carried out in various parts of the world have confirmed that there is a relationship between smoking of cigarettes and lung cancer, chronic bronchitis, certain diseases of the heart and arteries, cancer of bladder, prostrate mouth, pharynx and esophagus and peptic ulcer, etc. are also reported to be among the ill-effects of cigarette smoking. It has, therefore, necessary to provide, in the interests of the general public, that trade or commerce and production, supply and distribution of cigarettes shall not be made unless each package of cigarettes or its label bears thereon the specified warning that 'cigarette smoking is injurious to health'."

(21) The Jammu and Kashmir Weights and Measures Act

This repealed Act[104] is enacted to establish standard of weights and measures, to regulate interstate trade or commerce in weights, measures and other goods which are sold or distributed by weights, measures or number and to provide for matters connected therewith. Earlier the repealed Act provided primary unit of length, primary unit of mass and standard, unit of weight, unit of time and electric current, etc. However, the repealed Act provides for the establishment of standards of weights and measures on

---

103. A.I.R. 3 Manual 192 (4th Ed., 1979).
104. A.I.R. 32 Manual 674 (4th Ed., 1979).

metric system, regulation of interstate trade or commerce in weights, measures and other goods which are sold or distributed, penalties for use of non-standard weights or measures.

Therefore, this Act established standard of weights and measures thereby prohibiting the manufacture and use of non-standard weights. However, this Act goes more in breach than observance.

OBSERVATION

After making a careful study of long list of consumer legislations it is clear that in the State of Jammu and Kashmir as in the rest of this country consumer law is as old as the consumer himself. The question to what extent these enactments have protected an average consumer no satisfactory answer can be given. These Codes and enactments are primarily aimed at controlling production sale supply, etc. of several goods and services. However these legislations have not helped consumer in real sense. Firstly, because an average consumer is not knowing the law and may have hardly heard about these legislations. Secondly, it is a fact with which many will not disagree that high technicality, expensiveness and time consuming process has disappointed the consumer to go into the litigation. Thirdly, due to lack of enforcement agencies these legislations are going in constant violation in absence of checks and control and sometimes consumer crimes more often are committed in active protection of police and law enforcement agencies. Under these Acts there are more acquittals than conviction and the actual complainant usually consumer gets nothing which can be said to have redressed his grievance. Under these Codes and enactments no compensatory and direct remedy is available to the consumers to seek redressal against the offending traders, manufactures or provider of services. Under these Acts consumer has difficulty in challenging the government which have the monopoly in the service sector. In these blurred and bewildered circumstances Consumer Protection Act has proved a silver line to curb the rust. This Act will be dealt separately in next chapter.

CHAPTER

4

STATE CONSUMER PROTECTION ACT: A CRITIQUE

INTRODUCTION

The legislature of the State of Jammu and Kashmir enacted Consumer Protection Act on 19th of August 1987 which is equal to a similar Law passed by the Parliament in 1986. The Central Act applies to the whole of India except the State of Jammu and Kashmir. State Act is same as the Central Act with a few variations as it provides only for separate two-tire adjudicatory machinery—Divisional Forum at divisional level and the State Commission for the whole State whereas the Central Act provides a separate three-tire quasi-judicial machinery— National, State and District level. Among one of the measures (other measures include amendment of C.P.C. and Cr.P.C., increase in the number of Posts of Judges and Judicial officers, establishment of easily accessible special Courts and Tribunals. Further, adoption of alternative modes of disputes resolution such as arbitration and conciliation, Lok Adalts, etc.) taken by the State Government to provide cheap and accessible Justice to the downtrodden, backward and poor people is the enactment of the State Consumer Protection Act. The object of the Act as its preamble proclaims is the better protection of the interests of the consumer. The most important milestone in consumer movement in the State has been the enactment of the State Consumer Protection Act. The Act applies to all goods and services unless specifically exempted by the government by notification in the government Gazettee. The Act vests forums and commission with quasi-judicial authority to settle consumer disputes and complaints by providing speedy, simple, timely and inexpensive redressal. As this Act is directly and specifically on consumer protection in this chapter an attempt has been made to evaluate critically various provisions of this Act more conveniently in the light of model (Central Consumer Protection, Act) on Consumer Protection. Further while analysing various provisions relevant cases decided by the Apex Court, High Courts and Redressal agencies of various States have been quoted to support the arguments. I have not hesitated to express my own views on various sections of the Act.

PART I

(A) TITLE, EXTENT AND PREAMBLE, ETC. OF THE ACT

In this part title, extent and preamble, etc. of the Act will be briefly outlined.

(1) Title

Generally speaking various pronouncements of the Apex Court has made it clear that the title of a statute reflects its purpose. With this impression the title of the present Act gives a clear cut picture. Here title—Consumer Protection Act itself expresses the nature and purpose of the Act that it is meant to protect the interest of the consumers.

(2) Territorial Extent

The Consumer Protection Act, 1987 extends to the whole of the State of Jammu and Kashmir. What is the extent of Territory of the State a Section of the State constitution which deals with territory of the State will be quoted here.[1]

1. Justice A.S. Anand, 'The Constitution of Jammu and Kashmir', 3rd Ed., Universal Law Publishing Company Pvt. Ltd, Delhi.

Section 4: The territory of the State shall comprise all the territories which on the 15th day of August, 1947 were under the sovereignty or suzerainty of the Ruler of the State.

The above definition of the State Territory as enshrined in the State constitution is not giving a correct picture.[2] To have a better view of territorial extent as envisaged by the instant Act of Consumer Protection it is observed that the Act applies to all parts of the state of Jammu and Kashmir including Poonch, Rajouri and Leh Ladakh.

(3) Preamble

Preamble of the Act makes it clear that it seeks to provide for better protection of the interests of Consumer and for that purpose it makes provision for the establishment of Consumer Councils and other Authorities for the settlement of Consumer disputes and for matters connected therewith. For brevity and convenience preamble of the Act will be reproduced here:

> "An Act to provide for better protection of the interests of consumers and for that purpose to make provision for the establishment of Consumer Councils and other authorities for the settlement of Consumer disputes and for matters connected therewith."

The use of the expression for the protection of the interests of consumers reveals that the interests of the consumers were also protected even earlier under the provisions of several legislations relating to standardisation, grading; packaging and branding; prevention of food

2. *Id.* The extent of the territory has not been given in the constitution. This has not been defined in the Constitution of India either. The first schedule to the Constitution of India defines the territory of Jammu and Kashmir as: 'The Territory which immediately before the commencement of the constitution was comprised in the Indian State of Jammu and Kashmir. Prior to the accession of the state to India and after the partition of British India into India and Pakistan on the 15th of August, 1947, some parts of the state fell into the hands of the invaders, but the instrument of accession of Jammu and Kashmir State applied to the whole area of the state, including the area now under the occupation of Pakistan.

adulteration; short weights and measures; hoarding; profiteering; restrictive and unfair trade practices, etc. But these legislations failed to protect the ultimate consumers from defective goods or deficient services, over charging of prices and unscrupulous exploitation. The consumer needed better protection in all those matters which led to the enactment of the Consumer Protection Act. The Act is the very important socio-economic legislation with its main thrust on giving speedy redressal and compensation to the consumer,[3] Supreme Court while stressing the importance of the preamble in its decision in *Lucknow Development Authority* v. *M.K Gupta*[4] said:

> A scrutiny of the various definitions such as 'Consumer', 'Service', 'Trader', 'unfair practice' indicates that the legislature has attempted to widen the reach of the Act. Each of these definitions are in two parts, one explanatory and the other expandatory. The explanatory or the main part itself uses expressions of wide amplitude indicating clearly its wide sweep, then its ambit is widened to such things which otherwise would have been beyond its natural import.

(4) Application of the Act

Bare reading of Section 1 sub-section 2 of the Act makes it clear that the Act applies to all goods and services unless the State Government expressly exempts any category of goods or services from the applicability of this Act. Upto this time neither the Central Government nor the State Government has issued any notification but still conflicts and controversies created by some agencies and institutions have seriously affected the implementation of the Act.[5] The provisions of the Act thus have to be construed in favour of

3. Dr. V.K. Agarwal, Consumer Protection (Law and Practice as amended by The Consumer Protection, Amendment) Act, 1993, 2nd Ed, B.L.H. Publishers, Distributors Pvt. Ltd, New Delhi, p. 27.
4. (1994) 1 SCC; Dr. Avtar Singh, Law of Consumer Protection (Principles and Practice) 2nd Ed. (1997), Eastern Book Company, Lucknow, p. 3.
5. Cases consisting such conflicts and controversies will be dealt later on in the next Chapter V.

the consumer to achieve the purpose of the enactment as it is a social benefit-oriented legislation. The primary duty of the Court while construing the provisions of such an Act is to adopt a constructive approach without doing violence to the language of the provisions of the Act and producing a result contrary to the attempted objectives of the enactment.[6]

(5) Salient Features of the Consumer Protection Act

Following are the broad-based features of the Act[7]—

(i) For providing better interest to the consumers it provides quasi-judicial machinery in the shape of courts at Divisional and State level. Each divisional forum is presided over by the officer of the status of District Judge and that of State Commission (Forum) by the officer having rank of High Court Judge. These officials are designed as Presidents of their respective Forums. In each of these forums there are two public persons of eminence in the field of trade education, etc. to assist the Judges (Presidents).

(ii) The Act has within its ambit the services supplied by the government or the public sector apart from goods.

(iii) The Act provides a cheap remedy to the consumer unlike the Courts, the complaints before the appropriate fora can be filed in written even by the consumer himself.

(iv) It provides time bound disposal of cases. It lays down 90 days period from the receipt of notice by the opposite party (OP) within which to dispose of the case.

(v) Much significance is attached to the fact that the Consumer Protection Act provides for uniform period of limitation of 30 days for appeal from one forum to another thereby reducing time taken

6. *Supra* Note 4.
7. Dr. Keshav Sharma, Article, 'Consumer Movement of India-I', The Daily News Paper *Kashmir Times*, Thursday, 15th of March, 2001.

by the parties at the intermediate stages. It also discourages adjournments.

(vi) It is procedural law namely Civil Procedure Code which governs all civil litigation and which in most cases is responsible for protracting proceedings resulting inevitably into delay. A good sense prevailed on the wisdom of legislature that it choosed to keep the CPC with all its subtleties apart from the Consumer Protection Act providing only for its limited application in matters of summoning and enforcing attendance of witnesses, discovery and production of documents, etc.

(vii) The Consumer Protection Act has penalty provision providing for imprisonment ranging from one month to three years and a fine from Rs. 2000 to Rs. 10,000 to punish the traders who do not comply with orders passed by the Authorities.

PART II

This part deals with the definitions. These definitions will be discussed with support of case law wherever possible.

(B) DEFINITIONS

Following are the definitions as defined under Section 2 of the Act.

(I) Appropriate Laboratory

Act defines the term 'Appropriate Laboratory'[8] which includes any such laboratory or organization as is recognised by the government and includes any such laboratory or organization established by or under any law for the time being in force. The definition further provides that the appropriate laboratory as envisaged by the Act must be one

8. Clause (a) of Section 2(1) of Consumer Protection Act, 1987 (State Act).

which is maintained, financed or aided by the government. So any laboratory which is maintained or aided or financed by the State Government is the appropriate laboratory. Private Laboratories have no role to play under this Act. Any laboratory set-up under The Food Adulteration Act, etc. by the government will be deemed appropriate laboratory. However, non-availability of dependable and efficiently run testing laboratory has seriously handicapped law enforcement agency in the State of Jammu and Kashmir.

(2) Branch Office

The definition of 'branch office'[9] has been inserted by the Amendment Act, 1997. Branch office under the Act means—

(i) Any establishment described as a branch by the opposite party; or

(ii) Any establishment carrying on either the same or substantially the same activity as that carried on by the head office of the establishment.

The first part of the definition reveals that any establishment described as a branch by the opposite party will be a branch office for the purpose of the Act. The second part of the definition provides that any establishment carrying on either the same or substantially the same activity as that carried on by the head office of the establishment will be taken as a branch office. The definition of 'branch office' as given by the Act is useful as now a consumer/complainant can file complaint at any place where there is branch office and not necessarily where the cause of action arose. For this reason Section 9 clause (a) stands amended and now complaint will be lodged either at the place where the business is carried on directly or through a branch office.

(3) Who is a Complainant?

Under the Act 'complainant'[10] does not mean the actual

9. *Id.* Clause (aa) Inserted by The Jammu and Kashmir Consumer Protection (Amendment) Act, 1997.

10. *Id.* Clause (b) of Section 2(1).

aggrieved person only. Here 'Complainant' is the Consumer himself or any Voluntary Consumer Association (Registered) and the government if it makes a complaint. After the amendment in the State Act now any number of Consumers having the same interest may also be called complainant/ complainants. Thus under the Act following categories fall under the definition of complainant—

(i) A Consumer; or
(ii) Any Voluntary Consumer Association registered under the Companies Act, 1956 or any other law for the time being in force;
(iii) The government who makes a complaint; and
(iv) One or more consumers where there are numerous consumers having the same interest with the permission of the Divisional Forum on behalf of or for the benefit of all consumers so interested.

The reason behind widened range of *locus standi* is obvious that our legislatures were conscious and felt need to have a variety of group or some organized persons who will set the law in motion because ordinarily consumers are reluctant to put their grievances before the competent authorities and before Courts. It is to be submitted here that in view of the spirit of the Act same meaning will be assigned to the word 'Consumer' as it meant under the definition of consumer as defined under Section 2(1)(d) of the Act and not as provided under Section 10(a) which limits its scope while prescribing the manner of filing complaint by expressing that a complaint in relation to any goods sold or delivered or any service provided may be filed before a divisional forum by the consumer to whom such goods are sold or delivered or such services provided . . . The definition of consumer U/S 2(1)(d) is wide which covers even the user of goods and beneficiary of services also.

Regarding the voluntary consumer association it can be said with great pride that it is for the first time that these associations have been recognized and entrusted with an important task of protecting the consumers. However, it is the sorry state of affairs that though in the rest of our country there are numerous voluntary consumer associations which are working for and on behalf of the consumers but in the State of Jammu and Kashmir there is negligible number of these associations. It is not only consumer and voluntary consumer associations even government (as consumer of Goods and Services) can file the complaint but it is learnt that the government has never resorted to this provision so far. Now by way of amendment under the Central and State Act class action by consumers is permissible.

(4) What is a Complaint?

The 'complaint'[11] under the Act means any allegation in writing made by a complainant in regard to one or more of the grounds enumerated in the definition in the complaint.

Under the Act complaint must be made in writing specifying the name, description and address of the complainant and the opposite party. It must state those facts which arose and be supported by documents if any. It must also specify the relief which the complainant is seeking. Grounds for the complaint under the Act are enumerated in the Act itself which are as follows:

(a) Complaint against unfair and restrictive trade practices[12]

The meaning of the expression unfair trade practice for the purpose of the State Consumer Protection Act is similar to the definition as given in the Central Act. Central Act has borrowed this definition from Section 36 of the MRTP Act. In the Central Act prior to the 1993 amendment—to make the complaint under the Consumer Protection Act it was necessary that the complainant must have suffered loss or damage as a result of any unfair trade practice. Now by virtue of 1993 Amendment Act it has removed this difficulty and now a complaint can be made in respect of any unfair or restrictive trade practice whether the complainant has suffered loss or damage or not as a result of such trade practice. Under the State Act also such a provision shall be incorporated in future so that a consumer will file complaints

---

11. *Id.* Clause (c) of Section 2(1).
12. *Id.* Sub-Clause (i) of Section 2(1)(c)

not only for the loss or injury which he has already suffered but also in apprehension of that loss or injury. However, it may be noted that the scope of the State Act has been widened by 1997 Amendment, which covered within its ambit not only unfair trade practices but also restrictive trade practices adopted by the traders. The definition of restrictive trade practice has been incorporated in the newly inserted clause (nn) of Section 2(1) of the Act.

(b) Complaint against defective goods[13]

A complaint may be made in respect of the goods which suffer from one or more defects. 'Defect' means any fault, imperfection or shortcoming in the quality, quantity, potency, purity or standard which is required to be maintained under any law for the time being in force or under any contract express or implied or as is claimed by any trader. The term 'Trader' includes any seller, distributor, manufacturer and packer of goods. The 1997 amendment enables the consumer, etc. to file complaints not only after he has bought the goods but even if there is an agreement to buy goods.

(c) Complaint against deficient services[14]

Prior to the 1997 amendment, a complaint could be made only in respect of those services which were hired by the consumer and suffer from deficiency in any respect. Now a complaint can be made in respect of services hired or availed of or agreed to be hired or availed of suffer from deficiency in any respect. Deficiency means any fault, imperfection, shortcoming or inadequacy in the quality, nature and manner of performance.

---

13. *Id.* Sub-Clause (ii) of Section 2(1)(c), Amendment Act, 1997 substituted the words 'the goods bought by him or agreed to be bought by him' for the words 'the goods mentioned in the complaint'.
14. *Id.* Sub-Clause (iii) of Section 2(1)(c), substituted the words, 'the services hired or availed of or agreed to be hired or availed of by him' for the words 'the services mentioned in the complaint'.

(d) Complaint against excess-price[15]

A complaint may be made against a trader who has charged for the goods mentioned in the complaint a price in excess of the price—

(i) Fixed by or under any law for the time being in force; or
(ii) Displayed on the goods; or
(iii) Displayed on any package containing such goods.

Thus, when there is no fixing of price of an article by law, nor a display of price on the package containing the goods or on the goods themselves, the Act does not contemplate any complaint being instituted in respect of the price charged for the article on the ground that the price charged for is excessive. The consumer redressal forums constituted under the Act cannot undertake an investigation of the reasonableness of the price fixation made by a manufacturer, producer or dealer.

In a case[16] a complaint was filed by the respondent questioning the action of the Mahboobnagar Milk Chilling Center in charging 15 paisa extra per half liter of milk supplied sachets to the consumers at Mahboobnagar. The State Commission of Andhra Pradesh proceeded to examine the reasonableness of the price structure for the different varieties of milk and ordered that the prices were excessive. The National Commission observed that no reference was made to any law in force in the state of Andhra Pradesh fixing the price at which the different varieties of milk were to be sold nor there was any mention of the price on the sachets containing the milk sold to the consumers. The National Commission held that in the absence of any law requiring an article to be sold at or below a particular price fixed thereunder and when there was no declaration of price on the packet containing the goods or on the goods themselves, the Act did not contemplate that the Consumer Disputes Regressal Forum constituted under its provision

15. *Id.* Sub-Clause (iv) of Section 2(1)(c).
16. Milk Chilling Centre, Mahaboobnagar *v.* Mahaboobnagar Citizens Council (1991) 1 CPJ 219 (National Commission).

should undertake an investigation of the reasonableness of the price fixation made by a manufacturer, producer or dealer. The National Commission therefore, declared that the order of the State Commission was unwarranted by law and accordingly set aside the order of the State Commission.

(e) Complaint against the hazardous goods[17]

Sub-clause fifth inserted in clause C of Section 2(1) by the Amendment Act, 1997 enables a person to file a complaint of any goods which will be hazardous to life and safety, are being offered for sale to the public without giving adequate information about the contents, manner and effect of use of such goods. This is an important provision for the safety of the consumers from the hazardous goods. It can be said that this provision should have been made applicable also to those services which may be of dangerous or hazardous nature invoking risk to life and safety of the people.

(5) Who is a Consumer?

Who is a 'consumer'[18] under Act Section 2(1)(d) gives a comprehensive definition. Actual definition of word consumer under the Act will be reproduced here—

"Consumer" means any person who—

(i) buys any goods for a consideration which has been paid or promised or partly paid and partly promised or under any system of deferred payment and includes any user of such goods other than the person who buys such goods for consideration paid or promised or partly paid or partly promised, under any system of deferred payment when such use is made with the approval of such person, but does not include a person who obtains such goods for resale or for any commercial purpose; or

17. *Supra* Note 14, Inserted Clause (v) of Section 2(1)(c).
18. *Id.*, Section 2(1)(d).

(ii) hires or avails[19] of any service for a consideration which has been paid or promised or partly paid and partly promised, or under any system of deferred payment and includes any beneficiary of such services other than the person who hires or avails of the services for consideration paid or promised, or partly paid and partly promised or under any system of deferred payment, when such services are availed of with the approval of the first mentioned person.

"*Explanation*: For the purpose of sub-clause (i), "commercial purpose" does not include use by a consumer of goods bought and used by him exclusively for the purposes of earning his livelihood, by means of self-employment."

The term "consumer" is defined in Section 2(1)(d) of the Consumer Protection Act in two parts—one in reference to a consumer who purchases goods and the second in reference to a person who hires services. Thus, the Act covers transactions for supply of goods and rendering of services. It covers whole range of commodity market as well as service market. The definition is wide enough to include in 'Consumer' not only the person who buys any goods for consideration but also any user of such goods with the approval of the buyer. Similarly, it covers any person who hires or avails of any services for consideration and also includes any beneficiary of such services when availed with the approval of the hirer. Thus, any user of goods or any beneficiary of services other than the actual buyer or hirer, is a consumer for the purpose of the Act and he is competent to make a complaint before the Consumer Disputes Redressal Forums under the Act.[20]

It is thus evident that this definition gives an altogether new legal colour and scope to the term 'Consumer', which extends crystallized by this exhaustive definition. The legislature deliberately extends it to person who may have

19. *Supra* Note 14, Inserted the words 'or avails' of after the word 'hires' in the definition of Consumer under the Act.
20. *Supra* Note 3, pp. 59-60.

had no privity of contract with the original trader, manufacturer or the person who had hired out the service. On the other hand, the definition limits the scope in the context of purchaser of goods, by excluding from its wide range those persons who buy such goods for re-sale or for any commercial purpose and expressly denies them the benefit of the Act. It would thus be seen that the Act introduces a new concept and class of consumers and gives them a very price legal connotation. The word 'Consumer' herein becomes a legal term of art having a meaning different and distinct from that used in loose common parlance. This is a significant development of the Act and concept radically different to the earlier and ordinary existing laws in the field.[21]

The above definition of term 'Consumer' reveals that a person claiming himself 'Consumer' should satisfy that[22]—

(i) there must be a sale transaction between the seller and the buyer;
(ii) the sale must be of goods;
(iii) the buying of goods must be for consideration;
(iv) the consideration has been paid or promised or partly paid and partly promised or under any system of deferred payment; and
(v) the user of the goods may also be a consumer when such use is made with approval of the buyer.

Similarly, in case of services consumer under the Act is required to satisfy that—

(i) the consumer hired the services;
(ii) service is for consideration;
(iii) service is not rendering of any service free of charge or under a contract of personal service; and

21. *Id.* It is observed by S.S. Sandhawalia, J. in Jagdamba Rice Mills *v.* Union of India (1991) CPJ 273 (Haryana) CDRC 321CA.
22. *Id.*, p. 61.

(iv) even beneficiary may be a consumer when services are availed of with the approval of the first mentioned person.

However, in view of explanation[23] annexed to clause (d) of Section 2(1) of the Act 'Consumer' is not the person who purchases goods for the resale or commercial purpose. Since this explanation has been borrowed from the central Act in both cases it is evident that Parliament/Legislature has the intention to exclude commercial sales from the Act.

Now let us divide and discuss definition of consumer under the following sub-headings.

(a) Consumer of Goods[24]

A Consumer for the purpose of goods means any person, who—

(i) buys any goods for consideration which has been paid or promised or partly paid and partly promised or under any system of deferred payment; and
(ii) includes any user of such goods other than the person who buys them, when such use is made with the approval of the buyer, but;
(iii) does not include a person who obtains such goods for re-sale or for any commercial purpose. Commercial purpose does not include use by a consumer of goods bought by and used by him exclusively for the purpose of earning his livelihood by means of self-employment.

The above provision reveals that a person claiming himself 'consumer' should satisfy that—

(i) there must be a sale transaction between the seller and the buyer;
(ii) the sale must be of goods;

23. *Supra* Note 19.
24. *Supra* Note 22, p. 60.

(iii) the buying of goods must be for consideration;
(iv) the consideration has been paid or promised or partly paid or partly promised or under any system of deferred payment; and
(v) the user of the goods may also be a consumer when such use is made with approval of the buyer.

As already said the term 'consumer' does not include a person who obtains any goods for re-sale or for any commercial purpose. However, sometimes much difficulty arises in differentiating whether a sale is for personal use or for commercial purpose. The mere fact that a person buys a thing repeatedly is not sufficient to make it a trade sale or to take it out of the category of a consumer sale. In a case[25] the Court observed that where an activity is merely incidental to the carrying on of a business, a degree of regularity has to be established before it can be said that the activity is an integral part of the business and therefore carried on in the course of a business.

(b) User of Goods[26]

The definition of consumer given in the Act makes it clear that it includes not only the person who buys any goods for consideration but also any user of such goods when such use is made with the approval of the buyer. This was necessary because the goods purchased by a buyer or most likely to be used by his family members, relatives and friends. Under the general principles of the Law of Contract such user of goods are not entitled to sue the supplier or trader of such goods on the ground of "Privity of Contract." The rule of Privity of Contract provides that only parties to the contract can sue and not a stranger. Thus a third person who is not a party to the contract cannot sue. But now under the provision of Consumer Protection Act a complaint may be made by any user of goods with the approval of the buyer

25. *Supra* Note 4, p. 16; R&B Customs Brokers Company *v.* United Dominions Trust, (1988) 1 WLR CA.
26. *Supra* Note 20, pp. 62-63.

even though he is not a party to the contract for purchase of those goods.

(c) Goods Purchased for Earning Livelihood and Self-employment

By reason of the strange problem of distinguishing between business purchases and purchases for self-employment, the definition was amended in 1997 on similar lines as under the Central Amendment Act in 1993 by adding an explanation so as to include within the meaning of the term 'Consumer' a buyer for self-employment by providing that purchase for a commercial purpose would not include things purchased for earning livelihood by means of self-employment.

The 'Explanation' as added to Section 2(1)(d) seems to have been wisely inserted with a view to safeguard the interest of small consumers who buy goods for self-employment to earn their livelihood. Prior to the amendment, a person buying any goods for commercial purpose was excluded from the definition of 'Consumer' and was not covered within the ambit of Consumer Protection Act. This caused genuine difficulties to consumers who were purchasing goods for earning their livelihood say like a Taxi driver buying a car to run it as a taxi, or a rickshaw puller buying rickshaw for self-employment or a widow purchasing a sewing machine for her livelihood or a farmer purchasing fertilizers or seeds for his crops, etc. It was not desirable to exclude these and similar other categories of persons from the definition of consumer as they depend on the goods for earning their livelihood. At the same time, the intention behind the Act was to exclude big business and industrial houses carrying out business with profit motive from the purview of the Act. The insertion of the 'Explanation' has removed this difficulty and enables the consumers to file complaints before the Consumer Disputes Redressal Agencies under the Act where goods bought by them are exclusively for earning their livelihood by means of self-employment suffer from any defect.[27]

27. *Id.*, pp. 69-70.

(d) Consumer of Services

Another category of consumer laid down under the Act is that of hirer or user of services. Under sub-clause (ii) of Section 2(1)(d) of the Act, a consumer for the purpose of service means any person, who—

(i) hires or avails of any services for consideration which has been paid or promised or partly paid and partly promised or under any system of deferred payment; and

(ii) includes any beneficiary of such services other than the person who hires or avails of them, when such services are availed of with the approval of the hirer.

Now it is beyond any doubt that goods purchased for commercial purposes are excluded from the purview of the Act but Consumer Protection the services used for commercial purpose are not excluded from the scope of the Consumer Protection Act. A simple reading of the Act and especially the definition of a consumer of service U/S 2(1)(d)(ii) would show that a consumer of service for commercial purpose is not barred from claiming protection under the Act, on the contrary 'consumer of goods' for commercial purpose is specifically excluded from the purview of the Act U/S 2(1)(d)(i). However, the services rendered free of charge or under a contract of personal service are outside the purview of the Act.

In order to know what type of service is envisaged by the Act let us go briefly through the following sub-headings:

(i) What is Hiring of Services?[28]

The words hires or avails of any services occurring in Section 2(1)(d)(ii) shows that the term 'hire' has also been used therein in the sense of 'avail' or 'use'.

Accordingly the definition should be understood as stating that 'consumer' means any person who avails or uses any service.

28. *Ibid.*

The term 'hire' has not been defined in the Act. According to the Concise Oxford Dictionary, 'hire' means employ person for wages or 'fee'. In Collins English Dictionary 'hire' has been defined as 'to acquire the temporary use of a thing or the services of a person in exchange for payment or to provide something or the services of one self or others for an agreed payment usually for an agreed period'. As per Chambers Twentieth Century Dictionary 'hire' means to produce the use of services of at a price to grant temporary use of for compensation.

Hiring in its ordinary, plain and grammatical sense *inter alia,* involves letting of things or services for rent or wages. It is a payment for labour or for the use of goods. In economic parlance, it is the nature of rent and wages. 'Hiring' is thus, species of bailment and reward is an essential ingredient in hiring. Hiring creates a legal right in the hirer against the owner for the latter to render service for which the former had paid the hirer.

(ii) Taxes Whether Constitute Consideration for Service?[29]

In a welfare State, it is the responsibility of the government to provide adequate medical, health care and other facilities to all citizens. Such indeed has been the endeavor of all governments both at the Centre and at the State level even since the inception of a plain programme of development. The hospitals established by the government are funded from the consolidated funds of the Government of India/the State Government concerned and under the Constitution these consolidated funds comprise the revenues which are raised in the form of direct taxes as well as indirect taxes. Every person who is resident of State pays taxes if not directly at least indirectly since excise duty, customs duty, sales tax, etc. are levied on almost each and every single item of goods that a person has necessarily to purchase for one's day-to-day requirements.

Now the question is whether the direct and indirect taxes paid to the State by a citizen constitute 'consideration' for the services ostensibly rendered by the State to its

29. *Id.,* pp. 72-73.

citizens. As pointed out by the Supreme Court in *Commissioner, Hindu Religious Endowments, Madras* v. *Sri Lakhsmindra Thirtha Swamiar*,[30] that tax is the compulsory exaction of money by public authority for public purposes enforceable by law and is not payment for service rendered.

The legal position is now well settled that 'tax' in its true nature is a levy made by the State for the general purposes of government and it cannot be regarded as payment for any particular or special service. While, it is undoubtedly true that the government in a welfare state is under a duty to provide various forms of facilities to citizens and the expenditure incurred there on will have to be met from out of consolidated funds of the State, it cannot be said that a tax levied for the general purposes of the state construes 'consideration' for any specific purpose, benefit or service provided by the State.

Further, the consideration for hiring of services, be it called fee, charge or rent is that it is a voluntary payment, it is open to a person to make the payment and hire the services or to refuse to pay and forego the service. A tax on the other hand is a levy or imposition made by the government for public purpose. There is no element of voluntariness in the payment of tax. No tax-payer has the option to refuse to pay the tax legally imposed on him. It is therefore, clear that payment of tax to the government cannot be construed as consideration for the services rendered by the government.

(iii) Court-Fee: Whether Constitute Consideration for Service[31]

While dispensing the criminal justice the State is not charging any fee. The Court fee is charged from the litigants who intend to file action before the Civil Court. The question is whether the litigants are hiring services of the Civil Courts for consideration as contemplated under the Consumer Protection Act.

In order to appreciate this issue, it would be necessary to examine certain provisions of our constitution.[32] Under the

30. *Ibid*. (1954) SCR 1005.
31. *Id*., p. 75.
32. Constitution of Jammu and Kashmir, 1957.

constitution sovereign powers of the State has to be exercised through three agencies—Executive, Legislative and Judiciary. The said functions are thus divided amongst three organs of the state. Each has been given separate powers though not with mathematical precision, e.g in a state of emergency the President can exercise the legislative power by making ordinance. In order to meet the expenses of the State the legislature has been given power to raise the revenues by means of taxes. Article 365 of the constitution provides that no tax shall be levied or collected except by authority of law. Again the legislative power has been divided between Union and State under Seventh Schedule of the constitution. Item number 96 in the Union list, item number 66 in the State list and item number 47 in concurrent list reads as under:

> "Fee in respect of any of the matters in this list but not including fee taken in any Court."

It may be seen that legislature has been given power to levy fees in respect of any matter over which it has legislative power except the fees taken in the Court.

After discussing whether tax and fee constitute consideration it would not be out of place to mention and give a brief distinction between tax and fee briefly as possible.

(iv) Tax and Fee—Distinguished[33]

The distinction between a 'tax' and a 'fee' has been often considered by the Supreme Court of India and their observations are very valuable for distinguishing between the two. In its landmark judgment in *Commissioner, Hindu Religious Endowments* v. *Sri Lakshmindra Thirtha Swamiar,*[34] the Supreme Court observed:

A tax is the compulsory exaction of money by public authority for public purposes enforceable by law and is not payment for services rendered. . . . A fee may generally be defined as a charge for a special service rendered to

---

33. *Supra* Note 31, p. 75.
34. *Supra* Note 30.

individuals by some governmental agency. The amount of fee levied is supposed to be based on the expenses incurred by the government in rendering the service. . . . The distinction between a 'tax' and a 'fee' lies primarily in the fact that 'tax' is levied as part of a common burden, while a 'fee' is a payment for a special benefit or a privilege.

In the *Chief Commissioner of Delhi* v. *D.C.M.*,[35] the Supreme Court held that a legal fee must satisfy two conditions, namely, (i) there must be an element of *quid pro quo,* that is to say the authority levying the fee must render some service for the fee levied, however, remote the source may be; (ii) that the fee raised must be spent for purposes of the imposition and should not form part of the general revenues of the state. In *Southern Pharmaceuticals and Chemicals* v. *State of Kerala*[36] the Supreme Court set out the difference between 'tax' and 'fee' as under:

Tax—

(i) The essence of taxation is compulsion being imposed under statutory power.
(ii) Imposition is for public purpose without reference to any special benefit to be conferred on the payer of the tax. In other words, levy of tax is for the purpose of general revenue and there is no element of *quid pro quo* between the tax payer and public authority.
(iii) Tax is a part of the common burden and is regulated with reference to the capacity by the tax payer to pay.

Fee—

(i) Fee on the other hand is a charge for a special service rendered to individuals by some government agency.

---

35. *Id.*, p. 74 (1978) 2 SCC 367.
36. *Ibid.* (1982) 2 SCR 519.

(ii) It is based on the expenses incurred by government in rendering the service, though there may not be exact correlation between the expenses incurred and the quantum of fees collected.

(iii) The fees are uniform without reference to the ability to the different recipients (of service) to pay.

In *Sreenivas General Traders* v. *State of Andhra Pradesh,*[37] the Supreme Court reiterated that the distinction between a tax and a fee lies primarily in the fact that tax is levied as part of common burden while a fee is for payment for specific benefit or privilege although the special advantage is secondary to the primary motive of regulation in public interest. If the element of revenue for general purpose of the state predominates, the levy becomes a tax. The court further observed that in order to establish the *quid pro quo* concept, it is not necessary to establish exactly that the amount collected is spent on the services rendered. The authority collecting the fee must show that it is rendering a service in lieu of the fee that is giving some special benefit to the payer of the fee. The quantum of the fee collected and the expenses on the services rendered must have a mutual relationship, by and large the relationship between the levy and the services rendered is one of general correct not of mathematical exactitude. All that is necessary is that there would be a reasonable relationship between the levy of the fee and the service rendered.

In *Consumer Unity and Trust Society, Jaipur* v. *State of Rajasthan,*[38] the National Commission after considering the above decisions observed that the legal position must now be taken to be well settled that unlike a 'fee' a 'tax' in its true nature is a levy made by the State for the general purposes of government and it cannot be regarded as payment for any particular or special service while it is undoubtedly true that the government in the welfare state is under a duty to provide various forms of facilities to citizens and the

37. *Ibid.* (1983) 3 SCR 843.
38. *Id.*, p. 75; (1991) 1 CPR 241 (National Commission).

expenditure incurred thereon will have to be met from out of the consolidated funds of the state. It cannot be said that a tax levied for the general purposes of the state constitutes 'consideration' for any specific facility, benefit or service provided by the state. It thus, follows that the payment of direct or indirect taxes by the public does not constitute 'consideration' paid for hiring the services rendered in the government hospitals.

(e) Beneficiary of Services[39]

The Consumer of Services includes not only the hirer of services for consideration but also any beneficiary of such services provided that he is availing the services with the approval of the hirer. This is necessary to protect the interest of the user of services because under the general principles of the law of contract such user cannot sue the provider of services on the ground of 'Privity of Contract'.[40] Thus under the law of contract only the hirer of the services can sue and not the user of such services. But now such a user or beneficiary may seek relief against the deficient services under the Consumer Protection Act.

In *Dr. B.S. Sidhu* v. *Secretary, Central Government Post and Telegraphic Department*,[41] the Haryana State Commission held that a person other than the original consumer, who hires services can maintain a complaint for the alleged deficiency. The commission observed—

A plain reading of the aforesaid clause (ii) which specifically pertains to the hiring of services, would make it manifest that the statute visualizes two categories of 'consumer' thereby. Inevitably, the first one is the original consumer who hire such services for a consideration. The definition, however, does not stop at that. It provides further to bring within its ambit a second category also, namely, any beneficiary of such services, when these are availed with the approval of the original consumer. The definition, is thus, an

39. *Id.*, p. 78.
40. The Rule of Privity of Contract provides that only parties to the contract can sue and not a stranger.
41. *Id.*, p. 78 (1991) 2 CPJ 90 (Haryana CDRC).

inclusive and extensive one. Designedly it brings within its scope not only the person who has the privity of contract with the person hiring out the services, but also subsequent beneficiaries thereof, even though the latter may not be a party to the original contract or have a direct nexus therewith. In the true spirit of consumerism, the Act has not confined itself to the original hirer alone, but equally extended it to the subsequent beneficiaries of the services as well.

A nominee of an insurance policy being a person appointed by a policy holder to whom the payment of money secured by the policy is to be made in the event of his death is beneficiary entitled to avail the services with the approval of the person who hired such services for consideration and is thus a consumer.

Similarly, a person who is using the telephone of a subscriber with his approval is a consumer of telephone services and is entitled to claim compensation under the Act for the period for which his complaints remained un-attended by the telephone department.

(6) Consumer Dispute[42]

The term 'Consumer Dispute' has been defined in clause (e) of Section 2(1) of the Act. Consumer dispute means a dispute where the person against whom a complaint has been made denies or disputes the allegations contained in the complaint. The consumer dispute will arise when a complaint is made by a consumer before the consumer forums constituted under the Act and the opposite party denies or disputes the allegations contained in the complaint or omits or fails to respond within the stipulated time specified under section 11 of the Act.[43] In any of these situations the redressal forums will proceed to settle the consumer dispute in the manner specified in sub-section (1) or (2) of section 11. It may be noted that even in case the opposite party omits or fails to take any action to represent his case, the forum has to

42. *Supra* Note 18, Clause (e) of Section 2(1).

43. Similar Provisions are available under Central Act on Consumer Protection.

proceed in a manner as if to settle the consumer dispute.

In *Executive Engineer Gosikhurd Dam Division Wahi (Pawani)* v. *Shri Harigana Cement Ltd. Nagpur,*[44] the Irrigation Department of Government of Maharashtra has placed orders for the supply of 500 metric tons non-levy Cement for the Irrigation Project on the opposite party who is a manufacturer. An allotment of 3150 M.T. was made and an amount of Rs. 43,02,040 was paid being the 98% of the cost price of the non-levy cement agreed to be supplied by the opposite party. The Opposite Party supplied only 2020 metric tons. The complainant claimed the price of the balance quantity of cement with interest at the rate of 24% besides compensation of Rs. 3.00 lacs for breach of the contract. It was held that the complaint does not relate to any defects in the goods supplied but relates to a breach of contract of the sale of goods on the ground of failure to supply the full quantity of goods agreed to be supplied. So it was held that there is no consumer dispute as there was no allegation of any defective goods or deficiency in service.

In *A.N. Saigal* v. *Delhi Development Authority,*[45] D.D.A. was directed by District Forum to refund the amount which was charged by the Delhi Development Authority from the complainant as interest. In appeal to State Commission the appeal was allowed partly but the complainant feeling aggrieved has came before the National Commission by way of revision petition. This commission held that the pricing of a flat or plot does not fall within the four corners of the Consumer Protection Act. The decision given by this commission in *Gurinder Bedi* v. *Delhi Development Authority,* 1986-96 CONSUMER 3219(NS) has remarked in this case which is as follows:

We are of the opinion that the forums constituted under the Consumer Protection Act are not empowered to go into the question of fixation of the price of the flats. Deficiency in relation to 'service' has been defined in clause

---

44. 1986-96 CONSUMER 1900 (NS) quoted National Commission and Supreme Court on Consumer Cases 1986-96, Part II, Editor—Ms. Swarn Bhatia Nijhawan, International Law Book Company, Delhi.
45. *Ibid.* 1986-96 CONSUMER 3219 (NS).

(g) of section 2(1) of the Act.

In a number of cases[46] National Commission came to the conclusion on the facts and circumstances of the case that there is no consumer dispute and matters be agitated before other appropriate forums and not before the consumer forum.

In *Union of India, through General Manager, Western Railway Bombay and another* v. *Manoj H. Pathac,*[47] complainant purchased railway tickets and had reserved seats. Some person unauthorizedly entered the reserved compartment and forcibly occupied seats. When the complainant resisted he was attacked by them as a result suffered fracture leading permanent disability due to fracture of 0-12 vertebral column. It was held that the complainant had hired services of Railway Administration and if there is any negligence or deficiency in service on the part of the railway administration then it is a consumer dispute within the scope and ambit of Section 2(1)(d) of the Act.

(7) What is Defect?

The complaint under the Consumer Protection Act can be made in relation to those goods which suffer from one or more defects. The term 'defect' has been defined in clause (f) of Section 2(1) of the Act. 'Defect'[48] means any fault, imperfection or shortcoming in the quality, quantity, potency, purity or standard which is required to be maintained by or under any law for the time being in force or under any contract express or implied[49] or as is claimed by the trader in any manner whatsoever in relation to any goods.

The definition is wide enough to include any fault, imperfection or shortcoming in the quality, quantity, potency,

---

46. Hiralal *v.* The Administration, Municipal Council, Bhilwara and Others, 1986-95 CONSUMER 190 (NS); Kedar Nath Misra *v.* Union of India and Others 1986-95 CONSUMER 1276 (NS); Industrial Development Bank of India *v.* Shri Krishnemdu Ghosh and Another 1986-96 CONSUMER 2209 (NS); Vice-Chairman, Lucknow Vikas Pradhikaran *v.* Prabhat Kumar Jha and Another, 1986-96 CONSUMER 2463 (NS).
47. *Supra* Note 44, 1986-96 CONSUMER 2162 (NS).
48. *Supra* Note 18, Clause (e) of Section 2(1).
49. *Supra* Note 19, Inserted.

purity or standard. The quality, quantity, potency, purity or standard should be such which is required to be maintained by or under any contract express or implied or as is claimed by the trader in any manner whatsoever in relation to any goods. Where the quality, quantity, potency, purity or standard of any goods are not in accordance with law or promise made by the trader, the goods will be deemed as defective. There are many legislations[50] which are providing standards, quality, quantity, etc. of several goods. Where the goods did not fulfil the requirements as claimed or to be maintained they will be defective for the purposes of the Consumer Protection Act.

It has been observed that some times traders claimed particular quality, quantity of a product in the contract but it has not been followed in actual practice. The Amendment Act, 1997 has inserted the words under any contract express or implied in clause (f) of Section 2(1) with a view to bring such contractual claims of traders within the ambit of the Consumer Protection Act.

Further, the standards quality, quantity, etc. of the goods must correspond with the claims made by the trader in relation to those goods. Such claims may be made by advertisements, by printing on the packet of goods or otherwise. Where the standards, quality, quantity, etc. of the goods are not in accordance with such claims, the goods will be considered as defective. The claims may be either express or implied. Thus, the true import of the word 'defect' as defined in Section 2(1)(f) of the Act, is one of the widest amplitude and the standard prescribed may be either one specified by any law or as is claimed by the trader himself either expressly or impliedly.

(8) What is Deficiency under the Act[51]?

The complaint under the Consumer Protection Act can be made in respect of only those services which suffer from any deficiency. The term 'deficiency' has been defined in Section 2(1)(g) of the Act. The literal meaning of 'deficiency' is—incomplete, defective, wanting in specified quality or

51. *Supra* Note 48, Clause (g) of Section 2(1).

insufficient in quality, force, etc. The definition of 'deficiency' given above is wide enough to include any fault, imperfection, shortcoming or inadequacy in the quality, nature and manner of performance in relation to any service. The deficiency may be in quality, nature and manner of performance—

(i) which is required to be maintained by or under any law for the time being in force; or
(ii) which has been undertaken to be performed by a person in pursuance of contract or otherwise in relation to any service.

Thus, the deficiency may occur due to the violation of any standards as to quality, nature and manner of performance laid down in any of the existing laws. The deficiency may also be caused owing to non-performance of the promise made as to quality, nature, etc. of the services. Under the contract same cases of negligence in rendering the services may also fall within the ambit of the Act, for example, negligence by a doctor rendering medical services for consideration; an act of negligence by a repairer of goods; negligence by the telephone department in wrongful disconnection of telephone may amount to deficiency in service and are thus actionable within the purview of the Act.

(9) Divisional Forum[52]

The Act originally provides for a divisional forums (which are presently working) instead of district level forums as in the rest of the country. Here the State Act has made a big deviation from the Central Consumer Protection Act. Under the Central Act State Governments are required to set-up district consumer forums and if in any district there is work load by virtue of Amendment Act, 1993 (Proviso has been inserted) State Government may if it deems fit, establish more than one district forum in a district. Earlier for establishment of district forum State Government was to take prior approval of the Central Government but Amendment

52. *Ibid.* Clause (h) of Section 2(1).

Act has omitted these words and now State Governments under the Central Act of Consumer Protection have exclusive domain to set-up district forum. Now though the recent Amendment, 2002 in the State Consumer Protection Act provides for establishment of district forums but government has not taken steps to establish these forums so far.

(10) Goods

Clause (i) of Section 2(1) of the Act says 'goods'[53] means goods as defined in the Sale of Goods Act. However, the definition of 'goods' excludes money and actionable claims. Money, being a legal tender is an essential element of sale. Money consideration is the 'Price' which is payable for the sale of goods. Therefore, money itself cannot be a subject-matter of sale. But if notes or coins (which have ceased to be legal tender) are sold as collector's items, there seems no reason why they should not be regarded as goods for that purpose.

The term 'actionable claim' has been defined under Section 3 of the Transfer of Property Act. According to that definition 'actionable claim' means a claim of any debt other than a debt secured by mortgage of immovable property or by hypothecation of pledge of movable property or to any beneficial interest in moveable property not in the possession, either actual or constructive of the claimant which the Civil Court recognize as affording grounds for relief whether such debt or beneficial interest be existent, accruing conditional or contingent. In brief, an actionable claim means[54]—

(i) any unsecured debt; and
(ii) any interest in movable property not in possession of the claimant.

Such claims are to be governed by the provision containing in sections 130-137 of the Transfer of Property Act and therefore, they are outside the purview of the Sale of Goods Act.

53. *Ibid.*, Clause (i) of Section 2(1).
54. *Supra* Note 43, p. 102.

(11) Who is a Manufacturer[55]

The term 'Manufacturer' has been defined in clause (k) of Section 2(1) of the Act. Manufacturer means a person who:

(i) makes or manufacturer any goods or parts thereof, or

(ii) does not make or manufacture any goods but assembles parts thereof made or manufactured by others and claims the end product to be goods manufactured by himself; or

(iii) puts or causes to be put his own mark on any goods made or manufactured by any other manufacturer and claims such goods to be goods made or manufactured by himself.

Thus the manufacturer is the person who produces any goods or parts thereof or assembles any goods or parts manufactured by others or puts his own mark or trade marks on the goods manufactured by others.

The definition is wide and it is quite clear that in certain circumstances a person will be deemed for the purpose of the Act a manufacturer when in fact he does not done so. The reference to assemble goods makes it clear that person who produces a final product from components manufactured by others is to be treated as having manufactured that product. Similarly, in such cases there is no indication that actual manufacturer is also not liable and it would follow that for the purpose of the Act a particular product may be regarded as having been manufactured by two or more manufacturers. It would therefore seem that where a component/part is defective, then *prima-facie* the consumer at his choice could make a complaint either against the manufacturer of the component or against the manufacturer of the final product. In more cases the consumer will no doubt prefer to make a complaint against the final manufacturer rather than the manufacturer of the component either because he may have difficulty in

55. *Supra* Note 53, Clause (j) of Section 2(1).

identifying the component manufacturer or because while it may be clear that the final product was defective, it may be difficult to establish that the defect was caused by a fault in a particular component rather than faulty installation of that component or some other factor.

A person is deemed to have manufactured goods if he puts or causes to be put his own mark (e.g name or brand or trademark) on the goods made or manufactured by any other manufacturer and claims such goods to be goods made or manufactured by himself. In fact, such a person by putting his name or mark holds himself out to the public as the manufacturer of the goods. It seems reasonable that such a person should be treated as though he is the actual manufacturer where, for legitimate marketing reasons he chooses to induce the ultimate buyer to rely on his reputation rather than that of the real manufacturer whose identity is usually unknown to the buyer. Thus if for example, a super market claim sells its own branded goods without revealing the actual manufacturer. If the actual manufacturer's name is indicated then the super market simply will be a supplier.

A mark (whether name, brand or trademark) is deemed to be applied to goods if it is woven in, impressed on, worked into or annexed or affixed to the goods or if it is applied to a covering, label, reel or thing in or with which the goods are supplied. Covering includes bottle, glass, stopper, vessel, box, capsule, case, frame or wrapper and label includes a band or ticket.

The explanation appended to the definition of 'Manufacturer' clearly provides that where a manufacturer despatches any goods or part thereof to any branch office maintained by him, such branch office shall not be the manufacturer even though the parts so despatched to it are assembled at such branch office and are sold or distributed from such branch office. The basic idea of this explanation is to clarify that the liability of a manufacturer will continue even if he gets the goods or part thereof assembled, sold or distributed at any branch office maintained by him. Such branch office shall not be deemed to be a manufacturer.

---

56. *Id.* Clause (kk) of Section 2(1) Inserted.

(12) Who is Member of Consumer Forum?[56]

The Amendment Act, 1997 has inserted a new clause (kk) in Section 2(1) defining the term 'member'. According to the definition, 'member' includes the President and member of the State Commission or a Divisional Forum as the case may be.

(13) What Notification Stands under the Act?[57]

Clause (l) of Section 2(1) of the Act defines the term 'notification'. It means a notification published in the government gazette. Here government is the government of State of Jammu and Kashmir only.

(14) Who is a Person under the Act?[58]

The term 'Person' has been defined in clause (m) of Section 2(1) of the Act. 'Person' includes—

(i) a firm whether registered or not; or
(ii) a Hindu un-divided family;
(iii) a Co-operative Society; and
(iv) every other association of persons whether registered under the Societies Registration Act or not.

The definition is an inclusive one and not exhaustive. Thus, any person, not falling in the categories mentioned above, may still be a person within the meaning of the Act. In addition to an individual or natural person, the definition includes—a firm whether registered or not, Hindu un-divided family, a co-operative society, every other association of persons whether registered or not. The 'association of persons' means an association in which two or more persons join in common purpose or common action. Thus, the definition of 'person' extends to companies, firms, cooperative societies, joint families, any other association of persons.

---

57. *Id.* Clause (l) of Section 2(1).
58. *Id.* Clause (m) of Section 2(1).

(15) What is known by the term Prescribed?[59]

The term 'prescribed' means prescribed by rules made by the State Government of Jammu and Kashmir under the Act. Section 24 of the Act empowers the State Government of Jammu and Kashmir to make rules for carrying out the provisions of the Act. Thus the term 'prescribed' means prescribed by these rules made by the State Government. The Government of State of Jammu and Kashmir passed rules by a proper notification on 10th of March 1988 which are in force since the date.

(16) What is the Term Restrictive Trade Practice indicates under the Act?

The Amendment Act, 1997 has inserted a new clause[60] in Section 2(1) of the Act defining the term 'restrictive trade practice'. According to the definition 'restrictive trade practice' means any trade practice which requires a consumer to buy, hire or avail of any goods or as the case may be services as a condition precedent for buying, hiring or availing of any other goods or services.

The insertion of clause (nn) in Section 2(1) is significant as it enlarges the scope of the Consumer Protection Act by covering restrictive trade practices within its ambit. Generally, such trade practices are against the interest of consumers.

(17) What is the Service under the Act?

According to clause (o) of Section 2(1) of the Act, 'service'[61] means—

(i) service of any description which is made available to potential users; and
(ii) includes the provision of facilities in connection with banking, financing, insurance, transport, processing, supply of electrical or other energy, board or lodging or both, entertainment,

59. *Id.* Clause (n) of Section 2(1).
60. *Id.* Clause (nn) of Section 2(1) Inserted.
61. *Id.* Clause (o) of Section 2(1) Inserted 'housing construction' after the words 'board or lodging or both'.

amusement or the purveying a news or other information, but

(iii) does not include the rendering of any service free of charge or under a contract of personal service.

The service must be available to potential users who are willing to pay for the service. The service must be rendered for remuneration. Thus, if a company is running a bus which is meant to be used by the staff of that company only or it is running a canteen exclusively for its staff will not constitute rendering 'service' for the simple reason that the facilities are not meant to be hired by the potential users. The term 'service' as defined in the Act means 'service of any description'. Thus the service may not be rendered free of charge. The definition is wide but not exhaustive. It includes the provision of facilities in connection with banking, financing, insurance, transport, processing, supply of electrical or other energy, boarding or lodging or both, entertainment, amusement or the purveying of news or other information. These facilities are merely illustrative. In addition to these facilities there can be many more facilities which may be available to potential users and thus they may fall within the meaning of 'service' for the purpose of the Act. The services rendered by hotels, cinemas, laundries, etc. are also covered by the above definition. Though the services like medicine, law, accountancy, engineering, architect, estate agent, etc. have not been specifically enumerated in the above definition but it seems that these services are covered within the scope of the definition because these are available to potential users. However, the definition excludes two types of services, namely—

(i) rendering of any service free of charge; or
(ii) under a contract of personal service.

(a) Service Rendered Free of Charge[62]

Any service rendered free of charge is outside the

62. *Id.* Last portion of the definition of service as defined above under Clause (o) of Section 2(1)

scope of the Consumer Protection Act. It means for the purpose of this Act the service must be rendered for payment. It is a payment for labour, facility or use of goods. Where there is nothing on record to establish that the services rendered by the opposite party were hired for consideration, the complainant cannot maintain claim for any deficiency in service against opposite party.

(b) Contract of Personal Service[63]

The expression 'under a contract of personal service' has not been defined in the Act. However, the specific relief Act provides that a contract cannot be specifically enforced if it is so dependent on the personal qualifications or volition of the parties or otherwise from its nature is such that the Court cannot enforce specific performance of its material terms.

The contract of personal service is a contract to render the service in a private capacity to an individual excluding all others. It is somewhat plain that the phrase 'contract of personal service' in the definition would refer *inter-alia* to the relationship of a master and servant where the latter has entered into an agreement with the former for employment.

(18) What is State Commission?[64]

State Commission has been established in the State of Jammu and Kashmir under clause (b) of Section 7 of the Act. In the State, State Commission sits in the Summer zone at the Srinagar and for the period of Winter at Jammu. The State Commission in the State of Jammu and Kashmir as in other states is for the whole state. The State Commission in the State of Jammu and Kashmir is for the whole State as in other States there is one State Commission for the whole State consisting original, appellate and revisional powers. In the State of Jammu and Kashmir State Commission is the final appellate consumer forum. For the rest of the Country National Commission is the higher appellate consumer forum. Here in the State of Jammu and Kashmir appeals from the orders of State Commission lie directly to the Jammu and Kashmir High Court.

63. *Ibid.*
64. *Id.* Clause (p) of Section 2(1).

(19) What is Trader?

Clause (q) of Section 2(1) of the Act defines the term 'trader'[65] to mean a person who sells or distributes any goods for sale and includes the manufacturer thereof, and where such goods are sold or distributed in package form includes the packer thereof. Generally speaking, 'trader' means one who carries on trade. The definition of term 'trader' under the Consumer Protection Act is confined to goods only. Under this Act trader means any person who—

(i) Sells or distributes any goods for sale; and
(ii) Includes the manufacturer thereof; and
(iii) Where such goods are sold or distributed in package form includes packer thereof.

(20) What is Unfair Trade Practices?

The definition incorporated in clause (r) is apparently reproduction of the definition of 'unfair trade practice'[66] under the Central Act on Consumer Protection. As the Central Amendment Act, 1993 brought a change in the definition of unfair trade practice in the Central Act, in the same way State Amendment, 1997 in the State Consumer Protection Act brought a change to the effect words "adopts any unfair method or deceptive practice including any of the following practices" have been substituted for the words "adopts one or more of the following practices and thereby causes loss or injury to the consumers of such goods or services, whether by eliminating or restricting competition or otherwise." Before knowing these categories of unfair trade practices it is better to know first what is the meaning of expression 'unfair trade practices'.

(a) Meaning of Unfair Trade Practices

False means which is not true. The expression 'falsely represents' indicates that the representation is contrary to

65. *Id.* Clause (q) of Section 2(1).
66. *Id.* Clause (r) of Section 2(1) Inserted words "adopts any unfair method or unfair or deceptive practices including any of the following practices."

facts. A representation will be deemed to be false, if it is false in substance and in fact.[67]

The term 'misleading' means capable of leading into error. There is an obligation on the seller that if he advertises or otherwise represents, he must speak the truth. This obligation also requires that the representation must avoid half-truths. Sometimes, a statement may be literally true and yet may be false or misleading. An advertisement may be misleading because things are omitted that should be said or because advertisements are composed or purposely printed in such a way as to mislead. A representation containing a statement apparently correct in the technical sense may have the effect of misleading the consumer by using the tricky language. It is therefore, necessary to determine whether the representation complained of carries the possibility of misleading the buyer. The meaning of advertisements or other representations to the public, and their tendency to mislead or deceive are questions of fact to be determined by the consumer redressal forums.[68]

(b) Specific Categories of Unfair Trade Practices[69]

Following are some specific categories of unfair trade practices as given under the Act. The first category of unfair trade practice which are laid down in clause (i) of Section 2(1)(r) which relates to the practice of making false or misleading representation. All the sub-clauses (i)-(x) of this provision have a common element of factum of representation which must be false or misleading.

Thus, the representation may be made by making any statement, whether orally or in writing or by visible representation. It embraces not only words but also pictures associated therewith. The various forms of prohibition enumerated in clause (i) of Section 2(1)(r) have been discussed as follows:

67. *Id.*, p. 156.
68. *Supra* Note 37.
69. *Id.*, pp. 156-67.

(i) The provision prohibits such representation as that the goods are of a specified standard, quality, quantity and grade, etc. when that is not the case. A false representation as to the composition or ingredient of any goods will also fall under this sub-clause. A false representation would occur if a model is represented as a latest model or if a car is represented as been a particular year's model when it is in fact a model of an earlier year. All the components namely, standard, quality, grade, composition, style or model are not mutually exclusive rather they overlap in many situations. False representation as to silver content of utensils, silk contents of carpets, contents of juice, etc. are the instances which would fall within the ambit of this sub-clause.

(ii) This provision is intended to cover any statement which falsely suggests that the services are of a particular standard, quality, or grade. Sub-clause (i) is applicable to goods and sub-clause (ii) is applicable to services. For example, if private schools provide service, hold out certain promises to parents and charge for it. If they do not provide the promised service then it is a false representation and thus an unfair trade practice. Any arbitrary increase in the fees, imposition of charges for some non-existent facilities like liberty, sports and medical care will be cases of unfair trade practice.

(iii) This sub-clause is clearly aimed at prohibiting such practices as describing re-built, second-hand, renovated, reconditioned or old goods as new goods. The word 'new' has many meanings and therefore it is necessary to determine its meaning in the context of a given case. The 'new' is most frequently used in the sense that the goods are not old or un-used or not second-hand. The goods which have been used are not new. However, as stated above, much will depend on the particular facts. When a motor car is represented as 'latest model' it will be within the ambit of sub-clause (iii).

(iv) This sub-clause prohibits the representation that the goods or services have sponsorship, approval, performance, characteristics, accessories, uses or benefits which they do not have. Thus, a false representation that an electric machine has approval of the State Electricity Board, or any goods have ISI mark which they do not have, etc. are the instances of unfair trade practices falling within the scope of this sub-clause. A false representation that goods had been manufactured by well-known company could well be regarded as a representation as to 'sponsorship' or 'approval'. A representation as to performance or characteristics may be falsely in a variety of ways. It may relate to durability of goods or efficacy of services, etc. The provision also applies to representation that the goods or services have uses or benefits which they do not have.

(v) A seller or the supplier falsely claiming that he has a sponsorship or approval or affiliation which he does not have would be caught by this sub-clause. The provision overlaps to some extent with the provision of sub-clause (iv). Sub-clause (iv) is applicable when the statement represents that the 'goods' or 'services' have sponsorship or approval which they do not have. But sub-clause (v) applies to the statement which represents that the seller or the supplier has a sponsorship or approval which he does not have.

(vi) This sub-clause prohibits the practice of making false or misleading representation concerning the need for or the usefulness of any goods or services. It seems that the word 'need' is to be read in a broad sense in the context of sub-clause (vi) and that consequently need will be established if goods or services are desirable or preferable and the word does not imply any motion of an imperative question or necessity. This sub-clause has been designed to prohibit such practices and misrepresentions that certain repairs or the replacement of certain parts are necessary or useful when this is infact not the case.

(vii) This sub-clause requires that every warranty or guarantee of the performance, efficacy of length of life of a product or goods should be based on adequate or proper test, when such a warranty or guarantee is not supported by the proper test, it will be an unfair trade practice under this sub-clause. However, no standards or guidelines have been provided to determine the nature of adequate or proper test. Where a defence is raised to the effect that such warranty or guarantee is based on adequate or proper test, the burden of proof of such defence shall lie on the person raising the defence.

(viii) This sub-clause speaks of a warranty or guarantee or promise which is either materially misleading or there is no reasonable prospect of carrying out it. It also speaks of a promise to replace, maintain or repair an article or to provide certain service. Further this sub-clause deals with a warranty or guarantee of the performance, efficacy or length of life of a product or any goods that is not based on adequate or proper test but under sub-clause (viii) the representation must be materially misleading or that there was no reasonable prospect of carrying out it. Moreover, sub-clause (vii) is restricted only to the product or goods and does not apply to services whereas sub-clause (viii) covers service also.

(ix) This sub-clause prohibits the claims which materially misleads the public concerning the price at which a product or like products or goods or services have been or are ordinarily sold or provided. This sub-clause will clearly apply if an advertiser falsely claims that the price offered is less than his own previous or normal selling price. The claims as that 'goods' worth of Rs. 100, now

Rs. 50 are prohibited if no such reduction has really been made. Where the reduction is actually made but it is so insignificant that the customer would not normally regard it as a bargain price, the statement would be considered as misleading if the amount of reduction is not prominently stated or displayed.

(x) This sub-clause is intended to prohibit the practice of making any statement which gives false or misleading fact disparaging the goods, services or trade of another person. It may be direct statement or it may be indirectly or inferentially disparage the trade or business of another. Disparagement however, is distinguishable from other types of false advertising. 'Disparagement' generally involves casting aspersions on the quality or characteristics of goods or services of another whereas other types of false advertising usually comprise assertions of superior attitude for the advertiser's own goods or services. Inspite of this basic distinction commercial disparagement and false advertisement have the same effect as one's goods or services are falsely presented to the potential customers in a more favourable right than those of another.

(c) Overriding Effect of the Act?[70]

The Act in Section 3 makes it clear that the provisions of the Consumer Protection Act are in addition to the existing laws and they are to be applied harmoniously with a provisions of other legislations. Section 3 is reproduced here as follows:

SECTION 3: ACT NOT IN DEROGATION OF ANY OTHER LAW

"The provisions of this Act shall be in addition to and not in derogation of the provisions of any other law for the time being in force."

70. *Supra* Note 66, Section 3.

From the language of the above mentioned section it is clear that the provisions of the instant Act are supplementary in nature and have no overriding effect. The Act does not impede the remedies available to the consumer under the provisions of any other law for the time being in force. For example, a consumer may initiate proceedings in a Civil Court under the Law of Contract or Sale of Goods Act or any other existing law. The provision of Section 3 clearly indicates that the forum, remedies, adjudication, procedure, etc. provided under the Act is an additional dispensation. It is thus clear that the provisions contained in Consumer Protection Act do not in anyway abrogate the provisions of any other law for the time being in force.

(1) Breach of Contract and Consumer Protection Act[71]

The defect or default in goods or deficiency in service on the part of the opposite party may also amount a breach of contract under the general law but it will not in any way affect the jurisdiction of the consumer disputes redressal forums set-up under Consumer Protection Act. Once it is found that there is a purchase of goods or hiring of services for consideration and that loss has been caused to the complainant on account of defect in the goods or deficiency in services or unfair trade practices the aggrieved consumer is entitled to seek his remedy under the Consumer Protection Act by approaching appropriate redressal forum.

(2) No Conflict with other Laws[72]

The provisions of the Consumer Protection Act do not come in conflict with the provisions of any other law for the time being in force. These provisions are in addition to the provisions of any other law for the time being in force. It is for the consumer to choose a forum convenient to him to seek remedy for the loss suffered by him.

Here it would not be out of place to have a view about the scope[71] of Section 3 of the Act in hand. The provisions of

---

71. B. Sundharam Northy Section 3 of Consumer Protection Act, 1997 (2) CPR 112.
72. *Ibid.*

this section makes it clear that the provisions of this Act are intended to provide inexpensive and expeditious alternative remedy for consumers. Among all the provisions of Consumer Protection Act Section 3 is an important one dealing with the scope of the Act. The section provides that this Act is intended not to supplant but to supplement the existing laws. This Act therefore, does not touch or affect the rights created and the obligations imposed by other laws including the Law of Limitation. The Supreme Court in a judgment in *M/s Fair Air Engineer P. Ltd. & Another* v. *N.K.Modi,*[73] held that—

> "The provisions of the Act are to be construed widely to give effect to the object and purpose of the Act. It is seen that Section 3 envisages that the provisions of this Act are in addition to and not in derogation of any other law in force. . . . It would therefore, be clear that the legislature intended to provide a remedy in addition to the Consentient arbitration which could be enforced under the Arbitration Act or civil action in a suit under the provisions of the Code of Civil Procedure. We hold that the District Forum, State Commission and National Commission are judicial authorities for the purpose of Arbitration Act in view of the object of the Act and by operation of Section 3 thereof. We are of the considered view, it would be appropriate that these forums created under the Act are at liberty to proceed with these matters in accordance with the provisions of the Act rather than relegating the parties to an arbitration proceeding pursuant to a contract entered into between the parties."

Thus, the Supreme Court held that the forums under the Act are additional forums for cases coming within the purview of the Arbitration Act and Civil Courts.

From the above discussion briefly to say here that the Act has no overriding effect and is not in derogation of any other law for the time being in force.

---

73. 1996 III CPJ 1.

PART III

In this part brief account of establishment of State Consumer Protection Council and Redressal Agencies will be enunciated.

(A) STATE CONSUMER PROTECTION COUNCIL[74]

The Central Act on Consumer Protection envisages the setting up of the consumer protection councils at centre and States. The State Act of Jammu and Kashmir also provides for establishment of State Consumer Council.[73] The State Consumer Protection Council as in rest of the Country is a very important and potent body for promoting Consumer interests in the State.

(I) Composition of State Consumer Protection Council[75]

Prior to the Jammu and Kashmir Consumer Protection (Amendment) Act, 1997 The State Council was required to consist of the following members, namely,

(i) The Minister-in-charge of the Department of Food and Civil Supplies in the Government—Chairman

(ii) Such number of other official or non-official members representing such interests as may be prescribed—Members

Now by virtue of rules[76] in addition to the above members it shall consist of the following members, namely

(iii) Three Representatives of Autonomous Organizations concerned with consumer interests—Members

(iv) Three Representatives of consumer organizations or consumers—Members

---

74. *Supra* Note 70, Section 4.
75. Though now Consumer Protection (Amendment) Act, 1997 inserts Section 6a which provides for establishment of district consumers councils in each district but no steps have been taken to implement these provisions up to this time.
76. Rule 3, Jammu and Kashmir Rules, 1988.

(v) Two Representatives of women—Members
(vi) Three Representatives of farmers, traders and industrialists, one from each category—Members
(vii) Three persons capable to represent consumer interests not specified above—Members
(viii) The Secretary to Government, Food and Supplies Department—Member

(2) Number of Meetings of State Council[77]

Sub-section 1 of Section 5 of the Act makes it obligatory on the State Council to meet as and when necessary but not less than 3 meetings of the Council shall be held every year.

(3) Procedure for Meeting[78]

For better understanding the procedure as to how meetings are to be conducted by the State Council Rule 4 of the Jammu and Kashmir Rules, 1988 providing the procedure regarding the transaction of its business will be understood in this way that the meeting of the State Council shall be presided over by the Chairman, in his absence the Vice-Chairman, in the absence of the Chairman and the Vice-Chairman it is obligatory that the council shall elect a member to preside over the meeting. Each meeting of the State Council shall be called by giving not less than 10 days' notice in writing to every member. However, the notice shall specify the place, the day, hour and statement of business to be transacted there at. The same rule provides that no proceedings of the State Council shall be held invalid merely by reasons of any vacancy or defect in the constitution of the Council. The instant rule also provides that for the purpose of performing its functions under the Act, The State Council may constitute from amongst its members such working groups as it may deem necessary and every working group so constituted shall perform such functions as are assigned to it by the State Council. The findings of such working group shall be placed before the State Council for its consideration and the resolution passed by the State Council shall be recommendatory in nature.

77. Sub-section (1) of Section 5.
78. Section 5 of the Act and Rule 4.

(4) Tenure and Vacancy of Office of the State Council[79]

The term of the members of the State Council under rules is 3 years. However, any member may resign from the office before the above mentioned term. The vacancies so caused or otherwise, shall be filled from the same category by the government and such person shall hold office so long as the member whose place he fills would have been entitled to hold office if the vacancy had not occurred.

(5) Objects of the State Council[80]

Objects of the State Council will be discussed here under two Sub-headings—General Objects and Specific Objects.

(a) General Objects[81]

The State Council has been charged with promotion and protection of the rights of the consumers. Broadly speaking, the function of the Council is to investigate and make policy recommendations on the need for legislative or administrative action in the interest of consumers. This body has to play an important role in giving publicity to matters of consumer concern, furthering consumer education and protecting consumer from unscrupulous exploitation. The Amendment in both central and state Act has extended the scope of these rights by including 'services' and 'restrictive trade practices' in Section 6 of the Act. The Council has to perform a very responsible and important task in the consumer protection movement. The Council has to function as a catalyst in the consumer protection plan and to safeguard the interest of the consumers in the State. The Council can contribute significantly in providing better protection to the consumers in matters of availability, quality, quantity and prices of goods and services.

(b) Specific Objects of the State Council

The Act has recognized six rights of the consumers,[82]

79. *Ibid.*, Rule 5
80. *Id.*, Section 6
81. *Supra* Note 66, p. 193.
82. *Id.*, pp. 194-96.

namely—right to safety, right to be informed, right to choose, right to be heard, right to seek redressal and right to consumer education. The Primary object of the council is to protect these right of the consumers.

(i) Right to Safety

The right to safety means the right to be protected against the marketing of goods and services which are hazardous to life and property. Perhaps the most urgent need is for effective enforcement. While it is the concern of the government and its authorities to prevent dangerous goods from finding their way into markets the consumer is assured by this Act that if he has been victimized into purchasing goods which have injured his person or property, he will have a speedy and effectively remedy under the redressal hierarchy constituted under the Act. For example, adulterated food is dangerous to life and weak cement is dangerous to life as well as to property. The subject-matter of dangerous goods is generally taken care of under the Law of Torts since the time of *Donough* v. *Stevenson*. In the words of Winfield the principles has been extended from articles of food and drink and includes *inter-alia* tombstones, hair dye, industrial chemicals, lifts, motor cars and scented erasers and poisonous pencils. Likewise the term 'consumer' includes the ultimate user of the article or any one who is within physical proximity to it. Apart from these specific instances, the general principle of liability is the duty not to supply any consumer goods which fail to comply with the general safety requirements by not being reasonably safe having regard to all circumstances.

(ii) Right to Information

The consumer has been given the right to be informed by the producer about the quality, quantity, potency, purity, standard and prices of goods he buys so as to protect the consumer against unfair trade practices like false and misleading descriptions about the nature and quality of goods, exaggerated statements about their power or potency for example that the hair oil is capable of promoting hair growth or preventing hair loss. Where there is no such power to an appreciable extent or that the medical preparation is capable of curing baldness or that the goods are of some standard or purity when in fact the goods are not of that standard or purity. A misrepresentation as to price may occur, for example, in a concealed way in throwing open clearance, grand clearance or reduction sales or in an offer of a free gift along with particular product when in fact neither the prices are less than the original one's nor the so-called free gift is really free. Under these circumstances the right to obtain adequate information is an important right which enables the consumer to take intelligent decisions at the time of purchasing any goods or hiring any services.

Thus, the consumers must be assured of informative marketing and effective protection against practices which could adversely affect their economic interests and the exercise of choice in the market place.

(iii) Right to Choose

The right to choose means the right to be assured wherever possible, access to a variety of goods and services at competitive price. The Council as constituted under the Act has been charged with the responsibility of the organization of markets and market practices in such a way that all dealers are supplied with a variety of goods for the benefit of the consumer and that the goods with a variety are being offered at competitive prices. This is based upon the belief that best way to improve quality and value for money is to give the citizen wider choice through the mechanism of free competition. It is only then the consumer will have access to variety and will be able to enjoy the benefit of competitive prices.

(iv) Right to be Heard

The right to be heard also includes the right to be assured that the consumer interest will receive due consideration at appropriate forums. The council is also charged with the responsibility of assuring consumers that they would be heard as of right by the appropriate forums and the consumer will receive due attention and consideration from such forums. Thus, it is the duty of the

Council so to organize and compose the different forums under the Act so that an aggrieved consumer is heard as of right and receives due consideration at the hands of the appropriate redressal forums.

(v) Right to Seek Redressal

The consumer has been given the right to seek redress against restrictive or unfair trade practices or unscrupulous exploitation. The consumer should have some means of redress when goods fail to live up to their promise or indeed cause injury.

(vi) Right to Consumer Education

For the proper functioning of the legal system it is necessary that knowledge of the availability of a legal remedy should be so widely disseminated that people as a whole become conscious of their rights. By increased information as to rights and remedies the consumer will be better empowered to pursue his remedies. The enforcement of this duty (to provide consumer education to masses) is primarily the task of the government and other authorities constituted for the purpose.

(B) CONSUMER DISPUTES REDRESSAL AGENCIES[83]

To provide simple, speedy and inexpensive redressal of consumer grievances, the Act envisages a two-tier quasi-judicial machinery at the divisional and state level. It is noteworthy to mention here that consumer redressal agencies have been established in almost all the districts of neighbouring States of our country except in the State of Jammu and Kashmir. In this way in the State[84] there is establishment of Divisional Forum in each division and the appeals from the orders of the Divisional Forum goes to the State Commission and appeals from orders of State Commission lies to the Jammu and Kashmir High Court. First

83. *Supra* Note, Section 7.
84. Substituted—of eminence in the field of education, trade or commerce; similar provision under Central Act.

here we will deal with the composition, terms and conditions, etc. of the lowest level of redressal agencies—divisional forum.

(1) Composition of Divisional Forum[85]

Presently each Divisional Forum consists of a President and two members.[86] The President is required to be a person who is, or has been, or is qualified to be a district judge and other two members are required to be persons of ability, integrity and standing and have adequate knowledge or experience of dealing with problems relating to economics, law, commerce, accountancy, industry, public affairs of administration one of whom to be preferably a lady. Regarding the appointment of members of the Divisional Forum the Amended Act[87] provides that every appointment be made by the government on the recommendation of a Selection Committee consistsing of the following members—

(i) The President of the State Commission—Chairman

(ii) The Secretary to Government Law Department—Member

(iii) The Secretary to Government Supplies Department (in charge Consumer Affairs)—Member

(2) Tenure and Vacancy[88]

The term of office of every member of the forum is five years or up to the age sixty-five years whichever is earlier. However, both the Act and Rules provides that no member is eligible for re-appointment.[89] Every member is at liberty to resign his office in writing at any time by addressing the resignation to the government. This way vacancy may arise on account of resignation, death or by removal and any such vacancy so caused may be filled by appointment of a person

85. *Id.* Section (1-A) of Section 8.
86. *Supra* Note 83, Section 8.
87. *Supra* Note 85.
88. *Supra* Note 79, Rule 7(ii).
89. Similar provisions regarding the tenure, etc. provided under the Central Act.

possessing the qualifications as mentioned in Section 8(1) of the State Act.

(3) Salary, Honorarium and other Allowances

Under Sub-section 3 of Section 8 where the President of the Divisional Forum is a sitting judge of the Sessions Court, he shall enjoy all the benefits which he should have enjoyed as a sitting judge of Session Court. Where he is not a sitting judge of such Court he shall receive a honorarium equivalent to the amount of salary as he was drawing at the time of his retirement minus the pension per month. 'Prior to appointment, the President and the members of the Divisional Forum shall have to give an undertaking to the effect that he does not and will not have any such financial or other interest as is likely to affect prejudicially his functions as such'.[90] However, the terms and conditions of service of the President and the members or any member of the Divisional Forum shall not be varied to their disadvantage during their tenure of office.

(4) Jurisdiction of the Divisional Forum[91]

Jurisdiction means the extent of the authority to administer justice not only with reference to the subject-matter of suit but also to the territorial and pecuniary limits. It is a fundamental rule that a judgment of Court without jurisdiction is a nullity. . . . Under this Act while filing a complaint care is to be taken whether the Forum before which a complaint is to be lodged is having jurisdiction to entertain such complaint. For example, a complaint against any service free of charge or against a contract of personal service is outside the jurisdiction of the consumer forum.[92]

(a) Pecuniary Jurisdiction[93]

Sub-section 1 of Section 9 deals with the pecuniary jurisdiction. Originally it provided that the divisional forum has the jurisdiction to entertain complaints where the value of

90. *Supra* Note 88, Rule 7(i).
91. *Supra* Note 86, Section 9(1).
92. *Supra* Note 82, p. 213.
93. *Ibid.*

the goods or services and the compensation if any it claimed does not exceed rupees fifty thousand then Amendment Act 1997, substituted for the words 'rupees fifty thousand' the words 'value not exceeding rupees five lakh.' Now again by virtue of recent Amendment Act, 2002, Section 9 stands amended and for the words 'rupees five lacs' the words 'rupees ten lacs' have been substituted. So the complaint involving claims exceeding rupees ten lacs will lie to the other consumer forum that is the State Commission. It is pertinent to mention here that the pecuniary jurisdiction depends upon the amount of relief claimed and not upon the value of the subject matter nor upon the relief allowed by the forum.

(b) Territorial Jurisdiction[94]

Sub-section 2 of Section 9 deals with territorial jurisdiction of the divisional forum. It provides that a complaint shall be instituted in a divisional forum within the local limits of whose jurisdiction—

(i) the opposite party or each of the parties at the time of institution of the complaint actually and voluntarily resides or carries on business directly or through a branch office[95] or personally works for gain; or

(ii) any of the opposite parties, where there are more than one at the time of the institution of 'the complaint actually and voluntarily resides or carries on business directly or through a branch office[96] or personally works for gain provided that in such case either the permission of the Divisional Forum is given or the opposite parties who do not reside, or carry on business or have a branch office, or personally works for gain, as the case may be, acquiesce in such institution; or

(iii) the cause of action, wholly or in part, arises.

---

94. *Id.*, p. 214.
95. *Supra* Note 9 (for details of branch office).
96. *Ibid.*

Now let us have a bit of discussion about the various expressions as used in Sub-section 2 of Section 9 of the Act.

(i) Actually and Voluntarily Resides[97]

The words 'actually and voluntarily resides' are relevant at the time of the institution of the complaint. The residence gives the jurisdiction to institute a complaint under the Act. The term 'resides' indicates the place where a person normally lives. Further, it refers to the natural person and not to legal entities and government. A complaint under the Act can be laid against the government wherever the cause of action arose in whole or in part. This principle applies also to registered companies and corporations.

(ii) Carries on Business[98]

The expression 'carries on business' is intended to relate to business in which a man may contract and is liable to be used by persons having business transaction with him. The 'business' term is restricted to commercial business. To constitute 'carrying on business' at a certain place, the essential part of the business must take place in that place. A person may carry on business at a place where he has no office or regular establishment. The business need not be carried on personally. The phrase 'carries on business' is used as distinct from the phrase 'personally works for gain'. It does not involve actual presence or personal effort and a man may carry on business in a place through an agent or a manager or a servant but he must have an interest and some control upon the existence of the business.

(iii) Through a Branch Office[99]

Earlier consumer was to file complaint at the place where opposite party was carrying business but now by virtue of Amendment Act, 1997 it enables the consumers, etc. to file their complaints U/S 9(2) even at the place where a branch office of the opposite party is functioning.

97. *Id.* Clause (a) of Section 9(2).
98. *Id.* Clause (b) of Section (2)
99. Inserted *Supra* Note 85.

(iv) Personally Works for Gain[100]

The words 'personally works for gain' indicate that a person may be living outside the limits of jurisdiction but comes there to work for gain. For example, a pleader who lives outside the jurisdiction of High Court where he practices. It is necessary that work for 'gain' must be carried on personally. The word 'works' implies mental or physical effort. A complaint, thus may be instituted within limits of whose jurisdiction the opposite party at the time of the institution of the complaint, personally works for gain.

(v) Permission of the Forum or Acquiescence[101]

Where there are more than one opposite parties, a complaint may be instituted within the local limits of whose jurisdiction any of the opposite parties actually and voluntarily resides, or carries on business or personally works for gain. However, in such a case, the permission of the forum concerned is required. The permission may be granted even after the institution of the complaint and even at the stage of appeal. Where the permission is not granted, the complaint cannot be proceeded with unless the opposite parties who do not reside, or carries on business, or personally works for gain, acquiesce. Thus, where some of the opposite parties are within and others outside jurisdiction, either the permission of the concerned forum, or acquiescence of those who are outside the jurisdiction is required.

(vi) Cause of Action[102]

The expression 'cause of action' means every fact which is necessary to be proved to entitle the complainant to relief. It is, in other words, a bundle of essential facts which it is necessary for the complainant to prove before he can succeed in the case. It refers entirely to the grounds set forth in the complaint as the cause of action. The cause of action must be antecedent to the institution of the complaint.

100. *Supra* Note 82, p. 216.
101. *Ibid.*
102. *Id.*, p. 217.

It is to be submitted here that this Section does not take into consideration the residence of the complainant (the consumer) for whose benefit the Act is meant to give jurisdiction to file the complaint. The very object of the Act is consumer protection but a consumer who is the aggrieved person, who resides at a particular place, but has suffered by act/acts of the person done outside the jurisdiction of the District Forum where he resides cannot file a case within the jurisdiction where he resides. As the protection Act Section 9 stands he is required to file the dispute by going to the place where the opposite party resides or has his office or branch. A consumer may not have that tenacity to go such place outside his district/division or residence to agitate his grievance. So immediate necessity in the interest of the consumers and for the easy reach to the redressal forum Section 9 be amended by including a sub-clause (d) as follows:

Section 9(d)—'where the consumer resides'.[103]

(5) Manner in which Complaint is to be Made[104]

The complaint made to the Divisional Forum under Section 10 in a relation to any goods sold or delivered or agreed to be sold or delivered or any service provided or agreed to be provided may be filed with a Divisional Forum by—

(i) consumer to whom such goods are sold or delivered or agreed to be sold or delivered or such service provided or agreed to be provided;

(ii) any recognized consumer association whether the consumer to whom the goods sold or delivered or agreed to be sold or delivered or service provided or agreed to be provided is a member of such association or not;

(iii) one or more consumers where there are numerous consumers having the same interest, with the

103. Neelkanth Dhar, Article, A note on Section 11 of the Consumer Protection Act, 1986, Law teller, October 1995, Vol. 3, No. 10, p. 1009.

104. *Supra* Note 98, Section 10.

permission of the Divisional Forum on behalf of or for the benefit of all consumers so interested; and

(iv) the Government.

The Proviso appended with the Section provides that in relation to district of Leh, Kargil, Poonch and Rajouri a complaint under this section may be filed with the concerned Deputy Commissioner, who shall forward such complaints to the Consumer Forum having jurisdiction to entertain such complaint. However, it is to be submitted here briefly that this manner of filing complaints by the consumers of above mentioned places is likely to cause inconvenience to the complainants to file complaints before the competent consumer forum by sending their complaints through Deputy Commissioner.[105]

(6) Procedure on Receipt of Complaint[106]

The complaint made to the Divisional Forum is analogous in its nature to a plaint filed before a Civil Court but under this Act Section 11 provides the procedure which is to be followed on receipt of complaint by the Divisional Forum. It provides where a complaint does not require analysis or testing of the goods, it should be decided as for as possible within a period of 90 days from the date of the notice received by the opposite party and within 150 days if it requires analysis or testing of the goods.

The procedure to be followed on receipt of complaint may be classified into two parts—

(i) the complaint relating to service, or goods which do not require any analysis or test; or

(ii) the complaint relating to goods which require analysis or test.

Now it is proper to have a brief discussion about the above two points here one by one.

---

105. *Id.* Section 10 Provision appended.

106. *Id.* Section 11; seen also Section 8 of Amendment Act, 1997.

(a) When Analysis or Test is not required[107]

The Divisional Forum shall on receipt of complaint relating to any service or goods which do not require analysis or test refer a copy of the complaint to the opposite party directing him to give his version of the case within a period of 30 days. The period of 30 days cannot be curtailed. Where the notice did not provide 30 days time to the opposite party to file its reply, it will be a violation of Section 11(1)(a) and any order passed by Divisional Forum in the absence of opposite party is liable to be set aside. However, the period may be extended upto 15 days by the forum. Thus, in no case the opposite party be allowed to give his version after the expiry of 45 days. Where the opposite party admits the allegation made by the complainant, the forum has to decide the complaint on the basis of the merit of the case and documents provided present before it. But, where the opposite party denies or disputes the allegation contained in the complaint, or omits or fails to take any action to represent his case within the above stipulated time, the forum is bound to proceed and to settle the consumer dispute on the basis of the evidence drawn to its notice by the respective parties. In such a situation it is obligatory on the parties or their agents to appear before the forum on the date of hearing or any other date on which hearing could be adjourned. Where the complainant or his agent fails to appear on such dates, the forum may in its discretion either dismiss the complaint for default or decide it on merit. Where the opposite party or its agent fails to appear on the date of hearing, the forum may decide the complaint *ex-parte*.

(b) When Analysis or Test is Required[108]

Where the complaint alleges a defect in the goods which cannot be determined without proper analysis or test of the goods, the forum should obtain a sample of the goods

107. *Supra* Note 100, p. 242.
108. *Ibid*. A reading of Section 11 shows that the goods are to be referred to a laboratory only if the alleged defects cannot be determined without analysis or test of the goods. Where the defect can be seen by naked eyes there is no need to send it for laboratory.

from the complainant and if necessary, it may obtain more than one sample. On receiving the sample, the forum should seal and authenticate it in the manner prescribed by the Rules made by the State Government and fix a label on the container carrying the following information:

(i) name and address of the appropriate laboratory to which the sample will be sent for analysis and test;
(ii) name and address of the Forum;
(iii) case number;
(iv) name and description of the goods/articles kept in the sealed container; and
(v) seal of the Forum.

The sample sealed and authenticated in the above manner should be sent to the appropriate laboratory for analysis or test, with a view to find out whether such goods suffer from any defect. Samples of goods for test or analysis shall be sent by the Forum by registered post in a sealed packet, enclosed together with a memorandum in a outer cover addressed to the laboratory. The packet as well as the outer cover shall be marked with a distinguishing number. On receipt of the packet it shall be opened by an officer authorized in writing in that behalf and shall record the condition of the seal on the packet and then the laboratory is required to submit its report to the forum within a period of 45 days of the receipt of the sample or within such extended time as may be granted by the forum.

Sending goods (defective) for examining and conducting test about their purity, quality, etc. is a very important right conferred under Act. Any objection by the complainant regarding the correctness of the findings or methods of analysis or test adopted by the appropriated laboratory should be made in writing to the forum and the forum should give reasonable opportunity to the complainant as well as to the opposite party of being heard as to the objection made in relation thereto and take steps under rules of the Act.

(7) Findings of the Divisional Forum[109]

If after the proceedings conducted under Section 11 the Divisional Forum is satisfied that the goods complained against suffer from any of the defects specified in the complaint or that any of the allegations contained in the complaint about the services are proved it should issue an order to the opposite part directing him to do one or more of the things as enumerated in this section.

(8) Remedies Available to Consumer[110]

As above said under Section 12 of Consumer Protection Act, 1987 Divisional Forum on finding any defect in goods or deficiency in service has to issue direction to the opposite party. Directions are the remedies available to the consumers. Following are these remedies which are available to the consumer under this Act.

(a) Removal of Defects[111]

Where the goods complained against suffer from any of the defects pointed out by the appropriate laboratory the forum can issue an order to the opposite party to remove the defect from the goods in question. When the complainant alleges such a defect in the goods which cannot be determined by any analysis or test, the forum should decide the complaint on the basis of evidence brought to its notice by the respective parties and pass necessary order under the Act.

(b) Replacement of Goods[112]

Clause (b) of Section 12 provides that where the Divisional Forum finds that the goods complained against suffer from any of the defects specified in the complaint, it may direct the opposite party to replace the goods with new goods of similar description which shall be free from any defect. It is not clear when the forum can order for the removal of defect under clause (a) of Section 12(1) or when it

109. *Supra* Note 104, Section 12.
110. *Id.* [Clauses (a) to (d). Inserted (e) to (i)].
111. *Id.* Clause (a).
112. *Id.* Clause (b).

can ask for the replacement of goods under clause (b) of the same Section. It appears that it has been left to the discretion of the forum.

(c) Return of Price[113]

Under clause (c) of Section 12(1) of the Act if the Divisional Forum finds that the goods or services complained against suffer from any defect or deficiency specified in the complaint it may order to opposite party to return to the complainant the price, or the charges paid by the complainant. Obviously, the forum will pass such orders when the defect in the goods cannot be removed or the replacement of goods is not possible or even if possible it will not be a sufficient relief to the satisfaction of the complainant. Once it is proved that the goods were not of the standard quality but defective and are required to be returned to the seller, the customer is entitled to return of full price.

(d) Compensation for Loss or Injury[114]

Under clause (d) of Section 14(1) of the Act if the Divisional Forum is satisfied that the goods or the service complained against suffer from any defect or deficiency specified in the complaint, it may order the opposite party directing him to pay such amount as may be awarded by it as compensation to the consumer from any loss or injury suffered by him due to the negligence of the opposite party.

(e) To Remove of the Deficiencies[115]

Clause (e) of Amended Section 12 provides that where the Divisional Forum finds that the services complained against suffer from any defect or deficiency, it may direct to the opposite party to remove the defect or deficiency in the services in question. This provision has been inserted by the Amendment Act, 1997 on similar lines as provided by the amended Section 14 of the Central Act.

113. *Id.* Clause (c).
114. *Id.* Clause (d).
115. *Id.* Clause (e). Inserted

(f) Cease and Desist Order[116]

Clause (f) in Section 12(1) has been inserted by the Consumer Protection (Amendment) Act, 1997. According to this provision the Divisional Forum may direct the opposite party to discontinue the unfair trade practice or the restrictive trade practice or not to repeat it. Thus, clause (f) of Section 12 (1) of the Act authorizes the Divisional Forum to pass 'cease and desist' order. It means that the practice shall not be repeated in future.

(g) Not to Offer the Hazardous Goods for Sale[117]

Under this provision the Divisional Forum may by order direct the opposite party not to offer the hazardous goods for sale. It is to be noted that the term 'hazardous goods' has not been defined in the Act. Therefore, it creates difficulty to the Consumer Forums. However, it appears that it would include those goods which are likely to endanger the life, health or property of public.

(h) To Withdraw Hazardous Goods[118]

Divisional Forum may also direct the opposite party to withdraw the hazardous goods from being offered for sale. Prior to the Amendment Act, 1997 there was no such power conferred upon the Divisional Forum.

(i) To Provide for Adequate Costs to Parties[119]

In addition to the above directions Divisional Forum may award the adequate costs to parties. This is an important provision which enables this forum to award costs to the parties.

(9) Order by the Divisional Forum[120]

Every order made by the Divisional Forum U/S 12(1) shall be signed by its President and the member or members who conduct the proceedings. Where the proceeding is

116. *Id.* Clause (f).
117. *Id.* Clause (g).
118. *Id.* Clause (h).
119. *Id.* Clause (i).
120. *Id.* Sub-section 2 of Section 12. (For details)

conducted by the President and one member and they differ on any point they shall state the point on which they differ and refer the same to the other member for hearing on such point and the opinion of the majority shall be order of the Divisional Forum. (No act or proceeding of the Divisional Forum shall be hold invalid by reason of any vacancy of its President or member or any defect in the constitution thereof).[121]

(10) Procedure Regarding Meetings, etc.[122]

The Divisional Forum shall observe the procedure in regard to the transaction of its business as provided under rules. It provides that the meeting of the Divisional Forum shall be preside over by the President in his absence the senior most member (in order of appointment) shall preside over the meeting. Each meeting of the Divisional Forum shall be called by giving not less than 10 days' notice in writing to every member. The notice shall specify the place, the day, hour and statement of business to be transacted there at.

(11) Appeal to the State Commission[123]

Section 13 of the Act provides that any person aggrieved by an order made by the Divisional Forum may prefer an appeal against such order to the State Commission within a period of 30 days from the date of the order. Section 13 of the Act is to be reproduced here as follows:

Section 13: *Appeal*: Any person aggreived by an order made by the Divisional Forum may prefer an appeal against such order to the State Commission within a period of 30 days from the date of the order in such form and manner as may be prescribed.

Provided that the State Commission may entertain an appeal after the expiry of the said period of thirty days if it is satisfied that there was sufficient cause for not filing it within that period.

---

121. *Supra* Note 88 Sub-Rule (viii) of Rule 7.
122. *Id.* Rule 9.
123. *Supra* Note 119 Section 13 (For details) *Supra* Note 108, pp. 285-86.

The expression 'person aggrieved' does not mean a person who is disappointed or annoyed at decision. The term 'aggrieved' connotes some legal grievances, for example, deprivation of something, an adverse effect on the title to something and so on. He must show that the order affects his own right or confers a right on a person to which he is not entitled or is not in accordance with law.

The proviso appended to the Section 13 as mentioned above provides that the State Commission may entertain an appeal even after the expiry of 30 days if it is satisfied that there was sufficient cause for not filing it within the period. The party has to show as to why he did not file an appeal on the last day of limitation prescribed. In other words, it means that the party has to show sufficient cause for not filing the appeal on the last day but to explain the delay made thereafter day by day. The delay in filing an appeal should not have been for reasons which indicate the parties negligence in not taking necessary steps, which he could have or should have taken. What would be such 'necessary steps' will depend upon the circumstances of a particular case.

(12) Procedure for Hearing Appeal[124]

In exercise of the powers conferred by Section 24 of the said Act the State Government has made consumer protection rules. These Rules provide that under Section 13 of Act memorandum shall be presented by the appellant or his agent to the State Commission in person or be sent by registered post addressed to the Commission.[125] Every memorandum filed under Sub-rule (i) shall be in legible handwriting preferably typed and shall set forth concisely under distinct heads, the grounds of appeal without any argument narrative and such grounds shall be numbered consecutively.[126] Rules further provide that each memorandum shall be accompanied by a certified copy of the order of the Divisional Forum appealed against and such of the documents as may be required to support grounds of the

124. *Supra* Note 122, Rule 10.
125. *Id.* Sub-Rule 1.
126. *Id.* Sub-Rule 2.

memorandum.[127] When the appeal is presented after the expiry of the period of limitation as specified in the Act, the memorandum of appeal shall be accompanied by an application supported by an affidavit setting forth the facts on which the appellant relies to satisfy the State Commission that he has sufficient cause for not preferring the appeal with a period of limitation.[128]

The appellant shall submit six copies of the memorandum of appeal to the commission for official purpose.[129] On the date of hearing or on any other day to which hearing may be adjourned, it shall be obligatory for the parties or their agents to appear before the State Commission. If appellant or his agent fails to appear on such date, the State Commission may, on its discretion, either dismiss the appeal or decide it *ex-parte* on merits. If the respondent or his agent fails to appear on such date the State Commission shall proceed *ex-parte* and shall decide the appeal on merits of the case.[130]

The appellant shall not except by leave of the State Commission argue or be heard in support of any objection not set forth in the memorandum but the State Commission while deciding an appeal may not be confined to the grounds of objection set forth in the memorandum.[131] The State Commission may on such terms as it may think fit and at any state adjourn the hearing of the appeal but not more than one adjournment shall ordinarily be given and the appeal should be decided as far as possible within 90 days from the first date of hearing.[132] The order of the State Commission on appeal shall be signed and dated by the members of the State Commission and shall be communicated to the parties free of charge.[133]

127. *Id.* Sub-Rule (iii).
128. *Id.* Sub-Rule (iv).
129. *Id.* Sub-Rule (v).
130. *Id.* Sub-Rule (vi)
131. *Id.* Sub-Rule (vii)
132. *Id.* Sub-Rule (viii)
133. *Id.* Sub-Rule (ix).

(C) STATE COMMISSION[134]

The next higher forum in the hierarchy of Consumer Disputes Regressal Agencies in the State of Jammu and Kashmir is the State Commission. In this State as in the rest of the country State Commission has been set-up which in the State is the higher separate consumer forum. Its decisions are binding on both Divisional Forums presently functioning in the state.

(1) Constitution of State Commission[135]

The State Commission consists of a President and two or more members[136] The President for this forum shall be a person who is or has been a judge of a High Court and other members shall be persons of ability, integrity and having adequate knowledge of law and experience in law and consumer affairs.

(2) Appointment of President and Members[137]

Under the Section 14 of the Act the appointment of the President of the State Commission shall be made by the State Government[138] after consultation with the Chief Justice of the State High Court. However, consultation of the Chief Justice is necessary only if a sitting judge of the High Court is to be appointed as the President. It is to be submitted here that the State Act needs to be amended to the effect that for appointment of President of the State Commission consultation with the Chief Justice of the High Court be made necessary even though the retired judge of the High Court is to be appointed as the President. This sort of Amendment will help in making fair appointments to the office of the President of the State Commission. Regarding the

135. *Supra* Note 106; Inserted two or more members who shall be persons of ability, integrity and having adequate knowledge in law and experience in law and consumer affairs.

136. *Ibid.*

137. *Id.* By virtue of proviso now every appointment made under this section is required to be made by the government on the recommendation of the selection committee.

138. *Ibid.*

appointment of members of the State Commission the Amendment Act of 1997 now provides that State Government shall made every appointment on the recommendation of the Selection Committee consisting of the following, namely—

(i) Chief Secretary—Chairman
(ii) Secretary to Government Law Department—Member
(iii) Secretary to Government Food & Supplies Department (Incharge consumer affairs)—Member

(3) Terms and Conditions[139]

The State Government of Jammu and Kashmir has laid down Rules regarding the terms and conditions of service of the President and members of the State Commission. These rules provide that President and the members of the State Commission are required to give an undertaking to the effect that he does not and will not have any financial or other interests as is likely to affect prejudicially his functions as such.[140] The President and the members can hold office for a period not exceeding five years or such period as may be specified by the government in the notification.[141] However, any member may under his hand addressed to the government resign his office at any time and he may be removed from his office in accordance with the provisions of Rule 13.[142]

The terms and conditions of service of the President and the members shall not be varied to their disadvantage during their tenure of office.[143]

(4) Salary, Honorarium and other State Commission Allowances[144]

Where the President of the State Commission is a sitting judge of the High Court he shall enjoy all the benefits which he

139. *Supra* Note 133 Rule 12.
140. *Id.* Sub-Rule (i).
141. *Id.* Sub-Rule (ii).
142. *Id.* Sub-Rule (iii).
143. *Id.* Sub-Rule (iv).
144. *Id.* Rule 11.

should have enjoyed as sitting judge of the Hon'ble High Court. Where the President is not a sitting judge of High Court he shall receive a honorarium equivalent to the amount of salary as he was drawing at the time of his retirement minus the pension per month. Other members, if sitting on whole time basis, shall receive a consolidated honorarium or Rs. 3000 per month or if sitting on part time basis a consolidated honorarium of Rs. 100 per day per sitting. The Instant Rule 11 further provides that the President and the members shall be entitled to traveling and daily allowances on official tours at the same rates as are admissible to class first officer of the government

(5) Vacancies in the Office of State Commission[145]

A vacancy in the office of the President or a member may occur, after the expiry of the term, or by resignation, or removal. Any such vacancy caused by resignation or removal of the President or any other member of the State Commission under sub-rule 3 or otherwise shall be filled of by fresh appointment. Where any casual vacancy occurs in the office of the President of the State Commission, the senior most member as in case of Divisional Forum holding office (in order of appointment) for the time being shall discharge the functions of the President until a person appointed to fill such vacancy assumes the office of the President of the State Commission.[146] Sub-Rule (viii) of Rule 12 provides that when the President of the State Commission is enable to discharge the functions owing to absence illness or any other cause the senior most member (in order of appointment) shall discharge the functions of the President until the day on which the President resumes the charge of his functions.

(6) Jurisdiction of the State Commission[147]

The State Commission has been vested with three types of jurisdiction—Original Jurisdiction, Appellate Jurisdiction and Revisional Jurisdiction.

145. *Id.* Sub-Rule (v) Rule 12.
146. *Id.* Sub-Rule (vi).
147. *Supra* Note 134, Section 15.

(a) Original Jurisdiction

This jurisdiction of State Commission can be read under three sub-headings, namely, pecuniary jurisdiction, territorial jurisdiction and subject matter.

(b) Pecuniary Jurisdiction[148]

Under Section 15(a) of the Act the State Commission can entertain complaints where the value of the goods or services and compensation if any claimed exceeds rupees ten lacs but does not exceed rupees fifty lacs. It may be noted that prior to the Amendment Act, 2002 the pecuniary jurisdiction of the State Commission was five lacs but not exceeding rupees thirty lacs. It is also to be noted that originally prior to the above two Amendments originally pecuniary jurisdiction of the State Commission was above rupees fifty thousand but not exceeding rupees ten lacs.

It is appropriate to mention here that the pecuniary jurisdiction depends upon the amount of relief claimed including compensation and not upon the value of the subject matter, nor upon the relief granted when the complainant before the forum under the Act claims two reliefs in the alternative the forum has to consider for the purpose of jurisdiction the value of the relief which is higher.

(c) Territorial Jurisdiction[149]

There is no provision in the Act for determining the territorial jurisdiction of the State Commission. However, regarding territorial jurisdiction of the Divisional Forum whether the provisions of Section 9(2) can be made applicable to the State Commission there is no provision which could provide any guidance in this regard.

(d) Subject Matter

The provision of Section 15(a)(i) of the Act restricts the jurisdiction of the State Commission to complaints in respect of goods and services only. The State Commission can exercise its original jurisdiction in respect of any defect in

---

148. *Id.* Amended by Act, 1997.
149. *Supra* Note 147.

goods, deficiency in service, unfair trade or restrictive trade practice or charging of price in excess of the price fixed by or under any law or displayed on the goods or package containing such goods.

(e) Appellate Jurisdiction[150]

Under Section 15(a)(ii) of the Act, the State Commission shall have jurisdiction to entertain appeals against the order of any Divisional Forum within the State. According to Section 15 of the Act, any person aggrieved by an order made by the Divisional Forum may prefer an appeal against such order to the State Commission within the period of 30 days from the date of order. However, the State Commission may entertain an appeal after the expiry the said period of 30 days if it is satisfied that there was sufficient cause for not filing it within the period.

(f) Revisional Jurisdiction[151]

Under Clause (b) of Section 15 of the Act, the State Commission has jurisdiction to call for the records and pass appropriate orders in any consumer dispute which is pending before or has been decided by any Divisional Forum within the State of Jammu and Kashmir where it appears to the State Commission that such Divisional Forum has exercised jurisdiction not vested in it by law or has acted in exercise of its jurisdiction illegally or with material irregularity.

(7) Procedure Applicable to State Commission[152]

The procedure specified in Sections 10, 11 and 12 and under the Rules made for the disposal of complaints by the Divisional Forum are by virtue of the Section 16 applicable (with such modifications as may be necessary) to the disposal of disputes by the State Commission.

(8) Procedure Followed by State Commission[153]

The Act does not provide any special procedure to be

151. *Id.* Clause (b).
152. *Id.* Section 16.
153. Similar Provision is available under the Central Act on Consumer Protection.

followed by the State Commission. Section 16 of the Act however simply provides that the provisions of Sections 10, 11, 12 and the Rules made thereunder for the disposal of complaints by the Divisional Forum shall also be applicable to the State Commission. Section 10 provides the manner in which the complaint shall be made, Section 11 lays down the procedure and under Section 12 an order can be issued to the opposite party to do one or more of the things specified therein. All these provisions and the rules made there under, with suitable modifications are applicable to the State Commission. The Jammu and Kashmir Consumer Protection Rules have laid down in rules the procedure to be followed by the Forum/Commission. Where a complaint does not require analysis or testing of the goods, it should be decided by the State Commission, as far as possible, within a period of 90 days from the date of notice received by the opposite party and within 150 days if it requires analysis or testing of the goods. Where the opposite party admits the allegation made by the complainant the State Commission shall decide the complaint on the basis of the merit of the case and the documents present before it. If during the proceedings conducted under Section 11 the State Commission fixes a date for hearing of parties, it should be obligatory on the complainant and opposite party or his authorized agent to appear before the State Commission on such date of hearing or any other date to which hearing could be adjourned. Where the complainant or his authorized agent fails to appear before the State Commission on such day, the State Commission may in its discretion, either dismiss the complaint for default or decide it on merits. Where the opposite party or its authorized agent fails to appear on the day of hearing the State Commission may decide the complaint *ex-parte.* The State Commission may, on such terms as it may think fit and at any stage, adjourn the hearing of the complaint but not more than one adjournment shall ordinarily be given. Every proceeding shall be conducted by the President and at least one member thereof sitting together. However, where the member, for any reason, is unable to conduct the proceedings till it is completed the President and the other member shall conduct the proceeding *de novo*. Every order made by the State Commission shall be signed by its President and the member or members who conducted the proceeding. However, where the proceeding is conducted by the President and one member and they differ and refer the same to the other member for hearing on such point or points opinion of the majority shall be the order of State Commission. Orders of the State Commission shall be communicated to the parties free of charge.

(9) Appeals[154]

The original jurisdiction of the State Commission in terms of the monitory value of the dispute, namely a dispute between the value of rupees ten lacs to rupees fifty lacs. A person aggrieved of an order of the State Commission in respect of its either appellate or original jurisdiction can prefer an appeal to the High Court. Thirty days period from the order of the State Commission is allowed for carrying the matter before the High Court. A late appeal may also be entertained provided that the Court is satisfied that there was as sufficient cause for not preferring an appeal within the prescribed period. However, the appellant is required to explain the delay beyond the prescribed period of limitation and further that he has acted diligently for the purpose of filing the appeal.

(10) Mode of Filing Appeal[155]

The petition of appeal shall express clearly all the relevant facts leading up to the order appeared from and shall set-forth in brief the objection to the order appealed from and the grounds relied on in support of the appeal. The petition shall also state the date of the order appealed from as well as date on which it was received by the appellant. The petition of appeal must be accompanied by authenticated copy of the order appealed from and at least seven separate sets of the petition and the papers filed with it.

---

154. *Ibid.* Section 17.
155. More or less same procedure is to be followed here as in cases of appeal from Divisional Forum to State Commission.

After the appeal is registered, it shall be put up for hearing *ex-parte* before the Court which may either dismiss it summarily or direct issue of notice to all necessary parties or may make such order as the circumstances of the case may require.

(11) Finality of the Orders[156]

The Act provides that where no appeal has been preferred the orders of a Divisional Forum, or the State Commission may be enforced by a Divisional Forum or the State Commission and they are final. They will be enforced in the same way and in the same manner as order of these forums were decree or order made by a court in a suit pending therein and it shall be lawful for Divisional Forum or the State Commission to send in the event of its inability to the Court within the local limits of whose jurisdiction the opposite party resides or carries on business or personally works for gain and therefore the court to which the order so sent shall execute the order as if it were a decree or order sent to it for execution.

(12) Frivolous or Vexatious Complaints[157]

The Divisional Forum, the State Commission or the High Court may dismiss a complaint if the complaint is found to be frivolous or vexatious. The Act says that the Forum/Commission must record its reasons in writing for some dismissal. The Forum may also pass the order that the complainant shall pay to the opposite party such cost not exceeding ten thousand rupees as may be specified in the order. It means that now in addition to dismissal of the complaint which the forum declare frivolous or vexatious may award costs also to the opposite party.

(13) Penalties[158]

The Act provides in Section 21 that where a trader or a person against whom a complaint is made or the

156. *Supra* Note 154, Section 18.
157. *Id.* Section 20.
158. *Id.* Section 21.

complainant is supposed to comply with the order made by the Divisional Forum and/or the State Commission or the High Court fails or omits to comply with the order the said forum may punish him with imprisonment for a term which shall not be less than one month but which may extend to three year or with fine which shall not be less than two thousand rupees but which may extend to ten thousand rupees or both.

Part IV

In this part of the chapter some miscellaneous matters will be briefly mentioned.

(A) PROTECTION OF ACTION TAKEN IN GOOD FAITH[159]

The Scope of Section 22 is very wide and gives protection not only to members of the Divisional Forum the State Commission or the High Court but also to any officer or person acting under the direction of the said forum for executing any order made by it or in respect of any thing which is done or intended to be done in good faith. The condition only is that the protection is available in respect of anything done or intended to be done in good faith under the provisions of the Act or any rule or order made thereunder. The immunity is available against any suit, prosecution or legal proceeding in a Court of Law.

(B) POWER TO REMOVE DIFFICULTIES[160]

The object of Section 23 is to empower the government to make provisions to remove any difficulties which may arise in giving effect to the provisions of Act. Such powers however should not be inconsistent with the provisions of the Consumer Protection Act for removing the difficulties. The conditions for exercising these powers are enumerated as follows:

159. *Id.* Section 22.
160. *Id.* Section 23.

(i) Some difficulty must have arisen in giving effect to the provisions of the Consumer Protection Act.
(ii) It must be necessary or expedient to remove the difficulty.
(iii) The provisions made to remove the difficulty must not be inconsistent with the provisions of the Act.
(iv) The order to remove the difficulty must be made before the expiry of a period of two years from the commencement of this Act.
(v) The order must be published in the official gazette.
(vi) Every order made under this Section should as soon as may be laid before the legislature.

(C) POWER OF THE STATE GOVERNMENT TO MAKE RULES[161]

Section 24 of the Act empowers the State Government to make Rules for carrying out the provisions of the Act. Under this Section State Government has issued Rules in the year 1988 which are in existence and are titled as Jammu and Kashmir Consumer Protection Rules, 1988. These rules are very useful and are explaining various provisions of the Act.

(D) LAYING OF RULES[162]

Section 25 provides that every rule made by the State Government Under the Act should be the State Legislature. The provision is silent as to whether the state legislature has the power to make any modification or amendment of such rules. It seems that this power is implied and can be exercised by the state legislature.

OBSERVATION

From the above discussion it is clear that much has been done and much remains to be undone under the Central

161. *Id.* Section 24.
162. *Id.* Section 25.

Consumer Protection Act. Consumer Protection Act is a unique piece of social legislation which has excluded age-old doctrines like *Caveat Emptor, Privity* of Contract and to some extent Rule of Strict Liability and Principal of *Mens rea* also and has really given rise to the Rule of Negligence. If a person is held liable either for providing defective goods or deficient services he would be held liable for compensation under the Jammu and Kashmir Consumer Protection Act, 1987. The Preamble of Act suggests that this Act is to provide better protection of the consumer interest and in order to accomplish this purpose the Act provides for establishment of "Consumer Councils" and "Redressal Agencies." These words and expressions found in the preamble of the Jammu and Kashmir State Act are already in the preamble of the Central Consumer Protection Act, but in actual parlance in the state of Jammu and Kashmir, Consumer Protection (Principal) Act provides one consumer council for the whole state. In the rest of the country consumer councils and consumer forums are working at distric level. Regarding the establishment of one state commission in the state of Jammu and Kashmir position is same as elsewhere in other states of the country. Considering the need to have district level consumer councils for the state of Jammu and Kashmir as already provided under the Central Consumer Protection Act, the state legislature by way of amendment in the year 1997 has inserted Section 6-A which provides for the establishment of council to be known as District Council. So far as the objects of Consumer Council under the State Consumer Protection Act are concerned they are same and similar as those set for Consumer Councils under the Central Act, that is these councils are charged with promotion and protection of consumer rights. Similarly, Consumer Protection (Amendment) Act, 2002 provides for establishment of Consumer Forums at District level but it is seen that no steps have been taken so far by the government to establish these Forums.

Coming to the definition portion of the State Act it is appropriate here to trace the improvements made on the lines of Central Act. under the Central Act 'Branch Office' means any establishment described as a branch by the opposite party or any establishment carrying on either the same or substantially the same activity as that carried on by the head office of establishment. The word 'Branch Office' under the State Act carries the same meaning as given by the Central Act. The insertion of this clause has now encouraged consumers to file complaints at their own places if branch office of the opposite party is operated there. Earlier under the Principal Consumer Protection Act complainant was to file complaints at the place where opposite party/parties or any of the opposite party actually and voluntarily resides or carries business or personally works for gain, or where the cause of action arises but now by virtue of the Consumer Protection (Amendment) Act, 1997 on the lines of Central Consumer Protection Act complaint will lie even at the place within the local limits of jurisdiction branch office of the opposite party is carrying the same or substantially the same business as the opposite party. After the definition of Branch Office next comes the definition of 'complainant'. Now like the Central Act State Consumer Protection Act provides that the complainant includes in addition to consumer, voluntary consumer association and the government one or more consumers where there are numerous consumers. This means that now complainants can file a complaint in representative form, if they so choose. This position is already envisaged by the Civil Procedure Code and now by the Consumer Protection Act. It is a welcome development and this sub-clause (iv) to Section 2 sub-section 2 has widened the *Locus Standi* of the complainant. Similarly, amendment in 1997 has brought tremendous changes in clauses (c), (d), and (f) of section 2 sub-section 1 which has enlarged the scope of the State Act. Under both the state and Central Consumer Protection Act, 'Restrictive Trade Practices' indicates or means any trade practice which requires a consumer to buy, hire or avail of any goods or services as a condition precedent for buying, hiring or availing of any other goods or services. It would not be out of place to mention here that both the Acts have given similar specific definition of the Restrictive Trade Practices which is different from the definition as given in the MRTP Act. In addition to the above, State Act has borrowed from the Central Act provisions, which provides that complaint can be lodged for the goods 'bought by him' or 'agreed to be bought by him' and/or for the services 'hired or availed of' or 'agreed to be hired or availed of by him'. A big bold step is taken by the legislature by comprehending the definition of the word 'Consumer'. Now like the Central Act, State Consumer Protection Act provides that consumer means not only the person who actually buys goods but also the user of such good and similarly consumer of services means not only the person who hires or avails the services but also beneficiary of these services. Similarly, by increasing pecuniary jurisdiction of the Consumer Forums to meet the present needs of the society more consumers are expected to knock the door of Consumer Forums.

The above discussion gives impression that both State and Central Consumer Protection Act may be substantially same and similar but it is partly true. Consumers of the State of Jammu and Kashmir are still precluded from seeking justice of the National Commission and as alternative measure busy State, Jammu and Kashmir High Court has been empowered to hear appeals from the State Commission. As it is clear from Chapter 2 that there are increasing voices of consumers for improving consumer welfare in the State of Jammu and Kashmir. Establishment of district level Consumer Forum would significantly accelerate Consumer Protection. Only significant features of this Act will not help the consumers. Consumers of the far flung areas are slow in receiving benefit of this Act. So, authorities are expected to give serious thought and correct loopholes in the state Consumer Protection Act on the lines of Central Consumer Protection Act so that the importance of the consumers will be realized fully in the state of Jammu and Kashmir.

After the critical analysis of various provisions of the Consumer Protection Act in the light of model (Central) Act on consumer protection and Jammu and Kashmir Rules, 1988 it appears that this benevolent legislation intends to provide speedy and inexpensive remedy to the aggrieved persons against unfair trade practices, unscrupulous exploitation and deficient services. If this is the aim and purpose of this Act there is no reason why this Act has not been implemented in the state as in rest of the country. Amendment Act, 1997 has provided for establishment of district consumer councils and another Amendment in the year 2002 provides for establishment of district level Courts but it appears that these two amendments have not been carried into effect and this attitude on the part of government has created annoyance among the consumers. This social legislation which was intended to protect a large body of consumers from exploitation has remained ineffective. It is hoped a good sense will prevail on State Government to establish in actual practice district level Courts and also by way of Amendment these courts be empowered to pass interim orders.

CHAPTER

5

IMPACT OF LANDMARK JUDGMENTS: SOME REFLECTIONS

INTRODUCTION

In preparation of this research work I have gone through thousands of cases decided by various State Commissions, National Commission and Supreme Court but here in this chapter it is proposed to refer only those cases which have provided a new application of the existing range of responsibilities. With this avowed object in mind relevant cases decided by the National Commission and Supreme Court will be discussed and analyzed so that the question—what is the impact of these decisions on Consumer Fora in the State of Jammu and Kashmir will be better viewed and answered. However considering the fact that these courts have decided innumerable cases, so for the sake of brevity only those remarkable cases falling under headings—Defective Goods and Deficient Services will be undertaken here for discussion.

(A) Defective Goods[1]

A complaint can be made where the goods in question suffer from one or more defects. A defect in goods means any fault, imperfection or shortcoming in the quality, quantity, potency, purity or standard which is required to be maintained by or under any applicable law or as is claimed by any trader in any manner whatsoever in relation to the goods. Thus, standard, etc. may be either a legal prescription or trader's claim or consumer expectation. Now let us go through a bulk of cases under the above heading.

(I) Automobiles

On a survey of cases it has been found that under the category of goods most of the complaints are in connection with defective automobiles. In *Surender Agro Centre of Rewari & Another* v. *Sher Singh and others*[2] the complainants were in need of a tractor agreed to purchase it from the dealer. On seeing the very small size of the tractor the complainants refused to take delivery. On the assurance given by the dealer that he will take it back if the complainants do not find it suitable even after use. After the use of one day it was returned. The buyer was allowed to reject it as the tractor was found to be too small and therefore of no use for cultivation. Supreme Court in *Tata Engineering and Locomotive Co. Ltd. & Another* v. *Gajanan Y. Mandrekar*[3] upheld the order of State Commission that the seller has undertaken under the warranty to deliver the vehicle in good condition but when despite repairs the vehicle continued to give same trouble the complainant was rightly entitled to the compensation. However, in the circumstances of the case the apex court directed that one-third of the compensation be deducted towards the user of the vehicle by the purchaser during the period (eight long months after delivery) concerned. For the rest of the amount the order of the State Commission was upheld.

---

1. Clauses (f) and (i) of Section 2(1) Consumer Protection Act.
2. 1986-96 CONSUMER 2433 (NS) National Commission and Supreme Court on Consumer Cases. Ms. Swarn Bhatia, Nijhawan International Law Book Company.
3. (1997) 5 Supreme Court Cases 507.

In similar other complaints[4] about motor cars containing multiple defects price was ordered to be refunded and a demand for replacement was held to be not unreasonable but where due to improper handling the vehicle (its clutch plate) got damaged a number of times the same cannot be attributed to the manufacturing process. In *Amarnath Singh* v. *Mahindra and Mahindra and another*[5] complainant purchased a new Mahindra which after examined in the garage it was found that the engine was of a tractor and its bearings, crank shaft and other parts were of sub-standard size. National Commission held there is no difference between a tractor engine and a jeep engine except of a few adjustments. Further, it is the normal practice in the automobile industry of fitting undersized parts and it does not constitute a manufacturing defect. It is to be submitted that the view expressed by National Commission in this case is not good in law because this decision is likely to give legal base to those manufacturers who willingly and intentionally adopts such practices in order to cheat the buyer.

(2) Electronics[6]

Many complaints entertained by consumer Disputes Redressal Agencies are also about the quality of the goods supplied. Consumer expects his purchases to be suitable for his purpose or that they would give him reasonable use. But where goods are unreasonably dangerous they are likely to be regarded as defective by the objective test of analyzing the expectations of reasonably prudent user and the extent to which those expectations have not been met. In *T.T. Private Ltd.* v. *Akhil Bhartiya Grahak Panchayat & Another*[7] by the

---

4. M/s Escorts Ltd. and Another *v.* N.K. Dasapha, 1986-96 CONSUMER 2607 (NS); Same view was held in E. Aboo and Another *v.* Tata Engineering and Locomotive Company Ltd. and Others, 1986-96, CONSUMER 3084(NS)
5. 1986-96 CONSUMER 2373 (NS).
6. Various cases have been reported which are decided by the various Consumer Forums under the instant heading but for brevity we will here deal only few noteworthy cases.
7. 1986-96 CONSUMER 2367(NS); however in Smt. Gurmeet Kaur *v.* The Regional Office, T.T Ltd. and Another, 1986-96 CONSUMER

doctrine of *Res Ipso Loquitor* manufacturing company was held liable for the accident caused due to defective goods. In this case the complainant has purchased a new cooker of 5 liters capacity of 10 years guarantee. The cooker while cooking burst and exploded. Her wife received severe injuries. National Commission held injuries suffered due to the negligence of the company (Appellant herein) in supplying defective goods is established on record. The inference is irresistible that the accident was caused due to defective goods and compensation of one lac rupees was held to be on the conservative side.

(3) Machines

The supply of a different article than promised is a defective supply. In *M/s Kody Elocot* v. *Dr. C.P. Gupta*[8] the complainant purchased an ultra sound scanner machine with a warranty of one year. The machine stopped functioning after eight months of installation.

The National Commission observed that the unit did not perform satisfactorily after 8 months of its installation and thereafter started giving trouble and the defects could not be rectified. Therefore the machine was defective. Similarly, *Chocklingam Proprietor, Malandu Printers* v. *M. Amba Shankar and Others*[9] the appellant company purchased photo type machine. When defect after sometime occurred in the machine it was reported to the Regional Sales Manager who sent an engineer. The grievance of the appellant was that the respondents were bound to provide after sales service for all time to come and for failure to do so the respondent was guilty of negligence.

On hearing both parties and after going through the record National Commission came to the conclusion that the respondent had not refused to attend to the machines. They only demanded charges for servicing and charges for the

---

2001 (NS) there was no proof that the material used in the cooker was defective or sub-standard at the material time so there was no defect.

8. 1986-96 CONSUMER 2827 (NS).
9. 1986-96 CONSUMER 2284 (NS)

visiting engineer. The appellant was not prepared to pay those amounts after the warranty period of one year has long expired and when there was not subsisting contract of service between the parties.

In *M/s Jay Kay Puri, Engineer & Another* v. *M/s Mohan Breweries & Distilleries Ltd.*[10] the respondent Public Limited Company entrusted the work of centrally air conditioning the guest house established for its directors and officers to the appellants. However, when the cooling system of the air conditioning plant was put to use it did not function properly. It was repaired but even it did not work properly. National Commission from the material on record held that inference is irresistible that the goods, i.e. air conditioning equipment and machinery supplied were defective and there has been gross deficiency in service.

(4) Miscellaneous

In *Sahitya Pravarthaka Cooperative Society Ltd.* v. *K.N. Narayan Pillai*[11] the complainant purchased encyclopedia from cooperative society limited (appellant herein) which contained certain mistakes relating to subject-matter. National Commission held there is no law by or under which it can be said that the alleged mistakes in an encyclopedia will amount to a defect. But speaking respectfully and honestly the Hon'ble Commission has committed an error in not imposing any liability on the publisher. No doubt, publisher has published the encyclopedia on the basis of information said to have been received from various scholars in each subject but he was supposed to get the material scrutinized from knowledgeable person/persons in each subject before publishing the same.

Where complainant purchased certain items of furniture and on delivery found some defects in the furniture. National Commission held that the defects in the furniture supplied

---

10. 1986-96 CONSUMER 1954 (NS); In R.K. Kapoor *v.* R.N Mittal, 1986-96 CONSUMER 2297 (NS) price charged for air conditioner was ordered to be paid back for defect in it due to which it did not work.
11. 1986-96 CONSUMER 2059 (NS).

are of a minor nature but the relief granted be refunded of the entire cost of furniture.[12]

Many complaints though entertained by Consumer Disputes Redressal Agencies has been consequently dismissed on the ground complainant purchased goods not for earning livelihood but for commercial purpose. A fair distinction between consumer and non-consumer sales though seems necessary but it is difficult to make a clear-cut distinction and is always a question of fact to be decided in the facts and circumstances of each case. In *Laxmi Engineering Works* v. *P.G.G. Industrial Institute*[13] on the facts and circumstances of the case the Supreme Court on having regard to the nature and character of the machine and the material on record held it is not goods which the complainant purchased for use by himself exclusively for the purpose of earning his livelihood by means of self-employment.

However, in *Punjab Water Supply & Sewage Board* v. *Udaipur Cement Works*,[14] Supreme Court didn't appreciate with the observation of the National Commission to the effect that—

> "Where the transaction is one of the sale and purchase simpliciter no question of deficiency in service can arise so as to entitle the complainant to invoke the jurisdiction of the consumer forum where there was no case at all of any defect in the goods supplied."

It is to be observed that the rejection of said observation of National Commission by Supreme Court is based on merits. Changing conditions of trade in the 20th Century have altered the setting in which most sales take place was being deprived of the protection which it was the intention of the law that he should haye. Sellers of consumer goods exploited their superior economic power to contract

12. Rajiv Goel *v.* Col. M.M. Dutta, 1986-96 CONSUMER 3146 (NS).
13. 1986-96 CONSUMER 1554 (NS); To the same effect is the case titled Rjeev Metal Works and Others *v.* Mineral and Metal Trading Corporation of India Ltd. (1996) 9 SCC 422.
14. (1995) Supp. (1) SCC 117.

out of the liability for implied terms and by means of contractual exemption clauses transferred the risk of defect in their wares from their own shoulders to the luckless purchaser who might in consequence suffer heavy and irrecoverable loss. Hence the control of exemption clauses by legislation is a part of a wider programme of consumer protection. A sale is presumed to be consumer sale until the contrary is proved and the burden is on the consumer to show that his misfortune was the result of the defect in the goods supplied to him. But where the goods itself has not been supplied non-delivery is not a defect. Non-delivery is a typical breach of contract for which an action lies in damages. The only other remedy is an order for delivery of goods that is specific performance of the contract.

In *Colgate Palmolive (India) Ltd.* v. *Hindustan Lever Ltd.*[15] the most important grievance of the complainant before the commission was that the claim of the Colgate Palmolive Ltd. that its toothpaste is germ-fighter having the ability to stop bad breath and its ability to fight tooth decay are highly misleading quo the consumers and the trade, however, there was no evidence of a single consumer being mislead. The apex court held that in the event of a complaint being lodged by a trader in respect of unfair trade practice, it is for the trader to convince by way of evidence sufficient that there is involved an element of public interest, in the complaint in order to obtain the order of injunction and the commission in its turn has thus to consider as to whether or not, the public is being deceived or likely to be deceived and in the event the commission comes to a finding that there is likelihood of such a deception then and in that event only, the question of grant of an order of injunction arises.

(B) DEFICIENT SERVICES

A complaint can be filed under the Act in respect of unsatisfactory services. If the forum is convinced that any of the obligations contained in the complaint about the services are proved, it can provide any of the applicable types of

15. 1999 (3) CPR 70.

remedy specified in section 14. The consumer has to prove that the services suffered from a deficiency. The term service is defined as follows:[16]

> "Service means service of any description which is made available to potential users and includes the provision of facilities in connection with banking, financing, insurance, transport, processing, supply of electrical or other energy, board or lodging or both, housing construction entertainment, amusement or the purveying a news or other information but does not include the rendering of any service free of charge or under a contract of personal service."

The term "Deficiency" is also defined as follows:[17]

> "Any fault, imperfection, shortcoming or inadequacy in the quality, nature and manner of performance which is required to be maintained by or under any law for the timing being in force or has been undertaken to be performed by a person in pursuance of a contract or otherwise in relation to any service."

Supreme Court has made Analysis of Definition of word "service."[18]

In its decision in *Lucknow Development Authority* v. *M.K. Gupta*[19] the Supreme Court examined the scope of the term "service" in the context of a consumer protection legislation. Justice Sahai proceeded as follows:

> "It (definition of consumer) is in three parts. The main part is followed by inclusive clause and ends by exclusionary clause. The main clause itself is very wide. It applies to any service made available to potential

16. Section 2(1)(o) of Consumer Protection Act, 1987.
17. *Id.* Section 2(1)(g).
18. Dr. Avtar Singh, Law of Consumer Protection, 2nd Ed., Eastern Book Company, Lucknow, pp. 151-52.
19. (1994) 1 SCC 243.

> users. The word 'any' and 'potential' are significant. Both are of wide amplitude. The word 'any' dictionarily means 'one or some or all'."

In BLACK'S LAW DICTIONARY it is explained thus, word 'any' has a diversity of meaning and may be employed to indicate 'all' or 'every' as well as 'some' or 'one' and its meaning in a given statute depends upon the content and the subject matter of the statute. The use of the word 'any' in the context it has been used in clause (o) indicates that it has been used in wider sense extending from one to all. The other word 'potential' is again very wide. In OXFORD DICTIONARY it is defined as 'capable of coming into being, 'possibility'. In BLACK'S LAW DICTIONARY it is defined as 'existing in possibility but not in act'. Naturally and probably expected to come into existence at some future time, though not now existing, e.g., the future product of grain or trees already planted, or the successive future instalments or payments on a contract or engagement already made. In other words, service which is not only extended to actual users but those who are capable of using it are covered in the definition. The clause is thus very wide and extends to any or all actual or potential users. But the legislature did not stop there. It extended the meaning of the word further in modern sense by extending it to even such facilities as are available to a consumer in connection with banking, financing, etc. Each of these are wide-ranging activities in day-to-day life. They are discharged both by statutory and private bodies. In absence of any indication, express or implied, there is no reason to hold that authorities created by the statute are beyond purview of the Act. When banks advance loan or accept deposit or provide facility of locker they undoubtedly render service. A state bank or nationalized bank renders as much service as a private bank. No distinction can be drawn in private and public transport or insurance companies even the supply of electricity or gas which throughout the country is being made, mainly, by statutory authorities included in it. The legislative intention is thus clear to protect a consumer against services rendered even by statutory bodies. The test, therefore, is not if a person against whom a complaint is made is a statutory body but whether the nature of the duty and function performed by it is service or even facility.

In the foregoing pages an attempt is made to examine the question of amenability of public authorities to the jurisdiction created by the Act. In the chronological form service rendered by these public authorities to the society will be scrutinized in the following pages in some detail.

(I) Banking

Banking[20] is the business dealing with money and created transactions. In India, the modern banking is now 200 years old. The number of branches of commercial banks have gone up since 1994 and the activities of the banks have spread to the country side. All this has happened due to the extensive powers of control and regulation vested in the Central Monetary Authority—the Reserve Bank of India (RBI). It was nationalized in 1949. Commercial banking was mostly confined to private sector till 1969.[21] On 19th July 1969, 14 leading commercial banks were also nationalized. It was followed by nationalization of six more privately owned commercial banks in 1980.[22] The business of banking consists of borrowing and lending safe storage and money transfer, etc.

Growth of trade and commerce have in the recent years increased the business of banking. Banking constitutes the largest nationalized service sector in the country and banks are supposed to render a vital service to the society. More than a dozen of Acts[23] relating to banks and financial

---

20. It can be traced back beyond 2500 B.C. but modern banking originated in medieval times. It started taking its name from banca which means the money lending
21. Ab. Qayoom Ahanger, Article Greater Kashmir, 19 December 1999.
22. The purpose of nationalization was to bring these banks to the mainstream of commercial banking.
23. The Reserve Bank of India was originally established as share holder's bank in 1935. It was latter converted to a state owned bank by an Act of Parliament in 1949. Apart from this Act other Acts relating to banking are the State Financial Corporations Act, 1951, The State Bank of India Act, 1955, the State Bank of India (Subsidiary Banks) Act, 1959, the Deposit Insurance & Credit Guarantee Corporation Act, 1961, The Industrial Development Bank

institutions have been passed with a view to develop, guide and assist and control the growth of industry and trade and functioning of the economy of the country.

While defining term 'service' under section 2(1)(o) of the Consumer Protection Act the banking or financing services are specially included in the definition after defining 'service' in general term. When banks advance loan or accept interest on payments or deposits, safe storage and money transfer, etc. they undoubtedly render service whether they are public or private bank. The services that a bank renders to the customer is for consideration in as much as the credit balances in his accounts are lend to other parties and the bank earns interest more than it gives to the customer.

The bank cannot act arbitrarily either in considering the case of the customer or refusing to consider his case. Though the Consumer Disputes Redressal Forum may not in exercise of its summary jurisdiction attempt to adjudicate complaint involving complex question of facts or law, it will entertain the complaints where the banks has failed to honour its guarantee or delayed giving credit of the instruments deposited with it or refused to pay demand drafts on technical grounds or dishonoured cheques though funds were there, withheld fixed deposits after maturity, paid forged cheques, failed to carry out the instructions of the customer or safeguard the contents of lockers let out to the customer or without reasonable cause prevented the customer from operating his account or cheques deposited for credit where lost, it refused to return the security given by the customer which became excess in relation to his liability or made wrong entries or omitted to make entries in the customers

---

of India, 1964, The Banking Companies (Acquisition and Transfer of Undertaking) Act, 1980, The Regional Rural Banks Act, 1976, The Export Import Bank of India, 1981, The National Bank for Agricultural and Rural Development Act, 1981, The Industrial Reconstruction Bank of India Act, 1984., The National Housing Bank Act, 1987, The Banker's Books Evidence Act, 1891, Banking Companies (Legal Practitioner's Clients Accounts) Act, 1949, The Industrial Finance Corporation (Transfer of Undertaking & Repeal) Act, The Recovery of Debts due to Banks & Financial Institutions Act, 1993, The Special Court (Trial of Offences Relating to Transition in Securities) Act, 1992.

account in other words, the bank cannot act in a high handed manner it must deal with its customers with due respect and care and should avoid any harassment to customer. For improper or wrongful acts of the bank, it has to pay damages or compensation to customer and the recent trend is that the bank has been authorized to recover such compensation or damages paid to the customer from the salary of the employee responsible for such acts.[24]

Normally the Consumer Disputes Redressal Forum will not ask the bank to give credit facilities to its customers but where the bank has undertaken to grant loans and relying thereon the customer has altered his position and incurred certain liabilities, the forum may direct the bank to honour its promises. Some of the decisions given by National Commission and Supreme Court in which the liability of the bank has came into question can be scrutinized under the following headings:

(a) Denial of Credit Facility

In a series of reputed cases it has been repeatedly said that non-grant of financial accommodation or non-grant of loan by a bank does not amount to deficiency in service. See for example, The *Branch Manager, State Bank of India and others* v. *Sunderlah Kela*[25] and *Govind Electrodes Pvt. Ltd.* v. *General Manager, United Commercial Bank & Another.*[26] In the former case, the complainant prayed that the bank be ordered to restore the limit of the complainant which was stopped and that it may be ordered to sanction immediately the proposal of cash credit limit forwarded by the branch manager. National Commission held that it is for the bank to decide whether a particular party is eligible for the grant of credit within the framework of the credit policy laid down by the Government of India and the Reserve Bank of India (RBI).

In the later case, the complainant complained that for running his industry for manufacture of electrodes he had

---

24. M.L. Tannan, Banking Law and Practice in India, 19th Ed., Reprint (1998) Vol. 1, Indian Law House, New Delhi.
25. 1986-96 CONSUMER 2702 (NS).
26. 1986-96 CONSUMER 3152 (NS).

applied to the bank for working capital facility which was sanctioned to him but when he applied to the bank for enhancement of the limit for cash credit the bank refused. The non-cooperation of the bank as it was alleged adversely affected the production of the factory. The National Commission came to the conclusion that banks have the discretion to decide in good faith in the interests of safeguarding public funds whether a party should be given or continued credit facilities or not keeping in view its performance and above all whether or not the party concerned is justifiably eligible for additional credit facilities. Similarly, in *Branch Manager, Bank of Maharashtra* v. *Manohar Sita Ram Nandanwar*[27] the complainant (Respondent before National Commission) got the cash credit loan facility which was secured by FDR. The bank informed the complainant that the cash credit loan facility would cease in some future date which was mentioned and the amount of the FDR would be appropriated towards the amount outstanding in the cash credit loan facility in case the said account was not regularized on or before the date given. The National Commission held that it was open to the bank not to renew the cash credit facility after a period of one year and to adjust the amount in the FDR towards amount recoverable under the cash credit facility. The action of the bank was strictly in accordance with the terms of the arrangement of cash credit loan facility account and no deficiency in service on the part of the bank has been established in relation to the complainant.

Yet in another case[28] against bank for non-release of loan facility the National Commission concluded that bank was justified in declining to sanction the loan advance to the complainant in as much as he filed to provide the guarantee money as well as collateral security as had been demanded of him by the bank and without these conditions being fulfilled by the complainant for loan, the bank which had to act in conformity with the rules and regulations framed by the RBI could not have made the advance to the complainant.

---

27. 1986-96 CONSUMER 444 (NS).
28. C. Gopi Chettair *v.* The Manager, Federal Bank Limited and Another, 1986-96 CONSUMER 1424 (NS).

As in above cases, in a few other cases[29] the court has reiterated the same view that providing loan facility is in the discretion of the bank. The policy laid down by the Government of India and the guidelines of the RBI in the matter of bank credit are mere guidelines and the responsibility for taking decision vests with the bank or institution which has to give the credit eventually. The bank has to be the sole judge of the credit-worthiness of a party whether the unit proposed to be assisted by credit is economically viable or not is considered by the bank. Similarly, the refusal of the bank to enhance the existing sanctioned limits of credit or even to continue to grant to extent of the limits already sanctioned cannot constitute a breach of bank's obligations and hence it is not a deficiency in service.[30]

(b) Dishonouring Cheque

The most common relation between a banker and the customer is that of debtor and creditor. The customer is the creditor of the bank to the extent of the amount belonging to the customer deposited with the bank. A bank, therefore, has a duty to honour the customer's cheque and make the payment, if there are sufficient funds belonging to the customer, to meet such payment.[31] If there are sufficient funds to meet the cheque and the same is dishonoured by a bank, it can be held liable for the wrongful honour of the cheque and required to pay compensation for the damage caused thereby. In *State Bank of India* v. *N. Raveendran Nair*,[32] the Respondent-Complainant was engaged in business in textiles.

---

29. A.N. Sharma and Others *v.* D.M. Syndicate Bank and Another, 1986-96 CONSUMER 1674 (NS); Precession Industries *v.* Bank of Baroda, 1986-96 CONSUMER 2928 (NS); Surinder Singh *v.* Bank of Baroda and Others, 1986-96 CONSUMER 2137 (NS).
30. However in Mike's (P) Ltd. *v.* State Bank of Bikaner and Jaipur, 1986-96 CONSUMER 3187 (NS) the action of the bank in freezing the credit facilities without giving notice to the complainant was held mala-fide and accordingly he was entitled to the compensation of Rs. 10 lakhs.
31. Section 31 of Negotiable Instruments Act, 1881.
32. 1986-96 CONSUMER 3069 (NS).

He was purchasing textiles direct from the manufacturers and distributes them to retailers. With the above object he had obtained the draft payable at State Bank of India, Surat Branch. The said bank refused to honour the demand draft just on the ground that though the draft bore the signatures of two officials of the issuing branch, the specimen signature number of one of these officials was missing. On the question whether the State Bank of India, Surat Branch was negligent in rendering service while dishonouring that draft, the National Commission replied in affirmative. The State Bank of India, Surat had earlier honoured the demand draft issued by the State Bank of India, Travancore, which also did not bear the specimen signature on three occasions prior to the presentation of the disputed draft. So the commission held that the bank cannot be permitted to be whimsical while honouring one draft and dishonouring another draft of the same nature.

In another case[33] of the similar nature bank refused to make payment under two cheques. The apex commission held that the bank in the instant case has not been negligent in rendering service because the banker who was under an obligation to honour the cheques of its customers was equally bound not to encash them as he has received instructions later on to stop payment.

Since under rules when the drawer of the cheque countermands the payment, that is, issues instructions to the bank not to make the payment of a particular cheque issued by him, the authority of the bank to pay that cheque stands revoked. Any payment made by the bank after a due notice countermanding the payment was given cannot be considered good against the drawer.[34] This type of problem arose in *Osmanabad Distt. Central Co-operative Bank Ltd. & Another* v. *Ramachandra Dasharath Mane & Others.*[35] In this case partnership company had opened an account with the bank

---

33. Arun Sameer Associates Pvt. Ltd. *v.* Regional Manager, State Bank of India, 1986-96 CONSUMER 3231 (NS).
34. R.K Bangia 'Principles of Mercantile Law', 3rd Ed., 1995, Allahabad Law Agency, Allahabad.
35. 1986-96 CONSUMER 1852 (NS).

and alleged deficiency in the service of the bank on the ground that the withdrawals were allowed by the bank on the authority of one of the partners whereas according to the instructions given to them two partners should have authorized any withdrawal. National Commission was of the view that since copy of deed of dissolution of partnership firm was not received in time so the bank was justified in giving authority of withdrawal to only one partner in accordance with the special instructions as indicated in the account opening form that either of the partners shall operate the bank account with his signature.

(c) Received Amount not Credited

A bank must always have cash balances on hand in order to pay its depositors upon demand or when the amounts credited to them becomes due. Only in this way can confidence in the banking system be maintained. But when bank fails to credit the amount received under cheque or otherwise in one's account, its promises or obligations constitutes claims against it.[36] In *Sovintorg (India) Pvt. Ltd.* v. *State Bank of India, New Delhi,*[37] the bank failed to credit the amount deposited by the complainant for over a period of seven years. Holding the bank liable for not crediting the amount to the account and denying the complainant the benefit of this amount for over seven years the Supreme Court held that there was a grave deficiency in service.

Similarly, in *Laxmi Vilas Bank Ltd. & Another* v. *P.R. Krishanan & Another*[38] by reason of failure on the part of the bank to pay the amount due under the fixed deposit on the date when it matured for payment the complainant was entitled to receive interest at 18% on the full amount. In another case of similar nature namely, *Dr. K.T. Shivaiah* v. *Canara Bank,*[39] the complainant was sanctioned a pension. Out of this amount a sum was commuted. The bank did not credit the commuted value of the pension but nonetheless

36. *Supra* Note 33.
37. 1999 (3) CPR 56 (SC).
38. 1986-96 CONSUMER 3234 (NS).
39. 1986-96 CONSUMER 2026 (NS).

started effecting recovery of the pension per month. In the result he did not receive the commutation amount. While agreeing with the state commission that there was deficiency in service on the part of the bank in not crediting the commuted value of pension to the account of the complainant consider it just and fair that he should be allowed interest at 18% per annum on the commuted value of pension.

(d) Banker's Right of General Lien

Bankers have a right of general lien under the General Law of Banker's Lien. Such a right entitles the bank to retain things deposited with the bank as security for a general balance of account.[40] This right is available in the absence of a contract to the contrary. Therefore, if cheques or other securities have been deposited with a bank he can exercise lien over them. Bank can exercise lien even over those items for which the loans has been sanctioned say for e.g. building or capital assets. In *M/s Agnal Traders Ltd.* v. *R.K. Aneja & Another*[41] the complainant purchased a car by availing of loan from the bank. As the complainant defaulted in the payment of instalments the bank ultimately seized the car. The complainant filed a complaint questioning the accounts and adjustment of the loan, harassment of the complainant by the bank and the illegal act of seizing the vehicle. National Commission after assessing various receipts came to the conclusion that no excess payment was made by the complainant and the complainant is not a consumer as he has not alleged any deficiency in the service.

In the same way, in *Canara Bank* v. *G. Annaji Rao*[42] the National Commission held that bank has a general lien by virtue of which it is entitled to retain ornaments deposited by constituents as security in respect of any advance owing to the bank.

(e) Strikes or Lock-outs

In a modern economy, the dependence of their

40. *Supra* Note 31, Section 171.
41. 1986-96 CONSUMER 1931 (NS).
42. 1986-96 CONSUMER 1851 (NS).

operations even for a short period would not only produce serious adverse repercussions entailing very great hardship and lost to their customers, but would also completely paralyze the economic life of the country since strikes in public utility services have unfortunately become a very common and frequent phenomenon in our country. There is urgent and imperative need to evolve a workable scheme which would enable uninterrupted service being rendered to the constituents of every bank throughout the year during normal business hours on all working days notwithstanding as strike by the employees of the banks. Barring a few banking companies which are in the private sector the rest of the banking industry in the country is operated by nationalized banks. It is clearly the duty of the government to ensure that constituents of these banks are provided uninterrupted service and they are not put to inconvenience, hardship and loss by reasons of any stoppage of work by the employees of any of the nationalized banks.[43] In this connection the short question arose for consideration in *Consumer Unity & Trust Society* v. *The Chairman & Managing Director, Bank of Baroda, Calcutta & Another.*[44] The question was whether a banking company which renders service within meaning of clause (g) of section (2) of Consumer Protection Act is liable to compensate its customers for loss of service due to illegal strike by its employees.

It was held through R.M. Sahai, J., that the provisions of Section 14(1)(d) are attracted if the person from whom damages are claimed is found to have acted negligently and such negligence must result in some loss to the person claiming damages. Mere loss or injury without negligence is not contemplated by the section. The bank has not been found to be negligent in discharging of its duties. Therefore, even if any loss or damage was caused to any depositor but it was not caused due to negligence of bank then no claim of damages under the Act was maintainable.

---

43. Dr. V.K. Agarwal, Consumer Protection, 2nd Ed., BLH Publishers and Distributors Pvt. Ltd., New Delhi.
44. 1986-96 CONSUMER 1546 (NS).

(f) Other Grounds

The relation between the banker and the customer being complex in nature some times a confusion arises as to whether a particular duty was required to be performed by the bank or the customer. Such type of situation arose for consideration in *Pradeep Kumar Jain* v. *Citi Bank & Another.*[45] In this case the complainant borrowed money after making certain initial payments for the purchase of a car from the bank. He also obtained in respect of the car a policy of insurance from the Oriental Insurance Company and the policy was endorsed to indicate that the subject of higher purchase would be payable by the bank. The complainant issued two cheques with the impression that the policy would be automatically renewed in the name of the complainant with hire purchase endorsement in favour of the bank. Car met with an accident resulting in damage of car and death of five occupants. Supreme Court (on appeal) held merely because owner of vehicle passed cheque for insurance premium on to bank along with monthly instalment of loan obtained to purchase a vehicle, liability arising out of accident to third party cannot be vested with the bank on ground due to failure of bank to pay premium amount. Owner would be liable to compensate third party victims because it is the obligation of the owner to take insurance policy.

In another case,[46] due to fault on the part of the customer she was not entitled to encash the certificate after seven years as that certificate was in the name of Indian Credit Investment Ltd. and not in her own name. The National Commission held that since the documents on record were made in the name of the company which alone was entitled to act in accordance with the resolution of the Board of Directors of the company so the bank was justified in refusing the encashment at the instance of the complainant (Respondent).

It is to be submitted that in respect of banking service Consumer Disputes Redressal Forum especially National Commission has made the distinction between discretionary

45. 1999 (3) CPR 60 (SC).
46. 1986-96 CONSUMER 2590 (NS).

functions of banks such as granting of loans raising of credit limits and matters relating to repayment, etc. and deficiency of service in respect of honouring of demand drafts and making payments without exercising due care and diligence. In the former type it has refused to intervene and in the later type it has granted relief.

(2) Building and Housing Service

Housing service was not included even by way of an example in the original definition of the term service. The definition was amended in 1993 under central Act so as to specifically include "housing construction." The question of law that arose for consideration before the Supreme Court in several appeals tagged together and reported as *Lucknow Development Authority* v. *M.K. Gupta*[47] was whether the statutory authorities such as Lucknow, Delhi and Bangalore Development Authorities constituted under the State Acts to carry on planned city development are amenable to the Consumer Protection Act, 1986 in respect of any act or omission relating to housing activity such as delay in delivery of possession of houses to allottees, non-completion within the stipulated time or defective or faulty construction, etc. In the instant case, the Lucknow Development Authority had undertaken a housing project and invited applications for that purpose. The complainant applied in the prescribed form for allotment of a flat for which he made entire payment. However, possession of the flat was not given to him for which State Commission directed the authority to hand over possession of the flat without delay. The authority instead of complying with the order approached the National Commission and raised the question of jurisdiction. Petition however, was dismissed and the complainants cross appeal was allowed and the authority was directed to pay him Rs. 10,000 as compensation for harassment, mental torture and agony. That order of the National Commission became the subject of appeal to the Supreme Court. Several questions of law arose for consideration of the apex court which were answered in affirmative. The court held—

47. 1993-94 Company Law Digest, Vol. 23.

(i) There is no reason to hold that the authorities carried by the statute are beyond the purview of the Consumer Protection Act.

(ii) If such authority undertakes to construct building or allot houses or building sites to citizens of the state either as amenity or as benefit then it amounts to 'rendering of service' and will be covered under the expression 'service made available to potential users'. Since housing activity is a service it was therefore covered in the clause it stood before amendment. The amendment only clarified the position and did not add something new.

(iii) The commission or the forums constituted under the Act are empowered to award not only the value of the goods or services but also to compensate a consumer for any injustices meted out to him.

The court further held that if the direction to pay damages or compensation is issued against the state then the department concerned should pay the amount to the complainant from the public fund immediately and thereafter recover the same from those officers found responsible for such unpardonable behaviour by dividing it proportionately where there are more than one functionaries. Consequently, the decision of this State Commission in this case was upheld. R.M. Sahai, J. analysed the definition of service in the following terms:

> ". . . The entire purpose of widening the definition is to include in it not only day-to-day buying or selling activity undertaken by a common man but even such activities which are otherwise not commercial in nature yet they partake of a character in which some benefit is conferred on the consumer. Construction of a house or flat is for the benefit of the person for whom it is constructed. He may do it himself or hire services of a builder or contractor. The latter being for consideration is service as defined in the Act. Similarly, when a

statuary authority develops land or allots a site or constructs a house for the benefit of the common man it is as much service as by a builder or contractor. The one is contractual service and other statuary service. If the service is defective or it is not what was represented then it would be unfair trade practice as defined in the Act. Any defect in construction activity would be denial of comfort and service to a consumer. When possession of property is not delivered within the stipulated period the delay so caused is denial of service. Such disputes or claims are not in respect of immovable property as argued but deficiency in rendering of service of a particular standard, quality or grade. Such deficiencies or omissions are defined in sub-clause (ii) of clause (r) of section 2 as unfair trade practice. If a builder of a house uses sub-standard material in construction of a building or makes false or misleading representation about the condition of the house then it is denial of the faculty or benefit of which a consumer is entitled to claim value under the Act. When the contractor or builder undertakes to erect a house or flat then it is inherent in it that he shall perform his obligation as agreed to. A flat with a leaking roof, or cracking wall or sub-standard floor is denial of service. Similarly, when a statuary authority undertakes to develop land and frame a housing scheme, it, while performing statuary duty, renders service to the society in general and individual in particular. The entire approach of the learned counsel for the development authority in emphasizing that power exercised under a statute could not be stretched to mean service proceeded on misconception. It is incorrect understanding of the statutory functions under a social legislation. A development authority while developing the land or framing a scheme for housing discharges statuary duty the purpose and objective of which is service to the citizens. As pointed out earlier the entire purpose of widening the definitions is to include in it not only day-to-day buying of goods by a common man but even such activities which are otherwise not commercial but professional or service-oriented in nature. The provisions in the Acts, namely Lucknow Development Act, Delhi Development Act or Bangalore Development Act clearly provide for preparing plan, development of land and framing of scheme, etc. Therefore, if such authority undertakes to construct building or allot houses or building sites to citizens of the state either as amenity or as benefit then it amounts to rendering of service and will be covered in the expression 'Service made available to potential users'. A person who applies for allotment of a building site or for a flat constructed by the development authority or enters into an agreement with a builder or a contractor is a potential user and nature of transaction is covered in the expression 'service of any description'. It further indicates that the definition is not exhaustive. The inclusive clause succeeded in widening its scope but not exhausting the services which could be covered in the earlier part. So any service except when it is free of charge or under a contract of personal service is included in it. Since housing activity is a service it was covered in the clause as it stood before 1993."[48]

Thus in view of the Supreme Court's observation "Housing" would be a service within the meaning of the Act. This was the right interpretation borne out by the fact that the definition was amended and it now specifically includes "Housing Construction." Now large proportion of consumer disputes before Consumer Disputes Redressal Agencies are in connection with building and housing service. For a comprehensive study they are enumerated as follows.

(a) Deficiency in Service

A construction contract is a contract of services within the meaning of the Act and therefore user of service is a consumer. The failure to provide the building according to the contractual requirements is a consumer wrong amenable

48. 1993-94 Company Law Digest, Vol. 23.

to the remedies under the Act. In *Rajnish Chander Sharda* v. *Haryana Urban Development Authority*[49] the complainant was allotted plot but when he asked for possession of the said plot it was discovered that a factory existed on the plot. Then he was allotted other plot and when he asked for the actual possession again it was discovered that the plot belonged to another man. National Commission found Haryana Urban Development Authority guilty of gross deficiency in service towards the complainant beginning from 1979 to 1993 and held that it is amazing that Haryana Urban Development Authority made allotment of plots whose actual physical possession could not be given either because there was a factory or because the land was already in the possession of another party and the area was totally undeveloped. Consequently, the complainant was entitled to multiple reliefs. If 'the attitude of the builder is far from satisfactory in the transaction it is patently gross deficiency in service'.[50] In *M.D. Bhoopathy & Others* v. *Mrs. Sarada & Another*[51] the builders agreed to construct apartment building and pent houses but they could not honour the agreement and failed to put up the pent house. In the facts and circumstances of the case it was held that failure to build pent house amounted negligence and deficiency of service.

The National Commission has held that since the amendment of 1993 and the addition of clause (e) to section 14(1) a direction can be issued under the Act that the deficiency in service be rectified.[52] In *Yammuna Vihar Residents Welfare Association* v. *Vice-Chairman, Delhi Development Authority & Others*[53] the gist of the grievance put forward was that several of amenities which were originally promised to be provided in the colony relating to drainage facilities and

49. 1986-96 CONSUMER 3139 (NS).

50. Capt. C.P. Gupta *v.* Joint Secretary, Department of Local Government of Punjab and Another, 1986-96, CONSUMER 2357 (NS).

51. 1986-96 CONSUMER 2952 (NS).

52. Garden Estate Resident Welfare Association *v.* M/s Gulmohar Estate Ltd. (1997) 1 CPR 45, it was held non-execution of sale deed to the residents of colony of flats in terms of agreement is a deficiency in service and the opposite parties were directed to draft the sale deed.

53. 1986-96 CONSUMER 1731 (NS).

maintenance of proper hygienic condition environmental purity have not been kept up by the Delhi Development Authority and later by the Municipal Corporation of Delhi. Delhi Development Authority was directed to discharge their obligation by making available to the Municipal Corporation of Delhi necessary funds in respect of the deficiencies for the rectification of which responsibility was on the Delhi Development Authority prior to the date of transfer of the colony to the Municipal Corporation of Delhi.

However, no action will lie for doing of a thing which is beyond one's obligation. In *Arihant Corporation* v. *Umed Park Ghatlodie Co-operative Housing Society Ltd.*[54] the facts as gathered from the record are that the organizer offered a scheme to the members of the public wherein a representation was made that houses would be construed in accordance with the terms and conditions of Ahmedabad Urban Development Authority (AUDA) and all essential amenities such as water supply, soak-wells for discharge or drainage and electricity would be provided as per the regulation of Ahmedabad Urban Development Authority. However, only two soak-wells were provided. National Commission held two soak-wells to 164 tenements were sufficient for their needs. Further, since the management was handed over to the cooperative society it was their responsibility to clean the soak-wells. It was not the perpetual duty of the organizers to maintain the soak-wells.

Where the complainant never paid the amount due as shown in the allotment letter nor the future instalments the action of the building company to cancel the allotment cannot be said arbitrarily and *mala-fide*.[55] But where the complainant has suffered mental agony as huge amount borrowed by him from different agencies was lying blocked with the board and he was not getting any benefit from the deposits it is common knowledge that the prices of real estate are rising and the complainant cannot get a house at the amount deposited by him he would be entitled to claim deficiency in

54. 1986-96 CONSUMER 2278 (NS).
55. Mohan Kumar *v.* M/s Ansal Housing Finance and Leasing Company Ltd., 1986-95 CONSUMER 957 (NS).

service.[56] There are various complaints about deficient services claiming provider of services has thrust upon the consumer a plot/flat of less area than the one for which the consumer had paid the price. In *Mohammad Ibrahim Mulla* v. *Hamid Abubkar Memon and Another*[57] the case as set up in the complaint was that the complainant had purchased a flat from the builder. As per terms and conditions of the agreement the built up area including the Balcony should have been 715 sq. ft. However, after taking possession of the flat complainant found area of the flat less than agreed one by 48 sq. ft. Before National Commission the builder produced building rules and bye-laws of the Municipal Corporation which show that the area covered by stair case of any sort shall be considered as built up area. The commission held though the building rules and bye-laws are not much relevant for the purpose of disposal of this petition but it shows that the stair case was considered as built area while the plan was sanctioned by the corporation. Accordingly builder was not held liable for any deficiency in rendering of service.

In another case of similar nature namely, *Tulip Park Co-operative Housing Society Ltd.* v. *M/s Sai Overseas Import & Export*[58] the complainant, a co-operative housing society, had complained shortfall in services rendered by the builder and developer, which had agreed to construct and sell 64 flats to the complainant in a building. The complainant alleged that while under the agreement the builder had agreed to construct the flats having total saleable area measuring 34,361 sq. ft. but the saleable area actually measured comes to 29,788.34 sq. ft. For 4,572.66 complainants claimed refund of money. After considering the fact that the building was constructed as per the sanctioned plan and each flat has the area as given in the agreement and the complainant had agreed not to raise any dispute regarding saleable area, particularly when permitted area of construction was to the

56. S.P. Dhavarkar *v.* The Housing Commissioner, Karnataka Housing Board, 1986-96 CONSUMER 2867 (NS).
57. 1986-96 CONSUMER 2878 (NS).
58. 1993 (3) CPR 50.

extent of 34361 sq. ft. The Supreme Court held there was no deficiency in service in housing construction provided by the builder.

In *Srichand K. Bajaj* v. *S.M.N. Consumer Protection Council & Another*[59] also like the above case, no deficiency was proved. In this case the original plan envisaged car parking area intended for the use of the flat owners. However, towards the end of the construction, the builder converted seven car parking spaces into a ground floor apartment. According to the complainants all these were deviations from the approved plan and were unauthorized. The National Commission held that the complainant has not taken any step to get produced the approved plan from the builder to show that there was any violation about providing the parking spaces. Since only four allottees of the flats opted for garages and thus seven garages were not constructed and the space meant for those seven garages has been utilized as stated earlier by the builder amounts no deficiency.

However, a construction contract cannot be construed unfairly and arbitrarily so as to deny the basic facilities which are otherwise to be there. In *Lt. Col. Yogesh (Retd.)* v. *Hyderabad Urban Development Authorities*[60] the complainant was allotted a plot by Hyderabad Urban Development Authority for which he made full payment within time prescribed by the Hyderabad Urban Development Authority. He later inspected the plot and found that it was full of rocks and boulders. So he requested the Hyderabad Urban Development Authority to get the plot cleared and leveled before handing over to him or in the alternative he may be allotted another developed plot in lieu. Haryana Urban Development Authority invited the attention of the complainant to clause 15 of the conditions of the sale that the said prospectus of a

59. 1986-96 CONSUMER 2565 (NS); Another case titled S. Satyamoorthi and Another *v.* The Member Secretary, M.M.D.A., Madras and Others, 1986-96 CONSUMER (2560) (NS) was decided on similar way. Here National Commission held the layout plans were sanctioned and revised in exercise of the powers of statutory duty and there was no deficiency in service at all in exercise of statutory duty by the M.M.D.A. in sanctioning the building plans.

60. 1986-96 CONSUMER 2740 (NS).

developed residential site with basic amenities like roads, drainage, water supply and street lighting, etc. As is where is in the context in which it has been used in the brochure prefers to the length and breadth of the sizes of the plots which may vary according to the site situation or the frontage of the plots may be more in one case and less in the other case or one plot may be having an opening on the main road or the other on a main street. 'It is also deficiency in service where there is failure to deliver possession of allotted plot due to unauthorized encroachment on land and order to allot alternative plot suffers no illegality'.[61] 'Where Housing Board made refund of earnest amount to unsuccessful applicants within reasonable period of draw of lots there is in no way deficiency in service'.[62] Similarly, where the possession of the house was handed over to a person other than the one who had paid for the same, remedy by way of interest on the deposit amount was allowed.[63] Where the complainant purchased the plot in an open auction in 1983 and the plot was provided to him two years later in 1985 and that too with encroaches on it and the vacant possession was granted to him in 1991, he was allowed compensation amount of one lac rupees with interest at 18% on the amount deposited.[64]

(b) Liability where there is Delay

A housing organization providing plots and in some cases construction is required to provide the same within the stipulated time or where no time is given within a reasonable time ordinarily possession should be given within a month after full payment and in some cases it is remarked that there can be normal fluctuations of three months in the tentatively stipulated period in the completion of the houses. However, more often it depends on the facts and circumstances of each case. In *Delhi Development Authority* v. *Anoop Kumar*[65] the

61. HUDA *v.* Smt. Usha Leekha, 1999 (2) CPR 32 (National Commission).
62. Haryana Urban Development Authority *v.* Smt. Veena Kappar, 1997 (2) CPR 257 (National Commission).
63. S.K. Singhal *v.* Ghaziabad Development Authority, (1995) 1 CPJ 118 (National Commission).
64. R. Sivasubramaniyam *v.* T.N. Housing Board, (1995) 1 CPJ 396.
65. 1999 (2) CPR 24 (National Commission).

complainant had deposited money as registration money for a flat in the year 1979. He applied for change of locality in 1984. As no action has taken place despite reminders he wrote a letter in 1987 requesting the Delhi Development Authority to ignore his request for change of locality and allot him a flat but it was not allotted to him. The National Commission held long delay of five years in rejecting request of an allottee for change of locality and then non-inclusion of his name in subsequent draws amounts to deficiency in service.

'Where the possession of the flat is not delivered within the stipulated period the delay so caused is denial of justice'.[66] *In M/s Pushpa Builders Ltd. & Another* v. *L.R. Kapoor & Others*[67] the builder had undertaken to construct and provide flats to the complainants and notwithstanding the gaps of more than five years after 50% of the cost price had been deposited even the construction of the flats has not so far been commenced by the builder the National Commission held that the state commission could have with full justification, avoided compensation in addition to the amount of interest in favour of the complainant but it refrained from doing so and has only erred in favour of the builder by directing him only to refund the amount received by him by way of price of the flat with interest at 18% p.a. from the date of payment of the amount. Non-cooperative attitude adopted by the builder despite continuous and repeated contacts and communications to deliver possession amounts to deficiency in service.[68] As against this 'delay due to administrative exigencies and not on account of any *mala fide* action of any individual authority/builder does not amount to deficiency in service. A statutory authority is expected to perform its duties as expeditiously as possible and to take the

66. Dr. Ramesh Chander Ramniklal Shah and Smt. Ila Rameshchandra Shah *v.* M/s Lata Construction and Others, 1986-96 CONSUMER 2997 (NS).
67. 1986-96 CONSUMER 1549 (NS).
68. M.P. Bhaya *v.* Mrs. Malti Yogesh Karia, 1986-96 CONSUMER 2314 (NS); Wg. Comd. R.J Darukhanawala *v.* Manjith Singh, Representative of M/s Man Jog Builders, 1986-96 CONSUMER 2117 (NS).

action quickly'.[69] However, default, unjustifiable delay and harassment in the light of the facts and circumstances of the case is in no way excusable. In *Bihar State Housing Board & Others* v. *Prio Ranjan Roy*,[70] complainant was allotted house under LIG housing scheme but possession of the allotted house was not given to him and instead, it was allotted to else one. Under another order other house was allotted to him but it was in a most dilapidated condition which was not acceptable to the complainant. National Commission awarded compensation of Rs. 7 lacs along with refund of the amount deposited for allotment of the house to complainant. Supreme Court while accepting the agreement that the builder was negligent remanded the matter to National Commission for going into the aspect of compensation afresh.

The court held where damages are awarded there must be an assessment thereof and the order awarding damages must contain an indication of the basis upon which the amount awarded is arrived at in somewhat similar case *Bhagyashri A. Lohit* v. *Harivijay Builders*[71] a builder undertook to provide land and constructed bungalow. However, he let it out not to the complainant but to a tenant. He was directed to refund the whole of the money received from the client with interest at 12% from the date of payment till the date of refund and rupees 2,00,000 by way of loss caused to the client. In a large number of cases relating to housing construction National Commission on being convinced that there has been gross deficiency of service on the part of the builder directed the builder to pay compensation to complainants for mental agony and disappointment suffered by them in indefinitely waiting and not getting the flat.[72]

69. Haryana Urban Development Authority *v.* Smt. Nalini Aggarwal, 1997 (2) CPR 315 (SC).

70. (1997) 6 SCC 487.

71. 1993 CLJ 138 Maha.

72. Manoha B. Ghosalkar and Another *v.* Trimurti Associates, 1986-96 CONSUMER 2206 (NS); Smt. Govida Khurana and Another *v.* M/s Satiya Apartments (P) Ltd. and Others, 1986-96 CONSUMER 2109 (NS); M.M Singh and another *v.* Charanjit Kochhar Proprietor, M/s Charan Jit Kochhar Engineers and Contractors and Another, 1986-96 CONSUMER 2527 (NS).

Similarly, in *Rajasthan Housing Board* v. *R.C. Bhandari*[73] and *Harbans Singh* v. *Lucknow Development Authority*[74] there was delay in constructing and delivering possession. Interest at the rate of 6% and 15% was allowed respectively for the period covered by the delay.

As already said—what amounts to delay can be said in the particular facts and circumstances of the case. However, a reasonable delay is always permissible. In *Sarthak Behuria & Another* v. *The Orissa State Housing Board & Another*,[75] the grievance of the complainant was that there was unreasonable delay in construction of houses. National Commission found that the delay period of one year and three months cannot be said to be unreasonable delay in completion of such a big project. 'Where the delay in the completion of the flat has not been conclusively established the builder cannot be held liable'.[76] Similarly, 'where delay in handing over the possession of the flat was due to non-availability of water and electricity the responsibility for the delay caused by the Electricity and Water Supply Authorities cannot justifiably be placed on the housing board as these authorities are independent of the board'.[77]

Where house allottees suffered because of delay which was not due to helplessness they were entitled to compensation but where delay is due to the circumstances beyond the control of the builder no compensation is allowable.[78] The Supreme Court did not allow compensation or interest where delay in handing over possession of the plots to the allottees was caused due to interim orders of the court obtained by the landowners. It was averred in the

73. 1997 (1) CPR 61.
74. (1994) 1 CPR 98.
75. 1986-95 CONSUMER 510 (NS). Further in this case complainant failed to prove that there were any major defects in the house which required rectification or the cost of rectification.
76. 1986-95 CONSUMER 651 (NS).
77. 1986-96 CONSUMER 2764 (NS).
78. Gujarat Housing Board *v.* Akhil Bhartiya Grahak Panchayat (1996) 1 CPJ 103 (National Commission); Magtham Investment Ltd. and Others *v.* Super Construction Company Pvt. Ltd., 1986-96 CONSUMER 3065 (NS)

petition in *Ghaziabad Development Authority* v. *Sanchar Vihar Sahkari Avas Samiti Ltd.*[79] that the Ghaziabad Development Authority has violated the terms and conditions in as much it failed to put them in possession of the plots within the stipulated period. It was further complained that the authority has charged interest and penal interest for delayed payment of instalments. The Supreme Court held the view of National Commission that the interest cannot be charged from those who have applied for the plots under Self-Financing Scheme is an erroneous interpretation of the brochure. The entire brochure is required to be read as a whole as it relates to various schemes of housing to the eligible persons. A person who agrees on the basis of a brochure and goes ahead with acceptance and payments becomes bound by its terms by acquiescence and estoppel and cannot afterwards say that in a self-financing scheme no interest should be chargeable on balance instalments. Coming to the other point court was of the opinion that the National Commission has made no mistake in refusing interest or damages for delayed possession because delay was due to land acquisition proceedings and because of the interim orders obtained by the land owners.

(c) Imperfections or Use of Sub-Standard Material

Where the Housing Board uses a poor quality of material for construction or the construction work carried out by the builder is full of defects, imperfections and shortcoming in the quality of construction and is woefully deficient and inadequate in the quality, nature and manner of performance that was promised by the builder will amount to deficiency in service under the Act. In *Pushpa Builders Flat Buyers Association* v. *Pushpa Builders Ltd. & Others,*[80] the complainant proceeded against builders on the allegation that

79. AIR 1995 Supreme Court 2021.

80. 1986-96 CONSUMER 2402 (NS). In V.L Bhanu Kumar *v.* Dega Sundara Rama Reddy and Others, 1986-96 CONSUMER 1880 (NS) also National Commission held incomplete work in the construction of the flat amounts deficiency in service as well as imperfection in the service rendered.

none of the flats offered are complete or in a habitual condition. Accepting the report of the expert into the commission hold that the builder has been miserably failed in providing services to the complainant. Accordingly, the builder was directed to refund the amounts paid by the ten members of the association along with interest at the rate of 18% p.a.

Similarly, in *Welfare Association Brij Vihar, Ghaziabad* v. *Vice-Chairman, Ghaziabad Development Authority*,[81] the complainants for allotment of houses/flats under the scheme paid full amount in four half year instalments in a period of two years. In accordance with the terms of the scheme, the houses were to be completed within two years of the deposit but possession of the said houses/flats was given after one year's delay and infra-structural works necessary for the habitation and enjoyment of the houses/flats were not provided.

The commission held that no doubt there has been more than one year's delay on the part of the builder in completing and allotting the houses/flats however, such delay in construction are usual in this country and in any case it cannot be said that one year's delay in completion of construction is abnormal and that such delay can be deemed to be deficiency in service on the part of the Ghaziabad Development Authority. However, Ghaziabad Development Authority was held liable for making allotment of the flats before the infra-structural works were completed and that there were numerous defects in the houses constructed of which the allottees were forced to take possession on the threat of cancellation.

Once it is found by the Consumer Fora that there is deficiency in service on the part of housing board then its duty is to adequately compensate the consumer.[82] A failure to provide infrastructural facilities no doubt amounts to deficiency in housing service because without them the house cannot be beneficially enjoyed but at the same time if he fails

81. 1986-96 CONSUMER 3106 (NS).
82. Birja Shankeracharya *v.* Orissa State Housing Board, 1997 (1) CPR 124.

to prove that there is any defect in the flat allotted to him and those defects required remedial measures, the complainant cannot be entitled to deficiency in service.[83] In *Anuradha Builders & Others* v. *Ranjit Prasad & Another*[84] the complainants had occupied two flats but in which lifts were not installed by the Co-operative Housing Society. National Commission held on account of non-installation of the lift the flats are rendered unfit for occupation by persons of advanced age as is the case with the complainant but since the two flats had been in occupation of complainants for a long period it would not be proper or just to direct the Co-operative Housing Society to pay interest on the amount of purchase price of the flats paid which has been directed to be refunded by state commission.

In *The General Consumer Protection & Welfare Association & Others* v. *Ghaziabad Development Authority & Another*[85] the complaints of the complainants were:

(i) An increase in the cost of each house which has been described as arbitrary, exorbitant and illegal.
(ii) Inordinate delay in the construction and handing over of the possession of the houses in a habitual condition.
(iii) Construction of sub-standard houses and use of sub-standard materials.

After going through the evidence which disclosed considerable delay in the completion and allotment of houses, the delivery of possession made conditional on the payment of additional prices which amounts to unfair trade practice and the evidence regarding use of sub-standard materials in the houses under construction also remained unrebutted the National Commission held that Ghaziabad Development Authority has been deficient in rendering service in respect of housing construction and with the result appropriate relief's were granted.

---

83. 1986-96 CONSUMER 3113 (NS).
84. 1986-96 CONSUMER 3214 (NS).
85. 1986-96 CONSUMER 24 59 (NS).

Holding Ghaziabad Development Authority liable in another case[86] also National Commission held houses as constructed suffered from series of defects. Sub-standard materials and fixtures and fittings leading to percolation/ seepage of water from upper floors to lower floors. It is self-evident that these deficiencies were of very serious nature.

(d) Escalation of Construction Prices

Pricing of services is one of the factors over which consumer forums cannot play much role. The prices of land, building materials, labour charges, cost of transportation, the quality and availability of land, supervision and management charges are all factors of variable nature and they play their role in the working out of the price. Pricing is not a factor which falls within the purview of Consumer Redressal Forum.[87] In *Manohar Lal Sharma* v. *Delhi Development Authority & Another*[88] the grievance put forward by the complainant relates to the question of pricing of a flat allotted to a person by Delhi Development Authority. National Commission held the question of pricing cannot be gone into by the consumer forums. Since the prices of the flats are not fixed by any law and that even if any excess charge has been collected by way of price that will not constitute a ground for contending that there is a 'deficiency' in service on the part of the builder.

Those rendering house-building services have been allowed to increase charges equal to the amount of costs escalations provided there has been no delay on their own part in which case escalation during the period of delay may not be allowed. In *Smt. K. Saksena & Another* v. *Ghaziabad Development Authority & Another*[89] the main dispute between

86. Sanjay Nagar Residents Welfare Association *v.* The Vice-Chairman, Ghaziabad Authority, 1986-96 CONSUMER 2500 (NS).
87. *Supra* Note 18, p. 159; Seen also The Gujarat Housing Board *v.* Akhil Bhartiya Grahak Panchayat and Others, 1986-96 CONSUMER 2980 (NS)
88. 1986-96 CONSUMER 1016 (NS). In the Chairman and Managing Director, Tamil Nadu Housing Board and Another *v.* R. Venkataraman 1986-96 CONSUMER 2609 (NS) and Ramlal *v.* Chairman, Ghaziabad Development Authority and Another, 1986-96 CONSUMER 3157 (NS) the same view has been reiterated.
89. 1986-96 CONSUMER 2848 (NS).

the parties is about the price of plot. The complainant has deposited full price in lump sum for a particular plot. Infact, Ghaziabad Development Authority was not in a position to deliver the possession of that plot to her as big water tank of Irrigation Department was situated on the plot. Ghaziabad Development Authority allotted another plot and was asked to pay over and above the amount already deposited by her. In the light of the facts and circumstances of the case Ghaziabad Development Authority was found clearly deficient in rendering service and was directed to allot one plot to the complainant at the agreed rate and pay rupees 20,000 to her as compensation and she was given an option that if she could not accept the above proposal she will be entitled to the refund of the amount deposited by her with interest at the rate of 18% p.a. and she was entitled to compensation of Rs. one lakh.

Earlier in *The Gujarat Housing Board* v. *Akhin Bhartiya Grahak Panchayat & Others,*[90] National Commission while entitling complainants to compensation for delay in the construction and for the lesser area given to them held so far as the question of pricing is concerned it was held that it is the consistent view of this commission that Fora constituted under the Consumer Protection Act have no jurisdiction to go into the question of pricing of houses and plots.

In *DRS-87 Applicant's Association* v. *City Industrial Development Copn. of Maharashtra Ltd.*[91] the grievance of the complainant was two-fold. The first grievance was that there was delay in the construction of the houses and the second one is regarding escalation in the prices of the houses and some other charges said to have been levied by the C.I.D. Co. It was found by the National Commission that the delay occurred was caused due to the circumstances beyond its control and not due to its negligence. Regarding second grievance it was held that the quantum of consideration is not relevant in relation to services as had been defined under clause (g) of section 2(1) of the Act. The dispute about pricing

90. 1986-96 CONSUMER 2980 (NS).
91. 1986-96 CONSUMER 3088 (NS).

of a flat or a plot does not fall within the purview of the Consumer Protection Act and further the question of price is only relevant when the goods are purchased from a trader and the price charged is in excess of what has been fixed by any law or declared on the package.

However, in a number of cases[92] while relying on the judgment of the Supreme Court in the case of *Lucknow Development Authority* v. *M.K. Gupta*[93] in which it was ruled that once a plot or house is sold by any statutory authority and its possession is not delivered within the reasonable time it amounts to deficiency in service and also unfair trade practice. National Commission held where price of the flat raised about five times of the original price and where it was agreed upon earlier that no escalation charges were payable but inspite of its escalation charges were claimed from complainant is a deficiency in service.

From the above cases decided by the apex commission and the apex court it is observed that a person who applies for allotment of a building site or for a flat constructed by the development authority are enters into an agreement with a builder or contractor is a potential user and nature of transaction is covered in the expression 'service of any description' under section 2(1)(o) of the Consumer Protection Act. A government or semi-government body or local authority is as much amenable to the Consumer Protection Act as any other private body rendering similar services. The argument that the applicability of the Consumer Protection Act is confined to movable goods only a complaint filed for any defect in relation to immovable property such as house or building or allotment of sight could not be entertained by the Consumer Disputes Redressal Agencies is rejected by the Supreme Court in the following words:

> "When possession of property is not delivered within stipulated period the delay so caused is denial of

92. Ajay Khana *v.* Omega Commercial Pvt. Ltd. and Another, 1986-96 CONSUMER 2504 (NS); Jatinderdev Singh Masafir *v.* Ludhiana Improvement Trust, 1997 (1) CPR 137.
93. *Supra* Note 47.

> service. Such claims or disputes are not in respect of immovable property as argued but deficiency in rendering of service of particular house uses sub-standard material construction of a building or makes false or misleading representation about the condition of the house then it is denial of the facility or benefit of which a consumer is entitled to claim under the Consumer Protection Act."

(3) Courier Service

Courier service has been started by private operators. Though this service is expensive but at the same time it is efficient and there is a general acceptance that couriers would deliver parcels within 24 hours or at the most within two days. The essence of this service is safety and timely delivery of the package to the right person. This is borne out by the fact that the charges for this kind of service are several times more than ordinary mode of carriage.[94] But there is flood of cases before Consumer Disputes Redressal Agencies complaining loss of consignment or delay in delivering articles by couriers. Couriers in turn have objection that their liability should not be exceeded beyond the terms and conditions as contained in the courier consignment note. To our surprise couriers have usually limited their liability to a maximum of Rs. 100. Is this amount when awarded as compensation sufficient to redress consumer grievance when there is a clear case of gross negligence. Callous indifference and sheer dereliction of duty on the part of the courier in transporting or sending a consignment is question which is to be answered by a variety of cases.

In *M/s Skypak Couriers Pvt. Ltd.* v. *Consumer Education & Research Society & Others,*[95] there was loss of consignment containing passport visas, air ticket, degree certificate, etc. which were absolutely necessary for travel to one Mr. Khan. National Commission while holding courier liable for deficiency in the rendering of service held that it was obligatory on the part of the consignor to have disclosed the

94. D.N. Saraf 'ASIL', 1993, p. 64.
95. 1986-96 CONSUMER 1788 (NS).

contents of the packet and when it was not done the contention that they were lost by the courier cannot be supported. Relying on the above decision various cases have been decided on the same qua. In *M/s Air Pak Couriers (India) Pvt. Ltd.* v. *S. Suresh,*[96] complainant sent a consignment of papers described as "Important" which includes performance report and agreement letter from Jaipur to be transported and delivered to the complainant at Madras. The consignment did not reach the complainant. National Commission held complainant did not disclose in the consignment note the value of the documents sent by him through the courier, nor did he insure or indicate what was the nature of the documents. So the compensation of Rs. 1,00,000 awarded by State Commission was reduced to Rs. 100 as specified in the courier's rules. Where a packet containing some official record was delivered by the manager of the corporation to the courier company for delivery at the former's head office packet contained certain original records pertaining to the disciplinary proceedings and was not delivered. Complainant alleged the impossibility of rebuilding the records. The National Commission agreed with the findings of the state commission that the loss of the packet by the courier company amounts negligence and that there was deficiency of service on the part of the company. However, the commission was of the view that it was the responsibility of the complainant corporation to have arranged to keep a copy of the same with that office before parting with them and reduced the compensation of Rs. 1000 awarded by State Commission to Rs. 100 only.[97] Another decision against a courier has made it clear that unless the value of the consignment is made known before entrustment to the courier, he cannot be saddled with the liability for the actual value of the consignment.[98]

Above decisions are consistent with the view expressed by Supreme Court in *Bharati Knitting Co.* v. *D.H.L. Worldwide*

---

96. 1986-96 CONSUMR 3080 (NS).
97. Consumer Protection Council Tamil Nadu and Another *v.* M/s Indu Couriers Pvt. Ltd., 1986-96 CONSUMER 2925 (NS).
98. M/s Sky Pak Couriers Pvt. Ltd. *v.* M/s Loyal Machine Works Ltd., Coimbatore, 1986-96 CONSUMER 2957 (NS).

Express Courier Divn. of Air Freight Ltd.[99] wherein the complainant had consigned certain goods. The documents in relation thereto were sent in a cover. The cover did not reach the destination. Consequently, though duplicate copies were subsequently sent the season was over (summer season for which the manufacturer sent goods to the buyer) and consequently consignee paid less than the agreed price. The complainant demanded compensation for the difference of the loss incurred. Supreme Court (on appeal) held that on facts the National Commission was right in limiting the liability to the extent undertaken by the contract entered into by the parties and in awarding the amount for deficiency in service to that extent. The above decision has been followed in *Air Pak International Pvt. Ltd.* v. *K.P. Nanu & Another.*[100] Here the complainant booked the consignment of the ashes with the courier for carriage. The consignment never reached the consignee. According to the complainant the mortal remains of his wife are priceless but as the loss of the ashes caused mental agony and pain to the complainant he claimed a compensation of Rs. 50,000 for the loss. Applying the above decision the apex court restricted the award of compensation for the deficiency in service to Rs. 100 only in consonance with the terms and conditions of the consignment.

It is to be submitted here that the essence of this mode of carriage is safety and timely delivery of the package to the right person. This is borne out of the fact that the charges for this kind of service are several times more than the ordinary mode of carriage. In these circumstances it is expected that a good sense will prevail over our high esteemed judges to consider the quantum of compensation in the light of loss incurred in due spirit to the Consumer Protection Act.

(4) Educational Service

Role of educational service in our society is dynamic and not limited to the field of study only—that is its one aspect. In its institutional framework it is entrusted with the task of giving admission to different courses, conducting or

---

99. 1986-96 CONSUMER 2428 (NS).
100. (1997) 1 CPR 15.

holding examinations, issuing certificates or marks sheets which is purely administrative in nature and is performed by both teaching and non-teaching staff. This service require payment of prescribed fee more or less by the students or candidates (unless specified as free) and is provided by private, government or autonomous bodies. Days have gone when education was treated as mission. Like doctors teachers too are busy in private practice. They are opening academic/coaching centers for different courses where they are charging heavy tuition fee. No doubt still this profession is regarded as noble but where an employee of the educational department (board or university, etc.) commits any mistake which ruins or adversely affects the carrier of a student—Does this amount negligence or deficiency of a service? Education Act provides that no suit, prosecution or other legal proceeding shall lie against the government, any authority or any officer in respect of any thing which is in good faith done or intended to be done under any provisions of this Act or the rules framed thereunder. It is true only to the extent an institution or officer is within its/his authority under the Act. There is no guidance or remedy for deficient or negligent service under the said Act. So in order to understand, analyze, and answer the question whether 'Educational Service' is service within the meaning of Consumer Protection Act it becomes necessary to have a passing review of various cases on the point decided under the Consumer Protection Act.

The question whether a candidate for examination is a consumer came up for consideration in *Kumari Seema Bhatia* v. *Registrar, Rajasthan University*[101] where the National Commission upheld the view expressed by the State Commission in conducting the revaluation of the answer papers of a candidate who had appeared for an examination held by the university, the university was not rendering any service as defined in the Act for consideration nor there was any arrangement of hiring of service for consideration as contemplated by the Act. The question again camp up for

101. Order dated 12-04-1993 (National Commission) quoted 1986-96 CONSUMER 1916.

consideration before the National Commission in *Joint Secretary, Gujarat Secondary Education Board* v. *Bharat Narcottam Thakkar,*[102] where the above view was reiterated that in conducting the secondary school board examinations, evaluating answer papers, announcing the results thereof and thereafter conducting a re-checking of the marks of any candidate on application made by the concerned candidate, the board is not performing any service for hire and there is no arrangement of hiring of service involved in such a situation as is contemplated by section 2(1)(o) of the Act. The same view was reiterated in *Registrar, University of Board* v. *Mumbai Grahak Panchayat, Bombay.*[103]

In some other cases similar view has been expressed. In *Staff Selection Commission* v. *Smt. P. Lalita,*[104] the candidate did not received hall ticket necessary to enable her to appear the selection test and with the result she made complaint before the forum. Both the lower courts accepted the plea of the complainant that is direction to the staff selection commission to hold a fresh examination. National Commission held the issuance of a direction to Staff Selection Commission to hold a fresh examination for testing the suitability of the complainant for her being selected to the particular category of post was outside the scope of clauses (a) to (d) of section 14(1) of the Consumer Protection Act.

However, in *Akhil Bhartiya Grahak Panchayat & Another* v. *Secretary, Sharada Bhavan Education Society & Others*[105] a compensation of rupees 40,000 was allowed for unfair trade practice adopted by a private college. In this case two students were admitted to the college who passed the final examination and completed their practical training but could

102. *Ibid.* This view was followed in Maharashtra Board of Secondary Education *v.* Chairman Grahak Jagrutisangh (1994) II CPJ 1; Secretary, Board of Intermediate Education *v.* M. Suresh and Another–II (1995) CPJ 167; P.M. Noushaud and Another *v.* University of Kerala and Others–II (1995) CPJ 334 (by Maharashtra, Andhra Pardesh, Kerala and Delhi State Commissions respectively) and in other cases.
103. 1986-96 CONSUMER 1917 (NS).
104. 1986-95 CONSUMER 404 (NS).
105. 1986-95 CONSUMER 579 (NS).

not obtain registration after having qualified in the D. Pharmacy course due to the fact that this pharmacy college had admitted two students in excess of (30) the authorized maximum number of admissions in violation of the provisions of the Pharmacy Act and the rules made thereunder. The National Commission therefore, held that the facts establish clearly that there was unfair trade practice as well as deficiency in service on the part of the college authorities towards the students who were deliberately admitted to the course. Except this case there may be hardly any case where National Commission may have put the liability on educational authority. The view expressed in *Registrar, University of Bombay*[106] has been reiterated in other cases. In *Datapro Information Technology* v. *Rajinder Singh Saluja*[107] the complainant-student appeared for written paper, however, the date of viva examination was not communicated to him by the institute. National Commission held that there has been no deficiency on the part of the institute as it had displayed duly the circular of the education board on the notice board indicating the dates of the written and oral examination. There was no legal obligation on him to communicate the dates of viva examination to each student.

The decision given in *Shri Ramdrobaba Engineering College* v. *Sushant Yuvraj Rode & Another*[108] meets the same fate. Here the student obtained provisional admission to the Ist year of engineering for which he paid admission fee and security deposit. Thereafter the student secured admission in another college. In consequence, he requested the Engineering College to refund the fee and the security deposit paid by him. While the college was prepared to refund the caution money it was not agreeable to refund the admission fee on the ground that under the orders of the government of Maharashtra where a student leaves the institution and applies for refund of the fees after 30 days from the date of admission no fee is to be refunded. National Commission held that complainant student withdrew from the college to

---

106. *Supra* Note 87, pp. 136-37.
107. 1986-95 CONSUMER 658 (NS).
108. 1986-95 CONSUMER 1364 (NS).

join another institute voluntarily and as such there was no deficiency in service on the part of the institute. An interesting case on the point is also *Manisha Samal* v. *Sambalpur University and others*[109] where identical roll numbers were assigned to the complainant and two other students by the Sambalpur University for examinations. The final result was withheld by the university due to the non-clearance of the back paper but she apprehended that the marks awarded to her had been exchanged with those two other students who were given the same roll numbers erroneously. However, the university submitted a letter addressed to it by the Principal, Government College that the two other students with the same roll numbers did not appear in the examination. In view of this National Commission held that her apprehension that the marks she secured in examination papers had been awarded to other two students who had been assigned the identical roll number, in the examination is not true.

Recently in couple of cases National Commission by minority view held that a candidate who appears for the examination can be regarded as person who had hired or availed of the services of the university or board for consideration. In *Chairman, Board of Examinations, Madras* v. *Mohideen Kader*[110] the complainant was a student of the diploma course in electrical engineering. He went to the examination hall and the hall Supervisor told that the code number of that examination paper was (1) while the complainants hall ticket gave the number as (2) and that he was not eligible to write the examination. On subsequent verification, however, it was found that the code number for that paper was only (2) and it had been correctly entered in the hall ticket. It was the complainants case that the Invigilator had committed the mistake for which the board

---

109. 1994 Suppl. CONSUMER 1477 (NS).

110. 1886-96 CONSUMER 1911 (NS). The view expressed by Supreme Court in Bangalore Water Supply *v.* A. Rajappa and Others, A.I.R 1978 SC 548 is noteworthy to be mentioned here—"Education can be and is in its institutional form an Industry as defined in Section 2(i) of the Industrial Disputes Act."

was vicariously liable for the negligence. Both District Forum and State Commission allowed the complaint. National Commission by majority view held:

> "Whether a University or an institution affiliated to it imparting education is within the arena of consumer jurisdiction is a question which this commission will consider and decide when it directly arises before it. What this commission had decided in earlier cases is that a University or Board in conducting public examinations, evaluating answer papers, announcing the results thereof and thereafter conducting rechecking of the marks of any candidate on the application made by the concerned candidate is not performing any service for hire and there is no arrangement of hiring of any service involved in such a situation as contemplated by section 2(1)(o) of the Act. A candidate who appears for the examination cannot be regarded as person who had hired or availed of the services of the university or board for consideration."

However, the minority view given by Dr. (Mrs. R. Thameralakshi), member is that—

> "The words 'any services for a consideration' in the definition of 'consumer' points to the generally non-restrictive nature of the definition in relation to service. The words 'avails of' in section 2(1)(d)(ii) as alternative to 'hires' in the same section as also the words "has been undertaken to be performed in pursuance of a contract or otherwise in relation to any service in Section 2(1)(g) have the effect of bringing under the purview of the consumer forum, services rendered by bodies like universities which are established for rendering specified services and which services are availed of for a consideration, even in the absence of any arrangement or contract to hire such services a positive approach is needed in interpreting the provisions of the Act to capture to maximum extent the spirit underlying the enactment to render natural justice

to consumers and also to make those rendering these services accountable."

The same view was reiterated by the same member of National Commission in *Sh. Ravinder Singh* v. *Maharashi Daya Nand University, Rohtak*[111] wherein it was concluded that the answer to the basic question whether education is a service under the purview of the Act is in the affirmative and the answer to specific questions such as whether holding of examinations, declaration of results, etc. is a service is also in the affirmative, these specific issues being operational aspects of the basic matter. Very recently, the National Commission in *Miss Sonal Matapukar & Others* v. *Sri S. Nijalingappa Institute of Dental Service & Another*[112] held that concealment of true nature of the extent of sanctioned student strength in the prospectus issued in practicing fraud on students seeking admissions and thus a clear case of deficiency in service within the scope and ambit of Consumer Protection Act.

In the light of the above noteworthy minority view expressed in *Mohideen Kadre's case*[113] and subsequently in *Sh. Ravinder Singh's case*[114] there seems no logic or reason in excluding education from the category of service as envisaged by the Consumer Protection Act.

The scope of definition of 'service' in the Act has been discussed in extenso by the Supreme Court in *Lucknow Development Authority* v. *M.K. Gupta*[115] and more recently in *Indian Medical Association* v. *V.P. Shantha & Others.*[116] After pointing out that the definition of 'service' in the Consumer Protection Act is in three parts, the Supreme Court has observed in the former case:

---

111. 1986-96 CONSUMER 1948 (NS).
112. 1997 (2) CPR 24 (National Commission) Opposite Parties admitted 44 Students including complainants. to BDS course in excess of mentioned strength and consequently they were not allowed to appear in examination though all formalities where fulfilled by them.
113. *Supra* Note 110.
114. *Supra* Note 107.
115. 1986-95 CONSUMER 278 (NS).
116. 1986-95 (Suppl. CONSUMER 1569 (NS).

> "The main part is followed by inclusive clause and ends by exclusionary clause. The main clause itself is very wide. It applies to any service made available to potential users. The words 'any' and 'potential' are significant. Both are of wide amplitude. The word 'any' dictionarily means "one or some or all." In Black's law dictionary it is explained thus, word 'any' has a diversity of meaning and may be employed to indicate 'all' or 'every' as well as 'some' or 'one' and its meaning in a given statute depends upon the context it has been used in clause (o) indicates that it has been used in wider sense extending from one to all."

Referring to the inclusive part of the definition, the Supreme Court in the above said case observed:

> "The inclusive clause succeeded in widening its scope but not exhausting the services which could be covered in earlier part. So any service except when it is free of charge or under a contract of personal service is included in it."

The Supreme Court also made observations in the same case on the larger issue whether the public authorities under different enactment's are amenable to jurisdiction under the Act. Referring to the arguments placed before them in that case the local authorities or government and that therefore, they could not be subjected to the provisions of Act, the court observed:

> "In fact the Act requires the provider of service to be more objective and care taking. It is still more in public services."

They further observed:

> "Any attempt therefore, to exclude services offered by statutory or official bodies to the common man would be against the provisions of the Act and the spirit behind it."

Thus, though service of education has not been specifically included in the definition of service as provided under the Consumer Protection Act but it is within this definition as is clear from the words "Service means service of any description which is made available to potential users." So the need of the hour is that in future there should be positive judicial and quasi-judicial approach in interpreting the provisions of the Act to capture to a maximum extent the spirit underlying the enactment to render natural justice to consumers and also to make those rendering these services accountable.

(5) Electrical Service

Supply of electricity is a consumer service.[117] There are two important enactments dealing with electricity service— The Electricity Act, 1910 and The Electricity (Supply) Act, 1948. Though under both the above mentioned Acts there is a provision of arbitration for settlement of disputes if any arising between the board and Licensee but after passing of Consumer Protection Act exceedingly a large number of cases have been brought before the Consumer Disputes Redressal Agencies. An important and noteworthy point which deserves to be highlighted is that unlike other commercial matters a person who uses electricity for commercial purpose has been also treated as a consumer. See *Haryana State Electricity Board* v. *Jai Forging and Stamping's (P) Ltd., Yammuna Nagar,*[118] complainant claimed that due to illegal disconnection of electricity of the industrial premises he suffered loss apart from humiliation and loss of reputation of a reputable concern. National Commission upheld the order of state commission whereby he was entitled to Rs. 40,000 as loss plus Rs. 5000 in lump sum as compensation. Similarly, where the allegations of the complainant stood substantiated on the basis of the evidence oral and documentary he was entitled to an appropriate compensation.[119]

---

117. As provided by Section 2(1)(o) of Consumer Protection Act, 1986.
118. 1986-96 CONSUMER 2264 (NS).
119. Haryana State Electricity Board *v.* Taney Roshi Poultry Farm, 1986-96 CONSUMER 2237 (NS).

Since it is the first and main duty of the Power Department to supply electricity to its licensees any disregard to such obligation is a statutory violation. But it is true only where a licensee having fulfilled all the necessary conditions to get the power supply has been negligently denied or delayed this facility. Refusal to sanction supply unless all conditions are fulfilled is not a deficient service under existing rules. This impression also comes from the following cases on the point. In *Additional Chief Engineer & Others* v. *Ramalingam,*[120] there was delay in providing additional power supply to the complainant for ice factory. National Commission held that by making application along with earnest money deposit he had only became an intending consumer. In *Maharashtra State Electricity Board, Wardtha* v. *K.L. Ramani,*[121] National Commission while agreeing with the District Forum that there was delay and harassment on the part of the board in giving electric supply held that failure to grant electric connection to an applicant who had not filed a proper application for connection does not constitute deficiency in service.[122]

Where there is disconnection of power supply whether to a factory/mill or residence without notice it is wrongful and consequently actionable. In *Haryana State Electricity Board* v. *Naresh Kumar,*[123] board was held guilty of deficiency in service which it had undertaken to render to the consumer under The Indian Electricity Act and The Electricity Supply Act as also the statutory instructions of its own sales manual by disconnecting the electricity supply without any prior notice. 'Also disconnection of electric service within less than 7 days of the issue of the bill is deficiency in service'.[124] 'It is also deficiency in service if there is delay in getting defective transformers/meters repaired or replaced. It is the duty of the

120. 1986-95 CONSUMER 695 (NS); Seen also Additional Chief Engineer and Others *v.* Ramalingam, 1986-95 CONSUMER 695 (NS).

121. 1986-95 CONSUMER 1395 (NS).

122. Seen also Resi Engineering Works *v.* Commissioner, Coimbotare Corporation, 1986-96 CONSUMER 2675 (NS).

123. 1986-96 CONSUMER 1981 (NS).

124. Rajashtan State Electricity Board and Another *v.* Ramlikha Vyar, 1986-96 CONSUMER 2423 (NS).

Electricity Board to take prompt steps to have meters in question checked and if found defective to have them replaced by new meters having ISI Certification.[125]

Where the Electricity Board detects that any consumer had committed any malpractice with reference to his use of electric energy including unauthorized alterations, unauthorized extension and use of devices to commit theft of electric energy, the board may without prejudice to other rights of the consumer disconnect his electricity provided that the exercise of the power of disconnection shall be in accordance with the statutory powers. In *Haryana State Electricity Board* v. *Laxman Singh*,[126] the complainant had obtained prematurely a power connection by paying bribes/ illegal gratification to a junior engineer. Subsequently, the SDO visited the site and demanded Rs. 5000 and on the refusal to pay such charge the electric connection was disconnected. After going through the record and hearing of the parties the National Commission came to the conclusion that complainant had managed to obtain power connection by dubious means and the subsequent connection was therefore, fully justified and it cannot be deemed to be deficiency in service on the part of the electricity board. In *CESC* v. *Smt. Sunita Pal*,[127] the officers of the CESC found on surprise visit on the consumer premises that he was drawing electricity directly from the service cut-outs and in consequence disconnected the electricity in the said premises. State Commission on appeal directed the CESC to restore the electricity but the National Commission held the exercise of the powers of disconnection is in accordance with the statutory power and cannot be construed as any deficiency in service. However, a consumer/complainant cannot be held responsible for the unauthorized use of electricity by others. In V.*K. Ramchandani* v. *Municipal Corpn. of Delhi (DESU)*[128] the

125. Consumer Protection Council, Ahmedabad *v.* The Ahmedabad Electricity Company Ltd. and Another, 1986-95 CONSUMER 759 (NS); Consumer Assistance and Welfare Centre *v.* A.P. State Electricity Board, 1986-96 CONSUMER 3133 (NS).

126. 1986-96 CONSUMER 3258 (NS).

127. 1997 (2) CPR 92 (National Commission).

128. 1986-96 CONSUMER 2669 (NS).

complainant had obtained the electric connection for his farm house for tube well and the poultry farm and agriculture. The power supply was disrupted in his locality as a result of the overhead wires having snapped. The wires were subsequently repaired and the electric supply was restored in the area. However, the complainants electric supply was not restore . . . DESU failed to prove that the electric connection had been misused by the complainant . . . National Commission held there was no justification whatsoever for not restoring the connection subsequently. Complainants electric supply remained disconnected for three years for which he was entitled to damages.

Earlier we have seen consumer forums have been hesitant in issuing mandatory orders for supply of power where a person has not acquired status of a consumer[129]—but where the same or additional load has been sanctioned but not made available it amounts to deficiency in service. In *The Executive Engineer, Q and M Tamil Nadu Electricity Board & Others* v. *K.R. Mani,*[130] electricity board failed to produce the necessary records to establish that they were taking steps without any default and that delay in giving the additional load was unavoidable. However, where after submitting an application complainant did not press the board or its officers to give the electric connection immediately the supplier of electricity was not held liable for any deficiency.[131] Similarly, where there is delay on the part of complainant Electricity Board cannot be held liable for deficient service. In *M/s Genetic Industrial Gases (P) Ltd.* v. *The U.P. State Electricity Board & Others*[132] it was found that delay in supply of power to the unit of the complainant was occasioned due to the fact that the sub-station at the industrial estate was under

129. 1986-96 CONSUMER 2807 (NS).

130. *Id.,* p. 2807.

131. U.P. State Electricity Board and Others *v.* M/s Mona Confectionary Industries, 1986-96 CONSUMER 2985 (NS).

132. *Id.,* p. 2688 (NS); Seen also Alarcity Foundations (Pvt.) Ltd. *v.* The Chairman, Tamil Nadu Electricity Board, 1986-96 CONSUMER 3259 (NS). In Haryana State Electricity Board *v.* Pirthi Singh, 1986-95 CONSUMER 456 (NS) in which no deficiency was proved as it was not showed that the board has violated any rule, direction or instruction issued by it.

construction and the transformer was not available and when the sub-station was energized it was found that the complainant had not installed the L.T. switching system.

Various cases have been reported where disconnection has been based on imposition of arbitrary bills. In *Y.N. Gupta* v. *D.E.S.U.*[133] bills for electrical consumption were not prepared and served at the appointed time in accordance with the billing cycle and thereafter the consumer feel harassed with heavy arrears of bill. National Commission held that harassing the complainant with heavy arrears of bill amount deficiency in service. Not only the complainant has been harassed by presenting him with inflated bills requiring him to pay the same at extremely short notice but torturing him and his family members by arbitrarily and malafidely disconnecting his power supply and that too before the date specified for payment of the bill by DESU itself.

Briefly to say after perusal of cases supply of electricity has been held to be a consumer service even if the energy is being put to a commercial use.

(6) Financial Service

Financing Service is a service as mentioned u/s 2(1)(0) of the Act. Earlier under the heading of 'Banking Service' it is said that banks are necessarily allowed considerable discretion in deciding granting of loans, raising of credit limits and matters relating to repayment, etc. The same is true of Financing Institutions.[134] In the case of *Branch Manager, Tamil Nadu Industrial Investment Copn. Ltd.* v. *S.R. Subramanian*[135] the complainant approached the corporation for the grant of a loan for starting an oil mill industry. He deposited margin money but the corporation failed to advance him the balance of the amount. The National Commission held that it has been repeatedly pointed out by this commission that—

133. 1986-95 CONSUMER 551 (NS).

134. The Same view has been reiterated by National Commission in Pondichary Aerators *v.* M.D. Pondichary Industrial Development and Investment) 1991(1) CPR 613.

135. 1986-96 CONSUMER 2965 (NS).

> "Even after a bank or other financing institution has sanctioned the limits upto which a loan will be advanced by it to a borrower, it is still vested with the discretion to apply its mind from time to time and decide in its best judgment as to whether it will be reasonable, safe and prudent to make further advances to the particular borrower in the light of any failure on his part. So long as such discretion is exercised in good faith and for safeguarding the interest of public funds after due application of mind to all relevant factors, a decision taken by the bank or other financial institutions to discontinue making further advance to a particular borrower will not constitute deficiency in service."

Applying the aforesaid principles[136] to the facts of the present case, the National Commission was of the opinion that in view of the failure on the part of the complainant to show proper progress in the construction work of the factory and to comply with the conditions stipulated by the bank to open a special current account in order to enable it to make further advance to him, the bank cannot be said to have guilty of any deficiency in service in taking a decision to stop making any more advances to the complainant.

Similarly in *M/s Robinson India* v. *Rajasthan Financial Corpn. & Another,*[137] the complainant applied to the Rajasthan Financial Corporation for a loan for the manufacture of medicines and was sanctioned Rs. 7 lacs. The grievance of the complainant was that the Rajasthan Financial Corporation disbursed to him only Rs. 6.08 lacs and the balance amount was not disbursed. The complainant had also obtained sanction for a cash credit limit of Rs. 3 lacs from Punjab National Bank. The complainant alleged that the Rajasthan Financial Corporation and Punjab National Bank acted in collusion with each other with a view to cause him undue loss. On the merits of the case, National Commission found

136. The view has been taken from Special Machine Tools *v.* Punjab National Bank and Others, 1986-95 CONSUMER 766 (NS).

137. 1986-96 CONSUMER 2776 (NS).

that both the Rajasthan Financial Corporation and Punjab National Bank have acted as per the terms and conditions of the sanction of the loan and extension of cash credit facility. Further, it was the complainant who had defaulted in the repayment of principal with interest to the Rajasthan Financial Corporation and had also violated norms of financial discipline by operating his cash credit account with the Punjab National Bank in an unsatisfactory manner.

Where financial corporation could not give additional loan because the complainant failed to give additional security as it had misutilized the loan granted earlier there is no deficiency in service.[138] But where the default is on the part of the company or firm to carry out its obligations to repay the principal and interest on the amount deposited it amounts to deficiency in service.[139]

In another case[140] the question for the consideration of the commission was whether non-payment of subsidy is deficiency in service. It was held subsidy offered to be paid is not service as defined in the Consumer Protection Act. In the same way rescheduling of loans and relief in interest thereon is also not a service. It is in the nature of an accommodation and concession to a party.

Another issue that needs here mention is whether a prospective investor is consumer and can he claim any deficiency in service against a company. In order to answer this question let us move a step backward and see the decision of the MRTP Commission as given in *CERC* v. *T.T.K. Pharma.*[141] In this case it was held that shares before allotment are not goods as defined in the Sale of Goods Act, 1920. No doubt the MRTP, 1969 has been amended in 1991 in order to include in the definition of 'goods' shares before allotment but still the ruling of the above case prevails the most. In *Morgan Stanley Mutual Fund Kartik Das,*[142] the MSMF was

---

138. M/s Noath Industries *v.* Karnataka State Financial Corporation and Another, 1986-95 CONSUMR 1143 (NS).
139. Neela Vasant Raja *v.* Amogh Industries and Another, 1986-95 CONSUMER 446 (NS).
140. M/s Sowheny Export House (P) Ltd. *v.* Noida.
141. RTP 157/86; Order 15-05-1987.
142. (1994) CPJ 7 National Commission.

registered with Securities Exchange Board of India (SEBI) and was managed by the board of trustees. The Board have appointed Morgan Stanley Asset Management India Pvt. Ltd. (MSAM) as asset management company of (MSMF). The first scheme of the (MSMF) was approved by the board of trustees in the name of Morgan Stanley Growth Fund (MSDF). The (MSMF) and (MSAM) commenced marketing the scheme through circular advertisement to raise a capital of Rs. 300 crores by selling 30 crore shares of Rs. 10-each. A suit was brought by the complainant alleging that the scheme was not approved by (SEBI) and the basis of allotment of shares by the (MSMF) was unfair as the (MSMF) was intending to collect money by misleading the public. To the issue whether prospective investor could be said to be a consumer within the meaning of the Consumer Protection Act, the court replied in the negative. It held that only after allotment shares became goods and the question of violation of rights of investor would arise only after allotment.

However, keeping in view the comprehensive definition of service as provided under this Act and the fact that the financial service is within the inclusive clause of section 2(1) (o) it is to be submitted respectfully that the above case is based on wrongful judgment. Morgan Stanley is an internationally reputed financial service company. It employees more than 7,400 people to provide a wide spectrum of financial and advising services to round five hundred corporations, institutions, government and individual investors. Its main activities include investment, banking, financing services, merchant banking, undertaking asset management securities, sales and trading investment research, brokerage and correspondent services, commodities and foreign exchange trading, advising services and global custody. Thus, Morgan Stanley Mutual Fund is rendering financial services to the investors and therefore the complainant is a consumer.[143]

It is to be briefly stated that the financial service like banking service is within the ambit of Consumer Protection

143. S.S.H. Azmi, Article 'Morgan Stanley Mutual Fund *v.* Kartic Das: A critique, *Aligarh Law General*, Vol. XI, 1996, 127 at 133.

Act and is bound by the same rules and principles as are applicable to the banks.

(7) Insurance Service

The quick pace of industrialization of the modern age has rendered man and his property most vulnerable to different types of risk and uncertainties of life. Thus, while uncertainties of death, unemployment, sickness are constantly starting at the face of a man, his property is exposed to the risks arising from fire, water, accident, windstorm, Sea perils, earthquakes, floods, dishonesty, negligence, etc. resulting from acts of God. In the absence of any remedy or cooperative efforts of society, friends, relatives and others, these losses were borne by the victims concerned. But with the growth of the industrialized society and consequently a rapid increase in the number of situations in which the human life and property get exposed to risks and effective solution of reducing the burden of these losses has been devised by shifting these risks to agencies or persons willing or qualified to share them.[144] Presently in India Life Insurance Corporation, General Insurance Corporation of India and its subsidiaries are operating for pursuing the goals set for these agencies (at the time of nationalization) under various Acts.[145]

These Acts set out body of rules and principles for determining the disputes arising out of insurance contracts between individuals or groups and the insuring body. This Act—Consumer Protection Act also includes insurance within the definition of Section 2(1)(o). How far Consumer Disputes Redressal Agencies have commended themselves to impart consumer justice in matters relating to insurance service can be better viewed by going through a long list of cases decided by them. For convenience let us focus on them under the following sub-headings—

---

144. M. Arif Khan, 'Theory and Practice of Insurance', Educational Book House, Aligarh U.P.

145. Oriental Fire and Insurance Company Ltd., New India Assurance Company Ltd., United India Fire and General Insurance Company Ltd.

(a) Life Insurance

It is one of the most important and popular type of insurance. One of the deepest desires of a rational man is to ensure that his dependants are provided for in the event of his untimely death. Life assurance provides for ordinary life assurance, industrial life assurance and annuities.

(b) Marine Insurance

It is one of the oldest forms of insurance due to man's long association with the maritime trade and the perils of the sea. It includes Hull Insurance which insures the actual vessel and its equipments; Cargo Insurance for insuring the merchandise; Freight Insurance; which is self-explanatory.

(c) Fire Insurance

Includes the risk of destruction by fire and also loss of profits (consequential loss) policies.

(d) Miscellaneous Insurance

This general category includes fidelity insurance, unemployment insurance, employee's state insurance, plate glass insurance, motor car insurance, employees liability, public liability cash in transit, crop insurance, cattle insurance, beauty insurance, dog insurance, etc. But the cases which has been dealt by consumer forums are mainly concerned with vehicle insurance, consignment, burglary, etc. Let us go into the details of above mentioned types of insurance with support of cases.

(a) Life Insurance

Life policies are generally taken for the protection of the life. These contracts are based upon mutual trust and confidence between the insurer and the insured and are subject to good faith because the law cannot support fraud. In simple terms, utmost good faith in insurance means that each party to a proposed contract is legally obliged to reveal to the other all information which would influence the others decision to enter the contract whether such information is requested or not. In other words, utmost good faith requires each party to tell the other truth, the whole truth and nothing but the truth about the proposed contract. Accordingly, all the material facts should be disclosed by the insured and the insurer so that the person undertaking to shoulder the burden of risk may ascertain the nature and extent of it before fixing a price. So any non-disclosure of a material fact enables the under-writer to avoid the contract irrespective of whether the non-disclosure was intentional or inadvertent. In *Draupadi Devi Chaudhari* v. *United India Insurance Company Ltd.,*[146] the complainant had taken a mediclaim insurance policy from the insurance company covering risks of expenses incurred for hospitalization and domiciliary hospitalization. After some months complainants husband felt chest discomfort for the first time and was advised to undergo bye-pass surgery. The insurer repudiated the medical claim on the ground that he had been suffering from chest discomfort since ten years and this fact had not been disclosed in the proposal form. The repudiation of the insurance claim by the insurer was primarily based on the 'history' of the patient as recorded in the Hospital Discharge Card wherein it had been stated that Mr. . . . had "chest discomfort since ten years. . . ." National Commission found that the repudiation of the claim by the insurer in this case appears *bonafide* being based on the history in the discharge card of the hospital and that therefore, there was no deficiency in service on its part attracting the mischief of the Consumer Protection Act.

On merits also in *Divisional Manager, LIC of India & Others* v. *Smt. Sunita Sharma,*[147] it has been fully established that the insured had concealed material facts while taking the insurance policy.

In this case the complainant's deceased husband had taken out a policy on his own life. After his death the insurance company got the matter investigated which revealed that the deceased insured has suppressed material facts relating to the state of his health that he was suffering from mitral stanosis for about 17 years from breathlessness for 7 years and that about 9 months prior to the submissions of the proposal for the issue of the policy he had undergone

146. 1986-96 CONSUMER 391 (NS).
147. 1986-96 CONSUMER 359 (NS).

operation for appendicitis. This concealment of material facts while taking the insurance policy entitled the LIC to repudiate its liability under the policy.

Fraudulent misrepresentation of facts entitled LIC to repudiate the liability in *Smt. Kantaben* v. *Life Insurance Corporation of India Ltd. & Another*[148] also. The complainant was the widow of deceased who had during his life time taken a policy of insurance for Rs. 1 lakh. She being the nominee in the policy lodged a claim with the LIC. LIC repudiated all liabilities under the policy on account of the deceased having withheld correct information regarding his health at the time of effecting the assurance. The National Commission found that though allegation was made by the complainant that the services rendered by the insurer suffered from deficiency but there was no evidence to support that allegation. The policy taken by the deceased was vitiated by reason of suppression of material facts by the insured and the LIC was justified to repudiate its liability under the policy.

On similar grounds LIC repudiated the claim of the complainant in *Life Insurance Corporation of India* v. *Smt. Lily Rani Roy*.[149] The question whether submitting proposal and payment towards premium can be construed as a concluded contract. In a couple of cases before National Commission the question came for consideration. In *LIC of India & Another* v. *Smt. K. Aruna Kumari*,[150] facts in brief are these that the Respondent- complainant had submitted to the branch of LIC a proposal for insurance on own life. Unfortunately soon the husband died in an accident and the wife of the assured claimed the amount due under the policy of insurance in pursuance of the proposal and the premium accepted by LIC. LIC repudiated the contract on the ground that the assured was required to submit the age of certificate. Since it was not submitted so there was no acceptance of proposal. National Commission agreed with the point of refusal submitted by

148. 1986-96 CONSUMER 3004 (NS).

149. 1997 (1) CPR 40. National Commission held that LIC was right in repudiating the claim on the facts in respect of the information received from the hospital . . .

150. 1986-96 CONSUMER 2801 (NS).

the LIC and held that merely submitting the proposal and payment of an amount which was kept in deposit without appropriation towards the premium it cannot be said to be a valid contract of insurance.

The National Commission referred the decision held by the Supreme Court in *LIC's case*[151]:

> "The Contract of Insurance will be concluded only when the party to whom the offer had been made accepts it unconditionally and communicates his acceptance to the person the offerer. Though in certain human relationships reliance to a proposal might convey acceptance but in the case of insurance proposal silence does not denote consent and no binding contract arises until the person to whom an offer is made says or does something to signify his acceptance. Mere delay in giving an answer cannot be construed as an acceptance, as *prima-facie,* acceptance must be communicated to the offerer. Similarly, the mere receipt and retention of premium until after the death of the applicant or the mere preparation of the policy document is not acceptance.

However, earlier in *Life Insurance Corpn. of India* v. *Mrs. V. Jeeva,*[152] National Commission upholding the decision of the State Commission held that it was mistake on the part of LIC in not choosing to issue the policy immediately and that there is no illegality or irregularity when the two forums came to the conclusion that there was a concluded contract (as the premium was deposited) of insurance and deficiency in service.

It is to be submitted that keeping in view the constitutional mandate of the socio-economic justice the *Jeeva's case* has been rightly decided and the view expressed by National Commission in *Smt. K. Aruna Kumari's case* is based on erroneous judgment. A layman usually poor illiterate can hardly be expected to know that after accepting proposal and

151. AIR 1984 SC 1014.

152. 1986-96 CONSUMER 2533 (NS).

premium any formality remains to be fulfilled. It is upon the insurer who knows the technicality of the matter to get all formalities done and in case the same remains wanting it is in appropriate, unreasonable and unjust on the part of the insurer to avoid liability and say that the money deposited by the assured was kept in suspense account. In view of the social responsibility to provide reasonable security to policy-holders Insurance Corporations should provide better service but not by rejecting claims on frivolous and technical ground.

(b) Marine Insurance

Marine insurance is the oldest form of insurance. It covers loss or damage to vessels or to cargo or passengers, during transportation on the high seas. The risks insured against are those commonly known as perils of the sea. It does not include the ordinary action of the wind and water. Like other insurance contracts a full disclosure of all the material facts is more essential. However, it is only the fraudulent suppression, or knowledge of the suppressed facts which would entitle the Insurance Corporation to avoid the policy. In a number of cases relating to marine insurance the National Commission has over-emphasized the same view. In *M/s National Insurance Company Ltd.* v. *Premjibhai Ranchodhai Hodal Mangrol Matsyugandhi Mongrol,*[153] the fishing boats belonging to the complainant were insured. There was some disturbance in the sea. Efforts to tow the fishing board continued but owing to heavy swell at rough sea, mooring houses were frequently parted and all the fishing boats drifted along with heavy swell at midsea. The towing of the fishing boats was required to be abandoned and all the vessels sunk in the sea. The insurance company raised the contention that the complainants had not placed adequate persons on the vessel to man it which amounted to breach of manning warranty.

Upholding the decision of the state commission, National Commission held that the crew members tried to save the boats and retide the ropes but ultimately the efforts were required to be given up. The damage was caused only

153. 1997 (2) CPR 251 National Commission.

because of the rough sea weather and not because of any inadequacy of manning of the boats.

Similarly, in another case,[154] the insurance company does not disprove the fact that the engine shaft of the vessel had broken. So the National Commission held that it was not justified on the part of the insurance company to repudiate the claim of the complainant and that too after twenty months of the filing of the claim. If payments are delayed or withheld without satisfactory reasons, policy-holders will quite rightly loose confidence in the insurance company. Paying the claim is certainly one of the most important functions of marine insurance companies, it is essential that just claim be paid promptly and in full payment.[155] In *M/s Uniplas India Ltd.* v. *The National Insurance Company Ltd.*,[156] the complainant lodged a claim for the loss occasioned due to non-arrival of goods in respect of six Bills of Lading . . . The National Commission held that the insurance company has reduced the amount payable under the insurance policy arbitrarily, unfairly and has not settled the claim with reasonable expedition and thus has been guilty of deficiency in service.

Since marine insurance contracts are based on the principle of insurable interest under rules of marine insurance every person has an insurable interest who is interested in a marine adventure where he stands in any legal or equitable relation to the adventure. Thus, a person can take an insurance policy on his ship, an owner of goods can take policy on the cargo and the person entitled to receive freight can take policy on the freight. In a case[157] the insurance company has not paid the claim on the ground that the complainant had no insurable interest in the vessel as the true owner of this vessel was the person in whose name the vessel was registered. But the National Commission held that

---

154. United India Insurance Company Ltd. *v.* Smt. Kusemben J. Badiani, 1986-96 CONSUMER 3201 (NS).
155. 1986-96 CONSUMR, p. 265.
156. 1986-96 CONSUMER 1654 (NS).
157. Haji Dand Haji Haran Aboo *v.* United India Insurance Company Ltd., 1986-96 CONSUMER 3100 (NS).

the complainant had paid the premium by getting the vessel insured because the vessel was in his possession. He could not have done this if he had no insurable interest in the said property. From the totality of the facts the commission came to the conclusion that there was deficiency of service on the part of insurance company.

(c) Fire Insurance

The contract of fire insurance is infact an offshoot from the contract of marine insurance. The contract of fire insurance, like other contracts of insurance, differs from an ordinary contract in that it requires, throughout its existence, the utmost good faith (*Uberrima fides)* to be observed on the part of both the insured and in the insurers. A failure to comply with this requirement renders the contract voidable, for the insured as being the person interested in the subject matter, has some acquaintance with its nature and surroundings, and must, therefore, be taken, as against the insurers, to know what the matters are which are to be communicated to them. But the contract which the insurer make with insured must be clearly expressed. If the terms are ambiguous, the consumer cannot rely upon a construction which would effect, make the contract misleading or unfair.

In *M.K.G. Corporation* v. *United India Insurance Company Ltd. & Others,*[158] the National Commission held that the repudiation of the liability of the insurance company under the insurance policy was not *bonafide* and that it has placed a far-fetched and unreasonable interpretation on the insurance clause pertaining to insurance of stocks in process. Similarly, the insured cannot be allowed to take unfair advantage of a typing mistake in the insurance policy regarding the amount insured.[159]

In *United India Insurance* v. *Ajmer Singh Cotton & General Mills & Others, etc.,*[160] insurance company made the payments which were accepted by the insured with

158. 1986-96 CONSUMER 3204 (NS).

159. United India Insurance Company Ltd. *v.* M/s Mohan Lal and Sons, 1986-96 CONSUMER 1685 (NS).

160. 1993 (3) CPR 53 (SC).

declaration of receipt of the "sum in full and final discharge of claims upon them." After the payments were made the complainants (Insured) filed complaint before the state commission claiming interest at the rate of 18% p.a. against the insurance company. State Commission dismissed the claim but National Commission directed the company to pay the interest. The Supreme Court held that mere execution of the discharge voucher and acceptance of the insurance claim would not stop the insured from making further claim from the insurance company but it is possible under fraud, undue influence, misrepresentation, or the like. The same view was reiterated by National Commission in *The New India Assurance Co. Ltd.* v. *M/s Geetanjali Silk House & Another.*[161] The complainant had taken loan from the bank and insured the shop where he was carrying on cloth business. A fire broke out in the shop causing huge loss to the complainant. The complainant alleged that he had asked the bank that he was not agreeable to the payment offered by the insurance company but which the bankers had accepted. So he objected on the ground that he was coerced to agree the same in full satisfaction. National Commission held acceptance of the settled claim by co-insured will bind the other. In this case since there is no allegation that the complainants were coerced in any way to accept the sum so in no way (National Commission held) can be Insurance Company held liable for deficiency in service or imperfection in the rendering of service.

Though it is a fundamental principle of fire insurance that the insured in case of the loss covered by the contract, shall so far as the sum specified in the contract permits, be fully indemnified but shall never be more indemnified or on other words be never allowed to obtain benefit fraudulently or malafidely. In the light of the reports of the surveyors and investigator it was held by the National Commission in *Shiv Trading Company* v. *New India Assurance Co. Ltd. & Others*[162] that the fire was not accidental but it was arranged just to get benefit under the policy. On the same lines that is for similar

161. 1986-96 CONSUMER 2088 (NS).

162. 1986-96 CONSUMER 2293 (NS).

reason National Commission in *M/s Advance Rubber Industries* v. *M/s United India Insurance Company Ltd.*[163] found Insurance Company right in repudiating the claim. In this case the complainant had withheld material information from the Insurance Company that the family member of the landlord had poured kerosene oil over the rubber material which was mentioned in the F.I.R. immediately after the incident but was not disclosed to the insurance company.

However, in a large quantity of cases[164] decided by the apex commission it is noticed that there have been inordinate delays in the finalization of the claims of the insured. *M/s Tanawala Synthetic Textile Ltd.* v. *Oriental Insurance Co. Ltd.*[165] is relevant case on the point. In the instant case the insurance company sent a letter of repudiation to the complainant after a long delay of over three years. National Commission held long delay for not accepting the loss as assessed by the surveyors is itself a deficiency in service as per section 2(1)(o)(g) of the Act. On the facts and circumstances of the case in *M/s R.K. Industries* v. *The New India Assurance Co. Ltd.*,[166] the settlement of the claim was delayed deliberately for about 17 months.

In *M/s Shai Sabbari Syndicates* v. *M/s Oriental Fire & General Insurance Ltd.*,[167] the National Commission observed that the conduct of the insurance company in initially offering to settle the two claims and subsequently agreeing to have a re-survey done and finally agreeing to settle the claims at reduced payment exhibits deficiency of service in settling the claims and even when release of the amount was asked the

---

163. 1986-96 CONSUMER 2114 (NS).

164. M/s Asas Singh Cotton Factory *v.* United India Insurance Company and Others, 1986-96 CONSUMER 1754 (NS); M/s National Insurance Company Ltd. *v.* M/s Safari Industries (India) Ltd., 1986-96 CONSUMER 1860 (NS); The New India Assurance Company Ltd. *v.* Purushotam Goquldar Match Company, 1986-96 CONSUMER 2544 (NS); National Insurance Company Ltd. *v.* M/s Lal Chand Jain and Sons, 1997(1) CPR 1083; United India Insurance Company Ltd. *v.* M/s Beering Traders and Mills Stores and Another, 1997(2) CPR 132.

165. 1986-96 CONSUMER 2103 (NS).

166. 1986-96 CONSUMER 2760 (NS).

167. 1986-96 CONSUMER 2795 (NS).

same was not paid. This amounted to gross deficiency in service.

(d) Miscellaneous Type of Insurance

Apart from the main forms of insurance a number of insurance policy meant to cover a variety of other risks are also issued by the general insurance companies. Some of the important miscellaneous forms of policies among others are motor car insurance, goods in transit insurance, burglary insurance, etc. A survey of cases decided by National Commission under this heading is designed to undertake here:-

(i) Accidental Cases

The motor car insurance or automobile insurance is a contractual protection against losses connected with the use of automobile. Since usually on occurrence of any accident or loss of or damage to the vehicle, the insured must inform the insurer and the insured must take reasonable steps to prevent or mitigate as the case may be, any loss of or damage to the vehicle sometimes insurance companies repudiates the claims on the one or other ground of own damages that is the damages caused by the insured. In *National Insurance Co. Ltd.* v. *Rais Abbas Naqvi,*[168] the Respondent-Complainant had taken an insurance policy in respect of truck which was financed from a bank. The said vehicle met with an accident. The Insurance Company repudiated the claim alleging that the vehicle was passed for carriage of 12 tons and weight carried by the vehicle at the time of accident was 15 tons.

National Commission held that the policy of insurance lays down limitation as to the use. The licensed carrying capacity of the said vehicle for the goods was 12 tons but the investigation report showed it carried 15 tons. Since the truck was overloaded so the repudiation was based on material and cannot be termed as arbitrary. Similarly, carrying unauthorized passengers amounts violation of the terms and conditions of the policy.[169]

168. 1986-96 CONSUMER 2234 (NS).

169. The New India Assurance Company Ltd. *v.* A. Mohd. Yaseen, 1986-96 CONSUMER 2623 (NS).

As above stated it is the duty of the insured to intimate the insurer immediately if any change takes place regarding the insured property. In *The New India Assurance Co. Ltd.* v. *Mrs. S. Pushpa Devi Jamed & Another,*[170] the Complainant-Insured purchased lorry was taken by the financier and while proceeding on the way the vehicle met with an accident. The complainants shifted the goods to another vehicle and left the insured vehicle unattended for ten days. Someone as it was alleged set the vehicle on fire causing heavy damage to it. National Commission held that the fact regarding the change of possession of the lorry hire-purchaser to the financier was not intimated to the company before filing the claim so the repudiation by the company on this ground was genuine and reasonable.

To raise a claim before insurance company it is necessary under Section 64-VB of the Insurance Act that there should be valid insurance contract on date of accident. In a case,[171] it was observed that cheque for instalment premium was encashed one day after the alleged incident so there was no valid insurance contract and the repudiation of the claim by the insurance company did not constitute any deficiency of service. In *Hotel Southern Pvt. Ltd.* v. *National Insurance Co. Ltd. & Others*[172] also encashment of the cheque was dishonoured as there was no funds with the bank. Meanwhile accident took place but the claim was repudiated by the National Commission as there was want of premium on the day of accident. An interesting case from the discussion point of view here is *M/s Complete Insulation's Pvt. Ltd.* v. *New India Assurance Company Ltd.*[173] In the instant case a maruti car was purchased in the name of Mrs. Archana Wadhwa for which the Insurance Company had issued a comprehensive insurance policy. The premium for the insurance was paid by

---

170. 1986-96 CONSUMER 2620 (NS).

171. Bam Dev *v.* United India Insurance Company Ltd., 1997 (1) CPR 95.

172. 1986-96 CONSUMER 2803 (NS). In this case judgment of the Supreme Court in United India Insurance Company Ltd. *v.* Ayub Mohd. and Others, 1991 A.C.J. 650 was referred. In this case it was held in the absence of consideration for the policy Insurance Contract was void *ab initio.*

173. 1986-96 CONSUMER 2839 (NS).

the complainant company in whose favour the car was transferred. The complainant intimated the transfer of registration and asked for transfer of the insurance policy by two letters to which the insurance company did not reply. The car met with an accident and there was a total loss of car. The National Commission while setting aside the order of the state commission directed the insurance company to pay insured value of the vehicle. On appeal to Supreme Court provisions of section 103-A of the Motor Vehicle Act, 1939 (Old Act) and section 157 of the New Act were examined and it was found that since there was no such agreement as insurer had not transferred the policy of insurance in relation thereto the transferee the insurer was not liable to make good the damage to the vehicle. But we are in complete agreement with the National Commission in holding the insurance company liable for providing deficient services. As it is clear from the facts and circumstances of the case that the complainant intimated the insurer vide two letters about the transfer of registration and asked for transfer of the insurance policy but the insurance company did not reply to the said two letters. Anyway it is due to the delay or irresponsibility showed by the insurance company which is the root cause of complainants suffering.[174] In a large number of reported cases validity of the driving licenses were the main issue.

In *New India Assurance Co. Ltd.* v. *Smt. Pushpa Yashwant Ghatge*[175] and *Gurbhand Singh* v. *The Oriental Insurance Co. Ltd. & Others,*[176] National Commission held that the Insurance Co's. were right in repudiating the claims after considering survey reports from qualified surveyors in which the validity of the licenses were denied. To some extent on the similar facts complainant's grievance was not allowed to be redressed in *Sachin Balachandra Shah* v. *The Oriental Insurance Co.*[177] on the ground that driving licence of the driver was misused as in fact that person was not driving car at the time of accident and that person himself had written a letter to insurer that he

174. 1997 (2) CPR 151.

175. 1986-96 CONSUMER 1901 (NS).

176. 1997 (2) CPR 156.

177. 1999 (2) CPR 11 (National Commission).

was not driving car. National Commission held it is clear from the reports submitted on behalf of the insurance company that it has reasonable doubt to the genuineness of the claim and therefore, non-settling of the claim under the policy could not be due to deficiency in service or negligence.

However, insurance company in *The New India Assurance Company* v. *Sh. Hement S. Handra*[178] has been held liable for providing deficient service. In this case the complainant has insured his tempo vehicle with the insurance company. The said vehicle was involved in an accident. The insurance company rejected the claim on the ground that the driver of the tempo was holding motor car licence. But in view of sections 2(23), 2(21) and 10(2) of The Motor Vehicle Act, 1988 the apex commission held that the vehicle in the present case falls under the light motor vehicle so the repudiation of the claim by the insurance company has not been done on valid grounds and hence this amounts to deficiency in service.

(ii) Burglary, etc. Cases

Like other forms of insurance a desirous person also takes insurance policies to cover loss of consignment and collision and burglary. There is a steep rise in such type of insurance's and it is observed mainly due to the increase in filing complaints before the Consumer Disputes Redressal Agencies. In a couple of cases[179] relating to loss of consignment National Commission while declining negligence on the part of insurance company convinced the complainants to approach the ordinary civil court. In such cases it was found that due to the break up of war, purposes of the contracts were frustrated and consequently giving rise to the special and extra-ordinary nature of the facts and circumstances.

While denying delay and deficiency on the part of insurance company National Commission reached to the conclusion that the failure or the refusal on the part of the buyer to accept goods clearly conveyed the existence of *prima-*

178. 1986-96 CONSUMER 2211 (NS).
179. 1986-96 CONSUMER 26 (NS); Supp. (3) SCC 406.

facie dispute between the complainant and the buyer and the insurance company was not to be called upon to fulfil their contractual obligation before the conditions in the relevant provisions of the policy were complied with to their satisfaction.[180]

There are a large number of cases[181] which have been dismissed by the National Commission on the ground that the claim put forward by the complainants were not tenable. From the argument point of view it is unnecessary to set out in detail the contentions raised therein. In *M/s Modern Insulators Ltd.* v. *The Oriental Insurance Co. Ltd.,*[182] the insured factory had taken out an insurance policy known as 'All risks insurance policy'. The policy covered risks against loss during storage-*cum*-erection including trial and testing. After completion of the erection of 25M3 Kiln, was loaded with insulators for trial and testing and when it was opened it was found that complete structure of kiln furniture with insulators had collapsed and various items of kiln furniture were damaged. Insurance company refused to settle the claim stating that damaged property was not covered by the insurance policy. It relied on the exclusion clause was not included in the policy nor communicated to the insured. Insurance company cannot claim the benefit of the exclusion clause so as to avoid its liability under the insurance policy. Due to heavy rains the compound wall was damaged and collapsed in *M/s New India Assurance Co. Ltd.* v. *M/s Matchless Investment Finance and Leasing Ltd.*[183] also but on account of under-insurance it was found that it was *bonafide* for the insurer to deduct from the sums assessed by the surveyor.

In *M/s New Jaipur Dyeing & Tents Works* v. *The Oriental Insurance Company Ltd.,*[184] there was a burglary in the firm of complainants. The grievance of the complainants was that the

180. Rangudyog *v.* Export Credit Guarantee Corporation of India Ltd., 1986-96 CONSUMER 2230 (NS).
181. Parees Offset Pvt. Ltd. *v.* United India Insurance Company Ltd., 1986-96 CONSUMER 3211 (NS); M/s Fiorio Coloria S.P.Q. *v.* Oriental Insurance Company and Another, 1186.
182. 2000 (1) CPR 93 (SC).
183. 1986-96 CONSUMER 2302 (NS).
184. 1986-95 CONSUMER 887 (NS).

Insurance Company did not settled the claim within the reasonable time for which he claimed compensation. National Commission hold the view that since there was reasonable ground to doubt the genuineness of the claim, as such the non-payment of the insurance amount under the policies cannot be deemed to be a deficiency in service arising from negligence.

For the further examination of the subject-matter some more important cases are to be worth mentioning.

In *The Chairman Life Insurance Corpon. of India & Another* v. *Akhil Bhartiya Grahak Panchayat & Another,*[185] the complainant held 6 policies in servicing which the State Commission found deficiency in service rendered by the LIC to the insured as under:

(i) Unilateral increase in the premium payable on three policies by 50 paisa each which constituted a breach of contract of insurance.

(ii) Refusal on the part of LIC to give additional loans to the insured on the basis of the surrender value of the policies.

(iii) Failure of the Insurer LIC to furnish to the Insured the guaranteed surrender value of the policies and special surrender value of the bonus accrued on the policies from time to time.

(iv) Alleged rude behavour of an employee of LIC and failure of LIC to take action on the complaint made by the Insured.

National Commission held there has been no deficiency in the service on the part of LIC on the two major charges of deficiency in service-unilateral increase in the premium (on the policies by 50 paisa) due to rounding off and refusal to give additional loans on the basis of the special surrender value of the policies. Consequently a token compensation was awarded to the Respondent-Complainant in this case and that with reference to its deficiency in service established against the insurance in respect of items (iii) and (iv) above.

185. 1986-95 CONSUMER 858 (NS).

In a special leave petition Under Article 136 of The Constitution in *State of Orissa* v. *Divisional Manager, LIC and Another,*[186] the question before the Supreme Court was whether the State of Orissa (Appellant) is liable to pay compensation to the government servant (Respondent) under the Act and whether the claim is maintainable.

The court held that under section 2(1)(o) the excluded services are 'Service free of charge or under a contract of personal service'. Since the complainant in this case was government servant and therefore he was bound by the service conditions and the state was rendering services free of charge to the complainant. Under these circumstances it was held that the government servant has been excluded from the purview of the Act to claim any damages against the state under the Act. However, it was made open to complainant to claim in any other forum.

After perusing the above cases under the heading Insurance Service carefully one thing is observed and that is that the Consumer Disputes Redressal Agencies while deciding cases under different sub-headings as above mentioned have not faced much difficulty as in cases of life insurance. In these cases LIC has repudiated claims primarily on the ground that insured had hiddened the grounds of health. It is to be submitted here that LIC must employ competent doctors equipped with modern techniques so as to ascertain the state of health of a consumer. The standard proposal forms add to the miseries of the policy-holder. He is neither aware of his own health history nor is able to reply the questions asked in the proposal form.

(8) Medical Service

Unlike other services specifically mentioned in the definition section 2(1)(o) of the Act 'Medical Service' has always disputed applicability of the Act although there has been a remedy in Law of Torts for the negligence done by

186. 1986-96 CONSUMER 2141 (NS). In this case recent judgment of the Supreme Court in Indian Medical Association *v.* V.P. Shantha and Others (1995) 2 CCC; CONSUMER 673 (NS) was applied in which concept of personal service was considered.

the doctors. However, very few suits have been filed under The Law of Torts because it takes a long time to decide such cases. There is criminal liability also for the negligence committed by any person and a doctor can be prosecuted under sections 304-A, 336, 337 and 338 of Indian Penal Code. If the complainant is able to prove the negligence on the part of the doctor, he can be punished with imprisonment or fine or both according to the gravity of negligence and punishment prescribed under The Indian Penal Code, 1860.[187]

There are number of cases in the newspapers every day that after performing an operation the doctor forgot knife, towel, scissors or some other instrument in the body of the patient.[188] There are various cases[189] where the courts have held the doctor negligent in the performance of his duty under the Consumer Protection Act. Actually the controversy concerning the inclusion or exclusion of services rendered by medical practitioners and hospitals in general appears to have started from the decision of the Rajasthan State Commission in *Consumer Unity & Trust Society, Jaipur* v. *State of Rajasthan*[190] which needs to be referred here.

In this case a voluntary consumer organization made a complaint on behalf of a lady who underwent an abdominal tubectomy operation at the government hospital on part of the family planning programmes. It was alleged in the complaint that after operation she suffered serious complications on account of negligence on the part of the civil surgeon who had performed the operation and it was due to the lack of proper post-operation care and attention for which compensation was claimed. It was held by the concerned state commission that neither the lady nor his

---

187. Sheraz Lateef Ahmad Khan, Article, 'Patient as Consumer' (1996) (1) SCJ, p. 12.

188. Fareed Ahmad Khan, Article, 'Medical Services and Consumer Protection Act, 1986 (1997), Vol. 1, Part 4, SCJ.

189. Paschim Banga Khat Mazdoor Samity and Others *v.* State of West Bengal and Another, 1986-96 CONSUMER 2040 (NS). In this case it was held denial of immediate Medical Aid to complainant the Government Hospital was held liable for committing breach of the petitioner's right guaranteed under Article 21 of the Constitution.

190. (1991) 1 CPR 30.

husband can be said consumer under section 2(1)(o) of the Consumer Protection Act, as they had not hired services for consideration. On appeal, National Commission requested an advocate of the Supreme Court to assist the commission. The advocate proceeding before the National Commission laid emphasis on the following points:

(i) That tax could be regarded as payment of consideration the return for which tax-payer gets only the participation in the common benefits.
(ii) That it is guaranteed under the constitution that state should provide a good standard of life and health facilities.
(iii) That the words 'hires or avails' should be taken to mean any person who avails or uses any services.
(iv) That the expression 'service free of charge' no doubt appears to mean service without reward or remuneration (gratuitous service) but the word 'charge' has various other meanings for instance—duty, liability and burden, etc.
(v) That the Consumer Protection Act, 1986 is a beneficial piece of legislation (a measure of social welfare) which needs to be liberally construed for the protection of interests of larger number of people.

But the National Commission did not accept the above raised contentions specially that tax constitutes 'consideration' for any facility provided by the state and upheld the decision of the Rajasthan State Commission and observed:

> "The conclusion is evitable that persons who avail themselves of the facility of medical treatment in government hospitals are not consumers and that the said faculty offered in government hospitals cannot be regarded as service 'hired' for consideration. Hence, no complaint under the Act can be preferred either by any person or by a consumer association on his behalf . . .

The decision of the National Commission in the above

mentioned case was followed in a number of cases prominent among them are *Ram Kali* v. *Delhi Administration,*[191] *Soubhaya Prasad* v. *State of Karnataka,*[192] *Laxman T. Kotgiri* v. *Union of India,*[193] *Avtar Singh* v. *State of Punjab,*[194] *Dr. S. Venkataraman* v. *M. Chandrasekaram,*[195] *S.S. Kohlon* v. *Bawa Hospital,*[196] etc.

However, in *Sukunte Beherl* v. *Sashi Bhushan Rath,*[197] in which a lady wanted to terminate her pregnancy in a government hospital but was not permitted to do this despite the fact that another doctor advised for medical termination of the pregnancy. The opposite party on denying the allegations the District Forum dismissed the complaint as not maintainable. On appeal to Supreme Court it was held that obstruction to such medical termination of pregnancy would not be a negligence. Further the court said that the finding of the District Forum that the complaint under the Act is maintainable because she has not paid for such service is not correct where the state government has paid the doctor to render the service to the people who attend the hospital. Thus, the persons who were attending the hospital for treatment and advise were the beneficiaries of the service rendered by the doctor. Therefore, the complaint was a consumer within the meaning of section 2(1)(d).

Similarly, in *Cosmopolitan Hospitals* v. *Vasanth P. Nair,*[198] the National Commission expressed complete agreement with the observations of the Andhra Pradesh State Commission and especially the Kerela State Commission that "where a medical officers service may loosely be called personal, it will be incorrect, infractious and crude to describe it as personal service."

Thus, the National Commission, by its decisions in the above case, had endeavored to set at rest for the time being,

191. (1991) 1 CPJ, p. 809.
192. (1994) 1 CPR, p. 140.
193. (1993) 1 CPJ, p. 1001.
194. (1993) I CLJ 694.
195. (1994) III CPJ, p. 219.
196. *Id.*, p. 286.
197. (1993) II CPJ, p. 633.
198. (1992) 3 CLJ 80.

the controversy concerning the governance of private medical practitioners, hospitals and nursing homes by upholding the finding of The State Commission that the activity of providing medical assistance for payment carried on by hospitals and members of the medical profession falls within the scope of the expression 'service' as defined in Section 2(1)(o) of the Act and that in the event of any deficiency in the performance of such service, the aggrieved party can invoke the remedies provided under the Act by filing a complaint before consumer forum having jurisdiction. . . .

The decision of the National Commission in above-mentioned case has been approved by other state commissions. For instance, in *Sachin Agarwal* v. *Dr. Ashok Arora*[199] and *Ramanand B. Raikar* v. *Salgamkar Medical Research Centre.*[200]

Though both of the above named cases have been decided in favour of the consumer but there are a large number of cases which were rejected even at their preliminary stage for want of satisfactorily proof against doctors. Apart from strong opposition on the part of doctors and medical authorities against applicability of Consumer Protection Act to medical service the decision of Madras High Court in *C.S.K. Subramanian* v. *Kumaraswamy*[201] has given a deathblow to the consumerism in this field.

In this case several writ petitions were filed by doctors and medical authorities claiming immunity of medical service from the provisions of the Consumer Protection Act.

The Madras High Court held as:

(i) The services rendered to a patient by a medical practitioner or an hospital by way of diagnosis and treatment both medicinal and surgical would not come within the meaning of 'service' as defined in Section 2(1)(o) of the Act.

(ii) A patient who undergoes treatment under medical practitioner or an hospital by way of diagnosis

199. (1991) 1 CPJ 113.
200. (1993) 1 CPJ, p. 300.
201. (1994) 2 CLJ 294.

and treatment both medicinal and surgical cannot be considered to be 'consumer' within the meaning of Section 2(1)(d) of the Act.

(iii) The medical practitioner or hospital undertaking and providing paramedical services of any categories or kind cannot claim similar immunity from the provisions of the Act and they would fall to the extent of such services rendered by them within the definition of 'service' and a person availing of such service would be a 'consumer' within the meaning of the Act.

However, judgment of the above mentioned case of Madras High Court which had granted exemption to the medical profession from the application of the Consumer Protection Act has been answered by a landmark judgment in *Indian Medical Association* v. *V.P. Shantha & Others.*[202]

In the instant case the Supreme Court was called upon to decide the matter between Indian Medical Council Act and Consumer Protection Act. There were several appeals before this apex court from different state commissions, national commission and from various High Courts on the same issue of medical service, i.e. whether and if so in what circumstances a medical practitioner can be regarded as rendering service. Connected with this question is the question whether the service rendered at a hospital/nursing home can be regarded as 'service' u/s 2(1)(o) of the Act. The court in its judgment comprising a bench of three judges, namely, Kuldip Singh, S.C. Agarwal and B.L. Hansaria, JJ. speaking through his lordship Justice S.C. Agarwal held that doctors are accountable for any act of medical negligence under the Consumer Protection Act, 1986 and made the following conclusions:

(i) Service rendered to a patient by a medical practitioner except where doctor render service free of charge to every patient or under a contract of personal service, by way of consultation,

202. 1986-96 CONSUMER 1569.

diagnosis and treatment both medicinal and surgical would fall within the ambit of 'service' as defined in section 2(1)(o) of the Act.

(ii) The fact that medical/practitioners belong to the medical profession and are subject to the disciplinary control of the Medical Council of India and/or State Medical Councils constituted under the provisions of the Indian Medical Council Act would not exclude the services rendered by them from the ambit of the Act.

(iii) 'A contract of personal service' has to be distinguished from 'a contract for personal services'. In the absence of a relationship of master and servant between the patient and medical practitioner, the service rendered by a medical practitioner to the patient cannot be regarded as service rendered under a 'contract of personal service'. Such service is service rendered under a 'contract for personal service' and is not covered by exclusionary clause of the definition of 'service' contained in Section 2(1)(o) of the Act.

(iv) The expression 'contract of personal service' in Section 2(1)(o) of the Act cannot be confined to contracts for employment of domestic servants only and the said expression would include the employment of medical officer for the purpose of rendering medical service to the employer. The service rendered by a medical officer to his employer under the contract of employment would be outside the purview of 'service' as defined in Section 2(1)(o) of the Act.

(v) Service rendered free of charge by a medical practitioner attached to a hospital/nursing home or a medical officer employed in a hospital/nursing home where such services are rendered free of charge to everybody, would not be 'service' as defined in Section 2(1)(o) of the Act. The payment of a token amount for registration purpose only at the hospital/nursing home would not alter the position.

(vi) Service rendered at a non-government hospital/ nursing home where no charge whatsoever is made from any person availing the service and all patients rich and poor are given free service—is outside the purview of the expression 'service' as defined in Section 2(1)(o) of the Act. The payment of a token amount for registration purpose only at the hospital/nursing home would not alter the position.

(vii) Service rendered at a non-government hospital/ nursing home where charges are required to be paid by the persons availing such services fall within the purview of the expression 'service' as defined in Section 2(1)(o) of the Act.

(viii) Service rendered at a non-government hospital/ nursing home where charges are required to be paid by persons who are in a position to pay and persons who cannot offer to pay are rendered service free of charge would fall within the ambit of the expression 'service' as defined in Section 2(1)(o) of the Act irrespective of the fact that the service is rendered free of charge to persons who are not in a position to pay for such services. Free service, would also be 'service' and the recipient a 'consumer' under the Act.

(ix) Service rendered at a government hospital/health centre/dispensary where no charge whatsoever is made from any person availing the services and all patients rich and poor are given free service— is outside the purview of the expression 'service' as defined in Section 2(1)(o) of the Act. The payment of a token amount for registration purpose only at the hospital/nursing home would not alter the position.

(x) Service rendered at government hospital/health centre/dispensary where services are rendered on payment of charges and also rendered free of charge to other persons availing such service would fall within the ambit of the expression 'service' as defined in Section 2(1)(o) of the Act irrespective of the fact that the service is rendered free of charge to persons who do not pay for such service. Free service would also be 'service' and the recipient a 'consumer' under the Act.

(xi) Service rendered by a medical practitioner or hospital/nursing home cannot be regarded as service rendered free of charge, if the person availing the service has taken an insurance policy for medical care where under the charges for consultation, diagnosis and medical treatment are borne by the insurance company and such service would fall within the ambit of 'service' as defined in Section 2(1)(o) of the Act.

(xii) Similarly, where, as a part of the conditions of service, the employer bears the expenses of medical treatment of an employee and his family members dependent on him, the service rendered to such an employee and his family members by a medical practitioner or a hospital/nursing home would not be free of charge and would constitute 'service' under Section 2(1)(o) of the Act.

On the whole, the above judgment by bringing negligent doctors under the umbrella of Consumer Protection Act, 1986 has heightened the scope of consumerism. Following the *I.M.A.* v. *V.P. Shanta's* (1995) judgment in *Poonam Verma* v. *Ashwine Patel,*[203] a compensation of Rs. 30,000 was decreed against doctor.

In this case doctor (Respondent No. 1) was registered as medical practitioner with the Gujarat Homeopathic Medical Council as he had studied Homeopathy for 4 years in the Medical College at Anand and had, thereafter, obtained a diploma in Homeopathic Medicine and Surgery but had treated patient under Allopathic System prescribing Allopathic Medicines. The question for the consideration of the court was whether the doctor could prescribe and administer Allopathic Medicines if he had not studied Allopathy and had not pursued the prescribed course in

203. AIR 1996 Supreme Court 2111.

Allopathy nor had he obtained degree or diploma in Allopathy from any recognized Medical College and whether this will amount to actionable negligence? The court held since the law under which doctor was registered as a medical practitioner, required him to practice HOMOEOPATHY ONLY he was under a statutory duty not to enter the field of any other system of medicine. He having practiced in Allopathy, without being qualified in that system, was guilty of negligence *per se* and therefore, the appeal against him was allowed in consonance with the maxim *sic utere tuo ut aliunum non loedas* (A person is held liable at law for the consequences of his negligence).

The Supreme Court of India again in a recent case of *Parmanand Katara* v. *Union of India*[204] has emphasized that human life is more valuable and must be preserved at all costs and that every member of the medical profession nay every human being, is under an obligation to provide such aid to another as may be necessary to help him secure from fatal accidents, that it is the obligation of those who are in charge of the health of the community to preserve life and reminded every doctor of his total obligation and assured him of the position that he does not contravene the law of the land by proceeding to treat the injured victim on his appearance before him and that the formalities under the Criminal Procedure Code or any other local laws should not stand in the way of the medical practitioner attending an injured person.

Again in *Jyotsana Arvind Kumar Shah & Others* v. *Bombay Hospital Trust*,[205] the Bombay Hospital Trust has been directed to pay Rs. 7 lacs as compensation to the wife and children of a patient who died in the hospital for alleged carelessness and negligence. In this case one Mr. Arvind Kumar Shah was admitted to the hospital for an operation on his left hip. He was operated upon by Dr. K.T. Dholakia and died the following morning. The complainant had complained of pain and continuous bleeding from the wound till he died next day. The hospital authorities failed to appear before the

---

204. A.I.R. 1989 SC 2039.
205. 1999 (1) CPR 86 (SC).

commission, it proceeded *ex-parte* and directed the Bombay Hospital Trust to pay Rs. 7 lacs with interest of 12% p.a. from the date of the complaint till realization.

Similarly, in *M/s Spring Meadows Hospital (Noida) and Another* v. *Harjol Ahluwalia*,[206] the doctor made the diagnosis that the patient was suffering from typhoid and prescribed the medicine for treatment of fever. After some days nurse of the hospital asked the father of the minor patient to get the injection where upon the nurse injected the same to the minor patient. The patient immediately on being injected collapsed while still in the lap of his mother. The doctors diagnosed that the child had suffered a cardiac arrest. He was admitted to AIIMS for some days to stabilize the condition of the child but all in vain. The Supreme Court (on appeal) held that commission was right in awarding compensation in favour of the child taking into account the cost of equipments and the recurring expenses that would be necessary for the said minor child who is merely having a vegetative life. The compensation awarded in favour of the parents of the minor child is for their acute mental agony and the life long care and attention which the parents would have to bestow on the minor child.

Now, though it is well established that guilty doctors would be liable under Consumer Protection Act but it is only if negligence in treating the patient has been proved. In the following cases no negligence or deficiency was established and accordingly no relief was granted. Here first case of such type is *The Calcutta Medical Research Institute* v. *Bimalesh Catterjee & Others*.[207] In this case state commission awarded compensation of Rs. 2 lacs in favour of the complainant for negligence and deficiency in transplanting blood of wrong group. However, the National Commission held that State Commission had relied on a certificate issued by a doctor who is neither hematologist nor a pathologist. He does not mention the blood group of either the donee or the donor. No evidence has been brought on record to link the blood

206. 1998 (1) CPR 1 (SC).

207. 1999 (1) CPR 3 (National Commission).

transfusion with any of the resultant complications in the case nor has any evidence been led which would go to show the hospital or any of its doctors had been negligent.

In another case,[208] complainant was suffering from bronchial problem and breathing trouble. She took treatment from appellants herein, but her condition deteriorated however, her condition improved when she consulted other doctors. State Commission accepted complainants claim and awarded compensation of Rs. 2 lacs against each of two appellants herein. But the National Commission held that complainant had failed to tender evidence and State Commission had disposed the case on basis of certificates given by persons who were not medical men. Neither in discharge certificate given by hospital nor in prescription of the doctor there was any suggestion that treatment given to complainants by appellant was wrong. So doctor should not be held guilty of giving wrong treatment without some medical evidence to that effect.

Similarly, in *Tara Chand Jain* v. *Sri Ganga Ram Hospital & Another*[209] the complainant was having urinary trouble. The opposite party No. 2 with his team examined the complainant and advised him prostate operation. However, the tendency of continuous and regular flow of urine which had started immediately after the operation continued and could not be cured. Complainant alleged that sprincter muscle of complainant was cut during operation and that is why there was leaking of urine. National Commission held that no cogent, convincing and reliable evidence is produced in support of allegations made in complaint. So in the absence of medical evidence produced charge of negligence or deficiency on part of doctor could not be held proud.

It is to observed that in the light of the above discussion it can be safely said that extension of the jurisdiction of the consumer forum created under the Act to the medical practice is welcome step to bring in greater accountability in this important public utility service.

---

208. Subhashis Dhir and Another *v.* Smt. Sanjakta Sengupta and Others, 1999 (3) CPR 13 (National Commission).
209. 1999 (3) CPR 38 (National Commission).

However, the condition *quid pro quo*,[210] i.e., a consideration should have been paid in order to put liability on one's shoulder for negligent service under this Act has brought lot of confusion. Though there is very little difference between the obligations undertaken by a medical practitioner in private practice and those imposed on his colleagues and counterparts working in the hospitals run and administered either by the government or local authorities or philanthropic bodies but the source of consideration being entirely different in both services had made the medical authorities (government) to claim non-applicability of the Act. Since there is now major shift towards private medical health care facilities a National Sample Survey recently found that 70% of the out-patient Central government health services put the average rate of growth of private hospital at a high 70% in the 80's while that of government facilities grew by just 2%. Rama Paru, a public policy government expert in the Delhi-based Voluntary Health Association of India (VHAI) found that in Hyderabad as many as 80% of government surgeons were now consultants to private nursing homes making them liable under Consumer Protection Redressal Agencies as well. But it does not mean to circumscribe the limits of private medical practitioners and let the government doctors to go ahead even to the extent of committing negligence.

Keeping in view the aims and objectives of the Consumer Protection Act there is a greater need to bring the whole medical profession under this Act so that the human life is to be respected and protected with concern and care. Running a government health service is not a sovereign service so as to claim immunity from liability for sovereign acts. Medical men have to bring to their profession, like all other professionals, an amount of care and skill which is reasonable in the circumstances of the situation. A doctor can be held guilty of medical negligence only when he falls short of the standard of reasonable medical care. A doctor cannot be held to be negligent merely because in the matter of opinion he made an error of judgment or he has demanded

210. Dr. Sr. Louie and Another *v.* Kemolil Pathumma and Another, 1986-95 CONSUMER 54 (NS).

high charges even though the consideration paid to him is improper[211] but there is no reason why these government doctors will not be made accountable and why should those working in these hospitals get away with murders when it is through sheer negligence.

(9) Postal Service

Under the Indian Post Office Act, 1898 Postal Deptt. being indispensable agency for communication and financial service is meant to provide postal service to the public specially weaker sections of the country. But like medical and educational service postal service not specifically mentioned definition of 'service' as provided under Consumer Protection Act has claimed and contented statutory immunity and applicability of this Act U/S 6 of Post Office Act.[212] Moreover, the ruling of National Commission in *The Presidency Post Master* v. *Dr. U. Shanker Rao*[213] has given death blow to the avowed and celebrated purpose of Consumer Protection Act. In this case two revision petitions were disposed of by the common order as the points involved were similar.

In the first revision petition the complainant-director of National Medical Hospital decided to celebrate the 15th Anniversary of his hospital on 11th March, 1990. It is alleged that about 600 invitation letters were issued and put into post at the post office on 5th and 6th March, 1990 which were addressed to Industrialists and Bankers, etc. Most of the invitations are set to have reached invitees on 13th and 14th March, 1990 and the function in 11th March, 1990 proved to

211. Regarding the question of charging high fee in B.S. Hedge *v.* Dr. Sudhansu Bhattacharya, 1986-95 CONSUMER 545 (NS) it was held that it is not for the Consumer Forum to adjudicate on the question whether the consideration charged was reasonable.

212. The government shall not incur any liability by reasons of the loss, miss delivery or delay or damage to and postal article in course of transmission by post, except in so far as such liability may in express term be undertaken by the central government as hereinafter provided, and no Officer of the Post Office shall incur any liability by reason of any such loss. Loss, misdelivery, delay or damage unless he has caused the same fraudulently or by his wilful Act or default.

213. 1986-95 CONSUMER 395 (NS); Seen also Post Master General, Tamil Nadu *v.* Calvin Jacob, 1986-95 1235 (NS).

be a poor show as only 200 persons attended it. According to the complainant there was gross deficiency in service and negligence on the part of the postal department.

In the second revision petition it was alleged that due to the carelessness, negligence and misconduct of the postal authorities, registered letter containing the original lorry receipt of consignment sent by the complainant had fallen into the hands of some unscrupulous persons who used it.

District Forum in each case allowed the complaint and accordingly the damages claimed in each case was allowed. State Commission upheld the order passed by the lower court. National Commission held the claim petitions are not maintainable in view of Section 6 Indian Post Office Act as the services rendered by the post office are merely statutory and there is no contractual liability[214] so far as the speed post service by post department is concerned the National Commission held in *The Post Master, Station Kalhijuda & Others* v. *G. Hanumantha Reddy*,[215] the bar U/S 6 will not apply and it is open to the party aggrieved by the non-delivery or delay in delivery of an article sent by speed post to put forward a claim for compensation as against the postal department.

It is to be submitted that postal service is no doubt sovereign function of government but the provisions of Section 6 of Indian Post Office Act, 1898 constituted no defence when an action for compensation for deficiency of service or negligence is instituted under the Consumer Protection Act. Consumer Protection has been passed specifically to provide cheap, speedy, inexpensive and expeditious remedy against deficiency in service whether that is committed by the government or any private body provided only that the services are hired by the consumer. Any attempt to exclude statutory or official bodies to the common man would be against the provisions of the Consumer Protection Act and Postal Service is no exception to this rule.

---

214. The partner, Monickbag Automobiles *v.* Sub-Postmaster LSG and Another (1997) 1 CPR 6060 wherein it was held the services rendered by the post office are merely statutory and there is no contractual liability.

215. 1986-95 CONSUMER 1293 (NS).

(10) Telephone Service

The telephone service is a government monopoly. Like medical profession Telecommunication Deptt. has always contented the applicability of the Consumer Protection Act. The fact that disputes relating to telephones are to be settled U/S 7-B of the Indian Telegraph Act, 1885 does not oust the jurisdiction of Consumer Disputes Redressal Agencies[216] because Consumer Protection Act is in addition to the remedy provided under other existing law. The subscriber of the telephone hires the services from the Central Government for a consideration paid in the nature of installation charges, rental charges and call charges whereas Section 7-B applies only if there is any dispute concerning telephone line, appliance or apparatus between the Telegraph Authority and the subscriber.[217] In *Divisional Manager Telephones, Lucknow* v. *Madhu Enterprises, Lucknow*,[218] the National Commission held:

> "The non-mention of telephone facility in the inclusive portion of the definition is of no consequence in view of the very wide language used in the main part of the definition which takes in every form of service. Admittedly, the telephone service is not provided free of charge and hence the lost portion of the definition which excludes service rendered free of charge does not get attracted nor is this a case of contract of personal service."

Inspite of the above decision Telegraph Authority having developed phobia of this Act is striving against the jurisdiction of Consumer Disputes Redressal Agencies. How far the grievance of telephone consumers have been redressed under the Consumer Protection Act is to be enunciated by cases.

---

216. Seen also Telecom District Manager, Patna *v.* M/s Kaliyanpur Cement Ltd. (1986-96 CONSUMER 158 (NS).
217. Telecom District Manager, Mehasana and Another *v.* Shri Patel Shankerlal Kavalram, 1986-96 CONSUMR 2196 (NS).
218. Union of India *v.* Niresh Aggarwal (1991) CPJ 203.

(a) Disconnection of Telephone Service without Notice

Disconnection of telephone on the ground of non-payment of dues without intimation/notice to the subscriber amounts to deficiency in service. Disconnection of telephone without notice is violative of the principles of natural justice[219] But what amount to notice is a question not free from controversy. As per the Rule 443 of the Indian Telegraph Rules Telecommunication Deptt. is specifically entitled to disconnect the telephone without any notice. Once the bill has been served and there has been a default in payment of such bill. Following the rule National Commission in a number of cases[220] held (while rejecting the contention of the complainant that the telephone was disconnected without any advance notice to the complainant) there is no deficiency in service on the part of the department in disconnecting the telephone of the complainant on the ground of non-payment of the bill issued to the subscriber.

It is to be submitted here that even after due service of bills a separate notice of disconnection should be issued to the telephone subscriber calling upon him to pay the bill and it is only in the event of his non-comply with said demand within a period say for example one month from issue of such notice the disconnection should be taken into process.

However, where the action of the Telegraph Authority is arbitrary and not in accordance with the rules of Indian Telegraph specially Rule 443 it amounts to deficiency in service. In case of *Mahanagar Telephone Nigam Ltd. & Another* v. *M.R. Chedda & Another,*[221] the complainant having telephone facility requested for disconnection of the STD facility. He was informed that the STD facility had been withdrawn and telephone number has been also changed. He received telephone bills under the old number which were

219. *Supra* Note 43.

220. Seen Mahanagar Telephone Nigam Ltd. and Others *v.* Vijay G. Pradhan, 1986-96 CONSUMER 2968; General Manager, Telephones, Faridabad *v.* D.K Singh, 1986-96 CONSUMER 2768 (NS).

221. 1986-95 CONSUMER 384 (NS). Seen also Commercial Officer, Office of the Telecom, District Manager, Patna *v.* Bihar State Warehousing Corporation, 1986-95 CONSUMER 159 (NS), where complainant was entitled to Rs. 1000 for a short period disconnection.

highly abnormal and exorbitant. He did not pay the same and consequently telephone was disconnected. National Commission fully agreed with the State Commission that the STD calls cannot be attributed to the complainants.[222] Another case of grave deficiency is *District Engineer, Telecommunications Deptt. & Another* v. *Roshan Lal Aggarwal.*[223] Here Complainant was enjoying two telephones one at mill and another at residence. There was outstanding bill in respect of telephone charges for the telephone installed at mill. As the outstanding bill was not paid the telecommunication department disconnected both the telephones. National Commission upheld the decision of State Commission that as there was no outstanding bill against the telephone installed at residence so the telecommunication department disconnected the phone arbitrarily.

(b) Excessive Billing

Not only our day-to-day experience but our painstaking analysis of the cases reveal that most of the complaints before Telegraph Authority and Consumer Disputes Redressal Agencies are regarding excessive billing of the telephones. As far back as in 1986 Government of India, Ministry of Communications, Deptt. of Telephones had became aware of the difficulty experienced by the telephone subscribers about the issue of excessive telephone bills and issued instructions detailing the manner in which the complaints filed by the subscribers about excessive bills have to be dealt. It provides for[224]—

(i) Meter readings being taken every fortnight;
(ii) Identifying all subscribers whose current fortnightly readings show a sudden spurt; and
(iii) In case of such sudden spurts being noticed, placing the telephone line on observation and

---

222. In District Manager, Telephones, Patna *v.* L.K. Bagila (1992) 1 CPJ 189 (National Commission) also it was held that if the telephone which does not have STD facility shows STD calls amounts to deficiency in service on the part of Telephone Department.
223. 1986-96 CONSUMER 1993 (NS).
224. Vide circular No. 0/59/85-35, Dated 9th April, 1986.

> deputing responsible staff to the subscribers premises to check up that there has been no special occasion which might have given rise to such spurts. . . .

It is a common belief that some vile wretch workmen who may be a line man, technical person or some other person are vigorously providing unauthorized telephone connections to some miscreants (who themselves may or may not be among telephone subscribers) in return of reward or remuneration and thereby enabling them to misuse the telephones which are functioning in the name of others. With the result telephone owner applies for disconnection of the facility or faces the consequences by paying the excessive bill. Under these circumstances when an aggrieved subscriber approaches Court of Law/Redressal Agencies he is required to prove the allegations of deficiency made in the complaint and in case he fails to prove, the complaint goes dismissed.[225]

In an unique case interesting situation arose for consideration. The case is *Kasam Noor Mohd. Unad* v. *Union of India*[226] through Telecom District Manager, Telecom District, Jamnagar. The complainant who is collecting oil tins and supplying to the oil mills had got a telephone with STD facility. According to him, the normal bills for the said phone ranged from Rs. 200 to 400 but the bills dated 1.9.1990, 1.11.1990 and 1.1.1991 were respectively for Rs. 23,324, Rs. 15,668, Rs. 21,901, the correctness of which he challenged. The telephone was put under secret observation. As requested by the complainant his phone was taken for safe custody and then was disconnected. In the absence of any evidence to establish that any collusion has taken place between the employees of the Telecom Department and third parties in the alleged misuse of the said telephone. The State Commission concluded that the complainant must have used the telephone for overseas calls and was then trying to avoid the liability to pay the telephone bills. Before National

---

225. Ab. Aziz Suleman *v.* General Manager, Telecom, 1986-96 CONSUMER 3166 (NS).
226. 1986-96 CONSUMER 2337 (NS).

Commission complainant only reiterated the points made before the State Commission. The Apex Commission (National Commission) held that the order of the State Commission is based on a fair appreciation of the evidence before them.

However, the minority view expressed by the member B.S. Yadav, J. is more convenient and expeditious. The learned member of the commission held considering the fact that the complainant is mainly a hawker, it would look very doubtful that he would use the telephone in making ISD calls. Further as soon as the spurt was noticed in the meter reading the department make no investigations. Considering all the circumstances of the case the learned member came to the conclusion that the telephone of the complainant has been misused.

Another noteworthy case is *The District Manager, Telephones and Others* v. *Niti Saran*[227] wherein the National Commission uphold the decision of the State Commission that "to resolve the dispute of excessive billing Redressal Forums have been taking recourse to ascertaining the average number of calls made from the particular telephones over a period of time to see whether the bills complained against show any abnormal or marked deviation from the pattern of calling derived from the average number of calls in a particular period." However, after concluding the order in the instant case, The National Commission expressed the disquiet over the manner in which the Consumer Disputes Redressal Agencies have been disposing of the complaints from consumers regarding inflated bills issued by the Telecom Authority. In this connection the commission in the last para of the order wished to reiterate the observations made in *Telecom District Manager, Patna* v. *Kalyanpur Cement Ltd.*[228] and held:

---

227. 1986-96 CONSUMER 793 (NS); (1991) 1 CPJ 48.

228. Order date 08-11-1990 R.P. No. 44; Seen also General Manager, Mahanagar Telephone Nigam Ltd. *v.* Mauli Chand Sharma, 1986-96 CONSUMER 2710 (NS).

> "The Consumer Redressal Forums will not be legally justified in taking over the function of estimating by application of the rule of thumb the precise number of calls made unless there is adequate evidence of calls which may be either direct or circumstantial to show that the metering equipment was defective or there has been misuse of the particular telephone by some unauthorized person in collusion with the employees of the department particularly in cases where a subscriber has the STD facility."

The above decision was followed consistently in *Divisional Manager, Telephones, Lucknow* v. *Madhu Enterprises, Lucknow,*[229] *Telecom District Manager, Patna* v. *M.S. Mukerjee,*[230] *Deptt. of Telecom & Others* v. *Satya Narain Lal,*[231] *Union of India, through Accounts Officer, Rajkot Telephones, Rajkot* v. *Dhanjibhai K. Patil,*[232] *U.S. Dalal* v. *Telecom District Manager, Telephone Exchange, Rohtak, Haryana,*[233] *Union of India* (through Chief General Manager) *Telecommunication, Jaipur & Others,*[234] wherein it was held by the National Commission (National Commission) that unless and until there is evidence to show that the metering equipment is defective or there has been tampering with the telephone connection by third parties it would not be legally correct for the consumer forums to determine the bills on the basis of average of the calls made during the earlier periods nor is the consumer's forum justified in disregarding the fact that the bills will be heavy if the consumer avails of the STD facility . . .

To the same effect is *Accounts Officer, Telephone District, Panaji* v. *Sheela H.N. Gaunekar,*[235] where no defect in meter was proved and consequently no average billing was allowed to be made the basis for correct verification of calls. Since

229. 1986-95 CONSUMER 904 (NS).
230. 1986-95 CONSUMER 1179 (NS).
231. 1986-95 CONSUMER 725 (NS).
232. 1986-95 CONSUMER 1239 (NS).
233. 1986-96 CONSUMER 2447 (NS).
234. 1986-96 CONSUMER 2160 (NS).
235. (1996) 1 CPJ 49 (National Commission).

malfunctioning of the telephone or misuse of the telephone line is a dispute within the meaning of Section 7-B of the Telegraph Act so the correctness of the bill or inflated bill can be challenged before the Arbitrator whose award by purview of this Section shall be final.[236] In the case of *The Telecom District Engineer, Pondichery & Another* v. *R. Shangmugam*,[237] National Commission held it is not open to the subscribes to first approach 'The Central Government' for appointment of an arbitrator and then either during pendency of arbitration or after the award to file a complaint before the Consumer Disputes Redressal Agencies. The Commission referred the recent pronouncement of the Supreme Court in *M.L. Jaggi* v. *Maha Nagar Telephones Nigam Ltd. & Others* decided on 2.1.1996 where the court while dealing with the scope of Section 7-B observed that the resolution of the dispute by arbitration U/S 7-B is a statutory remedy provided under the Act and that in dispute as regards the amount claimed in the demand raised, the only remedy provided is by way of arbitration. By operation of Sub-section (2) thereof, the award of the arbitrator shall be conclusive between the parties to the dispute and shall not be questioned in any court. Later on in para 7 of the judgment the Supreme Court made the legal position clear by stating "it is seen that U/S 7-B the award is conclusive when the citizen complains that he was not correctly put to bill of the calls he had made and disputed the demand for payment the statutory remedy open to him is one provided U/S 7-B of the Act. By necessary implication,

236. 7-B—Arbitration of Dispute:

(1) Except as otherwise expressly provided in this Act if any dispute concerning any telegraph line, appliance or apparatus arises between the telephone authority and the person for whose benefit the line appliance or apparatus is, or has been provided. The dispute shall be determined by Arbitration and shall, for the purposes of such determination be referred to an Arbitrator appointed by the Central Government either specially for the determination of that dispute or generally for the determination of dispute under this Section.

(2) The award of the Arbitrator appointed under sub-section (1) shall be conclusive between the parties to the disputes and shall not be questioned in any Court.

237. 1997 (2) CPR 115 (National Commission).

when the arbitrator decides the dispute U/S 7-B, he is enjoined to give reasons in support of his decision since it is final and cannot be questioned in a court of law. The only obvious remedy available to the aggrieved person against the award is judicial review under Article 226 of the Constitution.

However, where the subscriber merely complains about the exorbitant bill meaning thereby that he complains only about faulty reading of meter, it only involves question as to whether the meter has been correctly and honestly read and the readings had been correctly and honestly noted down. Such dispute does not fall within the purview of Section 7-B.[238]

(c) Delays

Delay in providing telephone service after a subscriber has made full payment in shifting it or in reconnecting it after a bill has been duly paid is a deficiency in service. In *Vijay Sethi* v. *District Manager, Telephones and Another,*[239] the complainant had locked his STD facility by use of wrong code. He requested the Telecom Authority for unlocking the same on payment of relevant charges. He claimed inaction of the Telecom Deptt. which resulted into business loss. National Commission uphold the decision of the State Commission that there was inordinate delay in reopening the locked STD dynamic code and this was deficiency in the telecommunication service. Similarly in *Union of India* v. *Amam Dahiya,*[240] an award of Rs. 6000 was allowed by way of compensation as there was delay on the part of telephone authority to provide telephone connection in accordance with allotted priority. However, where complainant could not cite a single instance in which some one below him in the waiting list had been provided a telephone connection cannot be entitled to compensation for the harassment.[241]

---

238. The Divisional Engineer and Another *v.* Harikrishen Bhattad, 1986-96 CONSUMR 2098 (NS).
239. 1997 (1) CPR 103.
240. (1993) 1 CPR 117 (National Commission); 1986-95 CONSUMER 81 (National Commission).
241. B.S. Bindra *v.* Secretary, Union of India and Another, (1986-96) CONSUMER 3218 (NS); Seen also Divisional Engineer (C.F.) Calcutta, Telephones *v.* Dr. Malati Sinha, 1997(2) CPR 266 (National Commission).

As said in the beginning the same conclusion can be drawn here that the existence of the alternative remedy of arbitration under Indian Telegraph Act cannot stand in the way of speedy and effective remedy which can be granted under Consumer Protection Act. Keeping in view the object of the Consumer Protection Act that is to promote welfare of the society in as much as to remove the helplessness of a consumer which he faces against powerful business and public bodies—all government bodies are liable under the Act for any deficiency in services to those who purchase their services for consideration and officers-in-charge would be held personally liable if they cause any harassment to the users of the services in pursuing the matters with the department. Like postal services as discussed earlier telecommunication department is claiming immunity though it is amenable to the Consumer Protection Act in respect of any act or omission in respect of their service which amounts to deficiency in service. In order to improve the quality of life for the society there should be more accountability from our officials manning the public utilities and a bit more consideration for the consumers in the state.

(11) Transport Service

Transport Service is the service as envisaged by the Consumer Protection Act. It includes Air, Railway and Road Service. The service of each category though meant for carriage of passengers or goods is regulated by different Acts. So it is better to scrutinize the matter of our concern separately under three sub-headings.

(a) Air Service

This service is provided by both public and private sector. Presently apart from Airlines and Air India Service there are private and foreign operators who have undertaken to provide this service. There is a steeped rise of complaints before consumer forums by passengers and National Commission too has been called in a number of cases to decide and determine the liability of Air Authority on account of delay or deficiency. In a case[242] National

242. Indian Airlines *v.* Shri Rajesh Kumar Upathgay (1990) 1 CPJ 206 (National Commission).

Commission held that flights may get delayed due to various causes such as poor visibility in the airfield, bad weather, bird hits, sudden strike by any crucial section of Airport Authority all of which may be factors beyond the control of Airlines. In such a case the delay cannot be attributed to negligence of the Air Authority. There may however, be other reasons where the delay in operating the flight might have been caused by reason of the negligence on the part of Air Authority. In *Air India* v. *N. Uddavan*[243] the complainant entrusted to the Air Authority a cargo of leather garments for transport and delivery to Poland. As the consignee in Poland did not take delivery the complainant instructed the Air Authority to arrange for forwarding the cargo to Sweden for delivery to the another named consignee. Air India pointed out to the complainant that the said course could be adopted only if the complainant obtained an order from the Reserve Bank of India (RBI) specifically authorizing Air India to accept the payment in Indian currency without which it will constitute clear violation of the Foreign Exchange Regulations and Rules. During long interval of time the goods had suffered heavy demurrage charges plus penalties imposed by the customs authorities in Poland which became levyable under Polish Law if the goods were not cleared within 15 days after arrival. National Commission held that the fact the consignee failed to take delivery even after expiry of a reasonable period would not operate to keep alive the responsibility of the carrier for the goods who carried goods safely to the port of destination without any damage or delay in the carriage on its part. The same view was reiterated in *Air France Cargo* v. *M/s Pillaiyar Exports and Others*[244] wherein it was held that responsibility undertaken by the carrier came to an end on the expiry of reasonable period from the date on which intimation of arrival was given to consignee.

In view of the above two decisions let us apprise the situation where buyer/consignee refuses to get goods or consignment. A consigner is supported to have shipped the goods with reasonable and probable regard to the agreement

243. 1986-96 CONSUMER 2474 (NS).

244. 1986-96 CONSUMER 2915 (NS).

or order. But where contract frustrated for one or the other reason or mainly as consigner fails to accept goods a duty is casted on the carrier to arrange for transportation of goods back to the sender's place or any other place in accordance with the advise of the consigner. No doubt carriers duty ends under law when after goods have been reached safely to its destination and sufficient notice have been given to the consignee but in the above two cases carrier is duty bound to seek instructions from the consigner and thereafter to be more prompt in discharging its duties in order to prevent enormous financial loss to consigner. Any disregard to such duty even in the absence of contract should be held deficiency in service.

Want of care and lack of skill to handle one's job may amount to deficiency in service. Where complainant boarded air craft of Indian Air lines and thereafter sometime he was informed by official of Airport Authority that his luggage was lying unidentified on the ground and that he should disembark from the aircraft to identify his luggage. As he stepped out on the stair, the ladder was suddenly removed and he fell down on the stony ground and sustained serious injuries. It was held that the negligence leading to the fall of the complainant on the ground was entirely with the staff of the Airport and therefore they are responsible for such negligence which caused 10% incapacity and permanent disability to the complainant.[245] Similarly, where there was loss of a suit case which was booked from Delhi to Seoul Via Hong Kong and which contained samples of textile pieces for display at an International Textile Fair it was held that staff (of the British Airways) was negligent in not putting the baggage in the same flight by which the complainant was traveling.[246] In a couple of cases it becomes clear that where there is loss of cargo or any part of it even though it is custom bounded the liability before customs examination is

245. The Station Manager, Indian Airlines and Others *v.* Dr. Jiteshwar Ahir, 1986-96 CONSUMER 1975 (NS). In this case a compensation of Rs. 5 lacs was allowed.

246. Exportors Apparal Group Ltd. and Others *v.* British Airways, 1986-96 CONSUMER 1971 (NS).

that of shipper and of the carriers after examination. In *M/s Shobha Global* v. *M/s Air India & Others*[247] 8 out of 12 cartons were found missing which could not be exported. It was held consignment was entrusted by customs house agent to The Air India Authority so it was that which was guilty of deficiency in service resulting in loss to the complainant.

A great loss and hardship may also be faced by a passenger on account of rescheduling of flights. Where a travel agent makes wrong entry in the ticket regarding the departure of flight, etc. it is held the travel agent is liable for this mistake. In *Indian Airlines Corporation* v. *Patel Rambhai Shanker Lal and Another*[248] it has been held:

> "The Authority conferred on the ticketing agent by Indian Airlines was only to sell and issue tickets in accordance with the flight operation schedules and timings notified by the Airlines. In making the wrong entry regarding the departure timing of the flight in question, the travel agent has manifestly acted contrary to the instructions of his principal, namely, The Indian Airlines Corporation. The said wrongful act of the travel agent was beyond the scope of its limited authority and for any consequential loss to a third party arising therefrom, the liability will only be that of the travel agent and not of the principal. The complainant who had hired the services of the travel agent has a legitimate claim against the said agent for the deficiency in service consisting of wrong noting in the ticket."

The above view has been followed in *Air India* v. *Yogendra Hiralal Parekh*[249] and subsequently in The Chief Commercial Officer, *Indian Airlines & Another* v. *Lal Chand & Another.*[250] There are numerous cases before consumer forums

247. 1986-96 CONSUMER 2551 (NS); Seen Another Case titled International Airport Authority of India *v.* Inter-friegth Services Pvt. Ltd. and Others, 1986-96 CONSUMER 2857 (NS).
248. 1986-95 CONSUMER 437 (NS).
249. 1986-96 CONSUMER 2215 (NS).
250. 1986-96 CONSUMER 2245 (NS).

especially National Commission regarding the misconduct of the staff employed by Air Corporations. Latest case of misconduct is *Indian Airlines Corporation Ab. Majid & Another.*[251] Here complainant purchased the waited list ticket from The Indian Airlines. After a short period his wait listed ticket was confirmed and after all necessary formalities at the airport he loaded the aircraft. After 10 minutes the duty officer along with two other members of the staff asked the complainant to get up from seat and on his refusal the officers forcefully took him out of the aircraft by dragging him down as a result of which his shirt was torn and he was publicly subjected to insulting and humiliating treatment. National Commission held the version given by The Indian Airlines Corporation for confirming his wait listed ticket and directed the complainant to disembark from the aircraft for the purpose of providing seat to another passenger who allegedly had a confirmed ticket for the same flight has not been convincingly established as true. However, the complainant has satisfactorily proved his case that his shirt got torn as a result of the force applied to its arm by the staff of the Indian Airlines while he was being taken out from the aircraft and consequently decision of the State Commission was upheld. In another case against excesses committed by staff of Royal Dutch Airlines in verification proceedings of visa which caused delay and consequently the complainant missed two flights, it was held by Supreme Court that checking and screening for the validity of the travel documents is done as a measure of safety and security of the passengers as well as the legal obligation of the Airlines. Further since complainant failed to prove the alleged business loss due to his missing flight so there was no deficiency in service.[252] However, where in case *Indian Airlines* v. *S.N. Sinha*[253] complainant alleged that a piece of metallic wire got mixed up in the food served by the Indian Airlines and it

251. 1986-95 CONSUMER 692 (NS).

252. Ranveer Singh Bugga *v.* M/s KLM Royal Dutch Airlines and Another, 1997(3) CPR 26 (National Commission); 1999(3) CPR 102 (SC).

253. (1992) 4 CPJ 62 (National Commission).

pierced his gum while he was consuming the food the principal—Indian Airlines was held liable. Another important case on the point is *Common Cause* v. *Union of India & Others,*[254] where the complaint petition was filed by the well known consumer organization "common cause" seeking redressal of the grievance of air passengers who were put to great amount of inconvenience and hardship on account of disruption of a large number of flights of Air India caused by reason of a sudden strike. Coming to the claim for compensation made against Air India the decision in *Consumer Unity and Trust Society, Calcutta* v. *Chairman & Managing Director, Bank of Baroda,* 1986-95 CONSUMER 233 (NS) was refereed . . . in the light of which it was held that no negligence has been made out against Air India.

(b) Railway Service

The Railways provide the principal mode of transport in country. Inspite of hikes in passenger fare and freight, it still continues to be the cheapest mode of transport. With electrification of several roots, across the country it has reduced pollution and shortened the time of journey. It is a state owned enterprise and the responsibility of its administration and management rests with The Railway Board. The Railway Act, 1980 was the basic law which contained provisions regarding safety, fixation of rates, procedure for inquiries into accidents and payment of compensation for death or injuries sustained by passenger and for loss or damage to goods. It has now been replaced by The Railway Act, 1987 and Parliament has also enacted the Railway Claims Tribunals Act, 1987 for facilitating disposal of claims for payment of compensation.[255] Though it seems that these tribunals have exclusive jurisdiction over railway claims but there is neither any provision in this Act (which has been passed after Consumer Protection Act, 1986) excluding applicability of the Consumer Protection Act over railway disputes nor this service comes within the exclusionary part

254. 1986-96 CONSUMER 3047 (NS).

255. D.N. Saraf, Law of Consumer Protection in India, 2nd Ed. (1995) Tripathi Publications (Bombay), p. 33.

of the definition of 'Service' as provided under Consumer Protection Act, instead of it is within inclusive portion of definition. A correct interpretation of this blurred position created by both Acts is given by National Commission in *General Manager, South Eastern Railway* v. *Anand Prasad Sinha.*[256]

The expression service contained in section 2(1)(o) of the Consumer Protection Act specifically includes within its scope the provision of facilities in connection with transport. The Railway Administration as providing Transport facilities to the Public for consideration paid by them by way of the fare levied for the ticket. It is in fact one of the largest public utility undertaking in the country intending to render the service to the public by providing transportation by Rail through its large network. Therefore, passengers traveling by trains on payment of the stipulated fare charged for the ticket are 'consumers' and the facility of transportation by rail provided by the Railway Administration is a 'service' rendered for consideration as defined under the Consumer Protection Act.

Following the above decision *National Commission in Consumer Protection Council* v. *Indian Railways*[257] held the expression 'consumers' under the Consumer Protection Act, 1986 includes passengers who avail themselves of the facility of transportation offered by the railways. . . .

Since the first and foremost duty of the railway authority is to provide accommodation in trains routed to different places the same must be in accordance with the confirmed reservation. If wait listed passengers are given priority at the cost of those having confirmed booking it will amount deficiency in service. In *G.M. Southern Railways* v. *J.F. Albert Fernando*[258] complainants reserved 42 tickets which erroneously were allotted to others. For this gross negligence railway authority was held liable. However, where complainant alleged to have obtained confirmation

256. (1991) 1 CPJ 10 (National Commission).
257. (1992) 1 CPJ 120 (National Commission).
258. (1991) II CPJ 407.

telephonically which was denied by the railway official. National Commission held:[259]

> "The Railway Authority is under obligation to provide accommodation in railway trains against confirmed booking only and where a passenger is wait listed. Considering the conditions prevailing in the country it would be hazardous to make railway liable on the ground that the passenger claims to have obtained confirmation of reservation on telephone which such telephonic conversation is denied by a responsible official of the railway organization."

Another duty of the carrier here 'Railway Service' is to carry goods/passengers safely to its destination where complainant's were having reserved seats but some persons un-authorizedly entered the reserved compartment and forcefully occupied seats, when complainant's resisted they were attacked by these unauthorized persons and as a result complainant suffered fracture leading to permanent disability. National Commission held if any person enters into any reserved compartment un-authorizedly, then besides being liable for criminal prosecution he can be removed from the railway compartment by any railway servant or by any of the person whom such railway servant may call to his aid. In the instant case since administration neglected in checking the entry of unauthorized person in the reserved railway compartment and then failed to remove them forcibly for which they are duly empowered by the statue. Hence, there was gross deficiency.[260] However, penalizing complainant's for traveling in a train in which they were not entitled to travel cannot be held deficiency in service.[261] So far as the question of delay of departure and arrival of trains is concerned

259. Union of India through General Manager, Northern Railway and Another *v.* G.C. Sharma and Others 1986-95 CONSUMER 633 (NS).
260. Union of India through General Manager, Western Railway, Bombay and Another *v.* Manoj H. Pathack, 1986-96 CONSUMER 2162 (NS).
261. General Manager, Eastern Railway and Another *v.* P. Chattopadhyah, 1986-96 CONSUMER 2081 (NS).

National Commission is reluctant in conferring any liability on Railway Authority.[262]

(c) Road Service

The carrying of passengers or goods by buses, Taxies, Trucks, etc. is a consumer within the meaning of Consumer Protection Act and therefore any deficiency in the service is actionable under the Act. Every transaction of hiring of service may amount to a contract in the eye of law and any deficiency in rendering the service may be technically a breach of contract but merely for that reason the consumer cannot be denied the benefit of the protection conferred by the Consumer Protection Act.[263] In *Express Goods Service* v. *Standard Textile Mills*[264], the firm entrusted 8 consignments of goods of textile and knitted fabrics for carriage from Amritsar to Delhi and for onward delivery to the consignees. On the garb of fire the carrier misappropriated the goods. The carrier took the preliminary objection that the complainant is not a consumer within the meaning of Consumer Protection Act and that the goods in question were booked with the carrier for commercial purpose. Rejecting this contention National Commission held:

> "A combined reading of the definition of consumer as contained in Section 2(1)(d)(ii) read with 'service' as defined in Section 2(1)(o) persuades us to hold that it comprehends consumers of services of commercial and trade-oriented nature such as banking, financing, insurance, transport, etc. The services include within its

---

262. Seen Dr. Yatri Sang (Regd.) *v.* Northern Railway, 1992(1) CPR 270 (National Commission) and Union of India *v.* Ashok K. Singh (1995) 7 CPJ 3 (National Commission).
263. 1986-96 CONSUMER 3228 (NS). Seen also East India Transport Agency *v.* Jagdish Bhai M. Chandhan, 1986-96 CONSUMER 1942 (NS), M/s Birla Yamaha Ltd. *v.* M/s Patel Road Ways Ltd., 1986-96 CONSUMER 2164 (NS), wherein carrier failed to deliver consignments in accordance with the contract and accordingly they were held liable for deficient service performed by them as common carrier.
264. Cynco Textiles Pvt. Ltd. *v.* Economic Transport Organization and Others, 1986-95 CONSUMER 840 (NS).

scope the provision of facilities in connection with transport. The only service categories that have been excluded by the legislator from the definition are those rendered either free of charge or under a contract of personal services. No other exclusion can be inferred, if the legislature has not intended it either specifically or implication."

In the instant case since the transporter failed to carry the 8 consignments safely and to deliver the same to the consignees there has been deficiency in rendering of the service by it. The question whether the consumer Forum has jurisdiction to adjudicate upon a claim for compensation arising out of a motor vehicle accident the Supreme Court in *Thiruvalluvar Transport Corporation* v. *Consumer Protection Council,*[265] answered in negative through the judgment of A.M. Ahmadi, C.J., it was held:

The Motor Vehicles Act, 1988 can be said to be a special Act in relation to claims for compensation in respect of death or injury arising out of the use of a motor vehicle. The Consumer Protection Act, 1986 being a law dealing with the question of extending protection to consumer in general, could, therefore, be said to be a general law in relation to the specific provisions concerning accidents arising out of the use of motor vehicles found in chapter xii of the 1988 Act. Ordinarily the general law must yield to the special law . . .

Similarly, Consumer Disputes Redressal Agencies have no jurisdiction to entertain complaints against State Road Transport Corporation regarding the fare fixing which is to be fixed exclusively by this authority while taking into consideration only government orders etc.[266] However, if a passenger or consigner of goods is charged excessive prices than what has been fixed by State Road Transport

265. 1995 Company cases, Vol. 83, p. 82.

266. The General Manager, A.P. State Road Transport Corporation and Others *v.* The Secretary East Godawari District Consumer Aid, Advise and Welfare Society and Another, 1986-96 Consumer 3160 (NS) it was held that the question as to the reasonableness of the price charged for the performance of service cannot be agitated before a Consumer Forum.

Corporation he can make complaint before Consumer Disputes Redressal Agencies. In *Maharashtra State Road Transport Corporation* v. *B.G. Sarang,*[267] the complainant was traveling from Vengurala to Kundal and was charged Rs. 5.50 whereas on the return journey from Kundal to Vengurala he was charged Rs. 4.50 for the same distance. The National Commission held that the distance traveled for the purpose of charging fare shall be calculated from the stage point. In respect of vehicles going beyond Kundal the fare has to be calculated on the basis of distance between the boarding stage to the approved succeeding stage point as in respect of such route the stage point Kundal is only a sub-stage and is not an approved stage point. Therefore, the fare is calculated for 5 stages on the basis of distance. However, in respect of route Vengurala to Kundal the stage point Kundal is approved point and on the basis of the distance the fare is calculated for 4 stages. The fare being legitimately charged by the competent authority cannot be said to be a deficiency in service.

Cases will multiply if we will bring more cases on record which are available here but briefly to state that though the transport service is within the inclusive part of the definition under Section 2(1)(o) but The Railway Act and the Railway Claims Tribunals Act vests exclusive jurisdiction in the Railway Administration to entertain complaints on account of deficiency in service arising from loss, damage, deterioration or non-delivery of goods, etc.

(C) LAW DEDUCED FROM THE ABOVE DISCUSSED CASES

- 'Intentional' is doing for a purpose with an ultimate aim. The legislature by using the words 'deficiency' and 'negligence' clearly intended that the remedy for intentional malicious acts are outside the jurisdiction of Consumer Forums under the Act.
- Merely submitting the proposal and payment of an amount which was kept in deposit without

267. 1986-96 CONSUMER 2818 (NS).

appropriation towards the premium, it cannot be construed as a concluded contract of service.

- Even after a bank or other financing institution has sanctioned the limits up to which a loan will be advanced by it to a barrower, it is still vested with a discretion to apply its mind from time to time and decide in its best judgment as to whether it will be reasonable, safe and prudent to make further advances to the particular borrower in the light of any failure on his part. So long as such discretion is exercised in good faith and for safeguarding the interest of public funds after due application of mind to all relevant factors, a decision taking by the bank or other financial institution to discontinue making further advance to a particular borrower will not constitute deficiency in service.
- Fora constituted under the Consumer Protection Act, 1986 have no jurisdiction to go into the question of pricing of houses and plots sold or allotted on hire purchase system. Further, the question as to the reasonableness of the price charged for the performance of service cannot be agitated before a consumer forum.
- Where once the claim is paid and received in full and final settlement, there is no deficiency in service and no relief can be granted under the provisions of the Act.
- From where the goods were purchased for commercial purpose, if there is a warranty for its maintenance, the purchaser becomes a consumer in respect of the services rendered or to be rendered by the manufacturer or supplier during the warranty period.
- Where the cause of action has arisen due to the delay in delivery of goods and the relief claimed is also by way of interest on the price of the goods it constitutes a breach of contract in sale of goods.
- In the case of hospitals which provides treatment

to patients for payment there is no element of personal service.

- Once it is found that there is hiring of service for consideration and that loss has been caused to the complainant on account of neglect and deficiency in rendering the service the aggrieved consumer is entitled to seek his remedy under the Consumer Protection Act, 1986. The mere fact that the default or deficiency on the part of carrier may also amount to a breach of contract under the general law will not in any way affect the jurisdiction of the forums set-up under the special law, namely, Consumer Protection Act, 1986.
- The provisions of the Act are in addition to but not in derogation of any other law in force. A complainant has option to seek redress either under the Act or under the provisions of any other law including through arbitration as provided in the contract of insurance.
- A consumer can complain about a defect in the rendering of service event after the expiry of period of 6 months, provided the claim has been made within the time provided under the general law, i.e Law of Limitation.
- Purchase of seeds for the purpose of Agriculture is not a purchase of an article for commercial purpose.
- Insurance companies must compensate the insured within a reasonable period—it should be possible where there are not disputes to settle the claim within a period of 3 months.
- When amount towards payment of premium of insurance policy be cheque could be realized only after the date of incident, no valid contract of insurance could be said existing and repudiation of claim did not constitute deficiency in service.

OBSERVATION

Above we have dealt with a galaxy of representative

cases. The most important is the *Lucknow Development Authority* v. *M.K. Gupta* in which the Supreme Court emphasized the need for construing the provisions of the Consumer Protection Act in favour of the consumer. The approach made by the Supreme Court in the decision has been approved by Consumer Fora in the State in a number of cases, e.g *Mohd. Shafi and Mohd. Abass* v. *Regional Manager and Others,* State Commission while quoting the above decision observed that the Supreme Court has wisely stated that the Consumer Protection Act does entitle the complainant to claim compensation and also empowers the commission to grant the same. Similarly the decision passed by the National Commission in *Indian Assurance Company Ltd.* v. *Acharya Kumar Garg,* National Commission held once the claim is paid and received in full and final settlement there is no deficiency in service and relief cannot be claimed has been followed in a number of cases both by the State Commission and Jammu and Kashmir High Court under Consumer Protection Act (*Misger Gh. Mohi-ud-din and Others* v. *National Insurance Company*). If enlisted, cases will multiply which will show that the Consumer Fora in the State has actually/in substance followed decisions of the Apex Court and Apex Commission and decisions of these Courts have favourable/desired impact on Consumer Fora in the State. However, State Commission Srinagar wing in the case titled *Abdul Rashid Ganie* v. *Oriental Insurance Co. Ltd.* has followed the decision of Haryana State Commission Captioned *M/s Zamindera Tractors* v. *Oriental Fire and General Insurance Co. Ltd.,* 1993 in which it was held that full and final discharge gives quirts for the contractual payment under the policy but in no way extinguishes the consumer's right to claim in trust damage or loss due to the negligence of the insurance. Case titled *Indian Medical Association* v. *V.P. Shantha,* in which the Supreme Court has resolved the conflict and controversy by recognizing the medical service neither a contract of employment nor of personal service but rendering of professional service on payment. Here in the State in cases namely, *Sunita Kaur* v. *Dr. Arun Prasad and Others* and *Mrs. Shashi Sharma* v. *Bee Enn General Hospital* on the lines of *Shantha's case* compensation was awarded.

CHAPTER

6

QUASI-JUDICIAL ATTITUDE TOWARDS THE CONSUMER IN THE STATE OF JAMMU AND KASHMIR

INTRODUCTION

The last previous chapter on Consumer Protection Act revealed that it covered protection to the consumers in a wide spectrum of trade, commerce activities and the basic public utility services both by the public and private sector agencies. Besides, to facilitate protection from unethical conduct of producers, distributors and service providers and to curb exploitation of disputed cases by long and costly litigation, the Act provides for a mechanism of speedy, time-bound and cheap legal remedy. For the above purpose it provides for establishment of two-tier hierarchy of redressal agencies having quasi-judicial functions. Presently two Divisional Forums and one state commission is devoted to this task. In order to assess over the achievement and attitude of consumer fora towards the consumer in the State, in this chapter an endeavor is made to focus over the decided cases of consumer fora.

Consumer Fora in the State—Place of Sitting, etc.: In the State there are two Divisional Forums (one) in Jammu and another one in Srinagar province. Srinagar Divisional Forum is located in the Old Secretariat in a room followed by a partition and in this way there are two rooms where whole proceeding and office work is taking place. Similarly, Divisional Forum is situated near the Old Secretariat Jammu which is congested and ill in infrastructure. Since State Commission sits for six months in Srinagar and for next six months it moves to Jammu, this shuttling for six months here and there has created havoc not only among the employees of this forum but also to the consumers whose cases remain dragging on. State Commission both Srinagar and Jammu wing is also ill-equipped.

(A) DECIDED CASES OF DIVISIONAL FORUM, SRINAGAR

(I) Defective Goods

Cases under this heading will be read under some sub-headings:

(a) Automobiles

Under this heading a considerable number of complaints have been filed most of which stands decided in favour of the consumer. In *Mrs Prithipal Kaur* v. *Alson Motors and Another,*[1] the complainant had stated that opposite party No. 1 is an authorized dealer of opposite party No. 2 (Hindustan Motors Ltd., Bengal) and who deals with booking and supply of Contessia Classis Car manufactured by opposite party No. 2. The complainant desired to purchase Contessia Car and deposited Rs. 10,00,000. The car was not delivered within the stipulated time. Due to non-delivery of the car and also due to the insurgency and disturbed conditions which prevailed in the Kashmir Valley the complainant requested opposite party No. 1 to treat the order as cancelled and refund the amount paid but the same was not refunded. The Forum ordered the opposite party No. 2 to

---

1. O/F No . . . D/I 12-1-1992 D/D 25-10-95 (DF) Sgr.

refund the amount paid with 10% interest p.a. and compensation of Rs. 2,000.00 were awarded.

In another case captioned as *Badshah Begum* v. *Hanief Motors, Regal Chowk and Another*[2] when car was not delivered for quite sometime the complainant cancelled the order and requested for refund of Rs. 10,000 which he had deposited. Divisional Forum also directed the opposite party to pay Rs.10,000 with interest 15% p.a. and Rs. 10,000 were awarded as compensation. Two other cases namely, *Masudha Khursheed Shadad* v. *Maruti Udyoug Ltd., New Delhi*[3] and *Abdul Rehman Bhat* v. *Premier Automobiles, Bombay*[4] have been decided in consumers favour as opposite parties in both cases were found to have provided deficient services by neither providing motor car nor returning earnest money despite demands and commitment.

In all the above cases Divisional Forum directed the opposite party in each case either to supply the car within a time given by it or to refund money along with interest and compensation which it deemed fit and appropriate.[5]

(b) Electronics

Brief facts which have given rise to the complaint captioned as *Mohd. Amin Dar* v. *Front Lights, Gow Kadel, Srinagar*[6] are that the complainant purchased an electric heater from the opposite party for Rs. 700 and the accessories for Rs. 51. The complainant paid in cash and used the heater at his home. The heater did not gave sufficient heat to prepare tea or to cook any other eatables despite the fact that the step-up system was used. The complainant carried the purchased article back to the opposite party and lodged a complaint regarding mal-functioning of the heater.

The forum came to the conclusion that the totality of the circumstances indicated that unfair trade practice had

---

2. O/F No. 510/95 D/I 31-8-1995; D/D 21-7-98 (DF) Sgr.
3. O/F No. 997/97 D/I 4-8-1997 D/D 21-7-98 (DF) Sgr.
4. O/F No. 267/98 D/I 2-9-98 D/D 19-5-99 (DF) Sgr.
5. How many cases have been filed, disposed off and are pending before this Forum will be seen in the table later on.
6. O/F No. 326/94 D/I 28-3-94 D/D 3-4-95 (DF) Sgr.

been adopted by the opposite party in this case by selling an article under the cover of guarantee which proved to be false and the heater did not work at all. *Nazir Ahmad Parrey* v. *J.K. Third Arcades H.S.H.S., Srinagar*[7] is another case available on the point. In the instant case the complainant purchased a washing machine of trade mark whirlpool from Delhi.

Warranty period was 24 months. Since the complainant resided at Sopore he asked opposite party to transfer the services to their authorized dealer at Srinagar. He was given to understand that he was bound to deposit Rs. 200 as fees for transfer of services to the article from New Delhi to Srinagar. Within the warranty period complainant got repaired the machine from opposite party Sringar which charged Rs. 2500 for repairs. The complainant informed opposite party (Delhi) which in return informed the complainant to get back the money from opposite party Srinagar except transfer charge of Rs. 200. Opposite party (Dealer in Srinagar) was informed but it slept over the matter and did not refund the money. Divisional Forum directed the opposite party Srinagar to refund the amount of Rs. 2300 to the complainant along with interest at 12% and compensation of Rs. 3000 to redress inconvenience caused to the complainant.

(2) Deficient Services

Here also cases will be divided under some sub-headings.

(a) Banking

In *Abdul Hamid War* v. *Manager, Syndicate Bank, Srinagar,*[8] the petitioner has made deposits with the bank through their collector and has made the deposits of Rs. 30, Rs. 60, and Rs. 90 daily right from 1-6-1989 to 1-6-1990 which amounted to Rs. 3860 as alleged by the petitioner. Due to prevailing situation in Valley the deposits could not be continued and when he approached the bank to withdraw his

7. O/F No. 219/98 D/I 5-8-98 D/D 2-6-99 (DF) Sgr.
8. O/F No. 326/94 D/I 28-3-94 D/D 3-4-95 (DF) Sgr.

money he was told only Rs. 990 is balance with the bank. However, pass book bears the signatures against the deposits by the bank officials which amounts to the sum as claimed by the petitioner. The Divisional Forum held that the pass book issued to the complainant bears the initials of the duly authorized agent of the opposite party and as under vicarious liability the principal was held responsible for the omissions and commissions of his agent.

(b) Financing

Round 40 cases have been filed in Divisional Forum Srinagar against Janpriya Finance and Investment Ltd. Srinagar. Janpriya Finance and Investment Ltd., Calcutta is a registered company under relevant law. It opened its branches at Srinagar also. The company floated various social welfare schemes relating to endowment policies. People got attracted by the publications of Janpriya Finance Ltd. and purchased endowment policies. However, after sometime it closed its office at Srinagar without any notice to the complainants and hence complaints before the Divisional Forum. In each case the forum proceeded *ex-parte* and directed the opposite party to refund the amount deposited along with interest from the date of maturity till the whole amount is liquidated.[9]

Similar facts arose in the case *Mrs. Mumtaz Hussain* v. *Jammu and Kashmir Finance Company Ltd.*[10] The complainant got attracted by the publication of the Company and purchased an endowment policy. The complainant had undertaken to pay monthly instalments of Rs. 100 each to the company towards the maturity of the endowment claim which amounted to Rs. 400. Thereafter when the complainant approached the company at the branch office Nowhatta to deposit instalment she found that the company had closed its office at Srinagar. The complainant preferred complaint before consumer forum. The complaint was allowed and the

9. For example Mohd. Shafi Bhat *v.* Janpriya Finance and Investment Ltd., O/F No. 909/96 D/D 23-7-98 (DF) Sgr.
10. O/F No. 133/98 D/D 29-12-98 (DF) Sgr.

opposite party directed to refund the deposited amount along with 12% interest from the date of maturity of the policy and compensation of Rs. 1000 for redress of inconvenience, loss of time and money.

(c) Housing

Mohd. Shafi Mir v. *Jammu and Kashmir Housing Board Corporation, Jammu and Another*[11] is the case decided by Divisional Forum. He (the complainant) applied for allotment of a plot of land and he was asked to deposit 50% cost of the plot and he deposited half the price that is 50%. . . . Thereafter the second last instalment of the plot was received by the opposite party but the opposite party demanded interest because the same was deposited late to which the complainant showed inability to pay and demanded refund of the amount already paid as cost of plot. In response to notice the opposite party sent a letter to the counsel of the complainant agreeing to refund the amount received but without interest.

This forum held that the opposite party cannot be permitted by law to approbate and reprobate. They cannot take advantage of their commanding position and upper hand in the transaction. So the interest at the rate of 12% p.a. was allowed.

(d) Insurance

In a number of cases Divisional Forum has followed decision of the National Commission given in *New India Assurance Company* v. *Achhar Kumar Garg*[12] in which it was held

> "once the claim is paid and received in full and final settlement, there is no deficiency in service and no relief can be granted under the provisions of the Consumer Protection Act."

11. O/F No. 995/97 D/I 30-7-97 D/D 30-5-98 (DF) Sgr.
12. 1986-96 CONSUMER 1840 (NS).

With high regard to the above mentioned view Srinagar Divisional Forum has followed and applied the same trend in various cases. For example in *Misger Gh. Mohi-ud-din and other* v. *National Insurance Company.*[13] In the instant case complainants claimed that surveyors have made erroneous assessment while the complainants deserve more amount as indemnification. However, complainants had signed discharge vouchers in full and final settlement of their claims. Therefore, Divisional Forum held that they have waived the right to claim further indemnification.

Following also the decision of *Tasleema Jabeen* v. *National Insurance Company*[14] Divisional Forum Srinagar in a consecutive cases namely, *Ali Mohd. Ganie* v. *National Insurance Company*[15]; *Saif-ud-din Shah* v. *Divisional Manager, New India Assurance Company*[16] and *Gh. Mohd. Sheikh and Others* v. *National Assurance Company*[17] held—

> "The law is settled on this subject that execution of a discharge voucher by an insured in favour of the company discharges the insurance company of all the contractual liabilities arising under the agreement of insurance."

In *Dr. Gh. Mohd. Habi* v. *United India Insurance,*[18] the question for determination which arose that after its final settlement and after the receipt of payment was signed by the insured—Is it just and proper to withhold payment for non-production of the police report? Divisional Forum held that it was not a justifiable ground to withheld payment and complaint was allowed.

Again a common question of law has arisen in various cases of like nature and having identical facts. These complaints as per Srinagar Divisional Forum's report are 16

13. O/F No. 20/99 D/I 3-4-99 D/D 15-5-99 (DF) Sgr.
14. O/F No. 372/97 D/D 14-10-98 (Divisional Forum) Sgr.
15. O/F No. 391/98 D/D 18-5-99 (DF) Sgr.
16. O/F No. 129/98 D/D 25-5-99 (DF) Sgr.
17. O/F No. 57/98 D/I 26-3-98 D/D 28-6-99 (DF) Sgr.
18. O/F No. 282/98 D/D 7-5-99 (DF) Sgr.

in number.[19] All these cases related to the fire incident which had taken place at Chararisharif in the year 1995 in which the whole town was gutted. These cases have presented before this forum with the prayer for the direction against the insurance company for the payment of amount of indemnity. Controversy has arisen as to whether the relief granted by the government to the fire sufferers should be deducted from the amounts of indemnity to which the complainants are entitled.

Srinagar Divisional Forum held, the controversy has already been set at rest by the Honb'le High Court in judgment dated 11-3-1999 in all the related cases by holding the amount of *ex-gratia* relief granted by the government or by any other agency should not be deducted from the amount of indemnity which falls due to the complainants in terms of the reports submitted by the surveyors.

In the light of the judgement of the Honb'le High Courts, the Srinagar Divisional Forum allowed the complainants claims to the extent of surveyors report and interest was allowed on the amount assessed by the surveyor by the date of submission of the surveyors report till the date of payment and all the complaints were disposed off accordingly.

In a case,[20] it is found that the short controversy in the light of pleadings was that the complainant was not indemnified by the opposite party in terms of the report assessed by second surveyor in detail. After six months of the incident third surveyor was sent who could not properly assessed the loss. This forum was inclined to disagree to the report submitted by the third surveyor as it was according to the Honb'le Forum futile exercise on behalf of the company to have got the loss assessed again in a manner which was not warranted by law. In *M/s Ess Jay Sports* v. *United India*

---

19. For example Gh. Nabi Haji and Others *v.* National Insurance Company Ltd. D/I 26-8-98 D/D 20-4-99. Mohd. Maqbool Wani and Others *v.* Oriental Insurance Company Ltd. O/F No. 1103/91, 406/98, 197/98 D/D 20-4-99 three claims has been disposed under the said captioned case.
20. Ab. Gani Phafoo *v.* Oriental Insurance Company Ltd. Srinagar O/F No. 15/98 D/I 2-1-98 D/D 9-2-99.

Insurance Company Ltd.,[21] the only ground raised by the opposite party is that 'Fire Policy A' was issued in favour of the complainant in which less premium was attracted while in the instant case the company ought to have issued 'Fire Policy C' because of less premium. The forum held that terms and conditions not incorporated in the insurance policy are not binding on the insured and same cannot be raised at the time of settlement of the claim. Accordingly it was held that the opposite party can neither charge additional premium nor can they deduct the amount on the grounds of excess clause in order to validate the policy in question.

In various cases[22] insurance company could not finalize the claims of the claimants because CBI Authorities has seized the records maintained by the company. The forum in such cases while directing the opposite party in each case to indemnify the complainants by payment of already approved insurance claim with interest but didn't award compensation because delay in fact was due to the situation/fact not within the control of the opposite party. In *Editor Gh. Mohd. Arif* v. *National Insurance Compnay*[23] also, the forum did not award compensation on the ground that the contributory facts have been responsible in causing delay in the settlement of the claim.

Where the surveyor submitted an assessment report insurance company is bound by such assessment which was deputed by the company.[24] There are numerous cases which are allowed by the Hon'ble Srinagar Divisional Forum in favour of the consumer because in such cases it has been proved that insurance company has slept over the matter even though surveyors has submitted their reports of

---

21. O/F No. 128/98 D/I 30-5-98 D/D 7-5-99 (DF) Sgr.
22. Seen Bashir. Ahmad Ganie and Others *v.* Oriental Insurance Company O/F No. 990/97,991/97 D/I 29-7-97 D/D 18-11-98 (DF) Sgr; Mohd. Shafi Pir *v.* Oriental Insurance Company O/F No.1147/ 97 D/I 23-10-97 D/D 10-06-99 (DF) Sgr.
23. O/F No. 209/98 D/D 18-05-98 (DF) Sgr.
24. M/s Jhelum Valley Automobiles *v.* United Insurance Company Ltd. O/F No.374/98 D/I 21-10-98 D/D 30-05-99

assessment.[25] However, the question—whether the report submitted by the first surveyor is to be relied on or subsequent report submitted by the loss assessor is to be attached was answered in *M/s People's Medicate* v. *National Insurance Company*[26] where forum applied and cited the decision given in (Punjab) State Commission, DRA (II) (1998 CPJ—217).

Similarly, insurance company cannot repudiate a claim merely on technical grounds. In *Javaid Ahmad Peer* v. *Oriental Insurance Company*[27] the complainants shop which he had insured gutted due to fire. A surveyor of opposite party assessed the loss at Rs. 30,000. However, opposite party did not approve the claim merely because the Fire Brigade Department reported the date of occurrence 23-11-1992 as against the actual date of loss that is 21/22-11-1992. With the result the complainant was compelled by circumstances to knock at the door of this forum.

The forum after going through examination of witnesses, surveyors report and documentary evidence came to the conclusion that there was deficiency in service of the opposite party which has unnecessarily laid emphasis on the date shown by the Fire Service Department. In *Makroo Gift Center* v. *United India Insurance Company Ltd.*[28] Divisional Forum disallowed the deduction made on the ground of non-maintenance of proper accounts as unreasonable and regarding the delay for so many years on the part of opposite party compensation of Rs. 10,000 was awarded. In the same way Divisional Forum, Srinagar in *Dr. Tasleema Chasti* v.

---

25. Gh. Mohammad Salroo *v.* United Insurance Company O/F No. 1207/97 D/I 22-12-97 D/D 17-05-99 (DF) Sgr; Ab. Gani Bhat *v.* Oriental Insurance Company Ltd. D/I 28-10-97 D/D 10-05-99 (DF) Sgr; Mushtaq Ahmad Thoker *v.* Oriental Insurance Company O/F No. 1205/97 D/I 12-12-97 D/D 8-5-99 (DF) Sgr; Manoj Kumar Koul *v.* Oriental Insurance Company O/F No. 1013/97 D/I 17-07-97 D/D 14-10-98 (DF) Sgr.
26. O/F No. 114/98 D/I 20-05-98 D/D 19-06-99 (DF) Sgr. In this case Assam SCDRC II 1995 CPJ C/P 108 of 1992 was referred and applied.
27. O/F No. 331/94 D/I 8-4-94 D/D 14-02-95 (DF) Sgr.
28. O/F No. 98/98 D/I 28-04-98 D/D 06-05-99 (DF) Sgr.

United India Insurance and Another[29] held that the opposite party could not reasonably justify the averments as to how and why was a Licence to run a clinic by the complainants necessary in connection with the assessment of loss and payment of the same to them. Ultimately loss assessed by the surveyor was allowed at 10% p.a. on the said amount from the date of submission of the surveyors report.

Applying the law laid down by the Hon'ble High Court of Jammu and Kashmir in *Divisional Manager, United India Insurance Company Ltd.* v. *M/s Prince Tailoring House*[30] the Forum held that in cases of total damage caused to the insured property, responsibility of full indemnification cannot be evaded. Accordingly full amount of insurance claim along with interest and compensation of Rs. 10,000 was awarded in each case.[31]

It has been found that the Srinagar Divisional Forum has allowed complaints in almost all cases where insurance companies appeared to have delayed the matter which caused inconvenience, for example, *Bhat Steel Industries, Awantipora* v. *Oriental Insurance Company;*[32] *Abdul Rehman Dar* v. *National Insurance Company;*[33] *Mohd. Younis Bhat* v. *United India Insurance Company Ltd.;*[34] *Gani Printing Press* v. *United India Insurance Company*[35] and others are among such cases.

As in fire incidents, in insured vehicle accidents also the Srinagar Divisional Forum held that the company must finalize the case within 2/3 months from the date of submission of the report by the surveyor or if he has failed to do so, delay will amount to have caused mental agony to the complainants in each case. This view has been repeatedly held in a number of cases namely, *Sumair Singh* v. *Oriental*

---

29. D/I 08-01-98 D/D 23-04-98 (DF) Sgr.
30. D/D 23-03-1998 (DF) Sgr.
31. Jahangir Eenterprises and Others *v.* Oriental Insurance Company Ltd. O/F No 1107/97 D/I 29-07-97 D/D 11-12-98 (DF) Sgr.
32. O/F No. 436/98 D/I 19-12-98 D/D 08-05-99 (DF) Sgr.
33. O/F No. 820/96 D/D 30-07-98 (DF) Sgr.
34. O/F No. 245/98 D/I 20-08-98 D/D 24-05-94 (DF) Sgr.
35. O/F No. 149/95 D/I 16-06-98. Seen also Khani Pari Multipurpose Co-operative Society Wanpo *v.* Insurance Company Ltd. and Others O/F No. 1140/97 D/I 03-10-97 D/D 21-05-99 (DF) Sgr.

Insurance Company;[36] *Martand Fruit Agency* v. *Oriental Insurance Company;*[37] *Ab. Razaq Reshi and Others* v. *Oriental Insurance Company Ltd.;*[38] *Shabir Ahmad Wani* v. *National Insurance Company and Others.*[39] In *Nazir Ahmad Shah* v. *National Insurance Company Ltd.*[40] also the Divisional Forum after going through the whole set of averments and surveyor's report, complaint was allowed according to surveyor's report and Rs. 15,000 was awarded as compensation.

Cases captioned as *Mohd. Amin Lone* v. *National Insurance Company Ltd.;*[41] *Abdul Ahad Bhat* v. *Oriental Insurance Compnay;*[42] *Prethipaul Kaur* v. *Oreintal Insurance Company;*[43] *Malik Aftab* v. *United Insurance Company*[44] are also to the same effect.

In view of the decision given in *M/s Complete Insulation Pvt. Ltd.* v. *New India Insurance Company* (AIR 1996 Supreme Court 586) it was held that the cover of insurance in terms of the policy in question was not available to the complainant in the case captioned *Gh. Qadir Salmanai and other* v. *New India Insurance Company Ltd.,*[45] because he has admittedly sold the vehicle 6 years back to the date of occurrence in question.

Similarly in *Gh. Mohd. Ganie* v. *National Insurance Company Ltd.*[46] complainant was not in a position to prove the quantum of loss as alleged by him. So loss assessed by the surveyor was granted along with 12% interest from submission of surveyor's report. In *Ajit Feed Enterprises* v.

---

36. O/F No. 1087/97 D/D 27-08-98 (DF) Sgr.
37. O/F No. 1159/97 D/D 30-12-98 (DF) Sgr.
38. O/F No. 17/99 D/I 26-01-99 D/D 18-05-99 (DF) Sgr.
39. O/F No.1120/97 D/I 06-10-97 D/D 21-05-99 (DF) Sgr. Seen also Gh. Mohammad Dar *v.* United India Insurance Company O/F No. 589/95 D/I 16-11-95 D/D 15-10-98 (DF) Sgr.
40. O/F No.1037/97 D/I 26-08-97D/D 05-08-98 (DF) Sgr.
41. O/F No. 614/95 D/I 14-12-95 D/D 30-04-99 (DF) Sgr.
42. O/F No. 378/98 D/D 28-05-99 (DF) Sgr.
43. O/F No. 1181/97 D/I 17-11-97 D/D 04-01-98 (DF) Sgr.
44. O/F No. 60/98 D/I 01-04-98 D/D 12-12-98 (DF) Sgr.
45. O/F No. 1016/97 D/I 07-08-97 D/D 24-05-99 (DF) Sgr.
46. O/F No. 1080/97 D/I 18-09-97 D/D 21-07-99 (DF) Sgr.

Oriental Insurance Company Ltd.[47] resistance on the ground of bar of limitation was unfounded and the claim as per surveyors report was allowed. Recently in a couple of cases satisfactory amount of compensation has been allowed in *Abdul Ahad Baba* v. *National Insurance Company Ltd., Srinagar*[48] and in *Bashir Ahmad Sheikh Dabrune* v. *New India Assurance Company Ltd., Sonwar, Srinagar.*[49]

(e) Postal Cases

In *Mohd. Amin Dar* v. *Union of India and G.P.O., Srinagar,*[50] the complainant addressed a letter to the counsellor Embassy of U.S.A. situated at Shantinagar, New Delhi through registered mail from the branch office of post office Srinagar. When complainant received no reply he addressed another communication to U.S.A. Embassy at New Delhi and he was informed that documents were not received. The complainant made a representation to the opposite party to investigate into the matter. The matter was taken up by the opposite party with the concerned office. Before the final result of the enquiry the complainant filed the complaint. There was a great controversy regarding the maintainability of the suit in the forum. The learned council for complainant cited a Kerala High Court decision in *General Manager Telecom* v. *Consumer D.R. Forum (III),* (1997) CPJ 460 in which it was held that "both Consumer Protection Act and Indian Telegraph Act are special Laws but Consumer Protection Act, 1986 is more special so far as the disputed question is concerned. The Indian Telegraph Act deals with all aspects of telephone system and apparatus whereas the Consumer Protection Act deals with only with dispute raised by the consumers as to the services rendered to them. Therefore, Consumer Protection Act, 1986 is more special between the

---

47. O/F No. 368/98 D/I 08-10-98 D/D 24-05-99 (DF) Sgr. Seen also Gh. Nabi Bhat *v.* New India Assurance Company Ltd. O/F No. 255/93 D/I 22-06-93 D/D 18-9-95 and Mohd. Ramzan Ganie *v.* Oriental Insurance Company Ltd. O/F No. 235/95 D/I 13-8-98 D/D 30-04-99 (DF) Sgr.
48. O/F No. 47/2001 D/I 30-4-2001 D/D 30-10-2003 (DF) Sgr.
49. O/F No. 92/2001 D/I 29-6-2000 D/D 05-11-2003 (DF) Sgr.
50. O/F No. 412/94 D/I 3-10-94 D/D 17-07-98 (DF) Sgr.

two. Applying the settled principle that special law will prevail over the general law the machinery set-up under Consumer Protection Act to resolve the consumer dispute will prevail over Section 7-B of the Indian Telegraphic Act." Guided by the above decision the complainant was dealt under Jammu and Kashmir Consumer Protection Act, 1987 and Rs. 15,000 were granted in favour of the complainant against opposite party.

Where amount of money was deposited in the name of minors with the opposite party under a scheme and opposite parties issued certificates to that effect. Certificates indicate the amount of maturity of the deposits and the dates of maturity relating these certificates. On maturing some certificates the complainant required for disbursement of the mature amount as well as the amount concerning other certificates also as the amount were needed by him. The only ground of defence taken by the opposite party was that the complainant did not approach the opposite party but preferred this case. The forum accordingly directed the opposite party to refund the amounts of matured certificates along with interest at the rate of 12% p.a. from the date of maturity of other certificates not matured and only interest was directed to be paid on the refunded amount.[51]

(f) Telephone Cases

In this area round 115 complaints has been filed before Srinagar Consumer Forum. Out of this number only a few cases has been decided till this time. The reason for pendency of these cases is that tele-communication department has ever been contended the applicability of Consumer Protection Act, 1987.

In *Gulzar Ahmad* v. *Department of Telecommunication*[52] the brief facts which have given rise to this case are that the complainant applied for installation of Telephone connection which was enclosed with a demand draft of Rs. 3000 under

51. Abadullah Shah *v.* Secretary Postal and Telegraph Department O/F No. 19/99 D/I 2-2-99 D/D 20-4-99 (DF) Sgr.
52. O/F No. 351/98 D/I 26-2-98 D/D 04-07-98 (DF) Sgr. In this case order has been passd in *ex-parte*.

general category. Due to ailment of the complainants mother, the complainant as per instructions of opposite party deposited Rs. 12,000 under OYT (Own Your Telephone) and consequently he was promised that the telephone will be installed at the residential house of the complainant within a weeks time. After a weeks time he approached the opposite party many times. Constrained of these circumstances the complainant choose the last option available with him and lodged the complaint before the forum. Since the object of urgency in having a telephone under OYT category was frustrated by deficiency of service by the opposite party the Divisional Forum Srinagar in an *ex-parte* order directed it to refund Rs. 12,000 at 12% p.a. from the date of deposit till the whole amount is liquidated. Further Rs. 10,000 were awarded as compensation for mental pain and suffering apart from directing the opposite party to install a telephone in G.C. at complainants residence for which he had already paid Rs. 3000.

From the above decided cases it is clear that Divisional Forum Srinagar has delivered Justice in consistency with true spirit of the Consumer Protection Act. It has awarded compensation and interest without going into the technicality of things.

TABLE I*

Divisional Consumer Protection Forum, Srinagar

Sl. No.	*Item*	*Since Inception upto ending June 2003*	*Reporting Quarter ending September 2003*	*Progressive Total*
1.	No. of Cases Filed	3412	78	490
2.	No. of Cases Disposed	2936	92	3030
3.	No. of Cases Pending	474	—	460
4.	No. of Cases Decided within 90 days	172	20	191
5.	No. of Cases Decided within 150 days	1097	35	1132
6.	No. of Cases Decided within more than 150 days	1670	37	1707

* Progress Report of Cases as above mentioned has been collected directly from the office of the President Divisional Consumer Protection Forum Srinagar. Column No. 1 includes 23 cases remanded back by State Consumers Commission.

Table 1 showing number of institutions pendency and disposal of cases since inception till ending September 2003.

(B) CASES DECIDED BY DIVISIONAL FORUM, JAMMU

(1) Defective Goods

Under this heading *Ravi Paul Singh* v. *Kinetic Engineering Ltd. and another*[53] will be taken here. The case of the complaint is that he purchased one Kinetic FX and Engine from the opposite party who is authorizing selling dealer. From the very first day of its purchase the complainant has been suffering physically and mentally due to defects which the vehicle had in it. Whenever the vehicle slowed down the horn of the vehicle stopped functioning and it became very difficult to drive the vehicle on congested and busy roads of Jammu without horn. Vehicle was also emitting black smoke. These defects disclosed that the vehicle was not worthy and was having manufacturing defects. Vehicle was sent by the opposite party to the engineer and opposite party refused to deliver the vehicle unless issuance of satisfaction certificate by the complainant. The complainant on proving the allegations forum allowed the complaint and the opposite party was directed to deliver the vehicle to the complainant duly repaired and after removal of the defects complained of with a fresh warranty of one year for the defects complained of.

(2) Deficient Services

Our case study reveals that a large number of cases have been filed before this Divisional Forum. Here some noteworthy cases will be discussed.

(a) Banking

Raj Dev Singh v. *Manager, Jammu and Kashmir Bank, Shalamar Branch, Jammu*[54] is the noteworthy case. In this complaint averments made by the complainant are that he had sought admission in the institute of Chattered Financial Analyst of India for which he paid Rs. 8000 to the institute as

53. O/F No. 698/98 D/I 03-11-98 D/D 28-2-2001 (DF) Jmu.
54. O/F No. 540/99 D/I 31-8-99 D/D 1-3-2001 (DF) Jmu.

admission charges and second Rs. 5000 in five equal instalments of Rs. 1000. Due to some domestic unavoidable circumstances the complainant withdrew himself from the aforesaid course and wrote bank to stop payment. Bank by taking Rs. 100 as cheque stopping charges and even after four months the complainant found his pass book was showing payment of Rs. 1000. When complainant asked the bank about the grievance bank told him you must write to the institute for returning the payment of the cheque. Hence the complaint. The averments made by the complainant in his complaint stands proceeded by the evidence of the complainant and hence deficiency of service on the part of the opposite party in allowing passing of the cheques inspite of stopping payment instructions.

(b) Building

As per the complaint in *Jaswant Singh* v. *Indian Building Termites*[55] the complainant constructed a new house in the year 1996 and fitted wooden windows and doors in the house. The complainant contacted the respondent company for treatment of anti-termites works in the house and the expert visited the house of the complainant. The house was treated for anti-termite work for which Rs. 5000 was charged. Respondent company had issued a guarantee card annexed with complaint whereunder four years' guarantee was specified but even then windows and doors had the attack of termites due to which their condition was deteriorated. Briefly to state that the evidence has corroborated the contents of the complaint. By virtue of evidence harassment, mental torture and sufferings sustained by the complainant stands provide. Complainant was entitled to such damage caused and actual charges paid by him besides litigation charges.

55. O/F No. 33/2000 D/I 15-05-2000 D/D 29-08-2000 (DF) Jmu. In Uttam Singh Balorie *v.* Chief Technical Director O/F No. 27/2000 D/I 10-5-2000 D/D 17-8-2001, there was guarantee against the termite attack for which deficiency in service was claimed.

(c) Courier

In the complaint titled *Manoj Ratan* v. *Airborne Express Couriers*[56] the complainant was at Mohali and the relations of complainant booked a packet containing tickets of railway for complainant for 14-1-1997 through opposite party for onward delivery to the complainant. The consignment as booked by the opposite party never reached the complainant either before 14-1-1997 or even after and on 19-1-1997 the packet was returned with the remarks "Incomplete Address." Forum came to the opinion that address was not incomplete and return of the courier was not justified and amounts to deficiency of service.

(d) Financing

In a case[57] a bench of seven cases having identical controversy with same respondents though with different serial numbers and with same Advocates for the parties have been disposed off by the common final order.

Brief facts disclosed in all the aforesaid seven cases are that the non-applicants flouted a finance company in order to secure deposits. Non-applicants approached the complainants in the aforesaid cases for deposits of cash in their company and assured the complainant with a higher rate of interest would be reimbursed to them along with principal amount after expiry of a certain period. After the expiry of stipulated period they approached the non-applicants for refund of their amounts along with stipulated interest but the non-applicants disclosed that the company has failed and they flatly refused to reimburse them the amount. Non-applicants in their

56. O/F 38/97 D/I 29-4-97 D/D 19-3-2001 (DF Jmu.) As regards the objection that the complaint has not been filed by a proper person it has been held that complaint has been filed by Manoj Rattan. Since service had been hired by the consigner for benefit of the complainant that is Manoj Rattan the complaint does come within the definition of 'Consumer'as defined in the Consumer Protection Act. However parties had argeed to limited liability of the courier to the maximum of Rs. 500 so opposite party was directed to pay to the complainant compensation of Rs. 500 for deficiency of service.

57. Bansi Lal Tuli and Others *v.* Chairman and Directors Khidmat Investment Company Ltd. O/F No. 1505/92 D/I 20-10-92 D/D 22-03-95 (DF) Jmu.

objections pleaded that this forum has no jurisdiction to dispose off the complaints necessitating them to file the present complaints against the non-applicants.

Complainants produced evidence however non-applicants on the other hand produced no evidence in rebuttal.

Before disposing off the cases forum disposed off preliminary objections raised by the non-applicants. The preliminary objections so raised were as under—

(i) that the matter in controversy is false purely within the domain of company law and company law board constituted under the company Act alone has the jurisdiction to dispose off the complaints; and

(ii) that the complaints are not consumers within the definition of Consumer Protection Act so the matter does not fall within the ambit of Consumer Protection Act.

Regarding the first objection no argument was advanced by the learned counsel for the non-applicants. No provision of law has been quoted as to in what circumstances the company law board alone has the jurisdiction to dispose off the present complaints.

With regard to the second preliminary objection the learned counsel for the non-applicants submitted that the complainants are not consumers within the definition of Consumer Protection Act. Forum on this objection observed that the complainant had deposited a sum of money with the non-applicants who are the directors of the said company and had agreed to provide the agreed service to the complainants/depositors. The controversy in hand is not a case of loan of money advanced by the complainants to the non-applicants but is a clear case of hiring services of the non-applicants and of the company flouted by them. Respective files were found consequently to have proved their respective cases and have entitled to the relief sought for.

Another case similar to the above one is *Tara Chand Bamba and Others* v. *M/s Trimurti Finance and Investment Company and Others.*[58] In this case complainants became subscribers of the group community floated by the opposite party and deposits were made by them. Opposite Parties stopped their business and failed to repay the amounts received by them from the complainants. The complainants prayed for payment of Rs. 91,0000 with interest 24% p.a. Rs. 20,000 as compensation and Rs. 5000 litigation expenses.

The opposite parties have taken objections of maintainability of the complaint on the ground that it involved complicated questions of law and fact and so the complaint was not maintainable. Forum observed non-complicated question of law and fact is involved and allowed the complaint and opposite parties were directed to pay jointly and severally to the complaints the amount deposited respectively by them with interest 12% p.a. from the date of maturity.

One more available case is *Smt. Raj Rani Sharma* v. *M/s Aar Kay Traders, Head Office Moti Bazar, Jammu and Others.*[59] In this case also opposite parties transferred the properties and fled away from Jammu with all deposits of the depositors inclusive of the complainant. By the *ex-parte* evidence produced by the complainant which stands un-rebutted due to the absence of the opposite parties facts as alleged in the complaint stands proved and complaint was allowed.

(e) Insurance

As before the Srinagar Divisional Forum complaints against various Insurance Companies are also largely pending before Consumer Forum Jammu also. Cases under the above mentioned heading are so numerous that for the sake of convenience it is proposed here to go only through those cases which for one or the other reason deserve to be mentioned here.

58. O/F 685/98 D/I 4-3-98 D/D 15-11-2000 (DF) Jmu.
59. O/F 608/2001 D/I 8-5-2001 D/D 5-9-2001 (DF) Jmu.

In *Surjeet Kaur* v. *New India Assurance Company*[60] two complaints were disposed off by the same order.

Accident took place in both cases. Driver of the Truck succumbed to the injuries. The grievance of the complainants is that the opposite parties had refused to pay the claim of the vehicle and the claim of the deceased driver/insured.

In both complaints the plea of the opposite party was that at the time of accident the insured was himself driving the vehicle in contravention of terms and conditions of the policy without holding proper valid and effective driving license.

Forum held it is for the insurance company to prove that the driver who was driving the vehicle at the time of accident was not holding valid and effective license at the time of accident. The license produced by the complainants in the Court has not been challenged as fake or forged and on the face of it the license appears to be valid. Consequently opposite party has been found deficient in repudiating the claim of the complainants as the repudiation was unjustified and complaint was allowed.

In another case, opposite party was ready and willing to pay the claim on the basis of the report of the surveyor when complaint was lodged before the forum but denied to pay interest. The complaint is titled as *Syeed Abdul Rashid* v. *New India Assurance Company Ltd.*[61] In the instant complaint three storied residential house along with the house-hold goods were insured with the opposite parties. Some unidentified miscreants loaded with gun fired indiscriminately on the property of the complainants which caused great damage to the residential house and other property.

Opposite party filed objections and contended that the claim was pending for want of final investigation report from the complainant.

Forum held it was for the Police to either file charge sheet or final report in the competent Court. The document sought by the opposite party was not something which was

60. O/F No.456/98 D/I 10-10-98 D/D 19-1-2001 (DF) Jmu.
61. O/F, D/I (not mentioned on file) D/D 17-8-95 (DF) Jmu.

within possession or control of the complainant. The document sought was a public document copy thereof could have been obtained by the opposite parties themselves. Complaint was allowed and also interest of 12% p.a. on amount of Rs. 20,800.

However, complaints titled *Smt. Satender Kour Broca* v. *Life Insurance Corporation of India*[62] and *Anil Kumar* v. *National Insurance Company Ltd.*[63] where dismissed for no deficiency of service on the part of opposite parties.

In *M/s Home-N-Home Auqaf Building* v. *Oriental Insurance Company, Gangyal, Jammu*[64] main bone of contention was that Insurance Company was alleging that there was one car which engulfed in the fire in workshop but not the car of the complainant. Forum reached the conclusion after scrutinizing the evidence on record that the report submitted by the complainant appears to be correct because there is no Maruti Esteem Car registered with that number and the report submitted by the complainant appears to be correct.[65]

In another complaint in which deficiency of service on the part of insurance company was proved is *Bansilal* v. *The New India Assurance Company Ltd. and Jammu and Kashmir Bank,*[66] complainant purchased a Buffalo which was got insured by the opposite party No. 2 with the opposite party No. 1 on behalf of the complainant. Buffalo died and the complainant intimated the bank with regard to the loss suffered by him. The case of the opposite party No. 1 is that the complainant failed to furnish the sale purchase certificate and that is the reason for non-settlement of the claim. The forum held that it has not been disclosed by the opposite party No. 1 as to for what purpose the sale purchase certificate was required and how does non-production of certificate affected the settlement of the claim. Hence, deficiency was proved.

---

62. O/F 6037/96 D/I 31-8-96 D/D 22-7-98 (DF) Jmu.
63. O/F 27 D/D 30-1-2001 (DF) Jmu.
64. Not mentioned on Original file.
65. The Statemnt of the complainant was supported by final police report and the report of the surveyor appointed by the opposite party that the vehicle was involved in fire incident and loss caused to it.
66. O/F 939/2000 D/I 29-3-2000 D/D 12-3-2000 (DF) Jmu.

(f) Telephone

Under this heading like insurance cases, huge complaints are pending against telecom department, Jammu. Though a large remarkable cases are already disposed off in a wide range. Most of the cases are regarding excessive bills and delay in furnishing telephone connections.

Complaint titled *K.C. Sharma* v. *Union of India*[67] may be quoted here. Complainant has challenged the genuineness of telephone bill amounting to Rs. 11,687 on the ground that in the past before his telephone was shifted to the electronic exchange he had been receiving the telephone bills in the range of Rs. 2000 and after the shifting of his telephone to the electronic exchange he received the disputed bill which is patently excessive, inflated and wrong. During the enquiry the petitioner besides putting his attorney in the witness box, placed on record the Photostat copies of the past undisputed bills and disputed bill in support of his case. On the other hand, the non-applicant placed on record the detail billing in rebuttal. Forum found the statement from the documentary evidence placed on record by the petitioner and the detail billing filed by the non-applicant was not signed by any officer and as such non-applicants were directed to reduce the bill to Rs. 4,000.

In another complaint,[68] similarly circumstanced as above, complainant has succeeded in proving his case that the disputed bill is inflated and does not represent the actual use of telephone made by the complainant.

In *Bhupinder Singh* v. *Union of India and Others,*[69] complainant has claimed deficiency of service on the part of

---

67. O/F 4461/94 D/I 11-8-94 D/D 9-12-97 (DF) Jmu. It was observed by the Forum that Section 7(6) of Indian Telegraph Act provides for statutory arbitration of such disputes but the relief under Consumer Protection Act is in addition to the relief granted under the Telegraph Act and the provisions of Consumer Protection Act so not in any way comes in conflict with the provisions of Clause (b) of Section 7 of Indian Telegraph Act. Morever, the provisions of Clause (b) of Section 7 of Indian Telegraph Act are not mandatory.

68. Kewal Krishen Gupta *v.* Telecomunication, D.M. Jammu O/F 4621/94 D/I 28-10-94 D/D 25-2-95 (DF) Jmu.

69. O/F 672/98 D/I 05-2-98 D/D 31-01-2001 (DF) Jmu.

opposite party for having disconnected his telephone connection. His grievance as per facts and complaint is that he has always deposited the telephone bill well in time from the date of installation till date. However, on account of disconnection he has suffered a lot in the profession and has also suffered inconvenience.

Complaint was allowed and complainant was entitled to refund on account of rent of the telephone for the period, the telephone remained disconnected. Further, compensation of Rs. 15,000 for inconvenience due to wrongful disconnection of his telephone.

Now out of other cases regarding telephone department, complaint/case titled *M/s Bansal Builders* v. *Union of India and Telecom D.M.* is noteworthy. Here the complainant by the medium of a written complaint has approached this forum with allegations that he is a subscriber of telephone which is installed at his premises and the range of his telephone bills in the past had never exceeded Rs. 3000 whereas a false telephone bill for Rs. 1,93,350 was sent to the complainant which was enough to shock the nerves of the complainant who is a heart patient. When complainant approached concerned opposite party after two days he was informed that there had been a computer mistake which had resulted in the issuance of the wrong bill and the bill was slashed down to Rs. 3143 which was immediately paid by the complainant. In this case the oral and documentary evidence produced by the complainant, in the absence of any evidence of the respondent clearly goes to prove that on receiving the abnormal and inflated telephone bill issued by the respondent caused mental torture to the complainant who was a heart patient and in this way, clearly proves a lapse on the part of the respondent, entitling the complainant to compensation. Consequently, compensation of Rs. 10,000 were awarded.

Jammu Divisional Forum has received thousands of complaints and in majority of the cases consumer claims were allowed along with compensation and interest. What is important to note is that Jammu Divisional Forum like Srinagar Divisional Forum has passed balanced judgments more apparently in favour of Consumer.

Table* 2 showing number of institution pendency and disposal of cases since inception till ending September 2003.

TABLE 2*

Divisional Consumer Protection Forum, Jammu

Sl. No.	Item	Since Inception upto ending June 2003	Reporting Quarter ending September 2003	Progressive Total
1.	No. of Cases Filed	13,201	222	13423
2.	No. of Cases Disposed	9,468	136	9604
3.	No. of Cases Pending	3,733	86	3819
4.	No. of Cases Decided within 90 days	2,439	Nil	2439
5.	No. of Cases Decided within 150 days	3,871	2	3873
6.	No. of Cases Decided within more than 150 days	3,158	134	3292
7.	Average Time taken for disposal	8-9 months		

(C) CASES DECIDED BY STATE COMMISSION AT SRINAGAR

(I) Defective Goods

Under this heading case available here is *Nazir Ahmad Lone* v. *National Radio Electronic Company, New Delhi.*[70] The complainant was that he purchased a Photostat Machine from the authorized agent of the respondent firm in Srinagar. He was given assurance that the machine will run for full one year or/and will Photostat at least fifty thousand copies. He made a payment of Rs. 1,45,500 for this purpose. After sometime the machine broke down and developed defects and stopped working. He took the machine to Chandigarh and got it repaired there as here respondent make no such arrangement. The respondent in the guarantee card had promised that the machine will ordinarily work in proper

* Progress Report of Cases as above mentioned has been collected directly from the office of the President Divisional Consumer Protection Forum, Jammu.

70. O/F and D/I (not known) D/D 21-9-94 (SC) Sgr.

manner for at least one year or up to the date when it will Photostat fifty thousand copies. From the date it started giving trouble the complainant has been writing letters requesting the respondent to send some machine and get his machine repaired which of course the respondent never did.

In view of the circumstances appearing in the case respondents were directed by the commission to pay Rs. 50,000 to the complainant as costs of the damaged machine supplied to him and compensation of Rs. 20,000 plus costs and interest.

(2) Deficiency in Service

Under this heading only noteworthy cases will be dealt under different sub-headings.

(a) Air Service

Here case titled *Mohd. Abdullah Rishi* v. *Indian Airlines Corporation will be discussed first.*[71] Here complainants took a flight from Delhi to Srinagar by Indian Airlines. Five pieces of baggage's against five baggage tickets were booked with the opposite party. On arrival at Srinagar airport they were informed that the baggage had been left behind at Delhi and it will be arriving within a day or two but has not been delivered to him ever since that date. The attempt of the opposite party is that commission shall draw an inference about the goods not being their from the fact that no custom duty was paid. No claim form was filled and no weight and value was declared. It was held that it is a commonly known fact that for baggage which are booked by the passenger—it is for the airliner to notice the weight. The fact that the complainants were allowed to get out from the international airport clearly established the fact that they were cleared by the custom authorities. Consequently complaint was allowed and opposite party was directed to pay a sum of Rs. 80,000 and compensation of Rs. 10,000 were allowed.

---

71. O/F 100/95 D/I 10-10-95 (SC) Sgr.

(b) Banking

In *M/s Debo Nair Electrical Engineering Contractors* v. *Canara Bank Srinagar*,[72] the short point involved in this case is whether the failure of the opposite party to release the amount of FDR after a period of one year amounts to deficiency of service and whether this Act on the part of the opposite party has caused any loss and injury to the complainant.

The brief facts are that the complainant had a bank account with the opposite party which apart from him was required to be operated upon by his employee Anil Moti. It is said that the opposite party was under a contract that the account will be operated by these two persons. The complainant wanted a bank guarantee to be produced before I.T.D.C. Ltd. He accordingly asked the opposite party to take out Rs. 1.99 lacs from his accounts and issued an FDR for a period of one year. This was done to seek bank guarantee for I.T.D.C which was accordingly provided. The guarantee was for a period of six months. After one year when the FDR was matured he requested the bank concerned to make him the payment of the FDR which was denied on the plea that FDR was in the name of three persons, third one being Abdul Rashid, a stranger and that it cannot be paid unless all the three asked for the same. The case of the complainant is that he had never asked to include the third person in the FDR as he continues to be a stranger and the bank account from which the money was taken belonged to him and was being operated by him and his employee. FDR had matured in 1990.

Commission observed that nobody will believe this defence as nobody would like a stranger to be made an owner of the property possessed by him. It is not known as to who is this third person. Obviously commission observed mischief is committed by the bank employee. Accordingly bank was directed to pay the amount of FDR with 18% interest after one year of issuance and compensation of Rs. 10,000 were allowed for loss and injury due to the negligence of the opposite party.

---

72. O/F134/96 D/D 23-7-97 (SC) Sgr.

Interesting case on the point of discussion is *Noor Mohd. Mir* v. *Jammu and Kashmir Bank, Hazratbal.*[73] In this case as per version of the complainant he was having a saving bank account with opposite party. He was remitting his money into his account from Bombay and had been issued cheque books from withdrawals. According to him the balance in the account should have been Rs. 96,000 but it was only Rs. 46,000. His ledger account revealed that an amount of Rs. 30,000 and Rs. 20,000 were respectively withdrawn by two drawal forms despite the fact that he never draw the money and there was no occasion to do so in the presence of cheque book.

Commission observed it is rather admitted by the opposite party that some bank employees had committed fraud and embezzlement of lacs of rupees from the bank. It is also stated that a criminal case was filed but it was dismissed and the accused was acquitted. On facts and evidence of this case commission allowed the complaint and direct the opposite party to pay a sum of Rs. 1.00 lacs to the complainant and additional penalty of Rs. 5,000 as cost of the litigation.

Another case against bank authority which deserves to be mentioned here is *Syndicate Bank* v. *Inayatullah Jeelani*[74] and *Syndicate Bank* v. *Abdul Hamid War.*[75] These are two appeals which involve common question of fact and law and are decided by a common judgment.

The facts common to these appeals are that pursuant to scheme commonly known as Pigmay Deposit Scheme the respondents like many other people were depositing daily amounts with the agent of the appellant bank. The entries were being made under the hand and signatures of the agent and the agent in turn under scheme was to deposit the amounts so raised with the bank. This continued for some time but thereafter it discontinued due to security reasons and the agent of the bank who was raising deposits had left the Valley.

73. O/F 92/95 D/D 10-7-96 (SC) Sgr.
74. Appeal No. 146 of 1995 (SC) Sgr.
75. Appeal No. 147 of 1995 (SC) Sgr.

In appeal No. 146/1995 respondents alleges that he deposited a total of Rs. 5090 out of which he has drawn a sum of Rs. 3000 and in appeal No. 147/1995 deposits made accounts to Rs. 3860 but the bank in its ledgers has only given credit of Rs. 990.

After going through the file and taking into consideration respective contentions the Divisional Forum had arrived to the conclusion that full credit of the amounts raised from the respondents has not been given by the bank. Divisional Forum determined that under the settled law it is the liability of the master for the acts of agents. In this matter since agent misappropriated the money so bank is liable. State Commission held that the services are not only deficient but also unfair and appeals were dismissed.

In *Akbar Ali and Others* v. *Allahabad Bank and Janapriya Finance and Industrial Investment Ltd.*[76] a certificate was being issued to the persons from whom the amount was being raised by monthly instalments. The complainants had also deposited various amounts by instalments under certificate but even though the date of maturity was over the Janapriya Finance has not returned the money to the complainants. The amount so raised from the complainants was being deposited by the aforesaid company in the Allahabad Bank Branch, Srinagar. The account of the Janapriya Finance Company Ltd. is in the nature of FDR and Cash Certificates.

The case of the complainant was that despite the maturity period having since been completed the Janapriya Company has not fulfilled the requirement of returning them the maturity amount. After perusing the record on file commission observed that the Janapriya Finance Company has not provided service to the complainant which they had promised. Complaint was allowed and opposite party was directed to pay the maturity amount with interest at 10% from the date of maturity.

Another case against Janapriya and Bank of Allahabad is *Mrs. Haseena Bashir* v. *Janapriya Finance and Industrial Investment.*[77] Here case of the complainant is that she has paid

76. O/F No. 145/95 D/D 07-8-95 (SC) Sgr.
77. O/F No. 27/96 D/D 21-8-96 (SC) Sgr.

all the instalments for which she got duly signed receipts from the opposite party and when on the date of maturity she approached for payment she was told to wait for some time. Opposite party has not paid instead it has wind up of his office all over the State of Jammu and Kashmir. Complaint was allowed. However, in view of the fact that there are not much funds available and claimants are large, no order in respect of interest and compensation is made.

(c) Insurance

Under this heading maximum number of cases have been instituted and are still pending against various insurance companies. For the sake of brevity it is proposed to go through these cases under different sub-headings.

(i) Accidental Cases

Under this sub-heading first case here is *Gh. Nabi Bhat* v. *Divisional Manager, New India Assurance and Manager Co-operative Bank.*[78] In this case applicant was the owner of the truck. Truck met with an accident. Truck was insured with the New India Assurance Company and the complainant has been making payment. A surveyor was sent who made a final survey and lastly submitted his report. However, the company got the matter re-inspected. The company has stated that the company has not made the payment of the amount of loss to the tune as assessed by the surveyor.

The only controversy raised by the learned counsel for the opposite party was that the driver who was driving the truck was not holding the valid license on the date of alleged accident and he could drive heavy goods carrier and not passenger bus. Forum came to be satisfied by virtue of Motor Vehicle Act, 1930[79] in force that the driver was not required to have separate license to drive passenger bus as their was no separate category for them and heavy motor vehicle included the passenger bus as well. In couple of cases due to the fake driving license insurance company repudiated the claim. Cases are *Om Prakash Gupta* v. *Oriental Insurance*

78. O/F No. 255/93 D/I 22-6-93 D/D 18-09-95 (SC) Sgr.
79. Clausee (e) of Section 8(2).

Company Ltd.[80] and *Surjeet Kaur and Others* v. *New India Assurance Company.*[81] In the former case the vehicle owned by the complainant met with an accident and suffered heavy loss at Jammu Srinagar National Highway. The vehicle was insured is admitted and surveyor has assessed the loss and recommended that the complainant was entitled to this amount, but the claim was repudiated on the ground that the vehicle was being driven by one who was not having valid license. The commission dismissed the claim on the ground that a breach of contract made by the complainant for allowing a person to drive a vehicle who had fake license. It was held by the commission that if the license is shown to the employer of the driver who bonafidely believes such a renewed license as genuine which afterwards is found to be fake, breach is not wilful and hence it was held that the insurance company cannot escape the liability.

In the latter case, due to mechanical defect the vehicle fell down and was damaged. Driver who was also owner got grievously injured in the accident who succumbed to the injuries. The complaint has been filed by the widow and minor sons of the deceased driver/owner. The grievances of the complainants was that opposite party had refused to pay the claim of the vehicle and the claim of the deceased driver/insured is based on false ground that the vehicle has been driven by a driver not holding valid driving license at the time of accident. Opposite party averred that the complainants were notified to cooperate. It was in this state of things that the contention of opposite party was not accepted. Further it was observed that if the defence is accepted it will lead a large scope of corruption and crime.

In a couple of cases[82] complaints were allowed for the reason that insurance company have got the formalities completed but has not released the money.

---

80. O/F No. 1143/96 D/I ____ -96 D/D 17-1-2001 (SC) Sgr. Earlier Commission Dismissed the Complaint but Hon'ble High Court remanded back the case to this commission with the direction to decide the matter afresh.
81. O/F No. 1.224/98 D/I 29-6-98 D/D 26-7-2000 (SC) Sgr.
82. Abdul Wahid Bhat *v.* New India Assurance Company Ltd. D/D 28-11-2000 and Dr. Mohd. Afzal Khan *v.* United India Insurance Company Ltd. O/F No. 311/95 D/D 7-8-96.

(ii) Burglary and Theft

After going through the cases under this heading it will become clear how and to what extent insurance companies are causing delay in settling complaints which becomes the reason for the complainant to knock the doors of forums. In *Showkat Hussain Malik* v. *Oriental Insurance Company Ltd.,*[83] the complainant had taken an insurance in respect of his stocks in shop situated at Kupwara against burglary. The complainant raised a claim with an insurance company pursuant to which surveyor had reported loss but for no good reasons the settlement of his claim has been inordinately delayed. The opposite party in its version of the case has raised no substantial plea. All that is stated is that complainant is to strictly prove the insurance policy and the premium receipt and that they are not liable to pay any amount to the complainant. As a matter of fact after perusing the whole case it reveals that neither the existence of the insurance policy has been disputed nor is there any indication as to whether the case of complainant has been taken up for consideration at any stage. All that has been said is that the company is in no way liable for payment to the complainant. In this case while allowing the complaint commission directed the opposite party to pay the amount as assessed by the surveyor along with interest of 18% and compensation of Rs. 50,000 were awarded.

Complaints captioned *Nazir Ahmad Ganie* v. *Oriental Insurance Company;*[84] *M/s Ahad Dar and Sons* v. *Divisional Manager; Oriental Insurance Company*[85] and *Mohd. Yaqoob Bhat*

---

83. D/D 14-5-95 (SC) Sgr. In this case direction was given to the opposite party to initiate a domestic enquiry and locate the responsibility pin pointing the officers and officials who are responsible for putting the Insurance Company to this loss and for creating this awakward situation. The amount of compensation shall then be recovered from the pay due of such functionaries and if any functionaries has retired it shall be recovered from his pension and pensionary dues. Complaint titled Haji Gh. Mohammad Mandoo *v.* National Insurance Company Ltd. O/F No. 144/96 D/D 29-7-97 stands disposed off in similar way and claim was allowed with 18% interest.
84. O/F No.44/96 D/D 17-10-96 (SC) Sgr.
85. O/F No. 49/96 D/D 17-10-96 (SC) Sgr.

v. *Oriental Insurance Company Ltd.*[86] are also allowed at 18% interest. All these three complaints are disposed off by Justice Malik Sharief-ud-din (President).

In *Abdul Aziz Sheikh* v. *Oriental Insurance Company Ltd.*[87] and *Ali Mohd. Malik* v. *National Insurance Company and Others*[88] complainants in their respective complaints have proved unreasonable attitude and negligence on the part of functionaries of the company in discharging their duties. Consequently compensation of Rs. 50,000 and Rs. 30,000 were allowed apart from insurance claim/loss as assessed by the surveyor.

(iii) Cases Related Delay

It is found that some complaints made before the forum are such in which consumers have claimed compensation and interest for causing delay in settling the claim. In *M/s Lighter General Store* v. *National Insurance Company Ltd.*[89] complainant was left high and dry for five years. Under law insurance has to process the case at the most within three to four months. In the matter in hand it was observed that it is no use to offer a pittance to the insured. Since amount remained with the insured for more than five years for which the insured was mainly responsible and accordingly interest at the rate of 18% p.a. from the date of loss till the date of tendering cheque.

Similarly in *Mohd. Shafi and Mohd. Abass and Others* v. *Manager, Regional Manager and others.*[90] And also in *Abdul*

86. O/F No. 6/99 D/D 4-6-97 (SC) Sgr.
87. O/F No. 112/95 (SC) Sgr.
88. O/F No. 1145/95 D/D 29-08-95 (SC) Sgr. There are ample decisions which are disposed off in the similar manner as above because facts in all these cases were more or less the same. For example Mst. Sara Begum *v.* National Insurance Company O/F No. 31/96 D/D 10-6-97 (SC) Sgr; Parvez Ahmad Kuchay *v.* Oriental Insurance Company O/F No. 131/96 D/D 23-7-97.
89. O/F 277/95 D/D 7-6-96 (SC) Sgr; Seen also Gh. Mohi-ud-din Bhat *v.* United India Insurance Company Ltd. O/F No. 15/96 D/D 5-6-97 (SC) Sgr; Gh. Mohammad Bhat *v.* India Insurance Company Ltd. O/F No. 14/96 D/D 26-7-96 (SC) Sgr.
90. O/F No. 118/96 D/D 24-6-97 (SC) Sgr.

Hamid Wani v. *The Regional Manager, National Insurance Company Ltd.*[91] interest were allowed in all these cases.

There are ample cases in which compensation especially interest is allowed for delay caused by the insurance company in deciding validity of the driving license having been found fake and forged on verification and were asked to explain the position and they failed to do so within granted time limit so their claim was repudiated.

It was observed that as regards the accident the same is admitted and the postmortem report produced by the complainant which has not been rebutted proved that death of the deceased has been caused due to accident.

Further as regards assessment of loss to the vehicle as per special claim note produced by the opposite party compensation of Rs. 1,78,500 on total loss basis worked out by the final survey has been accepted as reasonable.

On the material, led by the parties forum came to the conclusion that the opposite party had been deficient in repudiating the claim of the complainants and accordingly complaint was allowed.

In one more decision similar to the above mentioned case the point was not whether the license is genuine or fake but the question remained whether complainant believed the license to be genuine or not. The case is *Vijay Kumar* v. *Oriental Insurance Company Ltd. and Others.*[92] In the instant case the complainant bonafidely believed the license genuine so there was no wilful breach of contract and complaint was allowed.

In *Mohd. Ismail Zarger* v. *Oriental Insurance Company and Others*[93] forum has wonderfully delivered and disposed off the case. In this case opposite party pleaded that non-cooperation of complainant is the reason that report was not submitted.

---

91. O/F No. 144/95 D/D 18-6-96 (SC) Sgr.
92. O/F No. 1315/96 (SC) Sgr. Further a sum of Rs. 30,000 was allowed to the complainant for loss and injury due to the negligency of the opposite party.
93. In Pushak Mahal Sopore *v.* United India Insurance Company O/F No. 341 D/D 8-7-96 (SC) Sgr. For delay of three years in settling the claim Rs. 70,000 compensation was allowed.

However, it was held that in normal course of cases the assured who is interested in getting the indemnification for the loss will be the last person that matters. In *Smt. Raj Dulari* v. *Noor-ud-din*[94] a claim was raised with the opposite party and the complainant submits that all the relevant and requisite documents were submitted to the surveyor within less than two months but the surveyor since that date slept on his claim and has not made any effort to accept the liability and make the payment. It was held that the entire defence set-up has been so tailored as to justify the delay without any valid reason and accordingly complaint was allowed.

Decision in cases *J.L Kachroo* v. *Divisional Manager, United India Company Ltd.*[95] and *Mehraj Krishen Bhat* v. *Oriental Isurance Company Ltd.*[96] was given on similar lines.

(iv) Fire Cases

While making survey of the cases against insurance company maximum number of cases fall under this sub-heading. In the case captioned *Jammu and Kashmir Bank, Main Bazar, Sopore* v. *United India Insurance Company Ltd.*[97] complainant has insured his building for a sum of Rs. 1.00 lac and another sum of Rs. 1.00 lac cover the risk in respect of furnitures, fixtures and fittings, machine, transformer and generator. In this case opposite party submitted that the case is under enquiry because it was found to be a closed proximity case in as much as insurance was carried out on 4th of Jan. 1993 and the incident took place on 6-1-1993.

Commission held that the fact that insurance was carried out only on 4-1-1993 is no ground for doubting that the insurance was carried in good faith. Even if this fact had raised any doubt it has taken opposite party three and half

94. O/F No. 112/95 (SC) Sgr.
95. O/F No. 675/97 (SC) Sgr.
96. O/F No. 1424/99 D/D 29-11-99 (SC) Sgr. Cases Gh. Mohammad Bagard *v.* National Insurance Company Ltd O/F No. 13/96 D/D 18-07-96 (SC) Sgr; Khursheed Ahmad Shah *v.* Regional Manager, United India Insurance O/F No. 301/95 (SC) Sgr. are disposed on similar way.
97. O/F No. 328/95 D/D 8-7-96 (SC) Sgr.

years in not arriving at the conclusion as to what it should do in the case. The reasons for non-acceptance of liability have been found to be unsustainable and complaint was allowed. Sum of Rs. 50,000 were awarded to the complainant for enormous loss, financial stress and physical and mental crises as he has taken the loan from the bank on which interest was accumulating.

On account of incident having taken place in Sopore on Sixth January it caused damage to hundreds of houses and business shops resulting in the burning and death of scores of people.

Cases captioned *M/s Gh. Hassan Sopore* v. *United India Assurance Company Ltd.;*[98] *Mohd. Ashraf Bhat* v. *United India Assurance Company Ltd., Srinagar;*[99] *Cosmic General Store* v. *United India Assurance Company Ltd.*[100] and *Gh. Rasool Mir* v. *United India Insurance Company Ltd.*[101] were decided on similar way as above mentioned case.

Facts of the case captioned *Abdul Gaffar Changal* v. *United India Insurance*[102] will be stated here briefly. Admittedly the complainants house was burnt as a result of the militant activities. Opposite party got the loss assessed but the company had declined to make the payment on the ground that a lady one Mehra Begum has disputed the insurance interest of the complainant that he was adopted son and was entitled only to half of the share of the property. It was observed revenue records were in favour of the complainant and possibly it was only done to create a ground for non-payment of the just claim of the complainant. It was held that an approved claim has been withheld on a manipulated and non-existent ground and consequently complaint was allowed.

Here before us are ample cases perusal of which reveals that complaints have been allowed on the ground that insurance company has taken much time to settle the matter.

---

98. O/F No. 346/95 D/D 8-7-96 (SC) Sgr.
99. O/F No.334/95 D/D 8-7-96 (SC) Sgr.
100. O/F No. 347/95 D/D 8-7-96 (SC) Sgr.
101. O/F No. 342/95 D/D 8-7-96 (SC) Sgr.
102. O/F No. 51/96 D/D 18-6-97 (SC) Sgr.

Cases are—*Mohd. Ramzan* v. *United India Insurance Company Ltd.*;[103] *Mohd. Aslam Mir* v. *Oriental Insurance Company Ltd.*;[104] *Nazir Ahmad Tak* v. *Oriental Insurance Company Ltd.*;[105] *Farooq Ahmad and Company* v. *United India Insurance Company Ltd.*;[106] *Smt. Raj Dulari* v. *National Insurance Company and another*[107] has been disposed off on similar lines as above mentioned cases. The case captioned *Talaq Bakery and Confectionary* v. *Oriental and General Insurance Company Ltd.*[108] is a very important case which needs to be mentioned here. During the validity of the insurance contract the business establishment of the complainant was destroyed due to fire and it was a total loss. He raised a claim with the insurance company and filed all the necessary and required documents. Till 1988 he was told that since the records of the opposite party were burnt in fire the matter is under consideration. After 1988 due to the insurgency in the Valley the respondents closed their office at Anantnag together with its divisional office at Srinagar consequent to which complainant approached the Regional Office of the company. In the meanwhile the opposite party opened a skeleton divisional office at Sonawar Srinagar and the complainant got in touch with it. Then his claim remained unsatisfied and the company has failed to accept its liability. Opposite party has taken the version that the complaint is time barred.

Commission observed that the records of the company got burnt and for a long time they were not in a position to deal with the claim of the complainant. Thereafter, the company closed its office and the complainant while approaching the regional office was told that his case is under consideration. In the absence of any communication from the opposite party the complainant is justified in

---

103. O/F No. 345/96 D/D 30-7-97 (SC) Sgr.
104. O/F No. 53/97 D/D 31-7-97 (SC) Sgr.
105. O/F No. 41/97 D/D 3-7-97 (SC) Sgr.
106. O/F No. 41/96 D/D 05-06-97 (SC) Sgr. Seen also Haji Qadir Joo Janwari and Company *v.* New India Assurance Company Ltd. O/F No. 337/96 (SC) Sgr.
107. O/F No. 112/96 D/D 5-6-97 (SC) Sgr.
108. O/F No. 81/95 D/D 18-6-96 (SC) Sgr.

treating the claim as pending for want of settlement. There is no evidence at what stage claim was repudiated and whether this fact was communicated to the complainant or not. In these circumstances complainant is justified to say that he was under impression that his claim is pending and thus he was forced to bring this litigation. Consequently commission held that the complainant was given to understand his claim is under process only supports the conclusion that the claim is not stale. In this case regarding the next point—complainant had not paid the premium. It was held that the insurance cover issued in this case was not denied by the opposite party and it was clearly mentioned that the complainant has paid a premium of Rs. 1,758. Consequently, complaint was allowed and sum of Rs. 2,96,000 with 18% interest from the date of loss till the payment was allowed plus Rs. 50,000 compensation.

One more case important to be noted here is, namely, *Shah Abass Hotel* v. *The Chairman, United India Insurance Company Ltd.*[109] Here the complainant had insured his hotel for a sum of Rs. 24.00 lacs which is not denied by the opposite party. The hotel was involved in an incident of fire and pursuant to a claim raised by him the surveyor assessed the loss at Rs. 9.00 lacs out of which 80% was paid to the complainant. The remaining 20% was withheld as it was stated that in reinstating policies the complainant is to carry out reinstatement, furnish the necessary bills and after verification 20% retained by the company is reimbursed.

Opposite party in their objections stated that the formalities were not completed by the complainant and bills did not indicate the mode of payment. Commission observed that the bills could not have indicated the mode of payment. Only the receipts of the payment would show how the payment were made. This led support to the suspicion that since there was no substantial and reasonable ground for withholding the claim it has been done for some other considerations.

109. O/F No. 220/95 D/D 15-7-96 (SC) Sgr.

Case captioned *Gull Mohammad* v. *United India Insurance Company Ltd.*[110] is noteworthy to be mentioned here. The case of the complainant is that in his absence as due to militancy he migrated to Jammu. It is unwarranted in law and is against principles of natural justice that the claim has been rejected.

Opposite party disputed the claim on two grounds. First that the claim is time barred and that the bills produced. by the complainant were found to be fabricated and fictitious and this was done under the terms of the contract.

After hearing the counsel for the parties and after giving careful consideration to the state of facts and law it was observed that the company has neither disputed the insurance cover, the validity of the policy nor was there any controversy in respect of the stocks having been lost in fire. However, as per report of the surveyor some of the bills from the dealers were found to be fictitious though there was total loss. Further it is observed that even though it is reported that some bills are fictitious but no evidence was given to that effect.

The case titled *Gh. Rasool Zarger* v. *Oriental Insurance Company and others*[111] has been decided on the evidence of the complainant only. In this case opposite party failed to produce the objections within the statutory period. Commission observed that the CBI has seized the records does not appeal to the commission as it no were stated that there was any complaint in respect of this case. In fact there could be no complaint of any fraud or bunglings in respect of this case as the case has not even been processed. So complaint was allowed with 18% interest.

Here is a case[112] in which insurance company has sent two surveyors and still failed to settle the claim of the complainant. In this case stocks of goods in the nature of silk,

110. O/F No. 91/95 D/D 24-10-96 (SC) Sgr; In Fayaz Ahmad Dar *v.* Oriental Insurance Company Ltd. O/F No. 58/96 D/D 11-6-97 (SC) Sgr. objection was that the loss is manipulated but opposite party was found incorrect.
111. O/F No. 36/96 D/D 23-7-97 (SC) Sgr.
112. M/s Special Diamond Silks *v.* United India Insurance Company Ltd. O/F No. 111/95 D/D 6-8-96 (SC) Sgr.

pashmina and other handicrafts to the tune of Rs. 10,25,000 was insured. The entire stocks were totally destroyed in a fire incident. A claim was raised and one Pritamber Lal Puri of New Delhi was asked to conduct the survey. The complainant produced the documents as required by the surveyor and the surveyor recommended the loss to the tune of Rs. 7.65 lacs. The opposite party failed to accept the liability despite this report of the surveyor. It however unilaterally and without notice to the complainant appointed one Rakesh Khana for finalization of the claim. Complainant complied the information of Mr. Khana but Mr. Khana did not visit the complainant nor complainant visited Mr. Khana. He however submitted a report which according to the complainant was prepared by Mr. Khana at his office based on presumptions and assumptions. According to the opposite party the necessity for appointing Mr. Khana as investigator was to verify whether some stocks had shifted from Hyderabad. It was observed by the commission that opposite party attempted to adopt the report of Mr. Khana which submitted it despite the fact that he never visited the complainant. All this shows opposite party has deliberately and wilfully adopted tactics of procrastination and delay in acceptance of its liability and has deprived the complainant and his rightful and just claim. Complaint was allowed and Rs. 1.00 lac was allowed as compensation as he suffered loss and injury for seven years.

Another case here is *Gh. Rasool Malik* v. *Oriental Insurance Company*[113] in which three surveyors were sent to make survey of the loss. In this case commission observed that there has been a deliberate and wilful attempt on the part of the insurance company to delay the settlement of the claim. It was in the interest of the insurance company to meet the just claim of the customer without loss of time. So complaint was allowed and Rs. 30,000 were awarded.

There are large number of cases decided by the Commission where complainants after accepting and executing a discharge receipt in full and final satisfaction of insurance claim have filed complaints before the commission

113. D/D 31-7-95 (SC) Sgr.

on the ground in each case that insurance companies caused delay in settling their claims. Some cases may be quoted here —*Abdul Rashid Ganie* v. *Oriental Insurance Company Ltd.*[114] Here the main dispute of the complainant was that even though he has given a discharge voucher in full and final satisfaction he is not debarred from claiming interest and compensation. In this case, *M/s Zamindera Tractors* v. *Oriental Fire and General Insurance Company Ltd.*[115] was quoted and Commission held that the insurance company has made no attempt to settle the case within the reasonable time and there is no explanation for the delay of 18 months in making the payment and there was no evidence that delay was attributable to the complainant so interest at 18% was allowed and Rs. 40,000 compensation also.

In another case[116] decided by the same commission, there was delay of 20 months. It was observed that under Insurance Manual the surveyor is bound to submit the report within 7 days and if he fails to do so and explanation is to be called from him and matter reported to the regional office. These rules as experience shows are followed in breach for the reasons not to be stated. According to well settled judicial precedents the company should not take more than 3 to 4 months to process the case. All these well settled norms are ignored by the functionaries of the opposite party. Normally

114. O/F No. 206/95 D/D 12-9-95 (SC) Sgr.

115. D/D 22-9-93 by Haryana State Commission and the judgment is delivered by learned J. Sandalwalia. In this case the point as to whether a complainant is stopped from filling complaint for interest after full and final satisfaction was elaborately discussed and it was finally concluded that a full and final discharge gives quietus for the contractual payment under the policy but in no way extinguishes the consumer's rights to claim interest, damage or loss suffered due to the negligence of the insurer.

116. Khursheed Ahmad *v.* United India Insurance Company Ltd. O/F No. 301/95 D/D 26-7-96 (SC) Sgr. Complaint captioned Mohd. Shafi and Mohd. Abbas *v.* Regional Manager and Others was also disposed off on similar lines. There was delay of 27 months. Seen another case on the point which is titled as Gh. Mohi-ud-din Bhat *v.* United India Insurance Company Ltd. and Another O/F No. 19/96 D/D 05-06-97 and Ab. Raheem Gujree *v.* United India Insurance Company 214/96 D/D 17-6-97.

in each case unsupportable justifications for the neglect is put forward though in this case opposite party has not chosen to do so and to tell us what action was taken from time to time. How then it can be said that the opposite party was not negligent in not dealing with the matter.

In the case titled *Abdul Hamid Wani* v. *National Insurance Company Ltd., Lal Chowk, Srinagar.*[117] Commission has shown how the functionaries of the company have delayed the settlement of the claim and wasted 22 months of the complainant and in this case also both interest and compensation was allowed.

Similarly in case *Gh. Mohd. Bhat* v. *United Insurance Company Ltd.* interest and compensation were allowed even though complainant has already issued receipt in full and final satisfaction.

In *Gh. Mohd. Bajard* v. *National Insurance Company, Sopore.*[118]

The complainant had insured his shop of Kiryana after procuring loan from Jammu and Kashmir Bank, Sopore. The shop was involved in an accident and intimation whereof was given to the company which appointed a surveyor and the loss was assessed at Rs. 15,000. The complainant stated that he submitted all the documents demanded by the company but the company sat on the matter and did not decide the same. Opposite party stated that the complainant's claim was repudiated by the Review Committee.

Commission observed that company has failed to satisfy the commission about the date of decision of repudiation and has withheld the report of surveyor. In view of the suppression of the report of the surveyor and all other documents relevant to the decision of the case complaint was allowed as per surveyor's report and 18% interest and Rs. 5,000 were allowed.[119]

---

117. O/F No. 277/95 (SC) Sgr.

118. O/F No. 13/96 D/D 18-7-96 (SC) Sgr.

119. Complaint captioned M/s Showkat General Store Handwara *v.* United India Insurance Company Ltd. O/F No. 114/95 D/D 13-6-96 (SC) Sgr. Stands allowed and Rs. 30,000 compensation was granted. In this case Company found documents fabricated but commission held that even though it was so it should have repudiate the claim within reasonable time.

In *J.B. Traders, Sopore* v. *United India Insurance Company*[120] surveyor submitted the report and loss was assessed at Rs. 6,02,27 on 2-6-1992 but company slept on the matter. In objection opposite party has not disputed neither the insurance cover nor the incident. It was also not in controversy that the surveyor made an assessment to the tune of Rs. 6,02,27. However, in objections it was stated that the company has approved for an amount of Rs. 4,89,305.

Commission observed it is not clear why the company reduced the amount as assessed by the surveyor. On the facts and circumstances it was found that the opposite party was deficient in providing services and complaint was allowed as per surveyor's report along with 18% interest and Rs. 50,000.

Cases captioned *M/s Rising Enterprises, Kaka Buildings, Court Road, Srinagar* v. *United India Insurance Company Ltd.;*[121] *M/s Kay Kay Enterprises Kupwara* v. *Oriental Insurance Company Ltd and others;*[122] *Bashir Brothers* v. *Oriental Insurance Company Srinagar;*[123] *Khursheed Enterprises, Sopore* v. *Oreintal India Insurance Company Ltd.;*[124] *M/s Galaxy Traders* v. *Oriental Insurance Company Ltd. and another;*[125] *Abdul Majid Dar* v. *Oriental Insurance Company*[126] were allowed also as in these cases respective insurance companies prolonged the matter unnecessarily for a long time.

The case of the complainant in *Manzoor Ahmad Kakroo* v. *New India Assurance Company Ltd. and another*[127] has been disposed off with the order that he shall get in touch with the Divisional Manager of the opposite party within a week as only objection in this case raised by the opposite party was non-cooperation of the complaint.

In another case titled *Basharat Industries* v. *National Insurance Company, M.A Road, Srinagar.*[128] Opposite party in

120. O/F No. 228/96 (SC) Sgr.
121. O/F No. 27/93 D/D 29-8-95 (SC) Sgr.
122. O/F No. 109/95 D/D 13-8-96 (SC) Sgr.
123. O/F No. 115/95 D/D 12-6-96 (SC) Sgr.
124. O/F No. 36/96 D/D 22-10-96 (SC) Sgr.
125. O/F No. 48/96 D/D 22-10-96 (SC) Sgr.
126. O/F No. 145/96 (SC) Sgr.
127. O/F No. 90/95 D/D 12-10-95 (SC) Sgr.
128. O/F No. 70/96 D/D 28-5-97 (SC)Sgr.

objections pleaded non-cooperation on the part of complainant. However, in this case non-cooperation was not evident and in this case complainant has insured his factory, building and machinery but the factory was forcibly occupied by the Security Forces as a result of which damage was caused to the building and to the machinery. Despite the report of surveyor matter was not settled. Commission observed that it is immaterial on which date damage was caused. Since security forces entered there during the validity of the insurance cover and whether it was caused in one day or in a number of days is immaterial. Neither the loss nor the validity of the cover is in dispute.

In *Mahraj Krishen Raina* v. *Oriental Insurance Company Ltd.,*[129] the case of the complainant was that he furnished all documents and surveyor has assessed the loss but still he was not paid. Opposite party provides complainant has failed to submit the police report. Company was asked to produce all documents before the commission but it failed to do so. It is observed that after surveyor's report nothing has been done. This created doubt in the mind of forum that case of complainant was deliberately and wilfully not processed and complaint was allowed.

In *M/s Assar and Company Fruit Commission* v. *Oriental Insurance Company*[130] complainant sent a truck load of fruit through Northern Kashmir Roadways duly insured with opposite party. During the course of transit the truck met with an accident resulting in damage to the truck and loss to the consignment. Opposite party appeared but subsequently disappeared from the scene. Complaint was allowed.

(d) Postal Service

In *Abdul Aziz Nahvi* v. *Chief Post Master General, Jammu and Kashmir Circle, Srinagar and Another*[131] the complainant had booked two parcels worth Rs. 262 and Rs. 186 respectively which were addressed to two different parties at New Delhi and Rohtak, Haryana. These parcels were never delivered to

129. D/D 05-10-95 (SC) Sgr.
130. O/F No. 348/95 D/D 25-7-96 (SC) Sgr.
131. O/F No. 235/95 D/D 04-6-97 (SC) Sgr.

the addressee with the result that the two complaints were duly registered by him with the opposite party. The opposite party did not bother to look into the matter for long but finally asked him to furnish the indemnity bond along with the receipts. Thereafter he was again asked to furnish an affidavit that he had not received any payment regarding these parcels. Despite this, the opposite party did nothing in the matter but in its version opposite party has not disputed the registration of the parcels. It is silent in respect of the fact as to whether these parcels were delivered to the addressee.

Commission observed on the facts of this case that the complainant has proved that he has been deprived of the value of these two parcels and for the last seven years he has been made to run from pillar to post in seeking redressal. It is observed that it may be anybody's guess that in sending so company must have spent some money to pursue the matter. Complaint was allowed and opposite party was directed to pay Rs. 448 value of the parcel and a sum of Rs. 1000 as compensation for emotional and mental stress.

Another case here is *Dr. Javaid Ahmad Calcutti* v. *Department of Post.*[132] The short question that arose in this case is as to whether the complainant is entitled to claim compensation for deficient service by the opposite party as a result of whose negligence he has suffered loss and injury. The complainant with a view to undergo post-graduation in medicines in U.S.A. has submitted his application form for appearing in education commission for Foreign Medical Graduate Examination (herein for short known as E.C.F.M.S.). The nearest destination from India where the examination were to be conducted was Singapore. Since the employment was very serious about taking this chance he sent his application through the GPO Srinagar by an International Speed Post. He was however, informed by a communication by the commission for Foreign Medical Graduates U.S.A. that since his application was received after the last date for registration it could not be registered. The complainant's case is that since there was 19 days between the date of registration and the date of booking of the speed post and if

132. O/F No. 235/95 D/D 04-6-97 (SC) Sgr.

opposite party were not negligent in the discharges of its duties in providing perfect services it should not have taken more than three days for the speed post to reach the destination. The opposite party has raised a dispute only to the extent delay in delivery of the speed post has been caused by U.S.A. Postal Services and they are in no way responsible for the same.

Commission observed that it is no defence that the fault is that of the U.S.A. Postal Services as the complainant. had hired the services of the Indian Postal Department. They may be deemed functionaries at the most as agents of the Indian Postal Services with whom the services were primarily booked. The complainant has lost valuable one year for which Rs. 30,000 were awarded as compensation.

(e) Cases Related to Passport

Case captioned *Gh. Hassan Mir and Others* v. *Green Channel Passport*[133] be quoted here. In this complaint the complainants approached the opposite party and hired their services for getting 3 Passports in the name of the complainants. The opposite party accepted to provide service on payment of double charges and assured that the complete passports will be delivered to the complainants. It is stated by the complainant that on the assurance of the opposite party the complainant arranged a business trip to London for the month of December, 1993 and also arranged various items of Kashmir Arts such as Carpets, Pashmina Shawl, etc. worth Rs. 12.00 lacs as cash credit and they were expecting to export it and earn profit but since the opposite party did not deliver the passports and complainants have to resell the goods at a loss of Rs. 2.00 lacs. In support of the case complainant has submitted a detailed affidavit in which he has reiterated these very facts. Commission got satisfied in *ex-parte* that it is a clear case of deficient service by the opposite party as a result of which complainants have suffered. In these circumstances complaint was allowed and opposite party was directed to refund the amount and also a sum of Rs. 30,000 as compensation for the loss and injury.

133. O/F No. 39/94 D/D 24-8-95 (SC) Sgr.

(f) Telephone

In *Abdul Khaliq Malik* v. *Chief General Manager Telecommunication,*[134] the complainant was a subscriber of, telephone which was suddenly disconnected. The complainant has stated that all the bills were paid against the proper receipts and there was nothing outstanding against the complainant, still he was billed in the sum of Rs. 10,055 for period between the 30th April 1993 to 25th August 1993. Complainant proved his case that there was nothing outstanding against the petitioner since his telephone was disconnected.

Commission allowed the complaint and passed order to the effect that the complainant shall pay a sum of Rs. 3,300 in full and final satisfaction of his outstanding and his telephone shall be reconnected. Further Rs. 10,000 were awarded.

(g) Transport

Among other trucks one truck was loaded with 90 quintals of Sugar as payment of freight of Rs. 25,000 out of which Rs. 22,000 was paid in advance and the balance was to be paid at the time of delivery. Opposite party failed to cause delivery of 90 quintals of sugar. The complainant brought the matter before the opposite party but opposite party did not respond. Opposite party refused to take service and hence was set in *ex-parte.* Opposite party was directed to pay Rupees 150,000 with 18% interest and compensation of Rs. 5,000.[135]

(h) Unfair Trade Practice

M/s Maruti Udyog v. *Mr. M.A. Malik and Another*[136] is an appeal against the order of Divisional Forum in which the appellant herein were directed to refund Rs. 43,949.62 and also pay Rs. 6,000 as compensation to the respondent. It is

134. O/F No. 72/94 D/D 17-6-96 (SC) Sgr.
135. M/s New J.K. Roadways Hazuri Bagh, Srinagar *v.* J.K. Major Transport Companies Association, Jammu O/F No. 57/96 D/D 18-6-97 (SC) Sgr.
136. D/D 21-8-95 (SC) Sgr.

alleged that at the time of booking he was promised the delivery of the car within a month but no delivery was made and the delivery was extended from time to time and meanwhile the prices of the Maruti Car increased and he was made to pay an excess amount of Rs. 40,000 and though earlier amount was deposited on 15-1-1991, car was finally delivered on 14-9-1991.

The main grievance of the petitioner was that had he been delivered car in time as promised he would not have to incur an extra expenses on account of enhanced tariff.

It is pertinent to mention here that Divisional Forum passed order in *ex-parte* and here appellant has not put in appearance since long and in normal course it was supposed to be dismissed in default but Commission, however, did not resorted to the option of dismissing the appeal for the reason this case involves a principle of law for which appeal came to be converted into revision as in the view of Commission Divisional Forum has acted in exercise of its jurisdiction irregularly.

Commission perused the memorandum of appeal in which it was mentioned that the reliance of the letter is misplaced. On perusal of letter it was sound clear that no commitment was made. The only expression used in the letter was that delivery is likely to be made in the month of July is not a firm commitment at all. In these circumstances it was found that the Divisional Forum has fallen in error by not looking at the contents of the letter and provision of the sale contract. Appeal was thus converted into the revision, order of Divisional Forum was set aside.

Table* 3 on next page showing No. of cases filed/ disposed its pending before State Commission (Srinagar and Jammu Wing) Jammu and Kashmir.

(D) CASES DECIDED BY STATE COMMISSION, JAMMU

Under this heading a number of cases have been disposed off and are still pending disposal before the commission. Out of disposed number of cases important among them will be taken up here.

TABLE 3

State Consumer Commission, J&K

Sl. No.	*Items*	*No.of cases filed since inception upto ending December 2002*	*Reporting Quarters January to March 2003*	*Progress total March 2003*
1.				
	a. Complaints	2883	11	2894
	b. Appeals	1391	20	1411
	c. Total	4272	31	4305
2.	No. of Cases Decided			
	a. Complaints	2583	31	2614
	b. Appeals	1145	44	1189
	c. Total	3728	75	3803
3.	Cases Pending			
	a. Complaints	300		280
	b. Appeals	246		222
	c. Total	546		502
4.	Cases Decided within 90 days			
	a. Complaints	469	10	479
	b. Appeals	176	14	190
	c. Total	645	24	669
5.	Cases Decided 90 days upto 180 days			
	a. Complaints	933	8	941
	b. Appeals	330	20	350
	c. Total	1263	28	1291
6.	Cases Decided in more than 180 days			
	a. Complaints	1181	13	1194
	b. Appeals	639	10	649
	c. Total	1820	23	1843

* The above combined list of cases (both Srinagar & Jammu Wing of SC) has been obtained directly from the office of State Commission Jammu and Kashmir Government.

(I) Defective Goods

In *K.K. Sahani* v. *S. Karan Singh and Others*[137] respondent-complainant purchased two tires for his truck in the month of March 1995. Same were fitted in his vehicle and the said truck left for Ludhiana in load of goods. On rechecking at Ludhiana both the tires came out of the rim due to some manufacturing defects in the tires. Tires were sent to the manufacturing company. They were examined by local engineer certified that the tires had no manufacturing defect. Same were returned to the respondent. Respondent agitated the matter before the forum that the tires had manufacturing defect. The forum allowed the claim petition and directed the appellant to replace the tires or to pay the costs of tires along with Rs. 2,000 as litigation charges. After hearing the counsel for appellant and perusing the record it was observed that short points raised in this appeal was that the respondent was not a consumer. Court/forum after perusing record of Divisional Forum and evidence/statement of respondent whereby he has admitted that he is the owner of the vehicle for which he purchased two tires. He had admitted that he is using the truck for commercial purpose. Hence the decision of the Divisional Forum was set aside.

In another case which is similar to the above mentioned one is *Satish Kaul* v. *Managing Director and Chairman, Bajaj Auto United Ltd. and Others.*[138] By the medium of appeal complainant prayed that he is aggrieved by the order of Divisional Forum whereby it was ordered that vehicle be repaired but complainant in appeal has prayed that vehicle repaired many a times but defects could not be removed. He prayed that opposite party be directed to replace the motorbike in question by giving a fresh one.

---

137. Apeal No. 1617/97 (SC) Jmu. Ofcourse judicial pronouncements from time to time show that the definition of 'consumer' has been stretched to include the goods which are used for commercial purpose but only for earning livlihood by the consumer.

138. Appeal No. 1960/99 D/D 17-4-2001. In Sushil Kumar *v.* Maruti Udyog and Another O/F No. 1263/97, complaint was allowed and opposite party was directed to replace the car of the complainant and Rs. 5000 were awarded as litigation costs.

It was observed that Divisional Forum has passed an appropriate orders which cannot be interfered with. Divisional Forum has taken note of this thing that the bike has not been returned to the respondent if it was not workable. It has been retained by the appellant/complainant so it cannot be replaced at the juncture of time without giving opportunity to the respondent to repair it.

However, in the below mentioned case complainant noticed cluton of the car was not functioning properly and it was giving unusual noise/jerks on running the engine. Considering that there is some major manufacturing defect in the engine and asked the opposite party for replacement. Complaint was allowed and opposite party was directed to make replacement within the period allowed.

In *Janki Motors Pvt. Ltd.* v. *Shafia Ahmad Raina,*[139] complaint was lodged before the Divisional Forum for demanding the balance money which opposite party avoided to refund. Hence complainant-respondent filed a complaint before the Divisional Forum by virtue of which Divisional Forum accepted his plea and directed the appellant (opposite party) to pay Rs. 7258.99 with 12% interest p.a. Further appellant was directed to pay Rs. 10,000 to the complainant as cost of litigation. In the present case, car was delivered after full payment. Invoice was issued showing the balance amount of Rs. 7258.99 as extra money payable to the respondent by the appellant. Opposite party filed no records that the sales tax was raised so the amount is not payable. Accordingly order of Divisional Forum came to be implemented by the direction of this forum.

In appeal captioned *Consumers' Welfare Association (Regd.) Jammu and Kashmir State Jammu* v. *Jakfeed Gas Services,*[140] it was found that there was delay in gas service by 23 days for which opposite party were found liable. For these reasons judgment of the Divisional Forum was set aside.

139. Appeal No. 2112/2000 D/I 15-12-2k (SC) Jmu.

(2) Deficient Services

This heading is to be further sub-divided under some headings:

(a) Air Service

Under this heading original complaint titled *Khalil Allaha Qazi (Advocate)* v. *Sh. Souran Singh and Another*[141] deserves to be mentioned first of all. In this case complainant filed complaint against non-petitioners for inadequate service rendered by them. Complainant has purchased five OK Air tickets from Srinagar to Jammu on/for 26th of October 1995. On this date he was flatly denied the issuance of boarding card in his favour but afterwards was given the same in the higher class in the same plane after charging higher excess money as illegal gratification. On hearing the complaint this commission directed both opposite parties to return the excess money or illegal gratification and Rs. 15,000 as compensation along with 18% interest. In this case payment was not made in time and execution was sought by the complainant. However objections[142] came to be filed in the execution applications and it was observed that opposite party No. 1 has never taken stand that he is not responsible to satisfy the order. It was further observed that opposite party No. 1 is resp^nsible to satisfy the order otherwise there is every apprehension that this award will be only on paper decree.

---

140. Appeal No. 2074/2000 D/D 22-3-2001 (SC) Jmu. In a couple of cases compensation came to be reduced from Rs. 5000 to Rs. 1500 and from Rs. 2000 to Rs. 1000. In M/s Maya Medicate *v.* R.N. Sharma, Appeal No. 1976/99 and warrner Lambet India *v.* Dr. Davinder Singh Appeal No. 2035/2000 D/D 15-11-2k.

141. O/F 1680/97 (SC) Jmu.

142. A para of which reads as under—"That the Petitioner has filed the execution and proceedings to be taken under Section 21, Consumer Protection Act against the Respondent No. 1 only, were as it was the main responsibility of the Station Master. MODI-LUFT, Srinagar Airport to make seats available to the Petitioner/Complainant. It would be in the fairness and in the interest of justice to first initiate proceedings against the Respondent No. 2. Respondet No. 2 is served with the notice and proceedings taken against him. Respondent No. 1 may kindly be called upon to satisfy the award given by the Hon'ble Commission.

(b) Banking

Important case here is titled as *Vijay Kumar Mital* v. *Chairman and Manager, Citizen Cooperative Bank Ltd.*[143] To summarize the allegations, complainant is aggrieved of that his four cheques were stolen from his cheque book and were encashed within four months period and the opposite party after forging his signatures in the name of fictitious persons. After theft immediately matter was brought to the notice of the police where the case U/S 379, 467, and 468 RPC was registered. By committing such forgery complainant was deprived of his money totaling to Rs. 15,210,000.

Objections were filed and complaint was resisted on two grounds. Firstly, that the complainant is guilty of latches and negligence himself. It is because of his carelessness that four cheques were stolen from his custody and he did not inform opposite parties before it was encashed. Secondly, opposite parties have taken a defence that there was not deficiency in service because the opposite parties had taken proper care and caution while comparing the signatures on the forged cheques with specimen signature of complainant retained in the bank.

In this case it was observed by the commission that a man is investing money and keeping it in the bank. Bank people derive benefits from such investment but they are allowed to release the money only when deposit holder gives mandate for that. When the cheque is forged one, it is not the signatures of the depositor, it means that it is not the mandate of the depositor to the opposite party to release his amount. Amount can be released only when there is mandate of depositor otherwise the bank is responsible and cannot absolve itself from the responsibilities. This is fortified by the

143. O/F No. 561/94 D/D 26-12-2000 (SC) Jmu. From facts of the case it was found that it is apparent that the Respondents have not disputed account No. of the complainant in their bank. It is not disputed that the cheques were not stolen and thirdly it is also not the bone of contention that the aforementioned cheques have been encashed by committing forgery. Further it is observed that evidence in this case shows that the complainant has not detected the misplacement of cheques during these four months but as soon as he came to know he informed both the opposite party and police.

view expressed by the Apex Court[144]—

> "Unless the bank is able to satisfy the court of either an express condition in the contract with its customer or an unequivocal ratification it will not be possible to save the bank from its liability. The banks do business for their benefit. Customers also get some benefit. If banks are to insist upon extreme care by the customers in minutely looking into the pass book and the statements sent by them, no bank perhaps can do profitable business. It is common knowledge that the entries in the pass books and the statements of account sent by the bank are either not readable, decipherable or legible. There is always an element of trust between the bank and its customer. The banks business depends upon this trust. Whenever a cheque purporting to be a customer is presented before a bank it carries a mandate to the bank to pay. If a cheque is forged there is no such mandate. The bank can escape liability only if it can establish knowledge to the customer of the forgery in the cheques. In action for the continuously long period cannot by itself afford a satisfactory ground for the bank to escape the liability."

(c) Building

In a case[145] complainant in response to an advertisement notice applied for a flat. His request was accepted and he was informed for the allotment of residential flat for ground floor. Agreement between the parties was executed on 23-03-98. He paid all the amount of Rs. 1,37,450 within three months and Rs. 1,32,300 within six months from the date of issuance of letter of intent. Similarly, Rs. 1,32,000 within

144. In Canara Bank *v.* Canara Sales Corporation and Others, AIR 1987 SC 1603.

145. Ramesh Chander Gupta *v.* Managing Director Housing Board O/F No. 2033/2000 D/D 16-4-2001 (SC) Jmu. In another case captioned Consumer Welfare Association (Regd.) *v.* Vice Chairman, Jammu Development Authority O/F No. 1191/96. Opposite party retained earnest money from 1980 to 31-10-1995 for which opposite party was held responsible.

twelve months before the execution of lease deed. According to the complainant possession was not handed over to him which opposite party was supposed to hand over to the complainant by March 1999. Forum observed that ordinarily possession should have given in March. Flats should have been complete in all respects by the end of March which was not done. Since complainant has not been offered the possession and by merely informing the complainant that the flat is complete in all respects does not mean that possession of the flat stands delivered to the complainant. For these reasons complaint came to be allowed and Rs. 50,000 was awarded as compensation plus Rs. 5,000 as litigation charges.

(d) Education

A case,[146] under this heading is to be quoted here. This appeal is filed against the order of Divisional Forum, Jammu by virtue of which Divisional Forum allowed the complaint and granted compensation of Rs. 3,000 to be paid to him. In this complaint it was averred that the appellant has been student of opposite party No. 2 from primary to tenth class but due to mistake of opposite party No. 2 his name has been got registered with opposite party No. 1 as Vikram Singh in place of Vikram Jeet Singh.

Appellant/complainant has contended that such mistake in the name has caused him not only mental harassment but also irreparable loss. He was not given admission in higher class nor was he given employment for two years unless his name was got corrected. For such deficiency of service he claimed Rs. 50,000 as compensation. Divisional Forum did not find any fault with respondent Nos. 1, 2 and directed respondent to pay Rs. 3,000 as compensation and Rs. 1000 as cost of litigation to complainant.

State Commission observed that appellant has suffered mentally and physically and has been put into humiliation.

146. Vikram Jeet Singh *v.* Jammu and Kashmir Board of School Education and Principal D.B.N. *v.* M., Jammu Appeal No. 2159/2k D/D Jan. 2001.

He has been deprived to get admission in higher class due to faulty certificate but he has not given the details of loss he suffered but at the same time it is an admitted fact that he was issued a faulty certificate and suffered due to the deficiency of service. So appeal was allowed and compensation of Rs. 10,000 was awarded taking into consideration that the school run by the trust.

(e) Insurance Service

Maximum number of cases filed before the forum are against various insurance companies. In cases titled *New India Assurance* v. *Hardeep Singh;*[147] *Vijay Kumar* v. *Oriental Insurance Company;*[148] *Om Prakash Gupta* v. *Oriental Insurance Company Ltd.;*[149] *New India Assurance Company Ltd.* v. *Krishen Gopal;*[150] bone of contention was that driver was not holding valid license and it was fake. Simple point involved in the above cases is that if a license is found to be fake whether insurance company is liable to compensate the loss caused to the owner of the vehicle. In one of the above cases—Krishen Gopal's case it has been observed that it is true the fake license is always fake but that is for purposes of the driver who cannot drive the vehicle on the fake license which has later on being renewed. Here the point is whether breach of contract has been committed by the insured who has employed the driver and allowed him to drive the vehicle. In Skandis case, Apex Court has made it clear that the breach is always wilful breach. Obligation of the employer at the time of employing the driver was to be cautious in examining the driving license of the driver/employee. The employer has been shown a driving license duly signed and stamped by the licensing Issuing Authority of Shimla and later on it was renewed by the state authorities. So he bonafidely believed as a prudent man that the license is genuine. So he employed the driver. Later on if the license is found to be fake on investigation company cannot escape liability for its being fake.

---

147. Appeal No. 2061/2000 D/I 4-1-2001(SC) Jmu.
148. O/F No. 1315/96 D/D 04-1-2001 (SC) Jmu.
149. O/F No. 1143/96 D/D 17-1-2001 (SC) Jmu.
150. Appeal No. 2068/2000 D/D 3-1-2001 (SC) Jmu.

Briefly to state that in all the above cases forum came to the conclusion that the question is not whether the license is fake or genuine but the question is whether the complainant bonafidely believed the license to be genuine or not. In all the above cases complainant bonafidely believed the license to be genuine so there was no wilful breach of contract.

In *Vijay Kumar* v. *Oriental Insurance Company*[151] the whole case law has been discussed and it was held by the forum that if the license is shown to the employer of the driver who bonafidely believes such a renewed license as genuine which afterwards is found to be fake, breach is not wilful.

Similarly, in Skandis case forum held that in such circumstances, insurance company cannot escape the liability. In *Smt. Bindu Bala* v. *Life Insurance Corporation of India*,[152] complaint was dismissed by the Divisional Forum on the ground that the acceptance of premium cannot be construed that the respondent has accepted the proposal and issued the policy. In this case premium was accepted on 17-3-1997 and risk is covered from 20-3-1997. Deceased died on 22nd of March. State Commission held that we are concerned from which date the risk is covered. Risk is covered from 20th March. If the form has been filed on 17th, premium has been accepted on 17th, there is nothing on record to show as to why the policy has been signed on 22nd March. Accordingly order of Divisional Forum was set aside and opposite party was directed to pay insured amount.

In *Gurjeet Kaur* v. *National Insurance Company*,[153] the claim was repudiated by the opposite party on the ground that death of the deceased did not took place due to any accident but he died due to brain tumor. State Commission came to the conclusion that we wonder as to why we should

151. O/F No. 315/96 D/D 4-1-2001.
152. Appeal No. 2131/2000 D/D 19-12-2k. In Ab. Wahid Bhat *v.* New India Assurance Company Ltd. and Others O/F No. 1979/99 D/D 28-11-2k. It was observed that complainant had completed all formalities but Insurance Company was late in releasing the money.
153. O/F No. 2067/2000 D/D 16-4-2001 (SC) Jmu.

not believe a police officer who was on patrolling duty has seen that the deceased getting a hit from military vehicle. Copy of the Rosnamcha is on the file. So finally court held that deceased died due to accident and is covered by insurance.

Case/appeal captioned *Smt. Mohinder Kaur* v. *National Insurance Company Ltd.*[154] is a very important case. Briefly stated Moti Singh, husband of the complainant was owner of the truck which was stolen away by some persons on 20th of Jan. 1998 and her husband had insured the vehicle with the respondent. Her husband lodged FIR at the police station and lodged a claim before apposite party. Ownership of the truck is not disputed. Insurance is not disputed. The only thing which is disputed is that the owner of the truck died in 1990 leaving a widow who lodged a complaint for the first time in the year 1998 which was dismissed in default and finally she lodged complaint in 1999. Complaint was dismissed for being barred by time. Commission observed through Justice M.Y. Kawoosa, that it is true that claim has been lodged later after several years but we have to keep in mind that Consumer Act is a newly created Act. There is less awareness about this Act before the general public who are mostly ignorant. In this case especially the owner of the vehicle has died after making the claim leaving a widow who was quite ignorant about these rights. Accordingly claim was allowed only to the extent as assessed by the surveyor.

Complaint captioned *Rajinder Koul Prop.* v. *United Insurance Company Ltd.*[155] is also a time barred case above one has been decided as dismissed on the ground that it was filed, before the forum in breach of condition No. 4(i) of the insurance cover which stipulates as under—

---

154. Appeal No. 2052/2000 D/D 13-2-2001 (SC) Jmu; In Ch. Giyan Chand *v.* National Insurance Company Ltd. O/F No. 2101/2000 D/D 22-2-2001. It was held that it is incumbent on the Insurance Company to make payment of 75% of loss withing 30 days from the date of theft. Since this rule was not adhered, so claim of the complainant was allowed.

155. O/F No. 548/97 D/D 2-12-99 (SC) Jmu.

> "On the happening of any loss or damage the insured shall forthwith give notice to the company and shall within fifteen days after the loss or damage or such further time as the company may in writing allow in that behalf deliver to the company."

Now let us have a view of cases arising out of fire insurance claims.

In *Brij Lal Raina and Others* v. *United India Insurance Company Ltd.*[156] complainants had jointly owned the house under the fire policy. Complainants due to militancy migrated to Jammu in the year 1990. In the year they were informed by neighbour that their house was dismantled and damaged by militants and they removed the material like G.C. Sheets, Timber and Bricks. Complainants due to security reasons did not visit the spot but got the FIR filed through the police concerned. Loss was assessed by the surveyor but later on opposite party repudiated the claim that this was a case of commission of theft and the case was registered under Sections 427 and 379 RPC. According to opposite parties theft and burglary is not covered by policy. The main objection of opposite party is that this is a case of commission of theft which is not covered by the policies. However, forum reached to the conclusion that it is to be seen as—whether the occurrence has taken place for committing any theft or it was subversive act by militants as is prevalent in the valley. Consequently commission allowed the complaint.

In a case,[157] commission rightly decided that the surveyor who earlier assessed the loss is the genuine report because there were two reports and out of two Commission allowed that one which is favourable to the consumer.

Complaints titled *Sh. Chaman Lal* v. *Oriental Insurance Company Ltd. and Another,*[158] *Mehbooba Shabnum* v. *National*

---

156. O/F No. 2000/99 D/D 23-2-2001 (SC) Jmu. In Ravinder Kumar Mantoo *v.* United India Insurance Company Ltd. O/F No. 812/95 D/D 30-11-2000 (SC) Jmu. complainant had proved deficiency of service and petition was admitted. Rs. 10,000 were awarded as compensation.
157. O/F No. 2099/2000 D/D 11-4-2001(SC) Jmu.
158. O/F No. 1801/98 D/D 17-4-2001 (SC) Jmu.

Insurance Company Ltd.;[159] *M/s Naresh Stone Crusher, Chinar Kangan, Srinagar* v. *Oriental Insurance Company Ltd.*[160] and *Gopi Nath Pandita* v. *Oriental Insurnace Company Ltd*[161] were also allowed against the respective insurance companies.

There are various complaints before the Commission regarding the damage caused to the property by fire or otherwise and out of disposed off cases some are noteworthy to be referred here. In *J.L. Kachroo* v. *Divisional Manager, United India Insurance Company Ltd.*[162] the only defence of the opposite party in this case was that no claim had been raised. Opposite party was prepared to get loss assessed by an independent surveyor in case the complainant furnishes the original receipt of postal certificate by which they had allegedly intimated the opposite party. Complainant produced two photo copies duly attested by Notary and on demand original receipt was handed over to the counsel of opposite party.

In this case/complaint only consistent stand of opposite party was that in case it is proved that intimation was given by the complainant it is prepared to assess the loss. Complainant proved to have given the intimation through postal certificate. Accordingly complaint was allowed as there remained no dispute then to be decided.

The complaint captioned *Makhan Lal Dass* v. *Oriental Insurance Company Ltd. and others,*[163] the insured house was set ablaze by unknown persons. Report was submitted by the surveyor but the opposite party did not pay the amount. Complaint was allowed and complainants case to the extent of Rs. 4,71,815 was assessed by the surveyor.

In *Vijay Kumar Bhat Lidhoc* v. *United India Insurance Company Ltd.*[164] house was involved in bomb blast. Till the death

159. O/F No. 198/99 D/D 9-12-2000(SC) Jmu.
160. O/F No. 2120/2000 D/D 23-4-2001 (SC) Jmu.
161. O/F No. 1763/97 D/D 24-11-99 (SC) Jmu.
162. O/F No. 1675/96 D/D 3-12-99 (SC) Jmu.
163. O/F No. 2071/2000 D/D 13-11-2000 (SC) Jmu.
164. O/F No. 1854/98 D/D 24-11-99 (SC) Jmu. In Mahraj Krishan Bhat *v.* Oriental Insurance Company Ltd. O/F No. 1924/99 D/D 29-11-99 (SC) Jmu. Complaint was allowed to some extent on similar basis as in this case.

of the complainant's father who was pursuing the matter and sent representation which included the representation grievance call of the opposite party. Thereafter, the matter was pursued vide their letters that the matter will be settled but the opposite party took no action in the matter. Surveyor was sent on spot after three years of the incident. However loss was immediately worked out by the state government. Accordingly forum directed the opposite party to pay Rs. 53,872 with 12% interest after four months of date of incident.

In complaint captioned *National Insurance Company Ltd.* v. *M/s New Union Bus Service,*[165] it was held that complainant is not a consumer. In this case, complaint was against the New Union Bus Service. The complainant had sent some consignment by the truck allotted by opposite party transport company. Truck met with an accident and the consignment was lost. Complaint before the commission was for asking the opposite party to compensate the loss though the consignment was insured. It was held that the complainant is not a consumer.

Now the cases which are to be quoted here are those in which privity of contract was the point of discussion. In *Showbani Joshi* v. *National Insurance Company Ltd.*[166] attorney filed the complaint which was dismissed by the forum. Before the commission it was observed that the attorney holder has been given power to run the vehicle, to get it insured, to appear and act in all courts—civil or criminal or in appellant jurisdiction appear before the finance companies, etc. It was held the attorney deed was executed validly by the owner of the vehicle who has privity of contract with the respondent. Accordingly judgment of Divisional Forum was set aside and the case was reminded back to the Divisional Forum to proceed ahead with the complaint in accordance with the law.

---

165. O/F No. 1357/96 D/D 06-12-2k (SC) Jmu.
166. Appeal No. 2062/2000 D/D 17-11-2000 (SC) Jmu. However in Rajinder Kumar *v.* National Insurance Company Ltd. Appeal No. 2009/99 D/D 2-2-2001 (SC) Jmu. claim was allowed in favour rightfull owner and it was found that there was not privity of constract between the complainant and the consumer.

(f) Medical

While scrutinizing cases of state commission a couple of cases/complaints have been found pertaining to medical negligence. In *Sunita Kalu* v. *Dr. Arun Prasad and Others*[167] complainant has come up with this complaint alleging therein that Gall Stone was detected in her gallbladder through sonogrpahy. She was attracted by an advertisement notice in Daily Excelsior Paper wherein opposite party No. 2 Bee Enn General Hospital had advertised the availability of services of opposite party No. 1 Laproscopic Surgery through small cuts without skin stitches by the process of Micro Caproscopic Surgery. Complainant deposited Rs. 5,000. After depositing total charges of Rs. 25,169 she was operated upon. On feeling fever and pain she was advised second operation. Grievance of the complainant was that the doctor who conducted first operation left the patient in Lurch and second operation was necessary because lever and intestine were teered due to the first operation.

Forum observed that need for undergoing second operation was felt due to complicacy in the first operation as admitted by Dr. Arun Prasad in his statement. Leaving patient in lurch after first surgery is definitely a deficiency in service for which a complaint was allowed and Rs. 2.00 lacs were allowed as compensation.

In another case,[168] surgical operation was conducted. After hardly one week when complainant got discharged she felt acute pain in her belly and lower abdominal part. X-ray/ Ultrasound showed a foreign body was seen in the left anterior wall of the uterous. Complainant alleged that due to lack of skill, carelessness and negligence opposite party had kept the stitching needle inside in her abdominal while conducting first operation for which he has to undergo second operation and Rs. 1.00 lac was awarded as compensation.

---

167. O/F No. 2008/98 D/D 26-4-2001(SC) Jmu. Similalry no privity of constract was found in Jammu and Kashmir Motors Pvt. Ltd. *v.* United India Insurance Company Ltd. Appeal No. 506/94 (SC) Jmu. where jeep was insured in the name of Essential Engineer Budgam.
168. Mrs. Shashi Sharma *v.* Bee Enn General Hospital Jammu O/F No. 1984/99 D/D 15-3-2001 (SC) Jmu.

(g) Post

In a case titled *Ragunandan Sharma* v. *Post Master Pucca Danga Jammu and Others*[169] the appellant had filed a complaint before Divisional Forum that he had to purchase a plot and needed a sum of Rs. 44,000 and in this regard he approached his friend at Agrah to arrange a sum of Rs. 10,000 for him. His friend agreed and sent a Bank Draft for Rs. 10,000 to the complainant by post which was lost in the transit. Friend at Agrah got duplicate and sent the same by speed post through the agency of postal service which according to the appellant was not at all delivered to him by post master. Hence the complaint was lodged. Divisional Forum dismissed the complaint on the ground that the complainant has not proved his claim and deficiency of service on the part of any of the respondent.

On appeal State Commission found that the finding of the Divisional Forum that there was nothing on the file to suggest that the post man had delivered the postal article to a wrong person, appears to be not well founded. Simply because Ayub Khan was not produced as a witness before the Divisional Forum was no ground to dismiss the complaint against the respondent No. 1 because other connected facts were already admitted. Complainant was deprived of the benefit for almost four years which resulted into the harassment and mental torture to the complainant. Compensation of Rs. 10,000 was allowed.

(h) Telephone

In *General Manager, Telecom* v. *Dr. Nagesh Chander Sharma*[170] Divisional Forum directed the appellant to pay Rs. 5,000 as compensation for inconvenience and hardship caused to the respondent due to deficiency in service by the appellant. In this case wrong telephone number was mentioned. Forum observed that appellant had not gone through his own record and mistake could have been detected at the initial state by the appellant. Consequently appeal was dismissed.

---

169. Appeal No. 1896/99 D/D 7-12-2k (SC) Jmu.

170. Appeal No. 2168/2000 D/D 1-1-2001 (SC) Jmu.

However in *T.C. Kotwal, Ex-District & Sessions Judge Advocate Jammu and Kashmir High Court* v. *Telecom District Manager, Jammu*[171] in appeal compensation of Rs. 1,000 was allowed in both cases in place of token compensation of Rs. 1,000 in both cases.

(i) Transport

In *Managing Director Jammu and Kashmir State Road Transport Corporation Jammu* v. *Divak Khajuria,*[172] there was delay in bus from Jammu to Phalgam at the very initial stage of starting the journey in Dackbanglow Jammu for which appellant herein was directed to pay compensation of Rs. 5,000 but in this appeal it was slashed down Rs. 1,000.

In *Sh. Pankaj Sharma* v. *The General Manager, Railways (North Zone), New Delhi*[173] complainant had to undertake a journey from Jammu to Bihar. He purchased two second class tickets with reservations from Jammu Railway Station. Complainant was informed that train will not proceed further and make his own arrangements. This shocked the complainant and his family. His wife was at advanced stage of pregnancy and it caused great inconvenience to the complainant. He lost his suit case while boarding another train in hurry. Suit case was carrying some valuables also.

Complaint was allowed to the extent for non-performance of contractual obligation of opposite party who had to carry the passengers to Baurani (State of Bihar). So State Commission granted compensation of Rs. 40,000 to the complainant.

(j) Miscellaneous

It is proposed to have mention of some cases under this heading. In *T.R. Gupta Contractors Limited* v. *Akbar Iqbal Road lines and Another.*[174] Briefly stated the complainant contractor

171. Appeal No. 531/94 D/D 22-9-2001 (SC) Jmu.

172. O/F No. 446/94 D/D 19-1-2001 (SC) Jmu. Complaint Om Prakash and Co. Kiryana Merchants *v.* Hindustan Transport was dismissed as he has receive amount from Insurance Company.

173. O/F No. 997/95 D/D 22-2-2001 (SC) Jmu.

174. O/F No. 1774/98 D/D 29-12-2000 (SC) Jmu.

company has been executing construction and other works as contractor in different parts of the country including Jammu and Kanpur and engaged the opposite party on the basis of a written contract to transport his machinery such as Crane and Boom from his work site Kanpur to work site Jammu. The opposite party transported and delivered to the complainant company only part of the said machinery and retained the rest which despite notice was not despatched to the complainant at Jammu which necessitated the complainant to file the present complaint. Objection was raised by the opposite party that the grievance of the complainant is for commercial purpose and so it is not a consumer problem. Commission observed that the service agreed to be rendered by the opposite party were for transportation of machinery. Consequently complaint was allowed and opposite party was directed to pay to the complainant sum of Rs. 1,79,500 as the cost of spare parts and fabrication charges and 1.00 lac as compensation for the loss of work.

(E) CASES DECIDED BY THE HIGH COURT (JAMMU AND KASHMIR)

Jammu and Kashmir High Court has decided some consumer cases under the consumer protection Act which are to be discussed here under some headings.

(I) Deficient Services

(a) Consumer Dispute

Here a case before us is *Jammu Development Authority* v. *Gouri Shankar*.[175] In this case respondent filed a complaint before the Divisional Forum. His grievance was that in pursuance of the scheme framed for the benefit of the weaker section of the society Jammu Development Authority (hereinafter referred as JDA) allotted a plot of land. Respondent/petitioner deposited a sum of Rs. 1752 but JDA did not deliver the possession of land. Petitioner was called to give further amount to which he objected. Forum gave the

175. 2002 (1) SLJ, 141.

decision to allot the land without calling upon him to pay additional amount. On appeal JDA submitted that in last twelve years there has been an appreciable increase in the price of the plot and therefore respondents must pay additional amount and he cannot get the plot at the old price.

The Honb'le High Court held that the respondent had deposited a sum of Rs. 1750 in the year 1985 and now by calling upon him to pay further amount at an enhanced rate when the respondents had paid the price as demanded would be totally unjustified.

Here is a case[176] which reveals as to how common people are being harassed and taken lightly.

Here respondents in this case hired helicopter services from Jammu to Katra and from Katra to Sanjchhat. First flight was cancelled for the technical defect and in the second flight the moment they entered to security zone they were told that the tickets stand cancelled as they received a message from Delhi that a very important person who has to travel in the helicopter. Petitioners made a protest for this but they were manhandled and forcibly dragged out from the airport.

It was held that while family kept waiting for the full day, keeping fast they received mental shock at eleventh hour when their tickets were cancelled after the second flight for these reasons compensation of Rs. 50,000 were allowed.

(b) Insurance

In *United India Insurance* v. *Chaman Lal Narang and Others*[177] Commission had allowed the case/appeal and appellants were directed to pay Rs. 2.57 lacs along with 18% p.a. from the date of fire incidence.

The facts of the said case in brief are that the respondents herein the owner of a residential house was insured and due to critical situation in the valley respondent-

---

176. 2002 (1) SLJ, 313.

177. 1996 SLJ 76. This is the Miscellaneous First Appeal under Jammu and Kashmir Consumer Protection Act, 1987. In this case it was held that this Act has been passed to provide for better protection of the interests of the consumer and for redressal of grivances of consumers.

complainant had to migrate from the place of (Anantnag) his residence in the year 1990 and he received information that his house had been destroyed by fire 23/24 of October 1991. Thereafter appellants satisfied themselves about the genuineness of the claim and asked respondent herein to submit his estimate. Surveyor had disallowed a number of items including sanitary fittings, doors and windows fittings, electric fittings and other items which were duly covered under the policy of insurance. The State Commission has decided the matter and the items deleted by the insurance company of the recommendation of the surveyor have been inducted in the award passed by it. Respondent herein was entitled by the state commission to the amount of Rs. 42,000 which was disallowed under different heads and in this way respondent/complainant was entitled to Rs. 2,15,000 plus Rs. 42,000 and amount of Rs. 10,000 as compensation.

Court observed that there are no reasons why the surveyor did not allow insurance claim of the electrical fittings and the sanitary fittings when it is a fact that insurance cover includes these items also. Therefore, arbitrariness done by the insurance company and non-allowance of items mentioned above by the surveyor were considered as deficiency in service by the company and the consumer can seek remedy from consumer forums in such cases.

Another case is *Khazir Mohd. Khirqa* v. *New Indian Insurance Company Ltd.*[178] In this case insured suffered loss by the devastating fire in town of Charisharief. The property involved in this case together with large number of property was insured and others uninsured property was destroyed in a devastating fire on 12th of May 1995. The loss assessors assessed the loss in each case and made recommendations for indemnification subject to terms and conditions of the policy. However, once the cases were complete, the insurers suddenly took the stand that they will deduct from the

178. 1997 SLJ 387. In case titled United India Insurance *v.* Gh. Mohammad Mir, SLJ 1999 276, property of insured damaged in fire at Charisharief, *ex-gratia* relief paid by government cannot be deducted from insurance claim.

accepted liability the amount of *ex-gratia* relief received by the insured from the State. The insured refused to accept this stand.

It was held that the insurers cannot avoid their liability. They can only do so under the terms and the conditions of the contract. The Court further held—

> "The doctrine of subrogation and the general principles of indemnity essentially presupposes the existence of a third party liability in law to compensate for the loss, even though it is not a party to the contract of indemnity. It is only the compensation received from such third party which will result in dismissing or reducing liability of the insurer. The fact that the assured cannot claim double indemnity amply makes it clear that the benefit, if any, received by the assured must be by way of compensation for the loss and the payment should be made by a party liable to make the loss good. Here in these cases it is nobody's case that the state has paid *ex-gratia* relief on the ground that it was liable to compensate for the loss."

One more important case is *National Insurance Company Ltd.* v. *Abdul Razaq Mir and Sons.*[179] Brief facts of the case are respondents were running furnishing business. The business was being run in the building situated at Lal Chowk, Srinagar. The building was insured separately. The building and the stocks lost in the fire. The claim in respect of the loss to building has been settled. However, the claim in respect of stocks came to be repudiated on the ground that the stocks were lying in third floor, which was not part of the shop and therefore not insured.

---

179. 1999 SLJ, 293. In Mohd. Yousf Dar *v.* Oriental Insurance Company, SLJ 2000 77, State Commission dismissed the complaint on the assumption that the house of the claimant was infact burnt on 27-10-95 when Insurance Policy in question was not in force. However on record Court found house was burnt on 27/28 December 1995 and it was approved by the Divisional Manager, Insurance Company. Court held that the finding of the State Commission cannot be sustained either in fact or law.

In this case reference was made to the decision of the Supreme Court in *M/s International Ore and Fertilizers (India) Pvt. Ltd.* v. *Employees State Insurance Corporation* (1997) 4 S.C.C (203), in which while interpreting the word 'shop' and explaining what it constitutes, the Apex Court observed that according to the shorter Oxford English Dictionary the expression 'shop' means a house or building where goods are made or prepared for sale and sold. It also means a 'place of business' or 'place where one's ordinary occupation is carried on'. In ordinary parlance a 'shop is a place where the activities connected with the buying and selling of goods are carried on.

Consequently keeping in view the nature and type of stocks offer for sale, Court held that it cannot be said that the stocks would not require the space or godown as part of the shop.

Regional Manager v. *Bashir Ahmad Rangraiz and Others*[180] is another case. In this case it was held that after a claimant has executed discharge voucher in favour of the insurance company towards full and final satisfaction of the claims no further claim can be agitated before the Consumer Protection Commission.

In *Rajinder Koul* v. *United Insurance Company Ltd.*[181] appeal was preferred against the order of the Jammu and Kashmir State Consumer Protection Commission, Jammu by which the complaint of the appellant against the respondent insurance company was dismissed on the ground that the claim was not within period of twelve months as contemplated by condition policy. It was held insurance policy providing that claim for loss or damage should be

180. SLJ Jan. to June 2, 2000, 47. Seen also Mohammad Yaseen *v.* National Insurance Company, SLJ 2001, p. 382. In the 13 cases in hand it was noticed that the amount has not been received under protest. In Divisional Manager *v.* Nazir Ahmad Shah, SLJ 2000, 47 for dealy in, settlement interest was allowed at 12% in three complaints and in appeal all the three were disposed off by the single judgment in which 18% interest was reduced to 12% interest. In United India Insurance Company *v.* Mohammad Mir, SLJ 1999, 276 18% interest was reduced to 12%.

181. SLJ 2000, July-December, p. 4561.

made within twelve months from the date of loss reported to company, after such period claim gets extinguished under the contract. In such situation the claim for enforcement of such right cannot be entertained by the authorities under Jammu and Kashmir Consumer Protection Act.

Case titled *Mohd. Muzamil* v. *National Insurance Company Ltd.*[182] is noteworthy to be quoted here. Briefly to say it appears from the facts of the case that the complainant insured his house, household goods and livestock for the period from 8-1-99 to 7-1-2000. In the month of March 1999 insured cow died. Loss caused to the complainant was intimated to the opposite party. Admittedly appellant filed the documents. Surveyor recommended the case as No Claim. Appellant approached the Divisional Forum. Divisional Forum dismissed the complaint on the ground that once it was repudiated complainant should approach the Civil Court. Opposite party contended contradiction in the date of postmortem of cow but Court found no contradiction while perusing the record. Consequently, it was held that insurance claim is repudiated arbitrarily without any reasonable ground, the consumer forum can sit over the judgment of surveyor and will look into the matter whether repudiation was justified.

Case titled *Life Insurance Corporation of India* v. *Bindo Bala and Others*[183] is an appeal preferred against the order of the state commission.

In this case respondents preferred a complaint before the Divisional Forum constituted under the Consumer Protection Act, 1987. The complaint was dismissed however on appeal, commission allowed the appeal. From the record it was found that premium was paid on 10th March and policy was issued on 22nd March but made effective from 20th March. Death of insured was caused due to electrocution on 20th March. The corporation refused to honour its commitment on the ground that no doubt, the premium was deposited on 17th March 1997 and no doubt, the proposal was registered on 20th March 1997,

182. 2002 (1) SLJ 315.

183. 2002 (1) SLJ 171.

the FDR was issued on 22nd March. It is on this basis that the claim is sought to be negatived. It was held that once the policy came into the effect w.e.f. 20th March, 1997 and insured deceased died thereafter his heirs would be entitled to the benefit of the policy. The judicial precedents do support that once payment in cash is made to the agent and it has gone into the coffers of insurance company then a contract would come into existence.

(c) Miscellaneous

Here is a case under Section 17 of consumer protection Act, 1987. The case is titled as *University* v. *Brinder,*[184] it was held that where period of limitation has not been mentioned the period fixed for preferring suits under law of limitation should be taken as reasonable guide. If the proceedings are initiated beyond the out limits fixed under law of limitation then these can be treated as suffering from delay and latches.

In *Union of India* v. *President Division Forum,*[185] appeal has been filed and styled under Section 17 of the Jammu and Kashmir Consumer Protection Act against the order passed by the said commission in exercise of its appellate jurisdiction because the appellant had moved the said commission against the order passed by the Divisional Forum. After hearing learned counsel for the parties and perusing the record, it was held that on plain reading of Sections 17, 15 and 2 of the Act, appeal in the High Court can lie only against the orders passed by the State Commission while it is deciding the matter on the original side in the complaint filed before it and not when it is deciding either an appeal filed by a person aggrieved by an order passed by the Divisional Forum or even while deciding an application for condonation of delay in filing the appeal.

In another case[186] it was held an interlocutory order passed by Divisional Forum or State Commission held not appealable. It is only those orders which are executable as a decree passed by a Civil Court of competent jurisdiction held appealable.

---

184. SLJ 1999 July-December 421.
185. 1995 SLJ, p. 108.
186. Nirmal Singh *v.* Manager, Central Cooperative Bank, SLJ 1997, 90.

In *Indian Airlines* v. *Farooq Ahmad*,[187] it was held if any amount is required to be deposited as a precondition for the maintainability of the appeal, the appeal will be taken to have been filed on the date the amount is deposited even though the memorandum of appeal is filed earlier.

(F) SOME GLARING JUDGMENTS OF CONSUMER DISPUTES REDRESSAL AGENCIES IN THE STATE OF JAMMU AND KASHMIR

First case here is *Abdul Rashid Ganie* v. *Oriental Insurance Company Ltd.*[188]

The short point involved in this complaint was as to whether the opposite party is liable to pay interest and compensation to the complainant even after the complainant has executed a discharge receipt in full and final satisfaction of his insurance claim under the contract of insurance. The main case of the complainant therefore is that even though he has given a discharge voucher in full and final satisfaction he is not debarred from claiming interest and compensation.

Adverting to the main point of controversy that commission take the view that this case stands concluded by precedent. The Commission quoted the case *M/s Zamindera Tractors* v. *Oriental Fire and General Insurance Company Ltd.* decided on 22-9-1993 by Haryana SCRC. In this case the point as to whether the complainant is stoped from filing complaint for interest, after full and final discharge gives quirts for the contractual payment under the policy but in no way extinguishes the consumers right to claim in trust, damage or loss due to the negligence of the insurer.

With the above mentioned observation of the State Commission, Haryana Commission while expressing complete agreement with the proposition of law laid down in aforesaid case made reference to a case *Girdari Lal Bansal* v. *Oriental Insurance Company Ltd.* decided by the same commission on 8th of July 1993 wherein the position in respect of the liability

187. SLJ 2001, 153.

188. J. Malik Shareef-ud-din passed/disposed of the instant case on 12-9-95 in O/F No. 206/95.

of the insurance company for payment of interest has been examined. Regarding this judgment the commission Jammu and Kashmir commented that his judgment is a very elaborate one the position of law has been thoroughly examined in respect of the liability on the insurance company regarding payment of interest. In this case the Haryana Consumers Commission has observed that according to the general law of insurance and the language of the insurance contract, the insurer will indemnify the insured against loss or damage and that this would mean that the insured is to fully indemnified. It was also observed that where an insured is reimbursed for the loss after years of the actual date of the loss it is not possible to say that the insured has been fully indemnified. Full indemnification means that the insured is to be reimbursed on the very date of the loss and certainly then insurer may choose to do the same or to accept the liability thereof.

State Commission Srinagar quoted the above judgment with approval to the effect that the entitlement to the indemnity for the loss incurred begins from the very date of loss itself and not on any other date, slippery date.

In the present case Commission observed that there is no explanation for the delay of 18 months in making the payments and there is no evidence that this delay was due to the complainant. On the facts of this case therefore, commission observed that the insurance company has deliberately and maliciously delayed the settlement of the claim and complaint was accordingly allowed.

In a similar case titled *Mohd. Shafi and Mohd. Abass* v. *Regional Manager and Others,*[189] J. Malik Sharief-ud-din observed that facts clearly go to show that the amount which had become due to the complainant on the date of loss was retained by the company for a period of more than 27 months and it had earned out of it. Under the Insurance Act the company is investing these amounts and is earning out of it. It would be unjust and against the equitable interests to allow it to retain these wrongful gains which results in the consequential loss to the insured. Further it is observed by

189. D/D 7-6-96 (J. Mr. Malik Sharief-ud-din).

the said learned president of the commission that it was in this situation that in case *Girdhari Lal Bansal* v. *Oriental Insurance Company,* Vol. 1, 1994 CPJ 118. Haryana Commission in one of its most elaborate judgments has examined this question and has come to the conclusion that since the insured is entitled to be indemnified from the very date of loss the mischief can be remedied only by allowing interest from the very date of loss after the liabilities are determined. Commission reported that this judgment of the Haryna Commission represents the sound principles of law. It is neither the language of the insurance contract nor the general legal position that can be invoked to frustrate the claim of the complainant for interest. The fact that for 27 long months the claim was not settled and the fact that even after the claim was processed and approved the head office of the company did not made the funds available by itself constitute a deficiency of service and the powers of the commission are straight way attracted.

While considering whether the complainant is entitled to compensation and on what grounds Commission quoted the Lucknow Development Authority case and felt that the Supreme Court while examining this question has clearly stated that the Consumer Protection Act does entitle the complainant to claim compensation and also empowers the commission to grant the same. This is a discretionary relief which can be granted over and above the relief which is basically asked for. This relief of compensation is made available on the ground that should the Commission came to the conclusion that the complainant suffered loss or injury as a result of neglect of the opposite party the compensation ought to be granted. The expression loss and injury has again been examined by the Supreme Court and it has opened that it has wider connotation attracting physical, mental and financial loss and even potential loss. The Supreme Court has further opened that there is no immunity attached to the functionaries who are entrusted with public power and that the compensation can be granted even in cases where the exercise of power has been honestly and bonafidely exercised but where it is a case of abuse of that power there is no escape at all. In the light of the above observation

Commission held that in this case the damage was done to the stocks in trade. For 27 months the man who expected the insurance company to come to his rescue and enforce the contract was starved, thrown out of business, deprived of his livelihood and was made to run from pillar to post and undergo huge expenses in persuading the company to settle his claim. In this process he was subjected to humiliation and indignities. He must have got a set back to the goodwill which he enjoyed in the business community. He must have lost his customers. All these factors taken together would lead to the only conclusion that the loss and injury caused to the complainant due to the deliberate neglect of the opposite party has been enormous and there is no way to measure it in terms of money. Consequently complaint was allowed on the basis of 18% interest and compensation of Rs. 30,000 was allowed.

Here is a case titled *Gh. Rasool Malik* v. *Oriental Insurance, Sonawar, Sringar.*[190] This case is a fit case to be cited here which shows the high handedness of the insurance company in settling the matter with the complainant. On the facts and circumstances of the case it is clear that insurance company deputed three surveyors to assess the loss and still the insurance company has not settled the claim. The Commission while allowing the complaint and compensation of Rs. 30,000 and Rs. 5,000 litigation cost noted down—

> "Insurance corporation is a nationalized corporation and the finances which its functionaries are entrusted with is not their private property. It is the peoples' money and people have right to keep a watch as to how this money is being spent. It is the duty of the functionaries of insurance corporation of which the opposite party is a subsidiary and also its functionaries to act in a manner so that their working is not open to the subscription."

190. 31-7-95.

Commission observed further that since it was within the knowledge of the functionaries that the statute entitles them to find this version of the case within a particular period why then they have not done so and why they have defaulted in contesting the case and providing us proper assistance for arriving at just conclusion is a matter which has to be taken seriously. Lastly, top functionary of the insurance corporation was directed to go into the matter and punish the defaulting officers.

Another case[191] similar to the above mentioned is also extra ordinary for its facts to be mentioned here. In the instant case insured stocks—silk, pashmina and other handicrafts to the tune of Rs. 10,25,000 were totally destroyed in a fire incident. The opposite party failed to accept the liability despite the report of the surveyor and unilaterally without any notice to the complainant appointed another person for investigation and finalization of the case. This information was conveyed to the complainant who fully complied with. Neither complainant visit the another person (investigator) nor the investigator on spot. However, he based the report on presumptions and assumptions and he has only tried to find fault with the report of the earlier surveyor.

Commission after having examined the evidence and hearing the both sides came to the conclusion that neither complainant visited the Hyderabad nor the surveyor came to Srinagar. He has prepared his report in his office. On the facts and circumstances of the case as above mentioned briefly the Commission was of the view that the opposite party has deliberately and wilfully adopted tactics of procrastination and delay in acceptance of its liability for more than seven years. Compensation of Rs. 1.00 lacs was awarded. However, controversy was raised on the point of awarding interest, Commission held, the general language of the insurance and the regulatory position of the law clearly envisages that the insured is to be indemnified fully. The full indemnification is only possible if the indemnification is on

---

191. M/s Special Diamond Silks *v.* Central Insurance Company Ltd., Srinagar, O/F No. 111/95 D/D 6-8-96.

and from the very date of loss. If the company withholds the acceptance of liability for seven long years the result is that it virtually deprives the opposite party of his rightful claim.

In the present case if the liability had been accepted within the reasonable time the insured could have put this amount to some useful purpose. Instead of allowing him to do so the company withheld the amount. . . . It is thus on the equitable grounds that interest is to be granted and it is different from the statutory right of grant of compensation for loss and injury.

In *Showkat Hussain* v. *Oriental Insurance Company Ltd.*[192] on facts Commission observed that after receiving the surveyor's report insurance company has totally felt unconcerned. This is a case in which the insurance company has totally betrayed itself and has forfeited confidence reposed in it by a consumer. In this case there is no reason advanced for the delay. Commission came to the conclusion that in this case there is inefficiency and lack of will but it is positively the outcome of some extraneous motive. It is a very sad case which provide ample evidence of the fact that the functionaries of the insurance company are not devoted to this job but are looking for something else. While allowing compensation of Rs. 50,000 the commission expressed that despite every day happening in these insurance companies functionaries are still suffered on the pay rolls of the state. This is a case in which functionaries have shown scant respect to the duties which they are expected to discharge.

One more interesting case is *Talak Bakery and Confectionary* v. *Oriental and General Insurance Company Ltd.*[193] Commission observed that it is an accepted position of law that Limitation Act is not applicable but still it is in the interests of public policy that the Commission shall not entertain stale claims. What remains to be seen in this case is as to whether this claim can be treated to be stale or not. It was found that since for time it was made open that the records were burnt and then office came to be closed and it was in this situation that the compliant approached the

192. D/D 14-9-95.
193. O/F No. 81/95.

regional office. Earlier in this case he was informed that his claim is under consideration. Under these circumstances the commission observed that the complainant is justified in treating the claim as pending for want of settlement. Consequently the contention regarding the claim being stale was rejected.

In the complaint titled *Ab. Aziz Nahvi* v. *Chief Post Master Jammu and Kashmir Circle, Srinagar,*[194] it was held that the fact that the parcels have been misappropriated is by itself enough evidence of fraudulent behaviour and this dishonesty on the part of postal authorities cannot be made subject matter of protection under Section 6 is a wrong interpretation. Consequently complaint was allowed.

OBSERVATION

Consumer Protection Act has been passed in the year 1987 and even after more than 10 years has elapsed. Consumer Protection in this State is a myth. while proceeding in the chapter it was expected that many conflicts and contraversies, delay, etc. may be there on the part of Consumer Fora in the State. However, in the course of case study, all doubts and apprehensions ended and a different picture got depicted. It is a fact that in the State of Jammu and Kashmir each Divisional Forum is for many districts and inspite of the fact the large population in the State is ignorant and uneducated about their rights, it is observed that flood of cases are instituted in these forums. Actually each forum consists one District Judge designed as President and two non-judicious members. How far these non-judicious members will deliver justice without knowing the intricacies and complexities of consumer law is a question which deserves to be answered. Coming to the relevant point for which case study has been undertaken it is clear from these cases that these forums while applying simple and almost similar procedure/trend have delivered justice consistently in the true spirit of the Consumer Protection Act. Case titled *Ab. Rashid Ganie* v. *Oriental Insurance Company* is a good example to

194. O/F No. 259/95 D/D 29-5-97 (J. Mr. Sharief-ud-din).

support this argument. Another example is *Regional Manager v. Bashir Ahmad Rangrez and Others* and also *Mohammad Yousf v. National Insurance Company Ltd.* is a case in which Jammu and Kashmir State Commission has taken a bold decision by holding that the entitlement to the indemnity for the loss incurred begins from the very date of loss itself and not on any other slippery date.

Regarding the delay and pendency of the cases the picture is very bleak but this delay is inevitable and attributed to various reasons, important among them is inadequate facilities of these Forums. The net result is that there is a liberal quasi-judicious attitude towards the consumer in the State.

CHAPTER

7

CONCLUSION AND SUGGESTIONS

To conclude, let us move a step backward towards the earlier chapters and especially chapter-wise observations. In previous chapters those factors has been briefly outlined which constitute root causes of consumer exploitation and harassment. In developed countries like U.K. and U.S.A. consumers themselves have strived to raise their standard of living but in our country usually in the State of Jammu and Kashmir consumers though expect fair deal, take things for granted without seeking information even though the goods are fake, spurious and adulterated. They take goods without asking about their purity even at the cost of their life and safety just because the goods are cheap and have excessive schemes, gifts and discounts, etc. It has been noticed that most of gifts with the schemes are not given to the consumers by the private business concerned people. They are all appropriated by the traders. This is because buyers do not check, read and study the products they buy. False guarantees and warranties are laid down without any intention to fulfil. Consumer is not ready to fight for his rights. It is estimated that forty percent of goods in our country are either sub-standard or adulterated but it is also expected that in the state of Jammu and Kashmir this figure may be more enlarged one because here major portion of the food, drugs and essential commodities are brought from outside the state and it is rightly commented about the people of the State that they are crazy to use foreign goods like shampoos, hair dyes, etc. without caring about their ill-effects and irreparable damage.

New products are coming in the market but consumer hardly knows about them. It is the backwardness and illiteracy on the part of the consumers which is responsible for this sorry state of affairs. Advertisements instead of informing consumers often misled them. Great care regarding standards both in goods and services is the ultimate name. In this connection rules, regulations and various enactments have been passed to do the needful by providing civil and criminal remedies. However, it has been recognized that inspite of encouraging legislative and governmental role consumers have failed to take advantage of the law. Rules concerning packaged goods are very clear and precise that all packaged items must be clearly marked as to their date of manufacture, date of expiry, contents in the product, MRP, etc. but most of these markets are full of such goods where packaging does not give any information and there are many items whose selflife is over, yet they are being sold and when the consumers use them they do not give the desired results. The consumer looses both ways, one in money spend, the other getting a useless item of no value. Who is to be blamed? Big producers or retailers who are driving huge profits, or government who is responsible partly because it has a big monopoly in trade and business and partly it is the duty of government to protect the life and lives of consumers and/or consumers themselves. In fact, all the three can play their respective roles to work in cooperation and for promotion of consumer protection.

What is said above about the defective and spurious goods the same is true as to the deficient services in public, private and cooperative utilities. In Chapter 5 we have seen this problem is more acute in case of monopoly services like banking, electricity, insurance, telephones, post, transport, etc. One pays even though the electricity and telephone service is not upto the standard mark. The same is true in transport service. One pays even though the price hike is unjustified. One could cite many examples when banks would be found rendering services which is neither courteous nor professionally upto the mark. In insurance service we have seen in the said chapter how inordinate and unjustified delay in appointing the surveyor is made by the various Insurance Companies.

In Chapter 2 after identifying some consumer problems and their possible solutions we have scrutinized provisions of various enactments with a view to spell out their efficiency and shortcomings. Briefly to state these legislations though primarily aim to control sale, supply and production of food, drugs and other essential commodities, etc. they vehemently failed to make a common man conscious enough to make a distinction between fair and foul, good and bad. Further, the tedious time consuming and uncertain procedure involved in reporting complaints under these enactments have discouraged even those consumers who are conscious of law and their rights. Not only this, these legislations have not kept pace with some of the sophisticated trade practices in respect of which consumers need protection. For this and many other like things Consumer Protection Act, 1987 was introduced in pursuance of U.N. General Assembly Guidelines on similar lines as Central Consumer Protection Act is for rest of the country. This Act is a comprehensive legislation which is to provide cheap and speedy remedy which enables the redressal agencies to impart justice. At present as discussed in Chapter 4 there is a two-tier, *quasi-judicial* machinery at divisional and state level to dispose of cases within a stipulated time and it provides protection to consumers against defective goods, deficient services, restrictive and also unfair trade practices. This Act covers also goods and services unless exempted by the government by notification in gazette. This Act does not replace the available remedy as provided under other Acts.

Despite the fact that Redressal Agencies under the Consumer Protection Act are busy and overloaded with their work consumer awareness and consumer resistance in the state is at its infancy. Our overall survey of thousands of cases in this work reveals that there is flood of cases against insurance service and rare instances are in other field of services. The greater the action the greater will be the consumer movements. Unless consumer awareness and consumer resistance becomes a mass movement the standard and quality of goods and services is not going to improve. If more exposure is given to fake items or spurious drugs and medicines, adulterated food items, underweight or overcharged goods then this public exposure will make it difficult for manufacturers or the traders and retailers, and others to market them. Today a choice before a consumer is between a sub-standard item and one that is known to be adulterated. Similarly though the Apex Court has brought all government and semi-government bodies under the purview of the Act these services continue to provide deficient services and have repeatedly claimed before the consumer forums that they are not answerable under the Consumer Protection Act as they are statutory bodies working under the direct control of the government. But this claim was firmly turned down by the Apex Court in *Lucknow Development Authority* v. *M.K. Gupta*.

Since the housing services are being rendered not only by statutory boards but also by private builders or contractors. Consumer forums have awarded not only the value of services but also compensation for the injustices suffered by the consumers. However, it has been observed from the cases relating to building and housing that the commission has refused to entertain complaints of class action suits which contain the question of law and fact relating to houses on the ground that issues raised were complicated questions of law and fact. Consequently, what has been given by legislature as a facility to the consumer has been taken away by the Apex Commission. The State Commissions on the other hand has entertained complaints filed by several consumers in a representative capacity. However, directions have been issued under the Consumer Protection Act (Central Act) for removal of latent defects which could not have been known at the time of taking possession of the house or land. The fact that the house allottee had signed a declaration at the time of taking over possession that the house was complete in all respects was held not to constitute any estoppel against recipient and the complainant has been entitled to all the expenditure incurred for removing such defects. By this ruling of Apex Commission consumer of housing service are likely to be greatly benefited. These services have been allowed to increase charges equal to the amount of cost escalation during the period of delay may not be allowed. The demand of a reasonably moderate escalation is not a deficiency in service. It would be so if it has been in the nature of an unscrupulous exploitation of the consumers. This approach seems to be justified because of the fact that inordinate delay, arbitrary and exhorbitant increase in costs are all consumer wrongs and therefore, jurisdiction of consumer forums cannot be denied on these matters.

Cases regarding the business of courier service for carriage of mail or parcels falls within the purview of the Consumer Protection Act and delay in delivery of the articles or non-delivery thereof amounts the deficiency in service. However, the procedure for acceptance of packets particularly of uninsured and undisclosed packets have created complicacy causing harassment to the consumer. The objection of the couriers that their liability is limited to Rs. 100 containing in the memo. Containing such a condition does not carry weight where such printed memo has been neither signed nor there has been any evidence to show that the terms therein were brought to the notice of consigner or the consignee or that the same were agreed upon by the consigner. In these cases a clause in the contract which restricted payment of compensation to a fixed amount should not be given effect.

Another category of service which has already became part of our discussion is education. No doubt, Consumer Protection Act does not expressly include education in the definition of service but I am in complete agreement with the minority view expressed in *Mohiuddin Kadeer's case*. The time has gone when education was treated a mission and vocation rather than profession, trade or business. There are various institutions who make lofty but false claims about the affiliation recognition, facilities and job prospectus with a view to allure the un-employed youth and thus mint money by charging exhorbitant sums from their students. Charging Rs. 300 to 500 per month (the month forming twenty days only rest holidays) from a group of as many as 100 to 250 students no limits whatever. In every nook and corner of our state coaching centers are seen everywhere. Thus placing educational system outside the purview of the Consumer Protection Act will do more harm than good to the society as a whole. So these institutions shall have to be accountable towards the students in the future.

As already mentioned while analyzing various cases under heading electrical service—supply of electricity has been held to be a consumer service even if the energy is being put to a commercial use. As in other services under this Act for example in cases of housing construction, etc. Consumer Disputes Redressal Agencies are refusing to decide the question of law and fact in life insurance cases. No doubt, the contract of insurance is the contract of *uberrimae fidie,* but rigor of the maxim suppression of *veri suggestio falsi* in life insurance cases can be subterfuged by directing LIC to employ competent doctors for ascertaining the state of health of consumers.

Here it is also important to comment on medical service. Perusal of a number of cases reveal that this medical profession is claiming immunity and has developed phobia of Consumer Protection Act. Supreme Court in a case has held that only private hospitals and nursing homes fall within the Section 2(1)(o) of this Act and the persons who avail themselves of the facility of medical treatment in Government hospitals are not consumers and the said facility cannot be regarded as service rendered for consideration. This view has sounded the death knell of emerging consumer jurisprudence. After all, doctors are paid by the government in a welfare state. By virtue of this decision only private doctors are made liable. In this case though the Apex Court has authoritatively set at rest the controversy regarding the applicability of the Consumer Protection Act to medical profession but this dichotomy made between private hospitals and government hospitals has no logic. There is no justification in a welfare state to exonerate a medical practitioner from liability for negligence while serving in a Government hospital.

So for as the postal and telegraphic services are concerned both are claiming immunity from the Consumer Protection Act. Regarding Postal Service National Commission in The Partner, *Monickbag Automobiles Case* (1997) observed that the services rendered by the post office are merely statutory and there is no contractual liability. Establishing the post offices and running the postal service the Central Government performs a governmental function and the government does not engage in commercial transaction with the sender of the articles transmitted by post is in the nature of charges imposed by the state for the enjoyment of the facilities provided by the Postal Department and not consideration of any commercial contract. The post office cannot be equated with a common carrier. But the attitude of the Redressal Agencies has been progressive in certain cases where postal authorities were held liable for their carelessness.

As postal department contended the applicability of this Act likewise telecom department denied the same. However, this contention has been rejected by the Apex Commission on the ground that the telephone service is not provided free of charge and nor is there any contract of personal service. The Consumer Protection Act gives the consumers' additional remedy besides those which may be available under other existing laws.

It has been repeatedly held that the consumer forums will not be legally justified in taking over the function of estimating by application of the rule of thumb the precise number of calls made unless there is adequate evidence to show that metering equipment was defective or there has been misuse of the particular telephone by some unauthorized person in collusion with employees of the department particularly in cases, where a subscriber has the STD facility. This is the reason that sometimes people get inflated bills for no valid reasons. However, this test evolved by the Apex Commission that it was for consumers of telephone services to establish that their inflated bills were due to the collusion between the post and telegraphic employees and third parties seems to be an erroneous one and has become handle for the telephone department through out the country as in the instant state to harass the consumers. The most unique and unfortunate future of this service is that unlike electricity or water meters which are installed in the premises of the consumer, the telephone meter is installed elsewhere away from the gaze or access of the subscriber from where it is possible to use the telephone of the subscriber without his knowledge. Moreover, the National Commission is divided as regards the texts to be applied in protecting consumer who complain of sudden excessive billing of their telephones. In the absence of any special circumstance one cannot justify an immediate disconnection of the telephone without notice. Not surprisingly therefore, a large number of subscribers apply for disconnection of this facility. It has been observed that it is the consumer who is at the utter mercy of these operators and officials of the telephone department.

Lastly, we have studied transport service with the help of decided cases and it is observed that the Railway Act and the Railway Claims Tribunals Act have nullified the express provision of the Consumer Protection Act that its provisions are in addition and not in derogation of any other law for the time being in force. The existence of this statutory bar against the award of compensation is resulting in gross injustice to the consumers.

The above discussion round defective goods and deficient services in the light of recent pronouncements of Supreme Court, National Commission and Consumer Forums of the State provides Consumer Protection Act is a principal consumer legislation and if effectively implemented will prove boon to consumers and will do wonders by providing better remedy to the aggrieved consumers. However, there is a greater demand for accountability not only on the part of private and public sectors but as well as services rendered by professional persons, unscrupulous businessman, unethical professionals and non-responsive governmental undertakings.

Thus to conclude it is proper to say that the State of Jammu and Kashmir which constitutionally has a special status has not raised above the level of satisfaction in providing and ensuring consumer protection in the state. The reason is obvious inspite of the significant role of consumer fora, there is acute lack of consumer awareness in the state. In order to create awareness and ensure consumer protection there is urgent necessity that government should establish more consumer courts in the state, so that justice will be accessible to the common man and it is natural when courts will be set-up at block and district level people will become more and more aware about the nature and purpose of these courts and also of their rights. Further there is need of making amendments and corrections in the penal laws dealing specifically with adulteration, labeling, packaging of goods, advertising, etc. so that the technical flaws will be removed and the persons entrusted with the responsibility of enforcing such laws—say for example Food and Drug Inspectors and/or non-judicious Members of Consumer Fora, etc. be recruited and provided high qualified and well trained in their respective fields. Not only this, media should play its important and legitimate role in awakening the masses. Business sector must establish their code of ethics which must be purely consumer-oriented. The most important thing is that if consumers and consumer organizations will remain vigilant major improvements will be brought in the quality of goods and standard of life. Furthermore, both government and private services including professionals be brought expressly under the purview of the Consumer Protection Act so as to avoid future unnecessary objections, denials and doubts about the amenability of the Consumer Protection Act. This way they will show improvements in terms of responsibility and competence.

Here it is noteworthy to say that the Consumer Protection Act is not a panacea for all ills. It needs to be geared up to serve the consumer better and remove islands of confusion from it. It is essential that the Consumer Protection Act should operate in full swing as early as possible so that its benefits percolate to the poor consumers. The Act must be given a fair trail and co-operation by all concerned so that justice may be easily available.

In the words of I.C. Saxena in his article "Consumer Protection Act, 1986: A View Point", the learned author stated:

"Consumer protection is our need,
In fact that is our creed,
Writing on the wall do we read,
New paths of joy consumer will tread."

Now before concluding the whole discussion on the subject matter the following suggestions for promoting consumer protection in the state are as follows:

- The State Level Consumer Protection Act made by the government has many flaws in it which deserves or need to be amended, on the lines of Central Act. Though Central Act itself needs amendment but the State government must incorporate some provisions (for example, third separate consumer forum) from it to benefit general masses.
- There is a need of creating awareness among the masses about consumer rights and creating confidence among them by disposing of the cases within specified time period. This is possible by making better position (by providing more facilities) of consumer forums in the state. So, government should exploit its resources in generating consumer awareness and redress the grievances of the people of State.
- There is an immediate need for the establishment of District Consumer Forums in each district of the State. Inspite the fact that Amendment Bill, 2002 provides for district level consumer courts government has not taken steps so far to act in accordance to it. This makes mockery of the Jammu and Kashmir Consumer Protection Act. So government should fulfil legislative mandate without delay because mere statutory words will not help actual establishment of forums in each district of the State will provide door to door justice to the consumers.
- Government and other agencies of consumer affairs should make all efforts to involve more and more people, particularly the youth who can carry the

message to the masses about their rights, laws, etc. in this connection. It is the educated and enlighted youth who can carry the message not only to city areas but also to the rural population as well.

- Government must create and strengthen more institutions which would serve people of far flung areas. It is observed that Food and Supplies Department is busy in various matters so the government for the very purpose of the Consumer Protection Act must also create an independent Consumer Affairs Ministry and make other departments to co-ordinate.
- Government should improve all services being rendered to the consumers.
- Necessary amendments should also be carried into the Consumer Protection Act whereby Consumer Forums should be empowered to entertain complaints having unlimited pecuniary jurisdiction.
- Consumer Forums should be established at Block and Tehsil level so that the consumers would have easy access to the authorities.
- There is hardly any voluntary organization in this State which is devoted to consumer cause. Steps should be taken by both government and Consumers to establish such Organizations so that the consumer grievances can be better redressed.
- There is dire need of setting up a separate product testing laboratory in the State.
- Consumer education should be given through posters, folk arts, street plays, T.V. dramas, seminars, etc. because no law can become forceful unless the consumer movement gains momentum.
- Consumer disputes and complaints should also be redressed by pre-litigation, negotiation, counseling, etc.
- Consumer Awareness camps should be organized in remote areas.
- Consumer Education should be introduced in educational institutions from primary to higher level as a subject in their curriculum.

- Educated youth specially students of colleges and universities should gear up for creating awareness among people about their rights and redouble efforts for mitigating their sufferings.
- Government should establish a consumer cell under Consumer Protection Act which will strive for achieving its objective and take effective measures towards welfare.
- Regular contacts with people in far-off places will enable consumer cell to know their miseries and finding solution to these.
- Government must make it obligatory for sellers and manufacturers to display price and stocks of essential commodities in other articles of mass consumption.
- The Government should authorize police and/or other independent agencies to look after and ensure that the consumers should not be defrauded by offering sub-standard goods even on low cheaper prices if those commodities affect the consumer health and wealth. Businessmen, producers, dealers, retailers should be compelled to maintain standards of quality, durability, etc.
- Government should fix as already suggested prices on almost all consumer commodities. Net retail price should be printed on packaged commodities instead of printing local taxes extra.
- The Government departments (Police squads, etc.) should be made more active and efficient in conducting raids. Corrupt officials must be summarily dismissed from service without going through lengthy procedures. The law must be amended for this purpose.
- The culprits should be given prompt and duly publicized punishment. Laws should be made more stringent for selling sub-standard products, adulterated products, underweight products, overcharging and misleading advertisement.
- There must be speedy trial and decisions on food adulteration cases preferably by specially assigned tribunals or forums.

- An advisory body with powers to hear the public should be set-up to regulate quality in food and essential commodities. Such an advisory body can advice the administration when it faces problems involving the safety of consumers or when changes in law or rules are planned. The concept of public hearing before a board should be effectively developed.
- All food products should carry information and care labeling. Provisions requiring the manufacturer to give his full address on the label should be made compulsory. Manufacturers, producers and even retailers must ensure that the product going into the market is wholesome, pure and properly labeled.
- Consumer should be protected from contractual abuses as one sided standard contracts.
- Business sector should participate in factual and relevant consumer education and information programmes.
- Special attention should be given by both the government and educated people/officials to the needs of disadvantaged consumers, in both rural and urban areas, including low income consumers and those with lower non-existent literary levels.
- Government should maintain and promote high ethical standards in pharmacy.
- Government should have proper control on distribution system of essential commodities before they will purchased by the innocent and ignored consumers.
- Lastly, Consumer Protection Act provides only compensatory provision and not for penal provision. It provides penality only in those cases where the defaulter fails to comply with the orders of the consumer forums. So in this Act penal provision and in other Acts say, for example, Prevention of Food Adulteration Act, etc. compensatory provision be incorporated.

APPENDIX I

THE CONSUMER PROTECTION ACT, 1986

No. 68 of 1986

[24TH DECEMBER, 1986]

An Act to provide for better protection of the interests of consumers and for that purpose to make provision for the establishment of consumer councils and other authorities for the settlement of consumers' disputes and for matters connected therewith.

Be it enacted by Parliament in the Thirty-seventh Year of the Republic of India as follows:

CHAPTER I

PRELIMINARY

1. Short title, extent, commencement and application

(1) This Act may be called the Consumer Protection Act, 1986.

(2) It extends to the whole of India except the State of Jammu and Kashmir.

(3) It shall come into force on such date[1] as the Central

1. The provisions of Chapters I, II and IV of this Act have come into force in the whole of India except the State of Jammu and Kashmir on 15-4-1987 vide Notification No. S.O. 390(E), dated 15-4-1987, published in the Gazette of India, 1987, Extraordinary, Part II, Section 3(ii).

Government may, by notification, appoint and different dates may be appointed for different States and for different provisions of this Act.

(4) Save as otherwise expressly provided by the Central Government by notification, this Act shall apply to all goods and services.

2. Definitions

(1) In this Act, unless the context otherwise requires,—

[1][(a) "appropriate laboratory" means a laboratory or organisation—

(i) recognised by the Central Government;

(ii) recognised by a State Government, subject to such guidelines as may be prescribed by the Central Government in this behalf; or

(iii) any such laboratory or organisation established by or under any law for the time being in force, which is maintained, financed or aided by the Central Government or a State Government for carrying out analysis or test of any goods with a view to determining whether such goods suffer from any defects;]

[2][(aa) "branch office" means—

(i) any establishment described as a branch by the opposite party; or

(ii) any establishment carrying on either the same or substantially the same activity as that carried on by the head office of the establishment;]

The provisions of Chapter III of this Act have come into force in the whole of India except the State of Jammu and Kashmir on 1-7-1987, vide Notification No. S.O. 568(E), dated 10-6-1987, published in the Gazette of India, 1987, Extraordinary, Part II, Section 3(ii).

1. Substituted by the Consumer Protectin (Amendment) Act, 1993 (w.e.f. 18th June 1993).

2. Inserted by the Consumer Protection (Amendment) Act, 1993 (w.e.f. 18th June 1993).

(b) "complainant" means—

(i) a consumer; or

(ii) any voluntary consumer association registered under the Companies Act, 1965 or under any other law for the time being in force; or

(iii) the Central Government or any State Government, who or which makes a complaint;

[1][(iv) one or more consumers, where there are numerous consumers having the same interest;]

(c) "complaint" means any allegation in writing made by a complainant that—

[2][(i) an unfair trade practice or a restrictive trade practice has been adopted by any trader;]

[3][(ii) the goods bought by him or agreed to be bought by him;] suffer from one or more defects;

[4](iii) the services hired or availed of or agreed to be hired or availed of by him] suffer from deficiency in any respect;

(iv) a trader has charged for the goods mentioned in the complaint a price in excess of the price fixed by or under any law for the time being in force or displayed on the goods or any package containing such goods with a view to obtaining any relief provided by or under this Act;

[5][(v) goods which will be hazardous to life and safety when used are being offered for sale to the public in contravention of the provisions of any law for the time being in force requiring traders to display information in regard to the contents, manner and effect of use of such goods.]

---

1. Inserted by *Ibid*.
2. Substituted by the Consumer Protection (Amendment) Act, 1993 (w.e.f. 18th June 1993).
3. Substituted by *Ibid*.
4. Inserted by *Ibid*.
5. Substituted by *Ibid*.

(d) "consumer' means any [person who—

(i) buys any goods for a consideration which has been paid or promised or partly paid and partly promised, or under any system of deferred payment and includes any user of such goods other than the person who buys such goods for consideration paid or promised or partly paid or partly promised, or under any system of deferred payment when such use is made with the approval of such person, but does not include a person who obtains such goods for resale or for any commercial purpose; or

(ii) [1][hires or avails of] any services for a consideration which has been paid or promised or party paid and party promised, or under any system of deferred payment and includes any beneficiary of such services other than the person who [2][hires or avails of] the services for consideration paid or promised or partly paid and partly promised, or under any system of deferred payment, when such services are availed of with the approval of the first mentioned person;

[3][*Explanation*—For the purpose of Sub-clause (i), "commercial purpose" does not include use by a consumer of goods bought and used by him exclusively for the purpose of earning his livelihood, by means of self-employment;]

(e) "consumer dispute" means a dispute where the person against whom a complaint has been made, denies or disputes the allegations contained in the complaint.

1. Substituted by the Consumer Protection (Amendment) Act, 1993 (w.e.f. 18th June 1993).
2. Substituted by *Ibid.*
3. Inserted by *Ibid.*

(f) "defect" means any fault, imperfection or shortcoming in the quality, quantity, potency, purity or standard which is required to be maintained by or under any law for the time being in force [1][under any contract, express or implied or] as is claimed by the trader in any manner whatsoever in relation to any goods;

(g) "deficiency" means any fault, imperfection, shortcoming or inadequacy in the quality, nature and manner of performance which is required to be maintained by or under any law for the time being in force or has been undertaken to be performed by a person in presence of a contract or otherwise in relation to any service;

(h) "District Forum" means a Consumer Disputes Redressal Forum established under clause (a) of section 9;

(i) "goods" means goods as defined in the Sale of Goods Act, 1930;

(j) "manufacturer" means a person who—

(i) makes or manufactures any goods or parts thereof; or

(ii) does not make or manufacture any goods but assembles parts thereof made or manufactured by others and claims the end-product to be goods manufactured by himself; or

(iii) puts or causes to be put his own mark on any goods made or manufactured by any other manufacturer and claims such goods to be goods made or manufactured by himself.

Explanation—Where a manufacturer despatches any goods or part thereof to any branch office maintained by him, such branch office shall not be deemed to be the manufacturer even though the parts so despatched to it are assembled at such branch office and are sold or distributed from such branch office;

1. Inserted by *Ibid*.

[1][(j) "member" includes the President and a member of the National Commission or a State Commission or a District Forum, as the case may be;

(k) "National Commission" means the National Consumer Disputes Redressal Commission established under clause (c) of section 9;

(l) "notification" means a notification published in the Official Gazette;

(m) "person" includes—

(i) a firm whether registered or not;

(ii) a Hindu undivided family;

(iii) a cooperative society;

(iv) every other association of persons whether registered under the Societies Registration Act; 1860 or not;

(n) "prescribed" means prescribed by rules made by the State Government, or as the case may be, by the Central Government under this Act;

[2][(nn) "restrictive trade practice" means any trade practice which requires a consumer to buy, hire or avail of any goods or, as the case may be, services as a condition precedent for buying, hiring or availing of any other goods or services;

(o) "service" means service of any description which is made available to potential users and includes the provision of facilities in connection with banking, financing insurance, transport, processing, supply of electrical or other energy, board or lodging or both, [2][housing construction] entertainment, amusement or the purveying of news or other information, but does not include the rendering of any service free of charge or under a contract of personal service;

(p) "State Commission" means a Consumer Disputes Redressal Commission established in a State under clause (b) of section 9;

---

1. Inserted by the Consumer Protction (Amendment) Act, 1993 (w.e.f. 18th June 1993)
2. Inserted by *Ibid*.

(q) "trader" in relation to any goods means a person who sells or distributes any goods for sale and includes the manufacturer thereof, and where such goods are sold or distributed in package form, includes the packer thereof;

[1][(r) "unfair trade practice" means a trade practice which, for the prupose of promoting the sale, use or supply of any goods or for the provision of any service, adopts any unfair method or unfair or deceptive practice including any of the following practices, namely:

(1) the practice of making any statement, whether orally or in writing or by visible representation which,

(i) falsely represents that the goods are of a particular standard, quality, quantity, grade, composition, style or model;

(ii) falsely represents that the services are of a particular standard, quality of grade;

(iii) falsely represents any re-built, second-hand, renovated, reconditioned or old goods as new goods;

(iv) represents that the goods or services have sponsorship approval, performance, characteristics' accessories, uses or benefits which such goods or Services do not have;

(v) represents that the seller or the supplier has a sponsorship or approval or affiliation which such sellers or supplier does not have;

(vi) makes a false or misleading representation concerning the need for, or the usefulness of, any goods or services;

(vii) gives to the public any warranty or guarantee of the performance, efficacy or length of life of a product or of any goods

1. Substituted by *Ibid.*

that is not based on an adequate or proper test thereof;

Provided that where a defence is raised to the effect that such warranty or guarantee is based on adequate or proper test, the burden of proof of such defence shall lie on the person raising such defence;

(viii) makes to the public a representation in a form that purports to be—

(i) a warranty or guarantee of a product or of any goods or services; or

(ii) a promise to replace, maintain or repair an article or any part thereof or to repeat or continue a service until it has achieved a specified result.

if such purported warranty or guarantee or promise is materially misleading or if there is no reasonable prospect that such warranty, guarantee or promise will be carried out;

(ix) materially misleads the public concerning the price at which a product or like products or goods or services, have been, or are, ordinarily sold or provided, and, for this purpose, a representation as to price shall be deemed to refer to the price at which the product or goods or services has or have been sold by sellers or provided by suppliers generally in the relevant market unless it is clearly specified to be the price at which the product has been sold or services have been provided by the person by whom or on whose behalf the representation is made;

(x) gives false or misleading facts disparaging the goods, services or trade of another person.

Explanation—For the purposes of clause (1), a statement that is—

(a) expressed on an article offered or displayed for sale, or on its wrapper or container; or
(b) expressed on anything attached to, inserted in, or accompanying, an article offered or displayed for sale or on anything on which the article is mounted for display or sale; or
(c) contained in or on anything that is sold, sent delivered, transmitted or in any other manner whatsoever made available to a member of the public,

shall be deemed to be a statement made to the public by, and only by, the person who had caused the statement to be so expressed, made or contained;

(2) permits the publication of any advertisement whether in any newspaper or otherwise, for the sale or supply at a bargaining price, of goods or services that are not intended to be offered for sale or supply at the bargain price, or for a period that is, and in quantities that are, reasonable, having regard to the nature of the market in which the business is carried on, the nature and size of business, and the nature of the advertisement.

Explanation—For the purpose of clause (2), "bargaining price" means—

(a) a price that is stated in any advertisement to be a bargain price, by reference to an ordinary price or otherwise, or
(b) a price that a person who reads, hears or sees that advertisement, would reasonably understand to be a bargain price having regard to the prices at which the product advertised or like products are ordinarily sold;

(3) permits—

(a) the offering of gifts, prizes or other items with the

intention of not providing them as offered or creating impression that something is being given or offered free of charge when it is fully or partly covered by the amount charged in the transaction as a whole;

(b) the conduct of any contest, lottery, game of chance or skill, for the purpose of promoting directly or indirectly the sale, use or supply of any product or any business interest;

(4) permits the sale or supply of goods intended to be used, or are of a kind likely to be used, by consumers, knowing or having reason to believe that the goods do not comply with the standards prescribed by competent authority relating to performance, composition, contents, design constructions, finishing or packaging as are necessary to prevent or reduce the risk of injury to the person using the goods;

(5) permits the hoarding or destruction of goods, or refuses to sell the goods or to make them available for sale or to provide any service, if such hoarding or destruction or refusal raises or tends to raise or is intended to raise, the cost of those or other similar goods or services.]

(6) Any reference in this Act to any other Act or provision thereof which is not in force in any area to which this Act applies shall be construed to have a reference to the corresponding Act or provision thereof in force in such area.

3. Act not in derogation of any other law

The provisions of this Act shall be in addition to and not in derogation of the provisions of any other law for the time being in force.

CHAPTER II

CONSUMER PROTECTION COUNCILS

4. The Central Consumer Protection Council

(1) The Central Government may, by notification, establish with effect from such date as it may specify in such

notification a Council to be known as the Central Consumer Protection Council (hereinafter referred to as the Central Council).

(2) The Central Council shall consist of the following members, namely—

(a) the Minister in charge of the [1][consumer affairs) in the Central Government, who shall be its Chairman, and
(b) such number of other official or non-official members representing such interests as may be prescribed.

5. Procedure for meetings of the Central Council

(1) The Central Council shall meet as and when necessary, [2][at least one meeting] of the Council shall be held every year.

(2) The Central Council shall meet at such time and place as the Chairman may think fit and shall observe such procedure in regard to the transaction of its business as may be prescribed.

6. Objects of the Central Council

The objects of the Central Council shall be to promote and protect the rights of the consumers such as,

(a) the right to be protected against marketing of goods [3][and services] which are hazardous to life and property;
(b) the right to be informed about the quality, quantity, potency, purity, standard and price of goods [4][or services, as the case may be] so as to protect the consumer against unfair trade practices;

---

1. Substituted by the Consumer Protection (Amendment) Act, 1993 (w.e.f. 18th June, 1993).
2. Substituted by *Ibid.*
3. Inserted by *Ibid.*
4. Inserted by *Ibid.*

(c) the right to be assured wherever possible, access to a variety of goods [1][and services] at competitive prices;

(d) the right to be heard and to be assured that consumer's interests will receive due consideration at appropriate forums;

(e) the right to seek redressal against unfair trade practices [2][or restrictive trade practices) or unscrupulous exploitation of consumers; and

(f) the right to consumer education.

7. The State Consumer Protection Councils

(1) The State Government may, by notification, establish with effect from such date as it may specify in such notification, a Council to be known as the Consumer Protection Council for (hereinafter referred to as the State Council).

[3][(2) The State Council shall consist of the following members, namely:

(a) the Minister incharge of consumer affairs in the State Government who shall be its Chairman;

(b) such number of other official or non-official members representing such interests as may be prescribed by the State Government.

(3) The State Council shall meet as and when necessary but not less than two meetings shall be held every year.

(4) The State Council shall meet at such time and place as the Chairman may think fit and shall observe such procedure in regard to the transaction of its business as may be prescribed by the State Government."]

8. Objects of the State Council

The objects of every State Council shall be to promote and protect within the State the rights of the consumers laid down in clauses (a) to (f) of section 6.

---

1. Inserted by *Ibid*.
2. Inserted by the Consumer Protection (Amendment) Act, 1993 (w.e.f. 18th June, 1993).
3. Inserted by *Ibid*.

CHAPTER III

CONSUMER DISPUTES REDRESSAL AGENCIES

9. Establishment of Consumer Disputes Redressal Agencies

There shall be established for the purposes of this Act, the following agencies, namely:

(a) a Consumer Disputes Redressal Forum to be known as the "District Forum" established by the State Government [1][* * *] in each district of the State by notification:
[2][Provided that the State Government may, if it deems fit, establish more than one District Forum in a district.]

(b) a Consumer Disputes Redressal Commission to be knwn as the "State Commission" established by the State Government [3][* * *] in the State by notifiation; and

(c) a National Consumer Disputes Redressal Commission established by the Central Government by notification.

10. Composition of the District Forum

[4][(1) Each District Forum shall consist of,—

(a) a person who is, or who has been, or is qualified to be a District Judge, who shall be its President;

(b) two other members who shall be persons of ability, integrity and standing, and have adequate knowledge or experience of, or have shown capacity in dealing with, problems relating to economics, law, commerce, accountancy, industry,

1. Omitted by the Consumer Protection (Amendment) Act, 1993 (w.e.f. 18th June 1993)
2. Inserted by *Ibid.*
3. Omitted by *Ibid.*
4. Substituted by *Ibid.*

public affairs or administration, one of whom shall be a woman.]

[1][(1A) Every appointment under sub-section (1) shall be made by the State Government on the recommendation of a selection committee consisting of the following, namely,—

(i) the President of the State Commission—Chairman.
(ii) Secretary, Law Department of the State—Member.
(iii) Secretary incharge of the Department dealing with consumer affairs in the State—Member.]

(2) Every member of the District Forum shal hold office for a term of five years or up to the age of 65 years, whichever is earlier, and shall not be eligible for re-appointment:

Provided that a member may resign his office in writing under his hand-addressed to the State Government and on such resignation being accepted, his office shall become vacant and may be filled by the appointment of a person possessing any of the qualifications mentioned in sub-section (1) in relation to the category of the member who has resigned.

(3) The salary or honorarium and other allowances payable to, and the other terms and conditions of service of the members of the District Forum shall be such as may be prescribed by the State Government.

11. Jurisdiction of the District Forum

(1) Subject to the other provisions of this Act, the District Forum shall have jurisdiction to entertain complaints where the value of the goods or services and the compensation, if any, claimed [2][does not exceed rupees five lakhs].

(2) A complaint shall be instituted in a District Forum within the local limits of whose jurisdiction—

---

1. Inserted by *Ibid*.
2. Substituted by the Consumer Protection (Amendment) Act, 1993 (w.e.f. 18th June, 1993).

(a) the opposite party or each of the opposite parties, where there are more than one, at the time of the institution of the complaint, actually and voluntarily resides or [1][carries on business or has a branch office on personally works for gain, or

(b) any of the opposite parties, where there are more than one, at the time of the institution of the complaint, actually and voluntarily resides, or [2][carries on business or has a branch office], or personally works for gain, provided that in such case either the permission of the District Forum is given, or the opposite parties Who do not reside, or carry on business or have a branch office), or personally works for gain, as the case may be, acquiesce in such institution; or

(c) the cause of action, wholly or in part, arises.[3]

[4][12. Manner in which complaint shall be made

A complaint in relation to any goods sold or delivered or agreed to be sold or delivered or any service provided or agreed to be provided may be filed with a District Forum by—

(a) the consumer to whom such goods are sold or delivered or agreed to be delivered or such service provided or agreed to be provided;

(b) any recognised consumer association whether the consumer to whom the goods sold or delivered or agreed to be sold or delivered or service provided or agreed to be provided is a member of such association or not;

(c) one or more consumers where there are numerous consumer's having the same interest, with the

1. Substituted by *Ibid.*
2. Substituted by *Ibid.*
3. Substituted by *Ibid.*
4. Substituted by the Consumer Protection (Amendment) Act, 1993 (w.e.f. 18th June, 1993).

permission of the District Forum, on behalf of, or for the benefit of all consumers so interested; or

(d) the Central or the State Government.

Explanation—For the purpose of this section, "recognised consumer association" means any voluntary consumer association registered under the Companies Act, 1956 (1 of 1956) or any other law for the time being in force.]

13. Procedure on receipt of complaint

(1) The District Forum shall, on receipt of a complaint, if it relates to any goods,

(a) refer a copy of the complaint to the opposite party mentioned in the complaint directing him to give his version of the case within a period of thirty days or such extended period not exceeding fifteen days as may be granted by the District Forum;

(b) where the opposite party on receipt of a complaint referred to him under clause (a) denies or disputes the allegations contained in the complaint, or omits or fails to take any action to represent his case within the time given by the District Forum, the District Forum shall proceed to settle the consumer dispute in the manner specified in clauses (c) to (g);

(c) where the complaint alleges a defect in the goods which cannot be determined without proper analysis or test of the goods, the District Forum shall obtain a sample of the goods from the complainant, seal it and authenticate it in the manner prescribed and refer the sample so sealed to the appropriate laboratory along with a direction that such laboratory make an analysis or test, whichever may be necessary, with a view to finding out whether such goods suffer from any defect alleged in the complaint or from any other defect and to report its findings thereon to the District Forum within a period of fifty-five days of the receipt of the reference or within such extended period as maybe granted by the District Forum;

(d) before any sample of the goods is referred to any appropriate laboratory under clause (c), the District Forum may require the complainant to deposit to the credit of the Forum such fees as may be specified, for payment to the appropriate laboratory for carrying out the necessary analysis or test in relation to the goods in question;

(e) the District Forum shall remit the amount deposited to its credit under clause (d) to the appropriate laboratory to enable it to carry out the analysis or test mentioned in clause (c) and on receipt of the report from the appropriate laboratory, the District Forum shall forward a copy of the report along with such remarks as the District Forum may feel appropriate to the opposite party;

(f) if any of the parties disputes the correctness of the findings of the appropriate laboratory, or disputes the correctness of the methods of analysis or test adopted by the appropriate laboratory, the District Forum shall require the opposite party or the complainant to submit in writing his objections in regard to the report made by the appropriate laboratory;

(g) the District Forum shall thereafter give a reasonable opportunity to the complainant as well as the opposite party of being heard as to the correctness or otherwise of the report made by the appropriate laboratory and also as to the objection made in relation thereto under clause (f) and issue an appropriate order under section 14.

(2) the District Forum shall, if the complaint received by it under section 12 relates to goods in respect of which the procedure specified in sub-section (1) cannot be followed, or if the complaint relates to any services:—

(a) refer a copy of such complaint to the opposite party directing him to give his version of the case within a period of thrity days or such extended period not exceeding fifteen days as may be granted by the District Forum.

(b) where the opposite party, on receipt of a copy of the complaint, referred to him under clause (a) denies or disputes the allegations contained in the complaint, or omits or fails to take any action to represent his case within the time given by the District Forum, the District Forum shall proceed to settle the consumer dispute,

(i) on the basis of evidence brought to its notice by the complainant and the opposite party, where the opposite party denies or disputes the allegations contained in the complaint, or

(ii) on the basis of evidence brought to its notice by the complainant where the opposite party omits or fails to take any action to represent his case within the time given by the Forum.

(3) No proceedings complying with the procedure laid down in sub-section (1) and (2) shall be called in question in any court on the ground that the principles of natural justice have not been complied with.

(4) For the purposes of this section, the District Forum shall have the powers as are vested in a civil court under Code of Civil Procedure, 1908 while trying a suit in respect of the following matters, namely:

(i) the summoning and enforcing the attendance of any defendant or witness and examining the witness on oath;

(ii) the discovery and production of any document or other material object producible as evidence;

(iii) the reception of evidence on affidavits;

(iv) the requisitioning of the report of the concerned analysis or test from the appropriate laboratory or from any other relevant source;

(v) issuing of any commission for the examination of any witness; and

(vi) any other matter which may be prescribed.

(5) Every proceeding before the District Forum shall be deemed to be a judicial proceeding within the meaning of section 193 and 228 of the Indian Penal Code, and the District Forum shall be deemed to be a civil court for the purposes of section 195, and Chapter XXVI of the Code of Criminal Procedure, 1973.

[1][(6) Where the complainant is a consumer referred to in subclause (iv) of clause (b) of sub-section (1) of section 2, the provisions of rule 8 of Order 1 of the First Schedule to the Code of Civil Procedure, 1908 shall apply subject to the modification that every reference therein to a suit or degree shall be construed as a reference to a complaint or the order of the District Forum thereon.]

14. Finding of the District Forum

(1) If after the proceeding conducted under section 13, the District Forum is satisfied that the goods complained againt to suffer from any of the defects specified in the complaint or that any of the allegations contained in the complaint about the services are proved, it shall issue an order to the opposite party directing him to [2][do] one or more of the following things, namely:

(a) to remove the defect pointed out by the appropriate laboratory from the goods in question;

(b) to replace the goods with new goods of similar description which shall be free from any defect;

(c) to return to the complainant the price, or as the case may be, the charges paid by the complainant;

(d) to pay such amount as may be awarded by it as compensation to the consumer for any loss or injury suffered by the consumer due to the negligence of the opposite party.

---

1. Inserted by the Consumer Protection (Amendment) Act, 1993 (w.e.f. 18th June, 1993).
2. Substituted by *Ibid.*

[1][(e) to remove the defects or deficiencies in the services in question;

(f) to discontinue the unfair trade practice or the restrictive trade practice or not to repeat them;

(g) not to offer the hazardous goods for sale;

(h) to withdraw the hazardous goods from being offered for sale; and

(i) to provide for adequate costs to parties.]

[2][(2) Every proceeding referred to in sub-section (1) shall be conducted by the President of the District Forum and at least one member thereof sitting together:

Provided that where the member, for any reason, is unable to conduct the proceeding till it is completed, the President and the other member shall conduct such proceeding de novo.]

[3][(2A) Every order made by the District Forum under sub-section (1) shall be signed by its President and the member or members who conducted the processing:

Provided that where the proceeding is conducted by the President and one member and they differ on any point or points, they shall state the point or points on which they differ and refer the same to the other member for hearing on such point as points and the opinion of the majority shall be the order of the District Forum.]

(3) Subject to the foregoing provisions, the procedure relating to the conduct of the meetings of the District Forum, its sittings and other matters shall be such as may be prescribed by the State Government.

15. Appeal

Any person aggrieved by an order made by the District Forum may prefer an appeal against such order to the State Commission within a period of thirty days from the date of the order, in such form and manner as may be prescribed:

---

1. Sub-sections (e), (f), (g), (h), (i). Inserted by the Consumer Protection (Amendment) Act, 1993 (w.e.f. 18th June, 1993).
2. Subs. by Act No. 34 of 1991 w.e.f. 15-6-1991.
3. Ins. by *Ibid*.

Provided that the State Commission may entertain an appeal after the expiry of the said period of thirty days if it is satisfied that there was sufficient cause for not filing it within that period.

16. Composition of the State Commission

(1) Each State Commission shall consist of-

(a) a person who is or has been a Judge of a High Court, appointed by the State Government, who shall be its President:
[1][Provided that no appointment under this clause shall be made except after consultation with the Chief Justice of the High Court;]

(b) two other members, who shall be persons of ability, integrity and standing and have adequate knowledge or experience of, or have shown capacity in dealing with, problems relating to economics, law, commerce, accountancy, industry, public affairs or administration, one of whom shall be a woman:
[2][Provided that every appointment made under this clause shall be made by the State Government on the recommendation of a selection committee consisting of the following, namely—
(i) President of the State Commission—Chairman.
(ii) Secretary of the Law Department of the State—Member.
(iii) Secretary, incharge of Department dealing with consumer affairs in the State—Member.]

(2) The salary or honorarium and other allowances payable to, and the other terms and conditions of service [3][***] of, the members of the State Commission shall be such as may be prescribed by the State Goverument.

---

1. Substituted by the Consumer Protection (Amendment) Act, 1993 (w.e.f. 18th June, 1993).
2. Substituted by *Ibid.*
3. Omitted by *Ibid.*

[1](3) Every member of the State Commission shall hold Office for a term of five years or upto the age of sixty-seven years, whichever is earlier and shall not be eligible for re-appointment,

(4) Notwithstanding anything contained in sub-section (3), a person appointed as a president or as a member before the commencement of the Consumer Protection (Amendment) Act, 1993, shall continue to hold such office as President or member, as the case may be, till the completion of his term.]

17. Jurisdiction of the State Commission

Subject to the other provisions of this Act, the State Commission shall have jurisdiction—

(a) to entertain—
  (i) complaints where the value of the goods or services and compensation, if any, claimed exceeds rupees [2][five laksh but does not exceed rupees twenty lakhs]; and
  (ii) appeals against the orders of any District Forum within the State; and

(b) to call for the records and pass appropriate orders in any consumer dispute which is pending before or has been decided by any District Forum within the State, where it appears to the State Commission that such District Forum has exercised a jurisdiction not vestd in it by law, or has failed to exercise a jurisdiction so vested or has acted in exercise of its jurisdiction illegally or with material irregularity.

18. Procedure applicable to State Commission

[3][The provisions of Sections 12, 13 and 14 and the rules made thereunder] for the disposal of complaints by the District Forum shall, with such modifications as may be necessary, be applicable to the disposal of disputes by the State Commission.

---

1. Substituted by the Consumer Protection (Amendment) Act, 1993 (w.e.f. 18th June, 1993).
2. Substituted by *Ibid.*
3. Substituted by *Ibid.*

[1][18A. Vacancy in the office of the President

When the office of the President of the District Forum or of the State Commission, as the case may be, is vacant or when any such President is, by reason of absence or otherwise, unable to perform the duties of his office, the duties of the office shall be performed by such person, who is qualified to be appointed as President of the District Forum or, as the case may be, of the State Commission, as the State Government may appoint for the purpose.

19. Appeals

Any person aggrieved by an order made by the State Commission in exercise of its powers conferred by sub-clause (i) of clause (a) of section 17 may prefer an appeal against such order to the National Commission within a period of thirty days from the date of the order in such form and manner as may be prescribed:

Provided that the National Commission may entertain an appeal after the expiry of the said period of thirty days if it is satisfied that there was sufficient cause for not filing it within that period.

20. Composition of the National Commission

(1) The National Commission shall consist of—

(a) a person who is or has been a Judge of the Supreme Court, to be appointed by the Central Government, who shall be its President:
[2][Provided that no appointment under this clause shall be made except after consultation with the Chief Justice of India;]

(b) four other members who shall be persons of ability, integrity and standing and have adequate knowledge or experience of, or have shown capacity in dealing with, problems relating to

1. Inserted by Act No. 34 of 1991.
2. Inserted by the Consumer Protection (Amendment) Act, 1993 (w.e.f. 18th June, 1993).

economics, law, commerce, accountancy, industry, public affairs or administration, one of whom shall be a woman:

[1][Provided that every appointment under this clause shall be made by the Central Government on the recommendation of a selection committee consisting of the following, namely—

(a) a person who is a Judge of the Supreme Court, to be nominated by the Chief Justice of India—Chairman.

(b) the Secretary in the Department of Legal Affairs in the Government of India—Member.

(c) Secretary of the Department dealing with consumer affairs in the Government of India—Member.

(2) The salary or honoarium and other allowances payable to and the other terms and conditions of service [2][* * *] of the members of National Commission shall be such as may be prescribed by the Central Government.

[3][(3) Every member of the National Commission shall hold office for a term of five years or up to the age of seventy years, whichever is earlier and shall not be eligible for re-appointment.

(4) Notwithstanding anything contained in sub-section (3), a person appointed as a President or a member before the commencement of the Consumer Protection (Amendment) Act, 1993, shall continue to hold such office as President or member, as the case may be, till the completion of his term.]

21. Jurisdiction of the National Commission

Subject to the other provisions of this Act, the National Commission shall have jurisdiction—

---

1. Omitted by the Consumer Protection (Amendment) Act, 1993 (w.e.f. 18th June, 1993).
2. Inserted by *Ibid.*
3. Substituted by *Ibid.*

(a) to entertain—
  (i) complaints where the value of the goods or services and compensation, if any, claimed exceeds rupees [1][twenty laks]; and
  (ii) appeals against the orders of any State Commission; and
(b) to call for the records and pass appropriate orders in any consumer dispute which is pending before or has been decided by any State Commission where it appears to the National Commission that such State Commission has exercised a jurisdiction not vested in it by law, or has failed to exercise a jurisdiction so vested, or has acted in the exercise of its jurisdiction illegally or with material irregularity.

[2][22. Power of and procedure applicable to the National Commission

The National Commission shall, in the disposal of any complaints or any proceedings before it, have—

(a) the powers of a civil court as specified in sub-sections (4), (5) and (6) of section 13; and
(b) the power to issue an order to the opposite party directing him to do any one or more of the things referred to in clauses (a) to (i) of sub-section (1) of section 14,

and follow such procedure as may be prescribed by the Central Government].

23. Appeal

Any person, aggrieved by an order made by the National Commission in exercise of its powers conferred by sub-clause (i) of clause (a) of section 21, may prefer an appeal against such order to the Supreme Court within a period of thirty days from the date of the order:

1. Substituted by *Ibid*.
2. Substituted by the Consumer Protection (Amendment) Act, 1993 (w.e.f. 18th June, 1993).

Provided that the Supreme Court may entertain an appeal after the expiry of the said period of thirty days if it is satisfied that there was sufficient cause for not filing it within that period.

24. Finality of orders

Every order of a District Forum, the State Commission or the National Commission shall, if no appeal has been preferred against such order under the provisions of this Act, be final.

[1][24A. Limitation period

(1) The District Forum, the State Commission or the National Commission shall not admit a complaint unless it is filed within two years from the date on which the cause of action has arisen.

(2) Notwithstanding anything contained in sub-section (1), a complaint may be entertained after the period specified in sub-section (1), if the complaint satisfies the District Froum, the State Commission or the National Commission, as the case may be, that he had sufficient cause for not filing the complaint within such period:

Provided that no such complaint shall be entertained unless the National Commissoin, the State Commission or the District Forum, as the case may be, records its reasons for condoning such delay.

24B. Administrative control

(1) The National Commission shall have administrative control over all the State Commissions in the following matters, namely:—

(i) calling for periodical return regarding the institution, disposal pendency of cases;

(ii) issuance of instructions regarding adoption of uniform procedure in the hearing of matters, prior service of copies of documents produced by one

---

1. Substituted by *Ibid.*

party to the opposite parties, furnishing of Enligh translation of judgements written in any language speedy grant of copies of documents;

(iii) generally overseeing the functioning of the State Commissions or the District Forum to ensure that the objects and purposes of the Act are best served without in any way interfering with their quasi-judicial freedom.

(2) The State Commission shall have administrative control over all the District Fora within its jurisdiction in all matters referred to in sub-section (1).]

25. Enforcement of orders by the Forum, the State Commission or the National Commission

Every order made by the District Forum, the State Commission or the National Commission maybe enforced by the District Forum, the State Commission or the National Commission, as the case may be, in the same manner as if it were decree or order made by a court in a suit pending therein and it shall be lawful for the District Forum, the State Commission or the National Commission to send, in the event of its imbiblity to execute it, such order to the court within the local limits of whose jurisdiction—

(a) in the case of an order against a company, the registered office of the company is situated, or

(b) in the case of an order against any other person, the place where the person concerned voluntarily resides or carries on business or personally worked for gain, is situated,

and thereupon, the court to which the order is so sent, shall execute the order as if it were a degree or order sent to it for execution.

[1][26. Dismissal of frivolous or vexatious complaints

Where a complaint instituted before the District Forum,

1. Substituted by the Consumer Protection (Amendment) Act, 1993 (w.e.f. 18th June, 1993).

the State Commission or the National Commission, as the case may be, is found to be frivolous or vexatious, it shall, for reasons to be recorded in writing, dismiss the complaint and make an order that complainant shall pay to the party such cost, not exceeding ten thousand rupees, as may be specified in the order.]

27. Penalties

Where a trader or a person against whom a complaint is made [1][or the complaint] fails or omits to comply with any order made by the District Forum, the State Commission or the National Commission as the case may be, such trader or person [1][or complainant] shall be punishable with imprisonment for a term which shall not he less than one month but may extend to three years, or with fine which shall not be less than two thousands rupees but which may extend to ten thousand rupees, or with both:

Provided that the District Forum, the State Commission or the National Commission, as the case may be, may, if it is satisfied that the circumstances of any case so require, impose a sentence of imprisonment or fine, or both, for a term lesser than the minimum term and the amount lesser than the minimum amount, specified in this section.

CHAPTER IV

MISCELLANEOUS

28. Protection of action taken in good faith

No suit, prosecution or other legal proceedings shall lie against the members of the District Forum, the State Commission or the National Commission or any officer or person acting under the direction of the District Forum, the State Commission or the National Commission or executing any order made by it or in respect of anything which is in good faith done or intended to be done by such member, officer or person under this Act or under any rule or order made thereunder.

---

1. Substituted by *Ibid*.

29. Power to remove difficulties

(1) If any difficulty arises in giving effect to the provisions of this Act, the Central Government may, by order in the Official Gazette, make such provisions not inconsistent with the provisions of this Act as appear to it to be necessary or expedient for removing the difficulty:

Provided that no such order shall be made after the expiry of a period of two years from the commencement of this Act.

(2) Every order made under this section shall, as soon as may be after it is made be laid before each house of Parliament.

[1][29A. Vacancy or defects in appointment not to invalidate orders

No act or proceeding of the District Forum, the State Commission or the National Commission shall be invalid by reason only of the existence of any vacancy amongst its members or any defect in the constitution thereof.

30. Power to make rules

(1) The Central Government may, by notification, make rules for carrying out the provisions contained in [2][clause (a) of sub-section (1) of section (2) clause (b) of sub-section (2) of subsection 4, sub-section (2) of section 5, clause (vi) of subsection (4) of section 13, section 19, sub-section (2) of section 20 and section 22 of this Act.

(2) The State Government may, by notification, make rules for carrying out the provisions contained in [3][clause (b) of sub-section (2) and sub-section (4) of section 7] sub-section (3) of section 10, clause (c) of sub-section (1) of section 13, sub-section (3) of section 14, section 15 and sub-section (2) of section 16.

---

1. Inserted by Act No. 34 of 1991, w.e.f. 15-06-1991.
2. Inserted by the Consumer Protection (Amendment) Act, 1993 (w.e.f. 18th June, 1993).
3. Inserted by the Consumer Protection (Amendment) Act, 1993 (w.e.f. 18th June, 1993).

31. Laying of rules

(1) Every rule made by the Central Government under this Act shall be laid as soon as may be after it is made, before each House of Parliament while it is in session, for a total period of thirty days which may be comprised in one session or in two or more successive sessions, and if, before the expiry of the session immediately following the session or the successive sessions aforesaid, both Houses agree in making any modification in the rule or both Houses agree that the rule should not be made, the rule shall thereafter have effect only in such modified form or be of no effect, as the case may be; so, however, that any such modification or annulment shall be without prejudice to the validity of anything previously done under that rule.

(2) Every rule made by a State Government under this Act shall be laid as soon as may be after it is made, before the State Legislature

APPENDIX 2

THE JAMMU AND KASHMIR CONSUMER PROTECTION ACT, 1987[1]

[16 of 1987]

[19th August 1987]

An Act to provide for better protection of the interests of consumers and for that purpose to make provisions for the establishment of consumer councils, and other authorities for the settlement of consumers disputes for matters connected therewith.

BE it enacted by the Jammu and Kashmir State Legislature in the Thirty-eighth Year of the Republic of India as follows—

CHAPTER I

PRELIMINARY

1. Short title, extent, commencement and application

(1) This Act may be called the Jammu and Kashmir Consumer Protection Act, 1987.

(2) It extends to the whole of the State of Jammu and Kashmir.

(3) It shall come into force on such date as the Government may, be notification in the Government Gazette, appoint and different dates may be appointed for different provisions of this Act.

---

1. Published in the Govt. Gazette dated 22-08-1987.

(4) Save as otherwise expressly provided by the Government by notification, in the Government Gazette, this Act shall apply to all goods and services.

2. Definitions

(1) In this Act, unless the context otherwise requires,—

(a) "appropriate laboratory" means a laboratory or organisation recognised by the Government and includes any such laboratory or organisation established by or under any law for the time being in force, which is maintained, financed or aided by the Government for carrying out analysis or test of any goods with a view to determining whether such goods suffer from any defect:

(b) "complainant" means—
   (i) a consumer; or
   (ii) any voluntary consumer associanon registered under the Companies Act, 1956 or under any other law for the time being in force; or
   (iii) the Government who makes a complaint;

(c) "complaint" means an allegation in wrting made by a complainant that—
   (i) as a result of any unfair trade practice adopted by any trader the complainant has suffered loss or damage;
   (ii) the goods mentioned in the complaint suffer from one or more defects;
   (iii) the services mentioned in the complaint suffer from deficiency in any respect;
   (iv) a trader has charged for the goods mentioned in the complaint a price in excess of the price fixed by or under any law for the time being in force or displayed in the goods or any package containing such goods.

   with a view to obtaining any relief provided by or under this Act;

(d) "consumer" means any person who—
   (i) buys any goods for a consideration which has been paid or promised or partly paid and

partly promised or under any system of deferred payment and includes any user of such goods other than the person who buys such goods for consideration paid or promised partly paid or partly promised or under any system of deferred payment when such use is made with the approval of such person, but does not include a person who obtains such goods for resale or for any commercial purpose; or

(ii) hires any service for a consideration which has been paid or promised or partly paid and partly promised, or under any system of deferred payment and includes any beneficiary of such service other than the person who hires the services for consideration paid or promised, or partly paid and partly promised or under any system of deferred payment, when such services are availed of with the approval of the first mentioned person;

(e) "consumer dispute" means a dispute where the person against whom a complaint has been made, denies or disputes the allegations contained in the complaint;

(f) "defect" means any fault, imperfection or shortcoming in the quality, quantity, potency purity or standards which is required to be maintained by or under any law for the time being in force as is claimed by the trader in any manner whatsoever in relation to any goods;

(g) "deficiency" means any fault, imperfection, shortcoming or inadequacy in the quality, nature and manner of performance which is required to be maintained by or under any law for the time being in force or has been undertaken to be performed by a person in pursuance of a contract or otherwise in relation to any service;

(h) "Divisional Forum" means a Consumer Disputes Redressal Forum established under clause (a) of section 7;

(i) "goods" means goods as defined in the Jammu and Kashmir Sale of Goods Act Samvat 1996;

(j) "government" means the Government of Jammu and Kashmir;

(k) "manufacturer" means a person who—

(i) makes or manufactures any goods or parts thereof, or

(ii) does not make or manufacture any goods but assembles parts thereof made or manufactured by others and claims the end product to be goods manufactured by himself, or

(ii) puts or causes to be put his own mark on any goods made or manufactured by any other manufacturer and claims such goods to be goods made or manufactured by himself.

Explanation: Where a manufacturer despatches any goods or part thereof to any branch office maintained by him, such branch office shall not be deemed to be the manufacturer even though the parts so despatched to it are assembled at such branch office and are sold or distributed from such branch office;

(l) "notification" means a notification published in the Government Gazette;

(m) "person" includes:—

(i) a firm whether registered or not;

(ii) a Hindu undivided family;

(iii) a co-operative society;

(iv) every other association of persons whether registered under the Jammu and Kashmir Societies Registration Act, Samvat 1998 or not;

(n) "Prescribed" means prescribed by rules made by the Government under this Act;

(o) "Service" means service of any description which is made available to potential users and includes the provision of facilities in connection with banking, financing, insurance, transport, procession, supply of electrical or other energy, board or lodging of both, entertainment, amusement or the purveying a news or other information, under a contract of personal service;

(p) "State Commission" means a Consumer Disputes Redressal Commission established in the State under clause (b) of section 7;

(q) "trader" in relation to any goods means a person who sells or distributes any goods for sale and includes the manufacturer thereof, and where such goods are sold or distributed in package form; includes the packer thereof;

(r) "unfair trade practices" means a trade practice which, for the purpose of promoting the sale use or supply of any goods or for the provision of any services, adopts one or more of the following practices and thereby causes loss or injury to the consumers of such goods or services whether by eliminating or restricting competition or otherwise, namely:

(1) the practices of making any statement, whether orally or in writing or by visible representation which:—

(i) falsely represents that the goods are of a particular standard, quality, grade, composition, style or model;

(ii) falsely represents that the services are of a particular standard, quality or grade;

(iii) falsely represents any rebuilt, second hand, renovated reconditioned or old goods as new goods;

(iv) represents that the goods or services have sponsorship, approval, performance, characteristics, accessories, uses or benefits which such goods or services do not have;

(v) represents that the seller or the supplier has a sponsorship or approval or affiliation which such seller or supplier does not have;

(vi) makes a false misleading representation concerning the need for, or the usefulness of, any goods or services;

(vii) gives to the public any warranty or guarantee of the performance, efficacy or length of life of a product or of any goods that is not based on an adequate or proper test:

Provided that where a defence is raised to the effect that such warranty or guarantee is based on adequate or proper test; the burden of proof of such defence shall lie on the person raising such defences;

(viii) makes to the public a representation in a form that purports to be—

(i) a warranty or guarantee of a product or of any goods or services; or

(ii) a promise to replace, maintain or repair an article or any part thereof or to repeal or continue a service until it has achieved a specified result, if such purported warranty or guarantee or promise is materially misleading or if there is no reasonable prospect that such warranty, guarantee or promise will be carried out:

(ix) materially misleads the public concerning the price at which a product or like products or goods or services, have been, or are ordinarily sold or provided, and for this purpose, a representation as to price shall be deemed to refer to the price at which the product or goods or services has or have been sold by sellers or provided by suppliers generally in the relevant market unless it is clearly specified to be the price at which the product has been sold or services have been provided by the person by whom or on whose behalf the representation is made;

(x) gives false or misleading facts disparaging the goods, services or trade of another person.

Explanation: For the purposes of clause (l), a statement that is—

(a) expressed on an article offered or displayed for sale, or on its wràpper or container; or

(b) expressed on anything attached to, inserted in, or accompanying, an article offered or displayed for sale, or on anything on which the article is mounted for display or sale; or

(c) contained in or on anything that is sold, sent, delivered, transmitted or in any other manner whatsoever made available to a member of the public shall be deemed to be a statement made to the public by and only by the person who had caused the statement to be so expressed, made or contained.

(2) permits the publication of any advertisement whether in any newspaper or otherwise, for the sale or supply at a bargain price, of goods or services that are not intended to be offered for sale or supply at the bargain price, or for a period that is, and in quantities that are, reasonable, having regard to the nature of the market in which the business is carried and size of business and the nature of the advertisement.

Explanation: For the purpose of clause (2), bargaining price means—

(a) a price that is stated in any advertisement to be a bargain price, by reference to an ordinary price or otherwise, or

(b) a price that a person who reads, hears, or sees the advertisement, would reasonably understand to be a bargain price having regard to the prices at which the product advertised or like products are ordinarily sold;

(3) Permits—

(a) the offering of gifts, prizes or other terms with the intention of not providing them as offered or creating the impression that something is being given or offered free of charge when it is fully or partly covered by the amount charged in the transaction as a whole;

(b) the conduct of any contest, lottery, game of chance or skill, for the purpose ot promoting directly or indirectly, the sale, use or supply of any product or any business interest;

(4) permits the sale or supply of goods intended to be used, or are of a kind likely to be used by consumers knowing or having reason to believe that the goods do not comply with the standards prescribed by competent authority relating to performance, composition, contents, design, constrtictions, furnishing or packaging as are necessary to prevent or reduce the risk of injury to the person using the goods;

(5) permits the hoarding or destruction of goods, or refuses to sell the goods or to make them available for sale; or to provide any service, if such boarding or destruction or refusal raises or tends to raise or is intended to raise the cost of those or other similar goods or services.

3. Act not in Derogation of any other Law

The provisions of this Act shall be in addition to and not in derogation of the provisions of any other law for the time being in force.

CHATPER II

CONSUMER PROTECTION COUNCILS

4. The State Consumer Protection Council

(1) The Government may, by notificatin in the Government Gazette establish with effect from such date as it may specify in such notification a Council to be known as the State Consumer Protection Council (hereinafter referred to as the State Council).

(2) The State Council shall consists of the following members, namely:—

(a) the Minister in charge of the Depatment of Food and Civil Supplies in the Government, who shall be its Chairman, and

(b) such number of other official or non-official members representing such interests as may be prescribed.

5. Procedure for meetings of the State Council

(1) The State Council shall meet as and when necessary but not less than three meetings of the Council shall be held every year.

(2) The State Council shall meet at such time and place as the Chairman may think fit and shall observe such procedure in regard to the transaction of its business as may be prescribed.

6. Objects of the State Council

The objects of the State Council shall be to promote and protect the rights of the consumers such as:

(a) the right to be protected against the marketing of goods which are hazardous to life and property;
(b) the right to be informed about the quality, 'quantity, potency, purity, standard and price of goods so as to protect the consumer against unfair trade practices;
(c) the right to be assured, wherever possible, access to a variety of goods at competitive prices;
(d) the right to be heard and to be assured that consumer's interest will receive due consideration at appropriate forums;
(e) the right to seek redressal against unfair trade practices or unscrupulous exploitation of consumers;
(f) right to consumer education.

CHAPTER III

CONSUMER DISPUTES REDRESSAL AGENCIES

7. Establishment of Consumer Disputes Redressal Agencies

There shall be established for the purposes of this Act, the following agencies, namely:—

(a) a Consumer Disputes Redressal Forum to be known as the 'Divisional Forum' established by the Government in each division of the State;

(b) a Consumer Disputes Redressal Commission to be known as the "State Commission" established by the Government.

8. Composition of the Divisional Forum

Each Divisional Forum shall consist of:

(a) A person who is or has been, or is qualified to be a District Judge to be nominated by the Government to be its President;

(b) a person of eminence in the field of education, trade or commerce;

(c) a lady social worker.

(2) Every member of the Divisional Forum shall hold office for a term of five years or upto the age of 62 years whichever is earlier, and not be eligible for reappointment:

Provided that a member may resign his office in writing under his hand addressed to the Government and on such resignation being accepted, his office shall become vacant and may be filled by the appointment of person possessing any of the qualification mentioned in sub-section (1) in relation to the category of the member who has resigned.

(3) The salary or honorarium and other allowances payable to, and the other terms and conditions of service of the members of the Divisional Forum shall be such as may be prescribed by the Government.

9. Jurisdiction of the Divisional Forum

(1) Subject to the other provisions of this Act, the Divisional Forum shall have jurisdiction to entertain complaints where the value of the goods or serviccs and the compensation if any, claimed is less than rupees fifty thousand.

(2) A complaint shall be instituted in a Divisional Forum within the local limits of whose jurisdiction—

(a) the opposite party or each of the opposite parties, where there are more than one at the time of the institution of the complaint, actually and voluntarily resides or carries on business or personally works for gain, or

(b) any of the opposite parties, where there are more than one, at the time of the institution of the complaint, actually and voluntarily resides or carries on business, or personally works for gain, provided that in such case either the permission of the Divisional Forum is given or the opposite parties who do not reside or, carry on business, or personally work for gain, as the case may be, acquiesce in such institution, or

(c) the cause of action, wholly or in part, arises.

10. Manner in which complaints shall be made

A complaint in relation to any goods sold or delivered or any service provided may be filed with a Divisional Forum by—

(a) the consumer to whom such goods are sold or delivered or such services provided;

(b) any recognised consumer association, whether the consumer to whom the goods sold or delivered or service provided is a member of such association or not; or

(c) the Government:

Provided that in relation to District of Leh, Kargil, Poonch and Rajouri a complaint under this section may be filed with the concerned Deputy Commissioner who shall forward such complaints to the Divisional Forum having jurisdiction to entertain such complaint.

Explanation: For the purpose of the section "recognised consumer association" means any voluntary consumer association registered under the Companies Act, 1956 or any other law for the time being in force.

11. Procedure on receipt of complaint

(1) The Divisional Forum shall on receipt of a complaint, if it relates to any goods—

(a) refer a copy of the complaint to the opposite party mentioned in the complaint directing him to give his version of the case within a period of thirty days or such extended period not exceeding fifteen days as may be granted by the Divisional Forum;

(b) Where the opposite party on receipt of a complaint referred to him under clause (a) denies or disputes the allegations contained in the complaint, or omits or fails to take any action to represent his case within the time given by the Divisional Forum, the Divisional Forum shall proceed to settle the consumer dispute in the manner specified in clauses (c) to (g);

(c) where the complaint alleges a defect in the goods which cannot be determined without proper analysis or test of the goods the Divisional Forum shall obtain a sample of the goods from the complainant, seal it and authenticate in the manner prescribed and refer the sample so sealed to the appropriate laboratory along with a direction that such laboratory make an analysis or test, whichever may be necessary, with a view to finding out whether such goods suffer from any defect alleged in the complaint or suffer from any other defect and report its findings thereon to the Divisional Forum within a period of forty-five days of the receipt of the reference or within such extended period as may be granted by the Divisional Forum;

(d) before any sample of the goods is referred to any appropriate laboratory under clause (c), the Divisional Forum may require the complainant to deposit to the credit of the Forum such fees as may be specified for payment to the appropriate laboratory, for carrying out the necessary analysis or test in relation to the goods in question;

(e) the Divisional Forum shall remit the amount deposited to its credit under clause (d) to the appropriate laboratory, to enable it to carry out the analysis or test mentioned in clause (c) and on receipt of the report from the appropriate laboratory, the Divisional Forum shall forward a copy of the report along with such remarks as the Divisional Forum may feel appropriate to the opposite party;

(f) if any of the parties disputes the correctness of the findings of the appropriate laboratory, or disputes the correctness of the methods of analysis or test adopted by the appropriate laboratoy, the Divisional Forum shall require the opposite party or the complainant to submit in writing his objection in regard to the report made by the appropriate laboratory;

(g) the Divisional Forum shall thereafter give a reasonable opportunity to the complaint as well as the opposite party of being heard as to the correctness or otherwise of the report made by the appropriate laboratory and also as to the objection made in relation thereto under clause (f) and issue an appropriate order under section 12.

(2) The Divisional Forum shall, if the complaint received by it under section 10 relates to goods in receipt of which the procedure specified in sub-section (1) cannot be followed, or if the complaint relates to any service—

(a) refer a copy of such complaint to the opposite party directing him to give his version of the case within a period of thirty days or such extended period not exceeding fifteen days as may be granted by the Divisional Forum;

(b) where the opposite party on receipt of a copy of the complaint referred to him under clause (a) denies or disputes the allegations contained in the complaint or omits or fails to take any action to represent his case within the time given by the

Divisional Forum, the Divisional Forum shall proceed to settle the consumer disputes:—

(i) on the basis of evidence brought to its notice by the complainant and the opposite party, where the opposite patty denies or disputes the allegations contained in the complaint, or

(ii) on the basis of evidence brought to its notice by the complainant where the opposite party omits or fails to take any action to represent his case within the time given by the Forum.

(3) No proceedings complying with the procedure laid down in sub-section (1) and (2) shall be called in question in any court on the ground that the principles of natural justice have not been complied with.

(4) For the purposes of this section, the Divisional Forum shall have the same powers as are vested in a civil court under the Code of Civil Procedure, Samvat 1977 while trying a suit in respect of the following matters, namely—

(i) the summoning and enforcing the attendence of any defendant or witness and examining the witness on oath;

(ii) the discovery and production of any documents or other material object producible as evidence;

(iii) the reception of evidence on affidavits;

(iv) the requisitioning of the report of the concerned analysis or test from the appropriate laboratory or from any other relevant source;

(v) issuing of any commission for the examination of any witness; and

(vi) any other matter which may be prescribed.

(5) Every proceeding before the Divisional Forum shall be deemed to be a judicial proceeding within the meaning of sections 193 and 228 of the Ranbir Penal Code, and the Divisional Forum shall be deemed to be a civil court for the purposes of section 195 and Chapter XVII of the Code of Criminal Procedure, Samvat 1989.

12. Finding of the Divisional Forum

(1) If, after the proceeding conducted under section 11, the Divisional Forum is satisfied that the goods complained against suffer from any of the defects specified in the complaint or that any of the allegations contained in the complaint about the services are proved, it shall issue an order to the opposite party directing him to take one or more of the following things, namely:—

(a) to remove the defect pointed out by the appropriate laboratory from the goods in question;
(b) to replace the goods with new goods of similar description which shall be free from any defect;
(c) to return to the complainant the price, or, as the case may be the charges paid by the complainant;
(d) to pay such amount as may be awarded by it as compensation to the consumer for any loss or injury suffered by the consumer due to the negligence of the opposite party.

(2) Every order made by the Divisional Forum under sub-section (1) shall be signed by all the members constituting it and if there is any difference of opinion the order of the majority of the members constituting it shall be order of the Divisional Forum

(3) Subject to the foregoing provisions the procedure relating to the conduct of the meetings of the Divisional Forum, its sitting and other matters shall be such as may be prescribed by the Government.

13. Appeal

Any person aggrieved by an order made by the Divisional Forum may prefer an appeal against such order to the State Commission within a period of thirty days from the date of the order in such form and manner as may be prescribed:

Provided that the State Commission may entertain an appeal after the expiry of the said period of thirty days if it is satisfied that there was sufficient cause for not filling it within that period.

14. Composition of the State Commission

(1) Each State Commission shall consist of:—

(a) a person who is or has been a Judge of a High Court, appointed by the Government, who shall be its President;

(b) two other members, who shall be persons of ability, integrity and standing and have adequate knowledge or experience of or have shown capacity in dealing with problems relating to economics, law, commerce, accountancy, industry, public affairs, or administration, one of whom shall be a woman:

Provided that no sitting Judge of a High Court shall be appointed under this sub-section except after consultation with the Chief Justice of the Court.

(2) The salary or honorarium and other allowances payable to and the other terms and conditions of service (including tenure of office) of the members of the State Commission shall be such as may be prescribed by the Government.

15. Jurisdiction of the State Commission

Subject to the other provisions of this Act, the State Commission shall have jurisdiction—

(a) to entertain—

   (i) complaints where the value of the goods or services and compensation, if any, claimed exeeds rupees fifty thousand but does not exceed rupees ten lakhs, and

   (ii) appeals against the order of Divisional Forum within the State; and

(b) to call for the records and pass appropriate orders in any consumer dispute which is pending before or has been decided by any Divisional Forum within the State, where it appears to the State Commission that such Divisonal Forum has exercised a jurisdiction not vested in it by law, or has failed to exercise a jurisdiction so vested or has acted in exercise of its jurisdiction illegally or with material irregularity.

16. Procedure applicable to State Commission

The procedure specified in sections 10, 11 and 12 and under the rules made thereunder for the disposal of complaints by the Divisional Forum shall, with such modifications as may be necessary, be applicable to the disposal of disputes by the State Commission.

17. Appeal

Any person aggrieved by any order by the State Commission in exercise of its powers conferred by sub-clause (1) of clause (a) of section 15 may prefer an appeal against such order to the High Court within a period of thirty days from the date of the order in such form and manner as may be prescribed:

Provided that the High Court may entertain an appeal after the expiry of the said period of thirty days if it is satisfied that there was sufficient cause for not filing it within that period.

18. Finality of Orders

Every order of a Divisional Forum, or the State Commission shall if no appeal has been preferred against such order, under the provisions of this Act, be final.

19. Enforcement of Order by the Forum or the State Commission

Every order made by the Divisional Forum, or the State Commission may be enforced by the Divisional Forum, or the State Commission as the case may be in the same manner as if it were a decree or order made by a court in a suit pending therein and it shall be lawful for the Divisional Forum or the State Commission to send in the event of its inability to execute it, such order to the Court within the local limits of whose jurisdiction—

(a) in the case of an order against a company, the registered office of the company is situated, or

(b) in the case of an order against any other person, the place where the person concerned voluntarily resides or carries on business or personally works for gain, is situated,

and thereupon, the court to which the order is so sent, shall execute the order as if it were a decree or order sent to it for execution.

20. Dismissal of frivolous or vexatious complaints

Where a complaint instituted is found to be frivolous or vexatious, the Divisional Forum or as the case may be, the State Commission may dismiss the complaint.

21. Penalties

Where a trader or a person against whom a complaint made fails or omits to comply with any order made by the Divisional Forum or the State Commission, as the case may be, such trader or person shall be punishable with imprisonment for a term which shall not be less than one month but which may extend to three years, or with fine which shall not be less than two thousand rupees but which may extend to ten thousand rupees, or with both:

Provided that the Divisional Forum, or the State Commission, as the case may be, may if it is satisfied that the circumstances of any case so require, impose a sentence of imprisonment or fine, or both, for a term lesser than the minimum term and amount lesser than the minimum amount, specified in this section.

CHAPTER IV

MISCELLANEOUS

22. Protection of action taken in good faith

No suit, prosecution or other legal proceedings shall lie against the member of the 'Divisional Forum' or the State Commission or any Officer or person acting under the direction of the Divisional Forum or the State Commission for executing any order made by it or in respect of anything which is in good faith done or intended to be done by such member, officer or person under this Act, or under any rule or order made thereunder.

23. Power to remove difficulties

(1) If any difficulty arises in giving effect to the provisions of this Act the Government may, by order in the Government Gazette make such provisions not inconsistent with the provisions of this Act as appear to it to be necessary or expedient for removing the difficulty:

Provided that no such order shall be made after the expiry of a period of two years from the commencement of this Act.

(2) Every order made under this section shall as soon as may be after it is made, be laid before each House of the Stale Legislature.

24. Power to make rules

The Government may, by notification, make rules for carrying out the provisions contained in clause (b) of sub-section (2) of section 4, sub-section (2) of section 5, sub-section (3) of section 8, clause (c) of sub-section and clause (b) of sub-section (4) of section 11, sub-section 3 of section 12, section 13, sub-section (2) of section 14 of this Act.

25. Laying of rules

Every rule made by the Government under this Act shall be laid as soon as may be after it is made, before each House of State Legislature, while it is in session for a total period of thirty days which may be comprised in one session or in two or more successive sessions and if, before the expiry of the session immediately following the session or the successive sessions aforesaid both Houses agree in making any modification in the rule of both Houses agree that the rule should not be made, the rule shall thereafter have effect only in such modified form or be of no effect as the case may be so, however, that any such modification or annulment shall be without prejudice to the validity of anything previously done under that rule.

Appendix 3

THE JAMMU & KASHMIR CONSUMER PROTECTION RULES, 1987

SRO 86.—In exercise of the powers conferred by section 24 of the Jammu & Kashmir Consumer Protection Act, 1987 (Act No. XVI of 1987), the Government hereby make the following rules, namely:

1. Short title and commencement

(1) These rules may be called the Jammu & Kashmir Consumer Protection Rules, 1987.

(2) They shall come into force from the date of their publication in the Government Gazette.

2. Definition

In these rules unless the context otherwise requires:

(a) "Act" means the Jammu and Kashmir Consumer Protection Act, 1987;

(b) "Agent" means a person duly authorised by a party to present any complaint, appeal or reply on its behalf before the State Commission;

(c) "Appellant" mean a party which makes an appeal against the order of the Divisional Forum;

(d) "Chairman" means the Chairman of the State Consumer Protection Council established under section 4 of the Act;

(e) "Memorandum" means any memorandum of appeal filed by the appellant;

(f) "Opposite Party" means a person who answers complaint of claim;

(g) "Respondent" means a person who answers any memorandum of appeal;

(h) "Section" means section of the Act;

(i) "Words and expressions" used in the rules but not defined herein shall have the same meanings as assinged to them in the Act.

3. The Constitution of the State Consumer Protection Council

(1) The Government may by notification in the Government Gazette establish the State Consumer Protection Council which in addition to the Chairman shall consist of the following members, namely:

(a) The Minister of State for Food and Supplies Department—Vice-Chairman

(b) One Member from Legislative Assembly and three from Legislative Council—Members

(c) Three Representatives of Autonomous Organisations concerned with Consmer interests—Members

(d) Three Representatives of the Consumer Organisations or Consumers—Members

(e) Two Representatives of Women—Members

(f) Three Representatives of Farmers, Traders and Industrialists, one from each category—Members

(g) Three persons capable to represent Consumer interests not specified above—Members

(h) The Secretary to Goernment, Food and Supplies Department—Member-Secretary

4. Procedure of the State Council

(1) The State Council shall observe the following procedure in regard to the transaction of its business:

(a) The meeting of the State Council shall be presided over by the Chairman, in his absence by the Vice-Chairman, in the absence of the Chairman, and the Vice-Chairman the Council shall elect a member to preside over the meeting.

(b) Each meeting of the State Council shall be called by giving not less than ten days notice in writing to every member.

(c) The notice shall specify the place, the day, hour and statement of business to be transacted thereat.

(d) No proceedings of the State Council shall be held invalid merely by reasons of any, vacancy or defect in the constitution of the Council.

(e) For the purpose of performing its functions under the Act, the State Council may constitute from amongst its members, such working groups as it may deem necessary and every working group so constituted shall perform such functions as are assigned to it by the State Council. The findings of such working groups shall be placed before the State Council for its consideration.

(f) The non-official members shall be entitled to A—class to and fro Bus fare and an allowance of one hundred rupees per day for attending the meetings of the State Council or any working group. Members of Legislature shall be entitled to travelling and daily allowances at such rates as are admissible to such members under the Salaries and Allowances of Members of Jammu and Kashmir State Legislature Act, 1966.

(g) The resolution passed by the State Council shall be recommendatory in nature.

5. Term of office of the State Council

(i) The term of office of the members shall be three years.

(ii) Any member may, in writing under his hand addressed to the Chairman of the State Council, resign from the Council. The vacancies, so caused or otherwise, shall be filled up from the same category by the Government and such member shall hold office so long as the member in whose place he is appointed would have been entitled to hold office had the vacancy not occurred.

6. The Salary or honorarium and other allowance payable to the members of the Divisional Forum—

(i) Under sub-section (a) of section 8 where the President of the Divisional Forum is a sitting judge of the Session Court, he shall enjoy all the benefits which 'lie' should have enjoyed as sitting judge of the Session Court. Where the President is not a sitting judge of the Session Court, he shall receive an honorarium equivalent to the amount of salary as he was drawing at the time of his retirement minus the pension per month. Other members, if sitting on whole time basis, shall receive a consolidated honorarium of Rs. 1500 per month or if sitting on part time basis, a consolidation honorarium of Rs. 50 per day per sitting.

(ii) The President and the members shall be entitled to travelling and daily allowances on official tours at the same rates as are admissible to Class I Officers of the Government.

7. Terms and conditions of service of the President and Members of the Divisional Forum

(i) Prior to appointment, the President and the Members of the Divisional Forum shall have to give an undertaking to the effect that he does not and will not have any such financial or other interest as is likely to affect prejudicially his functions as such.

(ii) The President and the Members shall hold office for a period not exceeding 5 years or upto the age of (65 as provided) years whichever is earlier, but shall not eligible for reappointment.

(iii) Notwithstanding anything contained in sub-rule (ii) the President or a Member may—

(a) by writing under his hand address to the Government resign his office at any time; and
(b) be removed from his office in accordance with the provisions of rule 13.

(iv) The terms and conditions of service of the President and Members shall not be varied to their disadvantage during their tenure of office.

(v) A casual vacancy caused by resignation or removal of the President or any member of the Divisional Forum shall be filled by fresh appointment.

(vi) Where any such casual vacancy occurs in the office of the President of the Divisional Forum, the senior-most Member (in order of appointment) holding office for the time being, shall discharge the functions of the President until a person appointed to fill such vacancy assumes the office of the President of the Divisional Forum.

(vii) When the President of the Divisional Forum is unable to discharge the functions owing to absence, illness or any other cause, the senior-most Member (in order of appointment) shall discharge the functions of the President until the day on which the President assumes the charge of his functions.

(viii) No act or proceedings of the Divisional Forum shall be hold invalid by reason of any vacancy of its President or Member or any defect in the constitution thereof.

(ix) In case of a difference of opinion among the Members of the Divisional Forum, the opinion of the majority shall prevail.

(x) The President or any Member ceasing to hold office as such shall not hold any appointment in or be connected with the management or administration of an organisation which has been the subject of any proceedings under the Act during his tenure for a period of 5 years from the date on which he ceases to hold such office.

8. Manner prescribed under clause (c) of sub-section (i) of section 11

(1) Samples of goods for test or analysis shall be sent by the Divisional Forum by registered post in a sealed packet, enclsoed, together with a memorandum in Form 1. In an outer cover addressed to the ______________________.

(2) The packet as well as the outer cover, shall be marked with a disinguishing member.

(3) A copy of the memorandum in Form 1 and a specimen impression of the seal used to seal the packet shall be sent separately by registered post to the ____________.

(4) On receipt of the packet it shall be opened by an

officer authorised in writing in that behalf by the __________________ who shall record the condition of the seal on the packet.

(5) After test or analysis, the result of the test or analysis together with full protocols of the tests applied shall be supplied forthwith to the Divisional Forum in Form 2.

9. Procedure of the Divisional Forum

(i) Under sub-section (3) of section 12 of the Act, the office of the Divisional Forum shall be located in two divisions, i.e. Jammu/Kashmir. Working days and office hours of the Divisional Forum shall be the same as that of the State Government.

(ii) The Divisional Forum shall observe the following procedure in regard to the transaction of its business.

(iii) The meeting of the Divisional Forum shall be presided over by the President. In his absence the senior-most member (in order of appointment) shall preside over the meeting.

(iv) Each meeting of the Divisoinal Forum shall be called by giving not less than 10 days notice in writing to every member.

(v) The notice shall specify the place, the day, hour and statement of business to be transacted thereat.

10. Procedure for hearing the appeal

(i) Under section 13 of the Act memorandum shall be presented by the appellant or his agent to the State Commissoin in person or be sent by registered post addressed to the Commission.

(ii) Every memorandum filed under sub-rule (1) shall be in legible handwriting preferably, typed and shall set forth concisely under distinct heads, the grounds of appeal without any argument or narrative and such grounds shall be numbered consecutively.

(iii) Each memorandum shall be accompanied by a certified copy of the order of the Divisional Forum appealed against and such of the documents as may be required to support grounds of the memorandum.

(iv) When the appeal is presented after the expiry of

the period of limitation as specified in the Act, the memorandum of appeal shall be accompanied by an application supported by an affidavit setting forth the facts on which the appellant relies to satisfy the State Commission that he has sufficient cause for not preferring the appeal with the period of limitation.

(v) The appellant shall submit six copies of the memorandum of appeal to the Commission for official purpose.

(vi) On the date of hearing or on any other day to which hearing may be adjourned, it shall be obligatory for the parties or their agents to appear before the State Commission. If appellant or his agent fails to appear on such date, the State Commission may, on its discretion, either dismiss the appeal or decide *ex-parte* on merits. If the respondent or his agent fails to appear on such date, the State Commission shall proceed *ex-parte* and shall decide the appeal on merits of the case.

(vii) The appellant shall not, except by leave of the State Commission, argu or be heard in support of any objection not set forth in the memorandum but the State Commission, while deciding an appeal, may not confine to the grounds of objection set forth in the memorandum:

Provided that the Commission shall not rest its decision on any other ground other than those specified in the memorandum unless the party who may be affected thereby, has been given, an opportunity of being heard by the State Commission.

(viii) The State Commission, on such terms as it may think fit and at any stage, adjourn the hearing of the appeal, but not more than one adjournment shall ordinarily be given and the appeal should be decided as far as possible, within 90 days from the first date of hearing.

(ix) The order of the State Commission on appeal shall be signed and dated by the Members of the State Commission and shall be communicated to the parties free of charge.

11. Salaries, honorarium and other allowances of the President and Members of the State Commission

(i) Where the President of the State Commission is a sitting judge of the Hon'ble High Court, he shall enjoy all the benefits which he should have enjoyed as sitting judge of the Hon'ble High Court, where the President is not a sitting judge of High Court he shall receive an honorarium equivalent to the amount of salary as he was drawing as the time of his retirement minus the pension per month. Other Members, if sitting on whole time basis, shall receive a consolidated honorarium of Rs. 3,000 per month or if sitting on part time basis, a consolidated honorarium of Rs. 100 per day per sitting.

(ii) The President and the Members shall be entitled to travelling and daily allowances on official tours at the same rates as are admissible to class I officer of the Government.

(iii) The honorarium or the salary, as the case may be, and other allowances shall be defrayed out of the contingency fund of the Government.

12. Terms and conditions of service of the President and Members of the State Commission

(i) Prior to their appointment, the President and the Members of the State Commission shall have to give an undertaking to the effect that he does not and will not have any financial or other interests as is likely to affect prejudicially his functions as such.

(ii) The President and the Members shall hold office for a period not exceeding 5 years or such period as may be specified by the Government in the notification, but shall be eligible for reappointment:

Provided that the President or a Member shall not hold office as such for a total period exceeding 10 years or after he attains the age of 65 years whichever is earlier.

(iii) Notwithstanding anything contained in sub-rule (ii) the President or a Member may—

(a) by writing under his hand addressed to the Government resign his office at any time;

(b) be removed from his office in accordance with the provisions of rule 13.

(iv) The terms and conditions of service of the President and the Members shall not be varied to their disadvantage during their tenure of office.

(v) Any casual vacancy caused by resignation or removal of the President or any other member of the State Commission under sub-rule (3) or otherwise shall be filled of by fresh appointment.

(vi) Where any such casual vacancy occurs in the office of the President of the State Commission, the senior-most Member (in order of Appointment) holding office for the time being, shall discharge the functions of the President until a person appointed to fill such vacancy assumes the office of the President of the State Commission.

(vii) When the President of the State Commission is unable to discharge the functions owing to absence, illness or any other cause, the senior-most Member (in order of appointment) shall discharge the functions of the President until the day on which the President resumes the charge of his functions.

(viii) No act or proceedings of the State Commission shall be held invalid by reason of any vacancy of its President or Members or any defect in the constitution thereof.

(ix) In case of any difference of opinion among the members of the State Commission opinion of the majority shall prevail.

(x) The President or any Member ceasing to hold office as such shall not hold any appointment in or be connected with the management or administration of an organisation which has been the subject of any proceedings under the Act during his tenure for a period of 5 years from the date on which he ceases to hold such office.

13. Removal of President or members from office in certain circumstances

(i) The Government may remove from office, the President or any Member who—

(a) has been adjudged an insolvent; or

(b) has been convicted of an offence which in the

opinion of the Government involves moral turpitude; or

(c) has become physically or mentally incapable of acting as the President or the Member; or

(d) has acquired such financial or other interests as is likely to affect prejudicially his functions as the President or a Member; or

(e) has so abused his position as to render his continuance in office prejudicial to the public interest.

(ii) Notwithstanding anything contained in sub-rule (1) the President or any Member shall not be removed from his office on the grounds specified in clauses (d) and (e) of sub-rule except on an inquiry held by the Government in accordance with such procedure as it may specify in this behalf.

APPENDIX 4

THE CONSUMER PROTECTION (AMENDMENT) ACT, 1993, NO. 50 OF 1993*

An Act further to amend the Consumer Protection Act, 1986.

Be it enacted by Parliament in the Forty-fourth Year of the Republic of India as follows:

1. Short title and commencement

(1) This Act may be called the Consumer Protection (Amendment) Act, 1993.

(2) It shall be deemed to have come into force on the 18th day of June, 1993.

2. Amendment of Section 2

In section 2 of the Consumer Protection Act, 1986 (hereinafter referred to as the principal Act), in sub-section (1),—

"(i) the office of chairman, director or member or any statement,

(1) for clause (a), the following clause shall be substituted, namely:

(a) "appropriate laboratory means a laboratory or organisation—
(i) recognised by the Central Government;
(ii) recognised by a State Government, subject to such guidelines as may be prescribed by the Central Government in this behalf; or

---

* Received the assent of President on 27th August, 1993.

(iii) any such laboratory or organisation established by or under any law for the time being in force, which is maintained, financed or aided by the Central Government or a State Government for carrying out analysis or test of any goods with a view to determining whether such goods suffer from any defect;:

(2) after clause (a), the following clause shall be inserted, namely:

(aa) branch office means—

(i) any establishment described as a branch by the opposite party; or

(ii) any establishment carrying on either the same or substantially the same activity as that carried on by the head office of the establishment;;

(3) in clause (b), after sub-clause (iii), the following sub-clause shall be inserted, namely; (iv) one or more consumers, where there are numerous consumers having the same interest;

(4) In clause (c),—

(A) for sub-clause (i) the following sub-clause shall be substituted, namely:- (i) an unfair trade practice or a restrictive trade practice has been adopted by any trader;;

(B) in sub-clause (ii), for the words the goods mentioned in the complaint, the words "the goods bought by him or agreed to be bought by him" shall be substituted;

(C) in sub-clause (iii), for the words [the services mentioned in the complaint], the words [the services hired or availed of or agreed to be hired or availed of by him] shall be substituted;

(D) after sub-clause (iv), the following sub-clause shall be inserted, namely:

"(v) goods which will be hazardous to life and safety when used, are being offered for sale to the public in contravention of the provisions of any law for the time being in force requiring traders to display information in regard to the contents, manner and effect of use of such goods;

(5) in clause (d),—

(A) in sub-clause (ii), for the word "hires" in both the places where it occurs, the words "hires or avails" of shall be substituted;

(B) after sub-clause (ii), the following Explanation shall be substituted at the end, namely:

Explanation—For the purposes of sub-clause (i), "commercial purpose" does not include use by a consumer of goods bought and used by him exclusively for the purpose of earning his livelihood, by means of self-employment;

(6) in clause (f), after the words "for the time being in force or" the words "under any contract, express or implied, or" shall be inserted;

(7) after clause (j), the following clause shall be inserted, namely:

'(jj) "member" includes the President and a member of the National Commission or a State Commission or a District Forum, as the case may be;';

(8) after clause (n), the following clause shall be inserted, namely:

'(nn) "restrictive trade practice" means any trade practice which requires a consumer to buy, hire or avail of any goods or, as the case may be, services as a condition precedent for buying, hiring or availing of other goods or services;';

(9) in clause (o), after the words "board or lodging or both", the words "housing construction", shall be inserted;

(10) for clause (r), the following clause shall be substituted, namely:

(r) "unfair trade practice" means a trade practice which, for the purpose of promoting the sale, use or supply of any goods or for the provision of any service, adopts any unfair method or unfair or deceptive practice including any of the following practices, namely:

(1) the practice of making any statement, whether writing or by visible representation which,—

(i) falsely represents that the goods are of a particular standard, quality, quantity, grade, composition, style or model;

(ii) falsely represents that the services are of a particular standard, quality or grade;

(iii) falsely represents any re-built, second-hand renovated, reconditioned or old goods as new goods;

(iv) represents that the goods or services have sponsorship, approval, performance, characteristics, accessories, uses or benefits which such goods or services do not have;

(v) represents that the seller or the supplier has a sponsorship or approval or affiliation which such seller or supplier does not have;

(vi) makes a false or misleading representation concerning the need for, or the usefulness of, any goods or services;

(vii) gives to the public any warranty or guarantee of the performance, efficacy or length of life of a product or of any goods that is not based on an adequate or proper test thereof:

Provided that where a defence is raised to the effect that such warranty or guarantee is based on adequate or proper test the burden of proof of such defence shall lie on the person raising such defence;

(viii) makes to the public a representation in a form that purports to be—

(i) a warranty or guarantee of a product or of any goods or services; or

(ii) a promise to replace, maintain or repair an article or any part thereof or to repeat or continue a service until it has achieved a specified result, if such purported warranty or guarantee or promise is materially misleading or if there is no reasonable prospect that such warranty, guarantee or promise will be carried out;

(ix) materially misleads the public concerning the price at which a product or like products or goods or services, have been or are, ordinarily sold or provided, and for this purpose, a representation as to price shall be deemed to refer to the price at which the product or goods or services has or have been sold by sellers or provided by suppliers generally in the relevant market unless it is clearly specified to be the price at which the product has been sold or services have been provided by the person by whom or on whose behalf the representation is made; and

(x) gives false or misleading facts disparaging the goods, services or trade of another person.

Explanation.—For the purposes of clause (1), a statement that is—

(a) expressed on an article offered or displayed for sale, or on its wrapper or container; or

(b) expressed on anything attached to, inserted in, or

accompanying, an article offered or displayed for sale, or on anything on which the article is mounted for display or sale; or

(c) contained in or on anything that is sold, sent, delivered, transmitted or in any other manner whatsoever made available to a member of the public,

shall be deemed to be a statement made to public by, and only by, the person who had caused the statement to be so expressed, made or contained;

(2) permits the publication of any advertisement whether in any newspaper or otherwise, for the sale or supply at a bargain price, of goods or services that are not intended to be offered for sale or supply at the bargain price, or for a period that is, and in quantities that are, reasonable, having regard to the nature of the market in which the business is carried on, the nature and size of business, and the nature of the advertisement.

Explanation.—For the purposes of clause (2), bargaining price means—

(a) a price that is stated in any advertisement to be a bargain price, by reference to an ordinary price or otherwise; or

(b) a price that a person who reads, hears or sees the advertisement, would reasonably understand to be a bargain price having regard to the practice at which the product advertised or like products are ordinarily sold;

(3) Permits—

(a) the offering of gifts, prizes or other items with the intention of not providing them as offered or creating impression that something is being given or offered free of charge when it is fully or partly covered by the amount charged in the transaction as a whole;

(b) the conduct of any contest lottery, game of chance or skill, for the purpose of promoting directly or indirectly the sale, use or supply of any product or any business interest;

(4) permits the sale or supply of goods intended to be used, or are of a kind likely to be used by consumers knowing or having reason to believe that the goods do not comply with the standards prescribed by competent authority relating to performance, composition, contents, design, constructions, finishing or packaging as are necessary to prevent or reduce the risk of injury to the person using the goods;

(5) permits the hoarding or destruction of goods, or refuses to sell the goods or to make them available for sale or to provide any service, if such hoarding or destruction or refusal raises or tends to raise or is intended to raise the cost of those or other similar goods or services.

3. Amendment of section 4

In section 4 of the principal Act, in sub-section (2), in clause (a), for the words the Department of Food and Civil Supplies, the words consumer affairs shall be substituted.

4. Amendment of section 5

In section 5 of the principal Act, in sub-section (1), for the words "not less than three meetings", the words at least one meeting shall be substituted.

5. Amendment of section 6

In section 6 of the principal Act,—

(i) in clause (a), after the word "goods", the words "and services" shall be inserted,

(ii) in clause (b), after the word "goods", the words "or services, as the case may be", shall be inserted;

(iii) in clause (c), after the word "goods", the "words and services" shall be inserted;

(iv) in clause (e), after the words "unfair trade practices", the words "or restrictive trade practices" shall be inserted.

6. Amendment of section 7

In section 7 of the principal Act, for sub-section (2), the following sub-sections shall be substituted, namely:

"(2) The State Council shall consist of the following members, namely:

(a) the Minister in-charge of consumer affairs in the State Government who shall be its Chairman;
(b) such number of other official or non-official members representing such interests as may be prescribed by the State Government.

(3) The State Council shall meet as and when necessary but not less than two meetings shall be held every year.

(4) The State Council shall meet at such time and place as the Chairman may think fit and shall observe such procedure in regards to the transaction of its business as may be prescribed by the State Government."

7. Amendment of section 9

In section 9 of the principal Act,—

(1) in clause (a),—
   (i) the words "with the prior approval of the Central Government" shall be omitted;
   (ii) the following proviso shall be inserted at the end, namely:
   "Provided that the State Government may, if it deems fit, establish more than one District Forum in a district.";
(2) in clause (b), the words "with the prior approval of the Central Government" shall be omitted.

8. Amendment of section 10

In section 10 of the principal Act, (1) for sub-section (1), the following sub-section shall be substituted, namely:

"(1) Each District Forum shall consist of—

(a) a person who, is, or has been, or is qualified to be a District Judge, who shall, be its President;

(b) two other members, who shall be persons of ability, integrity and standing, and have adequate knowledge or experience of, or have shown capacity in dealing with, problems relating to economics, law, commerce, accountancy, industry, public affairs or administration, one of whom shall be a woman.";

(2) after sub-section (1), the following sub-sections shall be inserted, namely:

"(lA) Every appointment under sub-section (1) shall be made by the State Government on the recommendation of a selection committee consisting of the following, namely:

(i) President of the State Commission—Chairman.

(ii) Secretary, Law Department of the State—Member.

(iii) Secretary incharge of the Department dealing with consumers in the State—Member.

9. Amendment of section 11

In section 11 of the principal Act,—

(1) in sub-section (1), for the words "is less than rupees one lakh", the words "does not exceed rupees five lakhs" shall be substituted;

(2) in sub-section (2),—

(i) in clause (a), for the words "carries on business or", the words "carries on business or has a branch office or" shall be substituted;

(ii) in clause (b),—

(A) for the words "carries on business", the words "carries on business or has a branch office" shall be substituted;

(B) for the words "carry on business", the words "carry on business or have a branch office" shall be substituted.

10. Substitution of new section for section 12

For section 12 of the principal Act, the following section shall be substituted, namely:

'**12. Manner in which complaint shall be made.**—A complaint in relation to any goods sold or delivered or agreed to be sold or delivered or any service provided or agreed to be provided may be filed with a District Forum by—

(a) the consumer to whom such goods are sold or delivered or agreed to be sold or delivered or such service provided or agreed to be provided;
(b) any recognised consumer association whether the consumer to whom the goods sold or delivered or agreed to be sold or delivered or service provided or agreed to be provided is a member of such association or not;
(c) one or more consumers, where there are numerous consumers having the same interest, with the permission of the District Forum, on behalf of, or for the benefit of all consumers so interested; or
(d) the Central or the State Government.

Explanation.—For the purpose of this section, "recognised consumer association" means any voluntary consumer association registered under the Companies Act, 1956 (1 of 1956) or any other law for the time being in force.

11. Amendment of section 13

In section 13 of the principal Act, after sub-section (5), the following sub-sections shall be inserted, namely:

"(6) Where the complainant is a consumer referred to in sub-clause (iv) of clause (b) of sub-section (1) of section 2, the provisions of rule 8 of Order I of the First Schedule to the Code of Civil Procedure, 1908 (5 of 1908) shall apply subject to the modification that every reference therein to a suit or decree shall be construed as a reference to a complaint or the order of the District Forum thereon."

12. Amendment of section 14

In section 14 of the principal Act, in sub-section (1),—

(i) in the opening portion, for the word "take", the word "do" shall be substituted;

(ii) after clause (d), the following clauses shall be inserted, namely:

"(e) to remove the defects or deficiencies in the service in question;

(f) to discontinue the unfair trade practice or the restrictive trade practice or not to repeat them;

(g) not to offer the hazardous goods for sale;

(h) to withdraw the hazardous goods from being offered for sale;

(i) to provide for adequate costs to parties."

13. Amendment of section 16

In section 16 of the principal Act, in sub-section (1),—

(i) in clause (a), the following proviso shall be inserted, at the end, namely:

"Provided that no appointment under this clause shall be made except after consultation with the Chief justice of the High Court;";

(ii) after clause (b), for the proviso, the following proviso shall be substituted, namely:

"Provided that every appointment under this clause shall be made by the State Government on the recommendation of a selection committee consisting of the following, namely:

(i) President of the State Commission—Chairman,

(ii) Secretary of the Law Department of the State—Member,

(iii) Secretary incharge of the Department dealing with consumers affairs in the State—Member.";

(iii) in sub-section (2), the brackets and words (including tenure of office) shall be omitted;

(iv) after sub-section (2), the following sub-sections shall be inserted, namely:

"(3) Every member of the State Commission shall hold office for a term of five years or upto the age of sixty-seven years, whichever is earlier and shall be eligible for re-appointment.

(4) Notwithstanding anything contained in sub-section (3), a person appointed as a President or as a member before the commencement of the Consumer Protection (Amendment) Act, 1993, shall continue to hold such office as President or member, as the case may be, till the completion of his term."

14. Amendment of section 17

In section 17 of the principal Act, in clause (a), in sub-clause (i), for the words "one lakh but does not exceed rupees ten lakhs" the words "five lakhs but does not exceed rupees twenty lakhs" shall be substituted.

15. Amendment of section 18

In section 18 of the principal Act, for the words and figures "The procedure specified in sections 12, 13 and 14 and under the rules made thereunder", the words and figures "The provisions of sections 12, 13 and 14 and the rules made thereunder" shall be substituted.

16. Amendment of section 20

In section 20 of the principal Act:

(i) in sub-section (1),—

(A) in clause (a), the following proviso shall be inserted, at the end, namely:
"Provided that no appointment under this clause shall be made except after consultation with the Chief justice of India";

(B) after clause (b), for the proviso, the following proviso shall be substituted, namely:
"Provided that every appointment under this clause shall be made by the Central Government on the recommendation of a selection committee consisting of the following, namely:

(a) a person who is a judge of the Supreme Court, to be nominated by the Chief Justice of India—Chairman,

(b) the Secretary in the Department of Legal Affairs in the Government of India—Member,

(c) Secretary of the Department dealing with consumers affairs in the Government of India—Members";

(ii) in sub-section (2), the brackets and words (including tenure of office) shall be omitted;

(iii) after sub-section (2), the following sub-sections shall be inserted, namely:

"(3) Every member of the National Commission shall hold office for a term of five years or upto the age of seventy years, whichever is earlier and shall not be eligible for re-appointment.

(4) Notwithstanding anything contained in sub-section (3), a person appointed as a President or as a member before the commencement of the Consumer Protection (Amendment) Act, 1993, shall continue to hold such office as President or member, as the case may be, till the completion of his term."

17. Amendment of section 21

In section 21 of the principal Act, in clause (a), in sub-clause (i), for the words "ten lakhs", the words "twenty lakhs" shall be substituted.

18. Substitution of new section for section 22

For section 22 of the principal Act, the following section shall be substituted, namely:

"**22. Power of and procedure applicable to the National Commission.**—The National Commission shall, in the disposal of any complaints or any proceedings before it, have—

(a) the powers of a civil court as specified in sub-sections (4), (5) and (6) of section 13;

(b) the power to issue an order to the opposite party directing him to do any one or more of the things referred to in clauses (a) to (j) of sub-section (1) of section 14,

and follows such procedure as may be prescribed by the Central Government.

19. Insertion of new sections 24A and 24B

After sections 24 of the principal Act, the following sections shall be inserted, namely:

"**24A Limitation period.**—(1) The District Forum, the State Commission or the National Commission shall not admit a complaint unless it is filed within two years from the date on which the cause of action has arisen.

(2) Notwithstanding anything contained in sub-section (1), a complaint may be entertained after the period specified in sub-section (1), if the complainant satisfies the District Forum, the State Commission or the National Commission, as the case may be, that he had sufficient cause for not filing the complaint within such period:
Provided that no such complaint shall be entertained unless the National Commission, the State Commission or the District Forum as the case may be, records its reasons for condoning such delay.

24B. Administrative control.—(1) The National Commission shall have administrative control over all the State Commissions in the following matters, namely:

(i) calling for periodical returns regarding the institution disposal, pendency of cases;
(ii) issuance of instruction regarding adoption of uniform procedure in the hearing of matters, prior service of copies of documents produced by one party to the opposite parties, furnishing of English

translation of judgements writen in any language, speedy grant of copies of documents;

(iii) generally overseeing the functioning of the State Commissions or the District Forum to ensure that the objects and purpose of the Act are best served without in any way interfering with their quasi-judical freedom.

(2) The State Commission shall have administrative control over all the District Forum within its jurisdiction in all matters referred to in sub-section (1).

20. Substitution of new section for section 26

For section 26 of the principal Act, the following section shall be substituted, namely:

"26. Dismissal of frivolous or vexatious complaints.— Where a complaint instituted before the District Forum, the State Commission or, as the case may be, the National Commission is found to be frivolous or vexatious, it shall, for reasons to be recorded in writing, dismiss the complaint and make an order that the complainant shall pay to the opposite party such cost, not exceeding ten thousand rupees, as may be specified in the order."

21. Amendment of section 27

In section 27 of the principal Act,—

(a) after the words "against whom a complaint is made", the words "or the complainant" shall be inserted.

(b) after the words "such trader or person", the words "or complainant" shall be inserted.

22. Amendment of section 30

In section 30 of the principal Act,—

(a) sub-section (1), after the words "the provisions contained in", the words, "brackets, letter and figures" clause (a) of sub-section (1) of section 2 shall be inserted;

(b) in sub-section (2), after the words "the provisions contained in", the words, "brackets letter and figures clauses (b) of sub-section (2) and sub-section (4) of section 7" shall be inserted.

23. Repeal and saving

(1) The Consumer Protection (Amendment) Ordinance, 1993 (Ord. 24 of 1993) is hereby repealed.

(2) Notwithstanding such repeal, anything done or any action taken under the principal Act as amended by the said Ordinance shall be deemed to have been done or taken under the principal Act as amended by this Act.

Appendix 5

THE JAMMU AND KASHMIR CONSUMER PROTECTION (AMENDMENT) ACT, 1997

(Act No. XIX of 1997)

CHATPER I

PRELIMINARY

An Act to amend the Jammu and Kashmir Consumer Protection Act, 1987.

1. Short title

This Act may be called the Jammu and Kashmir Consumer Protection (Amendment) Act, 1997.

2. Amendment of section 2, Act XVI of 1987

In section 2 of the Jammu and Kashmir Consumer Protection Act, 1987 (hereinafter referred to as the principal Act),—

(1) after clause (a), the following clause shall be inserted, namely:

"(aa) "branch office" means—

(i) any establishment described as a branch by the opposite party; or

(ii) any establishment carrying on either the same or substantially the same activity as that carried on by the head office of the establishment";

(2) in clause (b), after sub-clause (iii), the following sub-clause shall be inserted, namely:—

"(iv) one or more consumers, where there are numerous consumers having the same interests."

(3) in clause (c),

(A) for sub-clause (i), the following sub-clause shall be substituted, namely:—

"(i) an unfair trade practice or a restrictive trade practice has been adopted by any trader,";

(B) in sub-clause (ii), for the words "the goods mentioned in the complaint", the words, "the goods bought by him or agreed to be bought by him" shall be substituted;

(C) in sub-clause (iii), for the words "the services mentioned in the complaint", the words "the services hired or availed of or agreed to be hired or availed of by him" shall be substitued;

(D) after sub-clause (iv), the folowing sub-clause shall be inserted, namely:—

"(v) goods which will be hazardous to life and safety when used, are being offered for sale to the public in contravention of the provisions of any law for the time being in force requiring traders to display information in regard to the contents, manner and effect of use of such goods";

(4) in clause (d),

(A) in sub-clause (ii), for the word "hires", in both the places where it occurs, the words "hires or avails of" shall be substituted;

(B) after sub-clause (ii), the following Explanation shall be inserted at the end, namely:—

"*Explanation*.—For the purposes of sub-clause (i), "commercial purpose" does not include use by a consumer of goods bought and used by him exclusively for the purposes of earning his livelihood, by means of self-employment";

(5) in clause (f) after the words "for the time being in force" the words "under any contract, express or implied, order or" shall be inserted;

(6) after clause (k), the following clause shall be inserted, namely:—

"(kk) "member" includes the President and a member of the State Commission or a Divisional Forum as the case may be,"

(7) after clause (n), the following clause shall be inserted, namely:—

"(nn) "restrictive trade practice" means any trade practice which requires a consumer to buy, hire or avail of any goods or, as the case may be, services as a condition precedent for buying, hiring or availing of other goods or services,";

(8) in clause (o), after the words "board or lodging or both", the words "housing construction", shall be inserted;

(9) in the opening portion of clause (r), for the words "adopts one or more of the following practices and thereby causes loss or inquiry to the consumers of such goods or services, whether by eliminating or restricting competition or otherwise", the words "adopts any unfair method or unfair or deceptive practice including any of the following practices" shall be substituted.

3. Amendment of section 6, Act XVI of 1987

In section 6 of the principal Act,—

(i) in clause (a), after the word "goods", the words "and services" shall be inserted;
(ii) in clause (b), after the word "goods" the words "or services, as the case may be", shall be inserted;
(iii) in clause (c), after the word "goods", the words "and services" shall be inserted;
(iv) in clause (d), after the words "unfair trade practices", the words "or restrictive trade practices" shall be inserted.

4. Insertion of section 6-A in Act XV of 1987

After section 6 of the principal Act, the following section shall be inserted, namely:—

"6-A. Composition of District Consumer Protection

Council.—(1) The Government may, by notification in the Government Gazette establish with effect from such date as it may specify in such notification, a Council to be known as the District Consumer Protection Council, which hereinafter shall be referred to as District Council.

(2) The District Council shall consist of the following members, namely:—

(a) Deputy Commissioner of the District, who shall be its Chairman; and

(b) such number of other official or non-official members representing such interests as may be prescribed.

(3) The District Council shall meet as and when necesary, but not less than four meetings of the Council shall be hold every year.

(4) The objects of the District Council shall be the same as that of State Council."

5. Amendment of section 8, Act XVI of 1987

In section 8 of the principal Act,—

(i) in sub-section (1), for clauses (b) and (c), the following shall be substituted, namely:—

"(b) the two members who are persons of ability, integrity and standing and have adequate knowledge or experience of dealing with problems relating to economics, law, commerce, accountancy, industry, public affairs or administration, one of whom to be preferably a lady";

(2) after sub-section (1), the following sub-section shall be inserted, namely:—

"(1-A) Every appointment under sub-section (1) shall be made by the Government on the recommendation of a Selection Committee consisting of the following, namely:—

(i) The President of the State Commission—Chairman
(ii) The Secretary to Government, Law Department—Member
(iii) The Secretary to Government, Food, Supplies and Transport Department (Incharge Consumer Affairs)—Member".

(3) in sub-section (3), after the words "terms and conditions of service" the words "including tenure of office" shall be inserted.

6. Amendment of section 9, Act XVI of 1987

In section 9 of the principal Act,—

(1) in sub-section (1) for the words "rupees fifty thousand" the words "does not exceed rupees five lakhs" shall be substituted;

(2) in sub-section (2),—

(i) in clause (a), for the words "carries on business" the words "carries on business directly or through a branch office" shall be substituted;
(ii) in clause (b) for the words "carries on business" both places where it occurs the words "carry on business directly or through a branch office" shall be substituted.

7. Amendment of section 10, Act XVI of 1987

For section 10 of the principal Act, the following shall be substituted, namely:—

"**10. Manner in which complaint shall be made.**—Complaint in relation to any goods sold or delivered or agreed to be sold or delivered or any service provided or agreed to be provided may be filed with a Divisional Forum by,—

(a) the consumer to whom such goods are sold or delivered or agreed to be sold or delivered or such service provided or agreed to be provided;
(b) any recognised consumer association whether the consumer to whom the goods sold or delivered or

agreed to be sold or delivered or services provided or agreed to be provided is a member of such association or not;

(c) one or more consumers where there are nmerous consumers having the same interest, with the permission of the Divisional Forum on behalf of or for the benefit of all consumers so interested;

(d) the Government,

Explanation.—For the purposes of the section "recognised consumer association" means any voluntary association under the Companies Act, 1956 or any other law for the time being in force."

8. Amendment of section 11 of Act XVI of 1987

In section 11 of the principal Act, after sub-section (5) the following sub-section shall be inserted, namely:—

"(6) Where the complainant is a consumer referred in sub-clause (iv) of Clause (b) of sction 2, the provisions of rule 8 of Order 1 of the First Schedule to the Code of Civil Procedure, Samvat 1977 shall apply subject to the modification that every reference therein to suit or decree shall be construed as a reference to a complaint or the order of the Divisional Forum thereon."

9. Amendment of section 12, Act XVI of 1987

In section 12 of the principal Act,—

(1) in sub-section (1),

(i) in the opening portion, for the word "take" the word "do" shall be substituted;

(ii) after clause (d), the following clauses shall be inserted, namely:—

"(e) to remove the defects or deficiencies in the services in question;

(f) to discontinue the unfair trade practice or the restrictive trade practice or not to repeat them;

(g) not to offer the hazardous goods for sale;

(h) to withdraw the hazardous goods from being offered for sale;

(i) to provide for adequate costs to parties";

(2) for sub-section (2), the following sub-section shall be substituted, namely:—

"(2) Every order made by the Divisional Forum under sub-section (1) shall be signed by the majority of members constituting it and it shall be deemed to be the order of the Divisional Consumer Forum:

Provided that where the proceeding is conducted by the President and one member and they differ on any points, they shall state the point or points on which they differ and refer the same to the other member for hearing on such point or points and the opinion of the majority shall be the order of the Divisional Forum."

10. Amendment of section 13, Act XVI of 1987

In section 13 of the principal Act, the following proviso shall be inserted at the end, namely:—

"Provided further that no appeal shall lie unless the memorandum of appeal is accompanied by a certificate issued by the President of Divisional Forum to the effect that appellant has deposited with him 25% of the amounts payable under the order."

11. Amendment of section 14, Act XVI of 1987

Clause (b) of sub-section (1) of section 14 and provisio thereto of the principal Act, shall be substituted by the following, namely:—

"(b) two or more members who shall be persons of ability, integrity and having adeuate knowledge of law and experience in law and consumer affairs:

Provided that every appointment made under this section shall be made by the Government on the recommendation of the Selection Committee consisting of the following, namely:—

(i) Chief Secretary—Chairman

(ii) Secretary to Government, Law Department—Member

(iii) Secretary to Government, Food and Supplies Department (Incharge Consumer Affairs)—Member."

12. Amendment of section 15, Act XVI of 1987

In sub-clause (i) of clause (a) of section 15 of the principal Act, for the words "rupees fifty thousand" and "rupees ten lakhs" the words "rupees five lakhs" and "rupees thirty lakhs" shall respectively be substituted.

13. Insertion of section 16-A in Act XVI of 1987

After section 16 of the principal Act, the following section shall be inserted, namely:—

"**16-A. Validity of orders.**—Notwithstanding anything contained in section 16 no order passed by the State Commission and Divisional Forum shall be called in question simply on the ground that it has not been signed by all the members of the Divisional Forum or the State Commission, as the case may be, and all such orders shall be and shall always be deemed to have been validly passed if signed by the majority of the members."

14. Amendment of section 17, Act XVI of 1987

In section 17 of the principal Act, for the existing proviso, the following provisos shall be substituted, namely:—

"Provided that such appeal shall be heard by not less than two Judges of the High Court:

Provided further that the High Court may entertain an appeal after the expiry of the said period of thirty days if it is satisfied that there was sufficient cause for not filing it within that period:

Provided also that no appeal shall lie unless the memorandum of appeal is accompanied by a certificate issued by the Chairman, State Commission to the effect that the appellant has deposited 25% of the amount payable under the order."

15. Insertion of section 18-A in Act XVI of 1987

After section 18 of the principal Act, the following section shall be inserted, namely:—

"**18-A. Limitation period.**—(1) The Divisional Forum or the State Commission may not admit a complaint unless it is filed within two years from the date on which the cause of action arises.

(2) Notwithstanding anything contained in sub-section (1), a complaint may be entertained after the period specified in sub-section (1) if the complainant satisfies the Divisional Forum or the State Commission, as the case may be, that he had sufficient cause for not filing the complaint within such period:

Provided that no such complaint shall be entertained unless the Divisional Forum or the State Commission, as the case may be, records its reason for condoning such delay."

16. Substitution of section 20, Act XVI of 1987

For section 20 of the principal Act, the following section shall be substituted, namely:—

"**20. Dismissal of frivolous or vexatious complaints.**— Where a complaint instituted before the Divisional Forum or the State Commission, as the case may be, is found to be frivolous or vexatious, it shall, for reasons to be recorded in writing, dismiss the complaint and make an order that the complainant shall pay to the opposite party such cost, not exceeding ten thousand rupees, as may be specified in the order."

17. Amendment of section 21, Act XVI of 1987

In section 21 of the principal Act, for the words "against whom a complaint made" the words "against whom a complaint is made or the complainant" shall be substituted.

18. Insertion of section 23-A in Act XVI of 1987

After section 23 of the principal Act, the following section shall be inserted, namely:—

"**23-A. Vacancies or defects in appointment not to invalidate orders.**—No act or proceeding of the Divisional Forum or the State Commission, as the case may be, shall be invalid by reason only of the existence of any vacancy amongst its members or any defect in the constitution thereof."

APPENDIX 6

THE JAMMU AND KASHMIR CONSUMER PROTECTION (AMENDMENT) BILL, 2002.

(L.A. BILL NO. 10 OF 2002.)

A Bill to amend the Jammu and Kashmir Consumer Protection Act, 1987.

STATEMENT OF OBJECTS AND REASONS

The Jammu and Kashmir Consumer Protection Act, 1987 provides for the establishment of a State Commission and two Divisional Forums. But majority of the population is concentrated in rural areas who face a lot of inconvenience in getting their grievances redresed at the Divisional Forums. More importantly, the number of cases is too enormous for the Divisional Forums to dispose of within the stipulated period of 90 days. This has necessitated the establishment of Consumer Redressal agencies at the District Headquarters so that the poor people living in far flung areas can have easier access to these forums and can seek speedy redressal of their grievances. It may be relevant to mention that Consumer Redressal agencies have been established in almost all the Districts of neighbouring States.

1. Short title and commencement

(1) This Act may be called the Jammu and Kashmir Consumer Protection (Amendment) Act, 2002.

(2) It shall come into force from the date of its publication in the Government Gazette.

2. Amendment of section 2, Act XVI of 198

For clauses (h) and (kk) of section 2 of the Jammu and Kashmir Consumer Protection Act, 1987 (hereinafter referred to as 'the principal Act'), the following clauses shall be substituted, namely:—

(h) "District Forum" means a Consumer Disputes Redressal Forum established under clause (a) of section 7; and

(kk) "member" includes the President and a member of the State Commission or a District Forum as the case may be."

3. Amendment of section 7, Act XVI of 1987

In section 7 of the principal Act, for clause (a) the following clause shall be substituted, namely:—

"(a) A Consumer Disputes Redressal Forum to be known as the District Forum established by the Government in each district of the State:
Provided that the Government may establish Additional District Forum in any district."

4. Substitution of section 8, Act XVI of 1987

In section 8 of the principal Act, the following section shall be substituted, namely:—

"8. **Composition of the District Forum.**—(1) Each District Forum shall consist of—

(a) District and Sessions Judge or Additional District and Sessions Judge, having territorial jurisdiciton, who shall be its *ex-officio* President:
Provided that the Government may appoint any other person, who is or has been a District Judge, to be President of a District Forum; and

(b) two membes to be nominated from amongst persons of ability and integrity, having adequate knowledge or experience of dealing with problems relating to economics, law, commerce, accountancy, industry, public affairs or administration by the Government: Provided that one of the nominated members shall preferably be a lady.

(2) Every appointment under clause (b) of sub-section (1) shall be made by the Government on the recommendation of Selection Committee consisting of the following, namely:—

(a) President of the District Forum—Chariman
(b) Deputy Commissioner of the District—Member
(c) President District Bar Association—Member

(3) The Selection Committee under sub-section (2) shall prepare a panel of three names for nomination of every such member.

(4) Every nominated member of the District Forum shall hold office for a term of three years or up to the age of 65 years whichever is earlier:

Provided that a member may resign from his office in writing under his hand addressed to the President concerned and on such resignation being accepted, his office shall become vacant.

(5) Each nominated member shall be entitled to such honorarium as may be prescribed."

5. Amendment of section 9, Act XVI of 1987

In section 9 of the principal Act, for the words "rupees five lacs" the words "rupees ten lacs" shall be substituted.

6. Amendment of section 15, Act XVI of 1987

In sub-clause (i) of clause (a) of section 15 of the principal Act, for the words "rupees five lacs" and "rupees thirty lacs" the words "rupees ten lacs" and "rupees fifty lacs" shall respectively be substituted.

7. Amendment of sections 9, 10, 11, 12, 13, 14, 15, 16, 16-A, 18, 18A, 19, 20, 21, 22, 23-A, Act XVI of 1987

In section 9, 10, 11, 12, 13, 14, 15, 16, 16-A, 18, 18A, 19,

20, 21, 22, 23-A of the principal Act, for the words "Divisional Forum" and "Divisional Consumer Forum" wherever occurring, the words "District Forum" and "District Consumer Forum" shall respectively be substituted.

TABLE OF CASES

INDEX